Sweet Fuel

Sweet Fuel

A Political and Environmental History of Brazilian Ethanol

JENNIFER EAGLIN

OXFORD
UNIVERSITY PRESS

Oxford University Press is a department of the University of Oxford. It furthers the University's objective of excellence in research, scholarship, and education by publishing worldwide. Oxford is a registered trade mark of Oxford University Press in the UK and certain other countries.

Published in the United States of America by Oxford University Press
198 Madison Avenue, New York, NY 10016, United States of America.

Library of Congress Cataloging-in-Publication Data
Names: Eaglin, Jennifer, author.
Title: Sweet fuel : a political and environmental history of Brazilian ethanol / Jennifer Eaglin.
Description: New York, NY : Oxford University Press, [2022] |
Includes bibliographical references and index.
Identifiers: LCCN 2021060581 (print) | LCCN 2021060582 (ebook) |
ISBN 9780197510681 (hardback) | ISBN 9780197510704 (epub) |
ISBN 9780197510711
Subjects: LCSH: Biomass energy—Brazil. | Ethanol as fuel—Brazil.
Classification: LCC HD9502.5.B543 B638 2022 (print) | LCC HD9502.5.B543 (ebook) |
DDC 333.95/390981—dc23/eng/20211214
LC record available at https://lccn.loc.gov/2021060581
LC ebook record available at https://lccn.loc.gov/2021060582

DOI: 10.1093/oso/9780197510681.001.0001

1 3 5 7 9 8 6 4 2

Printed by Integrated Books International, United States of America

Contents

Acknowledgments

No man [or woman] is an island, and no book is written alone. There are too many people to thank for the time, support, reading, rereading, editing, and encouragement I have received along the way. Still, I have to try.

To my adviser, Peter Beattie, you saw this project from the beginning. Oh, how far it's come.

To my editor, Susan Ferber, and my external readers, this book is infinitely better for your editorial efforts and content suggestions.

To my team of colleagues who have kindly donated time to improving this book or just encouraged me to keep going: Nick Breyfogle, Casey Lurtz, Bart Elmore, Shawn Miller, Susanna Bohme, Tom Rogers, Gillian McGillivray, Cliff Welch, Chris Otter, Anne Hanley, Ed Murphy, Giorgio Rizzoni, Gail Triner, John Soluri, Joel Wolfe, Reighan Gillam, Elizabeth Hinton, Rashida Harrison, Marini Lee, Nikki Magie, Alex Galarza, Jonathan Square, Ebony Jones, Joan Flores, Cassi Pittman and our mighty little writing group, Katherine Marino, Clay Howard, Elizabeth Bond, Stephanie Smith, Chris Boyer, Kat Cosby, and so many more, I am undoubtedly a better scholar because of you all. I am also lucky enough to call many of you friends who have often made me a better human along the way.

There are also so many who have provided emotional support that reaches far beyond academia. To my OSU crew, my NYU crew, my MSU crew, my California crew, my São Paulo crew, and all the other friend networks that have lifted me up and sustained me along the way, thank you for always making sure I kept laughing.

To all my Brazilian contacts, this project would not exist without the warm Brazilian *jeito* that gives suggestions when there are no answers, welcomes when there seem to be no invitations, and always suggests a connection: Gabriela Santos, Marcos Amatucci and ESPM, Marcos Vinicius de Freitas and FAAP, Galeno Amorim, Ubaldo Silveira, Sr., Maurilio Biagi, Marcia Elldorf, Cliff Welch, Mari Habiro, the team at Canoeste, the Ribeirão Preto Archive, the National Archives, and more. *Obrigadão, gente.*

For all the financial support necessary to complete such an ambitious project: the Boren Fellowship, the Fulbright Foundation, the FLAS program,

UCLA Thayer Fellowship, the Woodrow Wilson Foundation, the Conference on Latin American History, and the Mellon Mayes Program have provided extensive external support that was critical to completing this project. During my time at Michigan State, I received numerous grants to support summer research trips. At Ohio State University, the Mershon Center, the Sustainability Institute, the Center for Latin American Studies, the College of Arts and Sciences, and, of course, the History department have been critical to bringing this project to completion and supporting its development along the way.

To my people, all the love to Jess, Chris, Jan, and Fulton, the team that pushes me to work harder and dream bigger every time. Stephanie, I'm lucky to have such a great cheerleader by my side. Thank you for the love and support. On to the next adventure.

Note on Text and Abbreviations

All translations from the original Portuguese are mine, unless otherwise noted. Any mistakes are my own.

II PND	Segundo Plano Nacional de Desenvolvimento (Second National Development Plan)
Anfavea	Associação Nacional dos Fabricantes de Veículos Automotores (National Car Producers' Association)
BNDE*	Banco Nacional de Desenvolvimento Econômico (National Economic Development Bank)
BHC	benzene hexachloride
BOD	biochemical oxygen demand
CASE	Companhia Agricola Sertãozinho (Sertãozinho Agricultural Company)
CDPA	Comissão de Defesa da Produção do Açúcar (Commission for the Defense of Sugar Production)
CEB	Comunidade Eclesial de Base (Ecclesiastical Base Community)
CENAL	Commissão Executivo Nacional de Álcool (National Executive Ethanol Commission)
CETESB	Centro Tecnológico de Saneamento Básico ([São Paulo] Technological Center for Basic Sanitation)
CNAl	Commissão Nacional de Álcool (National Ethanol Commission)
CNBB	Conferência Nacional dos Bispos do Brasil (National Conference of Bishops of Brazil)
CNP	Conselho Nacional do Petróleo (National Petroleum Council)
Copersucar	Cooperativa Central de Produtores do Açúcar e do Álcool do Estado de São Paulo (The Central Cooperative of Producers of Sugar and Alcohol of São Paulo)
CPDV	Centro de Documentação e Pesquisa Vergueiro (Vergueiro Documentation and Research Center)
CPT	Comissão Pastoral da Terra (Pastoral Land Commission)
CTA	Centro Tecnológico de Aeronáutica (Aeronautical Technology Center)
DAEE	Departamento de Águas e Energia Elétrica (Department of Water and Electrical Energy)

* BNDE was renamed BNDES (*Banco Nacional de Desenvolvimento Econômico e Social*, The National Bank for Economic and Social Development) in the 1980s.

ESALQ	Escola Superior de Agricultura "Luiz de Queiroz" (Luiz de Queiroz College of Agriculture)
ESP	Estado de São Paulo (São Paulo daily newspaper)
ETR	Estatuto do Trabalhador Rural (Rural Laborer Statute)
FEEMA	Fundação Estadual de Engenharia do Meio Ambiente (The State Foundation of Environmental Engineering)
FESB	Fomento Estadual de Saneamento Básico (State Promotion of Basic Sanitation)
FETAESP	Federação dos Trabalhadores na Agricultura do Estado de São Paulo(São Paulo State Agricultural Workers' Federation)
FSP	Folha de São Paulo (São Paulo daily newspaper)
Funproçúcar	Fundo para o Programa de Apoio à Agro-Indústria Açucareiro (Support Program for the Sugar Agro-Industry)
GEAT	Grupo Especial de Assistência Técnica (Special Technical Assistance Group)
GECEP	Grupo Especial de Controle Executivo dos Projectos (Special Group for Executive Control of Projects)
IAA	Instituto do Açúcar e do Álcool (Institute of Sugar and Ethanol)
IPI	Industrial Product Tax
IPT	Instituto de Pesquisas Tecnológicas (Institute for Technological Research)
PCB	Partido Comunista Brasileiro (Brazilian Communist Party)
Petrobras	Brazilian Petroleum Company
Proálcool/PNA†	Programa Nacional do Álcool (National Ethanol Program)
PT	Partido dos Trabalhadores (Worker's Party)
Sabesp	Companhia de Saneamento Básico do Estado de São Paulo (São Paulo State Basic Sanitation Company)
SEMA	Secretaria Especial do Meio Ambiente (Special Department of the Environment)
STI	Secretaria de Tecnologia Industrial (Department of Industrial Technology)
Surehma	Superintendência de Recursos Hídricos e Meio Ambiente in Paraná (Superintendency of Hydrolic Resources and the Environment in Paraná)
TRU	Taxa Rodoviária Única (Road Tax)
UNICAMP	Universidade Estadual de Campinas (University of Campinas)
USP	Universidade de São Paulo (University of São Paulo)
VTV	veículos de transporte do vinhaça (vinasse transport vehicles)

† Petrobras was spelled Petrobrás until the 1990s.

Map of Ribeirão Preto in the State of São Paulo
Source: Map by Bill Nelson.

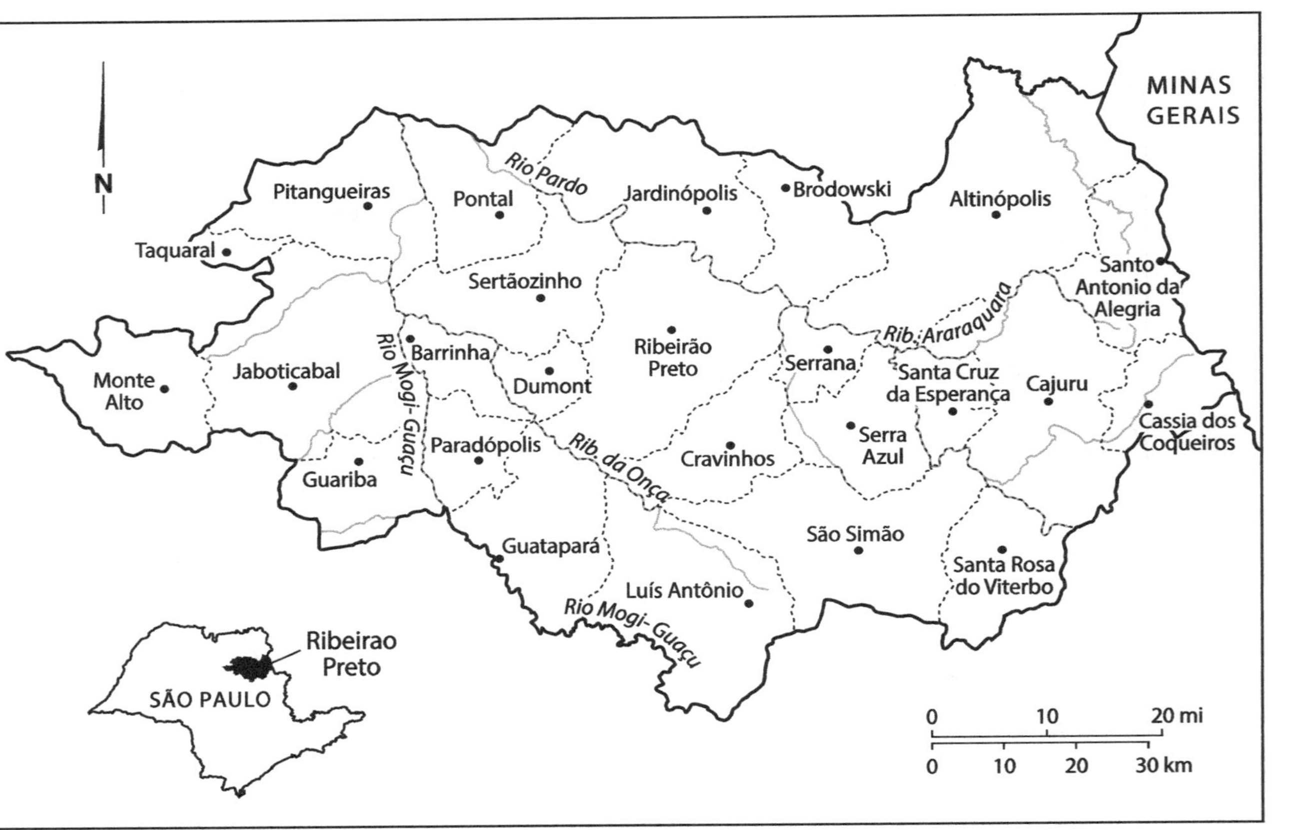

Map of major cities and waterways in the Ribeirão Preto region

Source: Map by Bill Nelson.

Introduction: Sugar and Energy

Fossil fuel-powered vehicles remain major contributors to the rapid warming of our planet. However, global car use shows no sign of slowing. Policymakers and specialists around the world have turned to biofuels generated from plant-based products such as grass, corn, sugar, and palm oil as part of the solution. Their lower carbon emissions than petroleum-based gasoline make possible continued high vehicle use with a reduced carbon footprint. In response, global initiatives such as the 2015 Paris Climate Agreement have encouraged the use of biofuels to power our present and future cars. Among the many biofuel varieties, sugar ethanol's higher efficiency than its competitors enabled Brazil, the world's largest sugar ethanol producer, to move to the forefront of climate-related biofuel promotion worldwide in the twenty-first century.[1]

Yet long before concerns about a warming climate incentivized such actions, Brazil looked to ethanol as a domestic fuel option. Sugar remains a key piece of the country's diversified green energy system: ethanol produces 60 percent less carbon emissions than petroleum-based gasoline and is more energy efficient than comparative biofuels such as American corn-based ethanol.[2] Sugar-based ethanol, referred to as *álcool* by Brazilians, has long been an important part of Brazil's sugar production. Beginning in the 1930s, the Brazilian government mandated a 5 percent mixture of ethanol in the national fuel supply. The success of this early state intervention later inspired the military regime (1964–1985) to aggressively expand the ethanol industry in the 1970s and 1980s. Large countries such as China and the United States have since sought to import or replicate Brazil's lower-carbon sugar-based ethanol as part of their efforts to reduce carbon emissions in the twenty-first century. However, such imitative efforts have included little critical reflection on what a turn to large-scale biofuel use required in Brazil.[3]

This book traces the development of Brazil's ethanol industry from its inception in the 1930s into the twenty-first century. It argues that private businessmen, politicians, and rural workers leveraged nationalist interests to create one of the world's most advanced alternative energy initiatives while at

Sweet Fuel. Jennifer Eaglin, Oxford University Press. © Oxford University Press 2022.
DOI: 10.1093/oso/9780197510681.003.0001

the same time ignoring how the industry contributed to environmental degradation and exploited rural populations. The ethanol industry grew from an effort to save a struggling sugar industry in the 1930s into a national energy solution with the creation of the state-led initiative called Proálcool (the National Ethanol Program) in 1975. The government implemented production incentives, financial support for producers, and fuel subsidies for consumers to integrate ethanol assertively and successfully into the economy. In the 1980s, the program evolved from one focused on supplementing fuel to one prioritizing fuel replacement after the launch of a domestically developed ethanol-fueled car in 1979. So rapid was the program's expansion that, by 1985, over 95 pecent of all new cars on the road ran exclusively on ethanol.[4]

Ethanol's rapid ascent paints a rosy picture for those who seek an energy model that moves away from dependence on fossil fuel, but praise for Brazilian ethanol typically obscures the contentious origins of the industry, which was neither green nor socially equitable. The industry has long been accused of extensive water pollution, which incited public outrage, protest, and eventually federal legislation. Proálcool was a direct product of the military dictatorship's economic development agenda, which systematically suppressed wages to expand business profits in the name of economic growth. Exploitative labor laws permitted sugar producers to rely on temporary agricultural laborers to drive the program's rapid expansion. Ultimately, growing demand for ethanol, falling international oil prices, and ethanol shortages due to droughts eroded consumer confidence in the alternative fuel option.[5] As the market for ethanol cars collapsed by 1990, the civilian democratic government, reinstated in 1985, acknowledged the economic and ecological limitations of the substitute fuel. Rather than scrap the program entirely in the 1990s, the government shifted it back to a fuel supplement program due to ethanol's importance to long-term domestic energy interests. In 2003, Volkswagen's Brazilian subsidiary launched the first flex-fuel vehicles that run on any combination of ethanol and/or gasoline, which reinvigorated Brazil's ethanol demand. By 2018, flex-fuel cars represented over 80 percent of Brazil's light vehicle fleet, and ethanol has become a core part of Brazil's energy model for the foreseeable future.[6] Furthermore, Brazil's basic national fuel is made of 25 percent ethanol. The nation's success has driven the United States, Europe, and Canada to adopt, or readopt in the case of the United States, these hybrid vehicles, though in lower relative numbers and usually lower ethanol mixture levels.

This book centers on the country's largest ethanol-producing region by the 1980s, Ribeirão Preto in the state of São Paulo, to tell the history of the industry's growth. The central government initially promoted ethanol production in the 1930s in part to industrialize the struggling Northeast sugar-producing region. By the 1950s, the more industrial, car-driving, urban markets of São Paulo and Rio de Janeiro transformed São Paulo into the center of national sugar and ethanol production.[7] As global sugar demand increased in the 1960s, powerful domestic São Paulo sugar producers aligned their interests with the military regime's nationalist development agenda to assert ethanol's possibilities as a larger part of the country's fuel infrastructure. After the 1973 oil shock, these agro-industrial producers shaped the government's creation and expansion of Proálcool. Thanks to a concentration of sugar producers who won government financing and proximity to the major city of São Paulo, Ribeirão Preto quickly dominated the program's expansion. The industry's growth made figurative sheikhs of paulista sugar and ethanol producers such as the Biagi family in Ribeirão Preto, later known as the "Brazilian Arabia" because of how much sugarcane the region produced.[8] Brazil is a hierarchical country in which a handful of extremely wealthy families have dominated the economy. These producers deftly connected their individual interests to larger national development projects associated with the industry since the 1930s. The history of the Biagi family's expansion of their sugar milling, technology, and distilling infrastructure, particularly their mill, the Usina Santa Elisa, reveals how the region became the center of the nation's alternative fuel industry and how the adverse effects of ethanol production contributed to the region's agro-industrial emergence.[9]

This historical case invites questions about the nature of development in Brazil. How did the state sustain support for the ethanol industry even in periods when the initiative was in opposition to popular political ideology? How did private actors, from producers to politicians to field workers and local community members, experience the growth of ethanol? What ecological costs did expanded ethanol production impose, and on whom? These questions must be understood in the context of national proponents who framed ethanol as a domestic energy source that defined Brazilian political ingenuity first as an economic initiative in the midst of a global energy crisis and later as an environmental boon in the age of climate change and carbon emissions.

As Brazil was a limited oil producer for most of the twentieth century, the development of its ethanol industry suggests the possibilities of moving beyond oil for fuel, and its shortcomings illuminate the limits of structural energy transitions in the present day. By linking sugarcane to the energy sector, the history of ethanol's development exposes a socially and ecologically fraught site of labor and land exploitation in the name of monocultural production. Yet this agricultural product became Brazil's most important agro-industrial product in the 1980s, a fuel in an age when control of energy defined political and economic possibilities for much of the world. Ethanol's history illustrates the shift from the energy politics of the twentieth century, when oil reigned supreme, to the energy politics of the twenty-first century, when alternative fuels have taken on greater importance.

Today, this industry stands as the lone example in the world of a large-scale alternative fuel initiative that successfully transitioned a country's domestic transportation fuel infrastructure away from petroleum.[10] However, the program's short-term sweeping success and long-term integration into the Brazilian energy system belies the complicated positive and negative effects the growth of ethanol has had on the population and the environment. Creation of the ethanol market required the ongoing cooperation of politicians, private businessmen, government agencies, scientists, agronomists, engineers, the automotive industry, farmers, sugarcane distillers, and field workers to successfully integrate the alternative fuel into the national fuel infrastructure. The history of Brazilian ethanol, this book argues, reveals how national pride in the alternative fuel program papered over the realities of the program's social and environmental costs.

From Early Industrial Product to Backward Industry in Brazilian History

Ethanol links sugarcane, an agricultural product of historical and cultural importance as the country's first major export, to broader twentieth-century national development objectives in Brazil. However, sugar has had a long history in Brazilian society. Its production has long been associated with industrial processing, but increased global competition made the sector synonymous with a backward, colonial industry by the beginning of the twentieth century. Ethanol's ascendance salvaged sugar's reputation.

Since Portuguese colonists first brought the plant, native to Southeast Asia, to colonial Brazil in the sixteenth century, sugar has always involved some degree of complex industrial processing.[11] A perennial plant, sugarcane, upon processing, produces sugar and multiple potentially useful sub-products such as molasses, alcohol (for fuel), *aguardente* (drinking alcohol), cellulose, protein for animal rations, and fertilizer.[12] It must be crushed within twenty-four to forty-eight hours after cutting in order to extract and process its juice into these traditional sugar products. To speed up the cutting and collection of cane, producers employ controlled burnings to break down the woody pulp, or bagasse (*bagaço*), outside the cane stalk. The cane then must be transported to the mill, cleaned of impurities, crushed, and processed according to the final sugar product desired. After crushing, the cane juice is concentrated into sucrose crystals to produce table sugar (white and brown sugar, depending on how refined this processing is). The remaining molasses is left for other sugar byproducts such as alcohol. In the nineteenth century, this process required around-the-clock work by an extensive slave population, with the field tasks performed during the day and mill grinding throughout the night. However, the larger, modern mills (*usinas*) of the twentieth century, which replaced older, smaller mills (*engenhos* and *bangues*), consolidated these processes and increasingly mechanized the milling process. This left the most intense labor for the field tasks, including the clearing of fields, planting, weeding, and cutting the cane.

Sugar alcohol requires additional processing. Alcohol may be distilled from any fermented sugar or starch products, be they potatoes, grapes, corn, or sugarcane itself. Lower-grade distillations make aguardente, or drinking alcohol made of sugarcane, including the famous Brazilian *cachaça* (made directly from cane juice) and rum, from fermented molasses. Higher-grade distillations of fermented sugar or molasses are potent enough to run engines.[13]

Alcohol distillation also produces the byproduct vinasse. Known variously in Brazil as *vinhaça*, *restilo*, *calda*, *vinhoto*, *vinhote*, *garapao*, *caxixi*, or *tiborna*, it is a brown liquid composed of over 90 percent water that is left over from heating the cane juice or fermented molasses to higher purity levels. The product includes a small percentage of organic materials, notably nitrogen, from the distilled cane residue. Lower-purity alcohols such as rum or cachaça produce lower quantities of this byproduct. Higher-purity ethanol alcohol produces 10 to 16 liters of vinasse per single liter of alcohol. Sugar and alcohol producers traditionally discard the liquid residue in nearby waterways. Initially considered more of a nuisance for its smell, akin to human feces, the byproduct has been produced and dumped in local waterways in small amounts as part of robust sugar production in Brazil for centuries.[14]

Northeast Brazil first earned its place as the colonial center of the Portuguese colony for its production of sugarcane for trade in the Atlantic slave trade. Sugar is considered the central factor in shaping Brazil's early colonial social formation in the sixteenth and seventeenth centuries.[15] Thereafter, sugar became Brazil's key agricultural export for the next three centuries, but dependence on sugar exports eventually created trouble for Brazilian producers, as other national exports became more profitable and high tariffs and low costs of land and labor diminished Brazilian sugar's hold on the increasingly competitive world market.[16]

In place of sugar, coffee emerged as Brazil's premier agricultural export in the nineteenth century. A backwater province during the imperial period, the state of São Paulo experienced a rapid expansion of economic and political influence with the emergence of coffee production in the mid-nineteenth century. The flat high plains and hills and fertile soils were well suited to coffee production, and an extensive railroad system developed to transport coffee to the state's coastal port, Santos. The city of São Paulo grew from a small town into a major city as a railroad hub for coffee transport from coffee-producing regions in the interior of the state.

Notably, Ribeirão Preto in the northeastern region of the state emerged as a dominant coffee-producing region after 1860. Located more than 200 miles from the port of Santos, the region was once completely covered by the dominating Atlantic Forest. Its first settlers came from the neighboring province of Minas Gerais after the end of the gold mining boom in the early nineteenth century. However, the region's rolling hills, tropical temperatures, favorable rainfall, rare frosts, and unique red soil rich in oxides made it ideal for agricultural production.[17] The municipality of Ribeirão Preto, officially founded in 1871, is tucked between two freshwater rivers, the Rio Pardo to the north and the Rio Mogi-Guaçu to the west and the south. Branches of a third major river, the Médio-Grande, run deep into the region, so the greater region sits in the three overlapping water basins.[18] These abundant natural resources allowed coffee planters to transform Ribeirão Preto into the most productive coffee region in the state, then the country, and finally the world. In 1909, the region accounted for over 40–50 percent of world coffee production, while Brazil as a whole accounted for 80 percent of the world market share.[19]

Coffee-related investments drove industrialization throughout the southern region, particularly São Paulo, as the sugar industry fell into disrepute, a symbol of an increasingly impoverished, underdeveloped Northeast region.[20] The Northeast dominated Brazilian sugar production for export and the bulk of domestic sugar consumption, but sugar production slowly expanded in the São Paulo countryside to meet growing local demand. Even as the Northeast's diminished importance in the national economy transformed sugar into a symbol of a backward, rentier economy, this agricultural product would become the model of technological development through sugar modernization and ethanol production within the century.

Coffee, not sugar, defined economic growth and opportunity in Ribeirão Preto, the state of São Paulo, and more broadly Brazil in the early twentieth century. The municipality of Ribeirão Preto transformed into the administrative center of the greater region as important municipalities such as Sertãozinho (1896) and Cravinhos (1897) emerged from the coffee plantations that surrounded it. São Paulo coffee planters, and thus Ribeirão Preto, claimed a large share of national political influence as coffee dominated the country's exports, and thus economic policy, during the First Republic (1889–1930).[21] As international coffee prices oscillated, federal support buoyed coffee's dominant position in the Brazilian economy, but paulista government officials and local politicians encouraged diversification of agricultural production in response to the coffee industry's crises. In response, São Paulo sugar production slowly expanded to meet growing local demand, especially among former coffee producers switching to sugar during coffee crises in the 1920s, much to the chagrin of dominant Northeastern sugar producers.[22]

Foreigners led the transition from coffee to sugar in São Paulo. Immigrants poured into São Paulo's interior to work the coffee fields through state-funded recruitment initiatives, and later they came to the city of São Paulo to take up industrial jobs. While domestic coffee owners focused on coffee production, some immigrants, particularly the large number of Italians recruited to the region, were the first to invest in large-scale sugar production in the paulista countryside. The country's largest single coffee producer in the early twentieth century, a German immigrant named Francisco Schmidt, opened the first large-scale sugar mill in the Ribeirão Preto region in 1906. The Engenho Central of Sertãozinho, a neighboring municipality to Ribeirão Preto, drew other former coffee workers to sugar production as well, including the Biagi family, who would come to dominate Brazil's sugar and ethanol production by the end of the century.[23]

Pedro Biagi was one of the nearly one million Italian immigrants who flooded Brazil's southern port of Santos between 1880 and 1900 in search of opportunities in São Paulo's coffee fields. Biagi and his family came from Padua in 1887 when he was 7 years old. After working the fields of the Campinas region for two years to pay off the costs of their Atlantic passage, he and his family moved to Sertãozinho to do the same job. After working in coffee fields, brickyards, and rum distilling, Pedro bought his own land in Sertãozinho and set up a sugar mill, the Usina Barbacena, with his partner, Mario Bighetti, in 1918.[24] The Usina Barbacena produced its first harvest in 1922, when they refined 6,400 sacks of sugar.[25] Over a decade later, Pedro's sons, including Maurilio Biagi, purchased the Usina Santa Elisa. In addition to sugar, the Biagis soon started producing ethanol.

Ribeirão Preto's importance as a sugar and ethanol hub in the state and the country closely follows the Biagis' ascent. The state won an increasing share of the domestic sugar market by the 1930s, and this share and the industry overall continued to grow. The flourishing of Ribeirão Preto relied on a set of complex economic, political, social, geographic, and environmental factors against which the expansion of Brazil's ethanol industry is set.

Sugar's roots as a foundational agricultural export define the industry's growth.[26] In the modern Brazilian economy, ethanol has become a commodity separate from and yet wholly connected to the sugar industry. The development of ethanol enabled sugar to recreate its image from a backward industry to the peak of agro-industrial energy development by the end of the twentieth century. This transition highlights three central themes in Brazilian history: development, environment, and labor.

Development and Ethanol

This book places ethanol at the center of twentieth-century Brazilian development efforts in order to reveal how the fuel source became a symbol of national industry and technology, even as the product typically remained outside of scholarship on national development in Brazil. Placing the ethanol industry in the context of the country's centuries of varied development strategies provides a window into how effective state intervention was in achieving this goal in practice.

Generally defined as "the politics of socioeconomic improvement," the idea of development has been most often associated with the degree of industrialization, per capita income, and the postwar era, and has tended to be based on standards of welfare in industrialized societies.[27] In truth, Brazil has gone through various policy models to support economic growth, later redefined as development.[28] As in most Latin American countries, Brazilian politicians initially pushed an agricultural export model, with sugar, rubber, cotton, and most notably coffee defining Brazil's export possibilities from the colonial era into the twentieth century. Slaves were exploited, immigrants recruited, and wealth produced, but levels of socioeconomic growth on a par with the Western world still eluded the country. Politicians and structural theorists shifted their attention to industrialization as the key to reaching westernized levels of development in the 1930s.[29] Factories were built, industries imported, and an entire new capital city constructed, but development, as defined by the developed world, still remained elusive. Politicians and theorists then set their sights on technology as the missing key to development in the 1970s. Scholars pointed to Brazil's overwhelming dependence on foreign technology as a central cause of the country's ever more unequal economy.[30] All the while, the country kept growing through extensive foreign financing, state-led enterprises, and agro-industrial development under the military dictatorship. However, the economic struggles of the 1980s reformed the state-led initiatives that had defined the Brazilian economy over the previous fifty years. By the 1990s, a wave of neoliberal reforms swept the country as IMF-ordained policies calling for less state intervention led to renewed market-oriented policies. Scholars derided the state-oriented development efforts that failed to achieve Western industrial development levels,[31] and only in the last ten years have they begun praising the government interventions that allowed the economy to industrialize through much of the twentieth century as a key to continued economic growth.[32] Re-examining this development trajectory through the ethanol industry illuminates a unique agro-industrial development path that at times aligned with the state's development strategy and at others contradicted its professed economic objectives.

The creation of an ethanol industry in the 1930s fulfilled both political and strategic development interests, a link which would remain a key element in Brazilian ethanol marketing through the century. The collapse of world prices for sugar and other important Brazilian commodities such as coffee pushed the government to redirect the export-oriented industry toward domestic production. Northeastern and southern sugar producers called for national support like that given to the coffee industry. The new provisional leader Getúlio Vargas had a particular interest in supporting Northeastern producers as a way to economically empower his political base and offset the influence of southern actors, particularly São Paulo coffee producers.[33] Furthermore, Vargas's budding economic agenda focused on the "development of a self-sufficient, modern and industrial domestic economy."[34] Additionally, ethanol repurposed underpriced potential sugar exports and lowered petroleum imports, which could improve the growing trade deficit.

In the 1950s, Brazil shifted to a more intense private-public allied development effort in a new iteration of the import substitution industrialization model that had been loosely executed under Vargas since the 1930s. Instead of the model of high import barriers to incentivize the creation of domestic industries, the government supported the arrival of foreign industries to establish domestic industries. The automobile, pharmaceutical, and mining industries exemplify the alliance of the federal government, private producers, and multinational firms aiming to push out domestic producers in favor of foreign producers.[35] Yet Brazilian sugar producers remained clearly in control of ethanol, as policy favored domestic control of the industrializing sugar sector. Here, producers used government financing and local network connections to push out foreign firms.[36]

Although the efficacy of state intervention has been debated, the ethanol industry presents a case where a nascent industry would not exist if not for the active intervention of the state. National policy successfully created a domestic industry through a state-led development agenda even when market forces, namely high barriers to entry into ethanol production, high sugar prices, and lower gasoline prices, should have deterred individual producers from producing ethanol. Thus, ethanol was a policy-driven undertaking that grew counter to neoclassical market logic in the name of national development.[37]

Scholars have generally agreed that Brazil has overwhelmingly relied on foreign technology to promote national development to its detriment, but the ethanol industry illustrates that Brazil's industrialization was not entirely dependent on the importation of foreign technology.[38] The industry spawned domestic innovations in ethanol-related fueling and processing technology that enabled its growth.[39] This included technology to repurpose the toxic byproduct vinasse as a fertilizer alternative and eventually export the product as an animal feed, as well as the domestic adaptation of the traditional gasoline-powered engine to run exclusively on ethanol and the related launch of the ethanol-fueled car in the domestic auto market in the 1980s. Since the 1930s, the Brazilian government actively connected growing interest in automobiles to a domestic fuel source through the promotion of sugar-based ethanol. Brazilian engineers began work on modifying a traditional engine to run exclusively on ethanol in the 1950s at the Aeronautical Technology Center (Centro de Tecnologia Aeronáutica [CTA]). Despite heavy investment by Volkswagen, the country's leading car producer by the 1970s, Brazilian scientists won the patent rights to the successfully altered engine in 1979. One Brazilian military official jubilantly claimed the patent put the country on an "equal footing with international manufacturers" to compete technologically and commercially on an international scale.[40] The Brazilian government and multinational companies then agreed to commercially launch cars with the adapted engine exclusively for domestic sale beginning the same year. The success of this initiative quickly transformed the ethanol car into a symbol of uniquely Brazilian development.[41] These innovations were a key part of the government's unwavering commitment to the development of ethanol from the 1930s onward, regardless of who was in power. Even today, flex-fuel technology, while developed originally in the United States, has integrated into the unique fueling infrastructure that has defined the industry's place in Brazil's energy sector.

Ethanol, the Environment, and Labor

Focusing exclusively on ethanol's connection to national development ignores the industry's long association with environmental destruction that directly affected rural communities in sugar-producing regions and beyond. As ethanol production expanded to service a growing Brazilian car fleet, sugar producers became negligent in disposing of the liquid waste from ethanol, and rural workers experienced deteriorating labor conditions in the expanding sugar sector. Scholarship on the connections between the energy industries, environmental destruction, and labor exploitation have traditionally focused on fossil fuel industries[42] while environmental histories have investigated sugar's detrimental environmental impact on deforestation, exhaustive monocultural production, and subsequent soil erosion.[43] By exploring the environmental and labor problems produced by the ethanol industry, this book offers a cautionary tale about a twenty-first-century alternative fuel industry's development.[44] Exposing the environmental costs of alternative energy development agendas challenges the presumption that non-fossil fuel options are superior to traditional fossil fuels' environmental costs.[45] Rural communities inserted themselves into debates about the ethanol industry's long-term growth by protesting its impact on local waterways and the labor conditions experienced by those facilitating the industry's development.

Environment

This book homes in on the connections between nature, nation, and environmental activism through the development of the ethanol industry over the course of the twentieth century. The environmental implications of the sugar sector have drawn the attention of Brazilian scholars from the very beginning of modern Brazilian historical writing. In the 1930s, the renowned sociologist Gilberto Freyre criticized how national interest in modernization and industrialization drove positive interpretations of the sugar industry despite its ecological realities.[46] As the field evolved, early environmental histories questioned the essential connection between nature, consumption, destruction, and Brazilian national identity in the 1980s and 1990s.[47] Alongside this scholarship, multiple waves of Brazilian environmentalism with both domestic and international origins have emerged.[48] The development of the ethanol industry, a major source of water pollution, illustrates how government officials favored economic development over the environment and how the public demanded government action.

By focusing on the connection of ethanol to larger water pollution issues, this book untangles idealized views of the industry. On the one hand, the industry heavily relied for decades on environmental degradation, through free vinasse dumping, to be able to grow into the alternative fuel industry it is today. On the other hand, public protests about environmental exposure in these rural sugar-producing regions challenged the political status quo that fundamentally supported industrialization over public health concerns. Even as rural citizens became ever less central to the state's industrial interests by mid-century, they continually found ways to draw attention to this environmental exploitation through community mobilization, legal action, and writing to local newspapers to demand federal action. While scholars have questioned local influence on national development agendas internationally, the ethanol case reveals that the environment drove local residents to intervene in the development of the program.[49] Technological solutions to the vinasse problem were in part the product of communities' pressure on producers, government, and researchers.[50] Incorporating this aspect of the industry's development writes people back into a history that can often overlook the population who directly experienced its growth to provide a fuller account of ethanol's impact.

An environmental perspective on the industry also exposes the limits of the program's policy-driven expansion under Proálcool. In 1960, when the government first shifted its focus back to sugar exports, sugarcane production in the country reached about 57.9 million tons. Between the 1975/1976 and 1984/1985 harvests after the program began, sugarcane production more than tripled nationwide, jumping from 68.3 million tons to 202.9 million tons. São Paulo production alone nearly doubled.[51] The program pushed the physical limits of rapid sugarcane expansion to meet growing fuel demands. Droughts in the Ribeirão Preto region put limits on ethanol production possibilities as the country descended into economic crisis and oil prices collapsed.[52] As a result, the fuel replacement program fell out of favor in the late 1980s, as consumers lost faith in the fuel alternative.

Industry and government officials repackaged the relationship of ethanol with pollution in the 1990s, revealing the way its importance at a national level continually reshaped its image in an increasingly urban nation that associated cars with modernity. When Proálcool experienced a financial crisis in the late 1980s, local communities' successful attempts to defend local waterways over the previous decades brought the industry's water pollution problem to national attention.[53] Yet producers and policymakers transformed the program that government officials and the Brazilian public deemed economically unsustainable in the early 1990s into a beacon of Brazilian environmental ingenuity of the twenty-first century. With the launch of ethanol cars and increased use of ethanol mixed in the national fuel supply, Brazilian scientists linked ethanol to decreasing levels of carbon-emitting car pollution in the highly polluted city of São Paulo in the late 1980s. As a non-fossil-based fuel, ethanol released no hydrocarbons directly into the air, so officials and private producers promoted the industry as a green one that improved the country's carbon footprint, despite its checkered history of water pollution and the use of fossil fuels in ethanol's production process.[54]

Assessing Proálcool's environmental imprint requires engaging with the food versus fuel issue that has defined the global biofuel debate in the twenty-first century. As biofuels attracted increasing attention after the oil shocks of the 1970s, scholars debated the net impact of redirecting land used to produce food products toward crops for fuel production.[55] In the 2000s, corn-based ethanol drove up the prices of the staple food, with a disproportionate impact on subsistence communities. Brazilian sugar ethanol supporters have argued this has not been the case in Brazil, where sugar is not a food crop and there is still ample farmable land to produce abundant food supplies. To be sure, monocultural sugar production, promoted in the name of fuel independence, pushed out diversified crop production, starting with beans and manioc and ending with a vibrant citrus economy. However, this book moves beyond this debate to illustrate how narrow assessments of the imprint of ethanol solely focused on the land use ignore the ethanol industry's historical connection to water pollution, which has been mostly erased from energy debates today.

Labor

The expansion of ethanol through Proálcool relied not just on environmental exploitation, but also on pliant, cheap labor. Social questions about the sugar industry drew national attention in the 1960s, and scholars have continued to assert the importance of sugar workers' protests in the 1964 coup and social movements during the 1990s.[56] However, labor is often left out of broader assessments of the ethanol program.[57] Cheap, abundant labor was critical to the program's success. The massive expansion of sugarcane required extensive reformations of the labor market. Government and producers were complicit in shifting the labor force used in cane fields from full-time workers to cheaper, temporary migrant laborers in the 1960s and 1970s. Sugar producers praised the expanded job market associated with increased sugar production in the 1970s and 1980s, but were silent about the grave labor conditions under which these mostly migrant laborers worked.

The 1984 rural labor strikes in Ribeirão Preto led by these short-term sugar workers offer an example of how workers inserted themselves into this development discussion. Rural workers were able to leverage the importance of ethanol production to win recognition and modest labor improvements as sugar unions and unionized autoworkers had years earlier. Without the formal recognition afforded by labor status, temporary, migrant workers were able to impact shifting public opinion on Proálcool. Rural labor scholars have established the exploitative nature of the sugar industry's expansion by examining temporary workers, known as *bóias-frias*, during the height of the ethanol program in the 1970s and 1980s, but they have not closely tied their mobilization to Proálcool's national image.[58] By strategically leading strikes at the beginning of sugar harvests in 1984 and 1985, rural workers in the region pressured sugar producers and fed growing public and private doubts that the program would be able to meet national production objectives. As the rural workers' strikes in Guariba revealed the precarious nature of the industry's labor conditions, national perceptions of the overall value of the program began to shift from the triumphalist rhetoric of the early 1980s to a more rigorous interrogation of the program's costs and benefits in the second half of the 1980s. Their mobilization, known as the Guariba strikes, forcefully introduced a neglected but critical group of program participants into the discussion of development and the industry's trajectory.

Placing ethanol's history in a rural setting highlights the local factors that affected the program's national development. Rural communities' resistance to vinasse dumping and rural workers' resistance to exploitative working conditions represent some of the earliest environmental and social justice protests in the country. Scholarship on environmental justice traditionally focuses on land displacement, the removal of indigenous groups, and Amazonian deforestation in Brazilian history,[59] while studies of labor and citizenship have disproportionately focused on urban dwellers.[60] By including disadvantaged communities outside of the city centers and beyond the scope of the country's mainstream environmental movements,[61] this case demonstrates that rural people were not absent from environmental or labor activism. Rural citizens found ways to demand clean water, basic wages, work condition improvements, and better healthcare, demands that have come to define the key aspects of social justice movements today. Their environmental and social pressures on a program that shortchanged them in the name of energy and development provide examples of the ways local communities both resisted and shaped the state-led development program. Local communities in Brazil were part of broader, international, non-Western state-led development programs that interrogated the costs and benefits of the alternative energy industry's development.[62]

* * *

This book traces the growth of the ethanol industry, from a state institution, the Institute of Sugar and Alcohol, in the 1930s, through the National Ethanol Program (Proálcool) of the 1970s and 1980s, to its transition to an independent fuel industry in the 2000s. During these decades, actors such as private producers like the Biagis, politicians, local fishermen, scientists and engineers, automotive executives, and field workers shaped and reshaped the industry's growth well beyond a simple state-led initiative. To illustrate this complex intertwining of actors and influences, the book is mainly chronologically organized, with two thematic chapters about labor and the environment that reach across these timeframes.

Chapter 1 examines the origins of the state's intervention in ethanol production under the Institute of Sugar and Alcohol (IAA) from 1930 to 1959. Sugar, ethanol, São Paulo, and particularly Ribeirão Preto became inextricably linked in this period. State officials first supported ethanol production as a means of diverting excess sugar production in the country after the collapse of global markets in the Great Depression. By World War II, ethanol proved its value as a potential domestic fuel source in the face of petroleum shortages that validated the government's early support and tied it to national security interests thereafter. In the state of São Paulo, the presence of the coffee infrastructure made a good deal of technical expertise available for sugar and alcohol production, shaping the region's future ethanol industry.

Chapter 2 examines the changing sugar and ethanol sector as sugar exports increased and petroleum came to dominate the fuel market, diminishing policy focus on ethanol in the 1960s and early 1970s. The collapse of US-Cuban relations enabled Brazil to capitalize on a larger international market, redirecting the protectionist policies that had supported ethanol in the 1930s and 1940s toward export-oriented growth in the 1960s. Sugar exports became a feature of the new military dictatorship's development plan during the late 1960s. By the early 1970s, booming sugar prices drove massive investment in the sector through state-led modernization programs such as Funproçúcar to mechanize production and consolidate large landholdings. Focusing on the Biagis' Usina Santa Elisa, this chapter shows how private actors used these programs to their benefit as they anticipated and shaped a future national ethanol program in the aftermath of the oil shock of 1973.

Chapter 3 examines the creation and expansion of the National Ethanol Program between 1975 and 1985. Proálcool began as a fuel supplement program after the 1973 oil shock and transformed into a fuel replacement program after the launch of the ethanol-fueled car in 1979. The Biagis utilized Proálcool funding to position the Usina Santa Elisa at the forefront of the sugar-ethanol sector. The Biagis emerged as major ethanol producers and technological market leaders by investing in new equipment and processing techniques as ethanol cars came to dominate the Brazilian car market by 1985.

Chapter 4 examines the broader environmental damage inflicted by the ethanol industry on local waterways. Sugar and ethanol producers dumped vinasse in waterways liberally for decades to the detriment of public health in sugar-producing regions. Regulation of vinasse dumping slowly expanded as constituents in these regions pushed back and formed a nascent environmental justice campaign. Ethanol producers' persistent abuse of local waterways damaged their public image and revealed the deeper truth that the successful transformation of the Brazilian energy sector carried very real environmental costs.

Chapter 5 focuses on the rural laborers' strike of May 1984 in Guariba, a sugar-producing hub within Ribeirão Preto, to illustrate Proálcool's social costs. The hiring of temporary migrant rural labor rather than the employment of a permanent workforce facilitated the exploitation of cheap labor on which the National Ethanol Program relied, a trend that was exacerbated by the country's economic crisis in the 1980s. Temporary rural laborers brought ethanol production in this dominant region to a halt in an effort to demand better working conditions and compensation. In the process, the workers' actions drew public attention to problems hidden during the years of the program's growth and contributed to shifting public opinion of the program by the late 1980s.

Chapter 6 explores the end of Proálcool as a fuel replacement initiative and its rebirth as an environmental program in the 1990s. Ethanol shortages in the late 1980s mired the program in debates about its long-term viability and ongoing value. The new democratically-elected president Fernando Collor dismantled the fuel replacement program but supported it as a fuel supplement program. However, propaganda for the revised program focused on ethanol's environmental contributions, namely, reducing air pollution in large city centers and its multiuse byproducts, despite the industry's long history of massive water pollution. With this new focus, the industry was able to successfully transition to a fully privatized industry by the end of the century. The 2003 launch of the new flex-fuel car which could run on any combination of ethanol and gasoline solidified ethanol's permanent place in Brazil's energy matrix in the twenty-first century.

Brazil successfully transformed ethanol into an energy commodity but that status also exposed the industry to the boom and bust cycles of the energy market in the 2010s. Ethanol's success as a green energy illustrates the winners and losers in alternative energy regimes and the importance of marketing in energy futures. The state's continued dedication to ethanol provides a telling example of the costs and benefits that such unyielding support has had on the nation's politics, economy, environment, and society. Ethanol supports created an alternative fuel industry for a country without substantial oil reserves for the better part of the twentieth century but exploited water and workers extensively in the process. As countries globally look for solutions to dependence on the fossil carbon regime, the history of Brazilian ethanol illustrates the challenges and possibilities of moving beyond carbon emitting petroleum to a future of alternate energy sources.

1
Early Sugar and Ethanol Policy, 1933–1959

> "It is one of the rare examples, in our country of an industry created and developed under the tutelage, support, and guidance of the State."
>
> Moacyr Soares Pereira, *O problema do álcool-motor* (1942)

In 1944, Maurilio Biagi, owner of the Usina Santa Elisa and the *fazenda* lands around it, followed an ill-advised government plan to expand manioc production to support the expansion of manioc flour, known as *farinha de mandioca*, for wartime consumption. When the plan fell through and he was stuck with excess manioc, he told a fellow Italian farmer in Ribeirão Preto, "Just, look, I believed in the government. I was left hanging."[1] Biagi abandoned the *farinha* plan, but he took a chance on another government promise about ethanol. It would eventually yield the gains he had anticipated and transform Biagi's new Usina into a premier agro-industrial center of sugar and ethanol production by the 1960s. The flourishing of the Usina Santa Elisa from the 1930s to the 1960s closely aligns with São Paulo becoming the leading sugar- and ethanol-producing state, with Ribeirão Preto as its hub.

Brazilian ethanol has a long history prior to the military government's national program in the 1970s. The technology for ethanol production existed by the early 1900s, and Brazil began to formally pursue research into and the development of sugar-based ethanol in the 1930s. Thereafter, sugarcane and ethanol policy were closely linked under federal management of the sugar industry. Early promotion of ethanol was not so much a proto-energy policy as a sugar support agenda. Hence, a history of ethanol production is also a history of state intervention in the sugar industry. Following initial interventions in 1931, federal policy, development, and market manipulation intertwined in the sector with the creation of the Institute of Sugar and Alcohol (Instituto do Açúcar e do Álcool [IAA]) in 1933. Thereafter, federal policy provided

Sweet Fuel. Jennifer Eaglin, Oxford University Press. © Oxford University Press 2022.
DOI: 10.1093/oso/9780197510681.003.0002

financial, agricultural, and technological support for sugar and ethanol, which linked the industries' production for the rest of the century.

This chapter reveals how state intervention transformed the sugar industry and gave birth to an ethanol market. IAA policymakers' interest in diversifying marketable products for the sugar sector and federal policies that inconsistently subsidized the fuel supply drove support for the ethanol industry. State intervention created and sustained the ethanol industry even as sugar lost political importance and could not be fully sustained in a free market. Government incentives gave regional entrepreneurs such as the Biagis the ability to expand their sugar and ethanol production capacity, which positioned Ribeirão Preto to become a dominant production region in the expanding sugar market of the 1960s and a prime investment site for Proálcool-driven ethanol production in the 1970s.

The state intervened to create the ethanol industry where demand did not yet exist. The market's creation under the IAA reveals the particular preference state officials gave to the industry during the Getúlio Vargas era. The new sugar policy supported Vargas's economic nationalist goals for a "self-sufficient, modern and industrial domestic economy."[2] Consequently, the sugar industry and ethanol interests led to the building of an important model of state intervention that shaped state-capitalist intervention in the 1960s. This was most apparent in São Paulo, where sugarcane and ethanol producers capitalized on the federal government's continuing support of ethanol production and invested in imported technology to further develop the sugar industry. The sugar and ethanol industry's ability to meet Vargas's dual interests and appease northeastern producers put it in a favorable position compared with other agricultural support programs of the Vargas era, including the dominant coffee industry. Yet producers such as Maurilio Biagi took their own initiative in mechanizing and modernizing the industry that would shape sugar and ethanol's industrial growth. Consequently, the sugar and ethanol industry follows a unique national agro-industrialization path.

São Paulo, Coffee, and Early Intervention in Agricultural Economic Planning

Key institutional transformations that began in São Paulo's coffee economy laid the foundation for the burgeoning paulista sugar industry. By the beginning of the twentieth century, the Brazilian coffee sector was in crisis. Production had outpaced world demand for a decade, but coffee accounted for almost 60 percent of the value of all Brazilian exports.[3] It was by far the country's most important agricultural industry, and São Paulo's economic and political power depended on it. To bolster the coffee industry, the São Paulo state government signed the 1906 Taubaté Agreement, which allowed state officials to purchase coffee from producers at a set minimum price and withhold coffee reserves from the international market in order to drive world prices back up. As São Paulo's coffee exports accounted for such a large percentage of national and world production, the state essentially acted as a global coffee cartel. While this was at first successful, later iterations became increasingly expensive and had less obvious impacts on world prices. By the late 1920s, the program had become a standard form of federal government support.[4]

The São Paulo coffee valorization programs were important precedents for subsequent federal intervention in the production of sugar and ethanol. The Great Depression led to the collapse not just of the price of coffee but of all agricultural export prices in 1930. Thereafter, President Vargas and the federal government would more actively intervene in the agricultural sector, extending protection to other crops, including sugarcane. Though initially hesitant about the coffee valorization schemes, the federal government took a central role in economic planning in the sugar industry in the 1930s.[5]

The international economic crisis set in just as a political crisis brought dramatic changes to Brazil with the presidential election of 1930. Vargas grabbed power with the backing of disillusioned opponents of São Paulo's growing political reach and the army after he lost the election.[6] His new provisional government took active steps to salvage the struggling sugar industry by increasingly focusing on the internal market using strategies it successfully employed for coffee. The first sugar protection legislation, Decree no. 20.401, passed on September 15, 1931, required that sugar mill owners, or *usineiros*, hold back 10 percent of the sugar produced for domestic sale from the market in order to drive prices back up. However, this decree indicated that such storage only applied to the producers in the regions overproducing for their domestic local markets, namely, northeastern producers. The government set a tax of $5 milreis (about US$2.50) per bag on producers who exclusively produced for domestic sale and refused to store their product.[7]

São Paulo producers largely financed this national tax. São Paulo's sugar demand continued to grow alongside its urban population. Many São Paulo producers refused to comply with the storage mandate and withhold sugar from sale in a growing local market. Northeastern mills producing for international markets were able to exclude their exported stocks from the domestic stock requirement.[8] Thus, the legislation bailed out overproducing and export-oriented northeastern producers at the expense of the expanding central-southern producers, much to the chagrin of paulistas.

Shortly after implementing this tax, the provisional government created the Commission for the Defense of Sugar Production (Comissão de Defesa da Produção do Açúcar [CDPA]) with Decree no. 20.761 on December 7, 1931. Intending to manage sugar policy more cohesively, the commission set up an administrative body that included federal government representatives from the Ministry of Labor, Industry, and Commerce, the Bank of Brazil, and the Treasury in addition to delegates from the principal producing states (in order of production capacity): Pernambuco, Alagoas, Sergipe, Bahia, Rio de Janeiro, and São Paulo.[9] Leonardo Truda, the representative from the Bank of Brazil, became the president of the commission.

Leonardo Truda was a guiding hand in early sugar intervention. Originally from Rio Grande do Sul, like President Vargas, Truda was one of many Rio Grande do Sul natives who rose to national political prominence under Getúlio Vargas in the 1930s. Trained in law, he worked as a journalist at the Rio de Janeiro newspaper *Diário de Noticias* before becoming a director at the Bank of Brazil. While there, he worked closely with sugar businesses and "came to understand the difficult situation of abandonment on the part of the public power that confronted the culture and industry of sugarcane."[10] Many credit Truda with the creation of the CDPA. Later, when the IAA took over the functions of the CDPA in 1933, Truda would remain the champion and most vocal supporter of sugar interests in the federal government.

As the primary financier of the agricultural industry and particularly the sugar industry, the Bank of Brazil played a critical financial and political role in the commission and later the Institute of Sugar and Alcohol. The Bank of Brazil first tied its financial power to agricultural policy as the entity through which Congress financed the coffee valorization programs.[11] Thereafter, it offered unprecedented levels of agricultural credit to large-scale producers, particularly in the sugar industry.[12] The Bank of Brazil did not valorize sugar but rather acted as a financial intermediary that collected the tax on sugar production and, from those funds, subsidized credit for sugar producers.[13] This positioned the bank at the very center of sugar policy, and after Truda, the Bank of Brazil delegate traditionally became the president of the IAA.

Ongoing disputes between the new federal government and São Paulo only exacerbated the economic struggles of the paulista sugar industry and undercut the CDPA's response. Regional and racial tensions led Vargas to strip paulistas of their federal powers and appoint João Alberto Lins de Barros, a Pernambucan lieutenant, as his caretaker governor (*interventor*) of São Paulo. The appointment of the "foreign" governor was accompanied by the newly centralized government's reduction of paulista politicians' control of the state's political and economic decisions.[14]

Contentious political relations between paulista politicians and the federal government devolved into civil war in 1932. On July 9, the paulista opposition led an armed resistance in the city of São Paulo against the provisional government's efforts to "reconstitutionalize" politics in the Constitutionalist Revolt. Over 10,000 paulista men fought the Brazilian army before Vargas managed to end the war in October. However, the revolt forced Vargas to appease paulistas to thwart further separatist efforts.[15] It undercut the IAA's new limitation policies, as fewer southeastern producers complied with the CDPA regulation to stockpile 10 percent of their sugar. If anything, it exposed the CDPA's inability to enforce legislation before the conflict. According to a 1932 report, 75 percent of producers escaped the sugar tax in the 1931–1932 harvest. Large producers still sold large quantities at a lower price, undercutting the IAA-established price of $30 milreis per sack. Truda and the CDPA initially could not enforce the sugar policy on a large scale since they lacked the infrastructure to regulate every sugar producer in the country.[16]

The CDPA implemented the initial sugar production limitation legislation as part of the envisioned defense of the sugar industry. However, the policy remained focused on rebalancing the industry and skewed toward reestablishing northeastern producers' dominance. Compliance with these policies, which was shaky after the 1932 São Paulo revolt, would continue to irritate paulista producers throughout the decade. While sugar limitations were an essential part of this defense, another factor was redirecting excess sugarcane toward alcohol production for fuel or ethanol. Although this connection would become more explicit under the IAA, ethanol had already gained some support amongst some specialists and government officials in the 1920s.

Ethanol Production before 1933

The technology behind ethanol production, namely, the ability to use ethanol derived from an agricultural base rather than petroleum to drive internal engines, dates back to the invention of the internal combustion engine.

Researchers in France and Germany tested the use of ethanol with internal combustion engines in the early 1900s. Henry Ford, Thomas Edison, and Alexander Graham Bell were all early supporters of ethanol use rather than that of oil.[17]

Brazilian scientists and engineers began experimenting with ethanol as a combustible fuel source in the 1920s. The paulista engineer Eduardo Sabino de Oliveira conducted research on it in collaboration with the engineer Heraldo de Souza Mattos and Professor Ernesto Lopes da Fonseca Costa at the private Escola Politécnica de São Paulo and the public National Technology Institute in Rio de Janeiro in the 1920s.[18]

While corn and potatoes drove ethanol experiments elsewhere, Brazilian scientists focused on ethanol from sugarcane. Fermentation converts sugar into ethyl alcohol. Initially, producers used molasses, which is left over after sugar juice extraction and ferments when mixed with yeast. Thereafter, distillation separates the alcohol from water for higher concentrations of alcohol. Drinking alcohol is distilled to around 74 to 95 percent purity (or alcohol by volume). Hydrated alcohol (a form of ethanol commonly used in medicines and other industrial products) is the most concentrated grade of alcohol possible through distillation, ranging from around 93 to 96 percent purity and 7 to 4 percent water, respectively. Anhydrous alcohol (another form of ethanol more traditionally used for fuel) requires dehydration using an additional dehydrating agent to reach over 99 percent purity. In Brazil, this additive was most traditionally benzol, which had to be imported into the country from the 1930s.

Until the late twentieth century, ethanol was most often produced from other cane byproducts, such as molasses or drinking alcohol, rather than directly from sugarcane. This is in part because of the higher value of other byproducts, particularly aguardente, on the domestic and foreign market until the 1930s. In fact, many producers preferred to use molasses as animal fodder or dump it in the riverways rather than purchase the equipment necessary to process the molasses into sugar ethanol's industrial (hydrous) and fuel (anhydrous) forms.[19]

While Brazilians use ethanol in two forms, the costs of producing anhydrous ethanol are notable. For industrial use, consumers traditionally used hydrous (or hydrated) ethanol. Carburant mixtures of the 1920s and early 1930s used hydrous ethanol along with other substances, such as gasoline and kerosene. However, cars ran better on gasoline mixtures using anhydrous (dehydrated) ethanol. Water in the hydrated version created mixture problems with gasoline, since it pooled at the bottom of tanks particularly at cooler temperatures and thus impaired the performance of the traditional car engine.[20] Yet, the additional processing required for anhydrous production was expensive, requiring additional dehydration equipment at the sugar mill plus the cost of importing benzol. Thus, despite its superior performance as a fuel option, anhydrous ethanol was not the preferred product for early ethanol producers.

As automobile ownership grew in the 1920s, the demand for fuel drove expanding gasoline imports and increasing interest in ethanol as a gasoline supplement.[21] President Epitácio Pessoa, a native of Pernambuco, referenced ethanol's importance in a speech to Congress in 1922: "The importance of the use of ethanol is highlighted by Brazil's colossal gasoline imports. Supporting the use of ethanol would also give a boost to our sugar industry."[22] After President Pessoa explicitly connected sugar and ethanol, private organizations, state governments, individuals, and firms expanded various forms of ethanol additives in gasoline. These efforts included research conducted by the Fuels and Minerals Experimental Station under the Ministry of Agriculture in Rio de Janeiro as well as state-level tax exemptions and subsidies to increase ethanol production and consumption for cars in selected northern states and Rio de Janeiro.[23]

Following his coup in 1930, Getúlio Vargas and his provisional government formalized state interests in ethanol as part of a sugar support initiative. Facing diminished access to international markets, the government looked to ethanol to address multiple pressing political and economic issues. Politically, the ethanol industry bolstered an ailing sugar sector and created a domestic industry that aligned with Vargas's interest in industrializing as part of a larger national self-sufficiency agenda. Economically, it addressed a major balance of trade issue. With the onset of the Great Depression, the international market for the country's major export and foreign exchange earner, coffee, collapsed. Although Brazil was a small petroleum consumer and international oil prices remained low in the 1930s, expanded ethanol consumption lowered petroleum imports and repurposed underpriced potential sugar exports to improve the growing trade deficit, which in 1930 exceeded US$100 million to the great alarm of policymakers.[24]

Federal promotion of ethanol began with Decree no. 19.717 of February 20, 1931. President Vargas's decree, supported by the Ministry of Agriculture, required that gasoline importers add a minimum of 5 percent mixture of domestically produced anhydrous ethanol to commercial gasoline.[25] The decree encouraged *álcool-motor* production for use in standard engines. This fuel was a mixture of regular gasoline and alternative sources such as ether and kerosene. *Carburante nacional* included gasoline and anhydrous ethanol exclusively, while less official variations included gasoline and less expensive inputs such as hydrous ethanol and kerosene.[26] The decree allowed importers to add other products to the requisite ethanol and gasoline mixture if the Ministry of Agriculture approved the formula used. To incentivize compliance, gasoline importers received a sales tax exemption on ethanol for all these mixtures.

Decree no. 19,717 went to great lengths to incentivize anhydrous ethanol production. This included an increase in the import duty of cylinder heads used in low compression rate engines which ran on gasoline and a 20 percent decrease in duty for those with higher compression rates that could thus run on ethanol; an exemption from import duty for all material and equipment used in the construction of usinas producing anhydrous ethanol; and a minimum reduction of 50 percent in the transport cost of denatured ethanol, or that mixed with other substances, relative to pure gasoline.[27] These tax breaks were meant to encourage production through the market rather than extensive state intervention.

While ethanol variations expanded relatively quickly, these initial government incentives generally failed. So the provisional government enacted an incentive program with Decree no. 20.356 on September 1, 1932, which offered a "prize of 50 million reis to the first plant to manufacture and redistill anhydrous ethanol that is established in each of the states of Rio de Janeiro, Pernambuco, or São Paulo, with the capacity to produce, at minimum, fifteen thousand liters daily of alcohol (anhydrous) by March 31, 1932."[28] The competition being open to producers in Rio de Janeiro, Pernambuco, and São Paulo meant that the targeted production markets were near large consumer markets in the country. Yet no producer met the deadline. The incentive at 50 million reis (roughly US$4,000) was not enough to cover the additional cost of equipment installation. Paulista producers preferred to dump excess alcohol rather than incur the costs of processing it into ethanol.[29]

Following the initial decree, President Vargas and the Ministry of Agriculture established the Commission of Studies on Alcohol-Motor (Comissão de Estudos sobre o Álcool-Motor) and the Fuels and Minerals Station (Estação de Combustíveis e Mineiros) in August and September 1931, respectively. The Ministry of Agriculture supervised the two entities, which they established to improve the infrastructure so criticized in the first incentive program. This included a "technical inspection service" to enforce fiscal penalties against violators of the regulations.[30] Both led research and experiments on optimal levels of ethanol mixed with gasoline.

Like the sugar policies of the early 1930s, these early interventions yielded limited results. As the scholar Tamás Szmrecsányi notes, these early decrees on ethanol "did not produce practical results until the advent of the IAA, in 1933" because of the "lack of technological infrastructure and . . . the insufficient economic stimuli offered by the Government."[31] Mixtures remained inconsistent in different markets. Distribution depended on major usineiros in primary sugar production markets such as Pernambuco, while the primary consumer markets in Rio de Janeiro and São Paulo struggled to expand production quickly. Moreover, there was little penalty for non-compliance, which hindered these early efforts.[32] However, more formal intervention would yield better results in both regulating the sugar industry and constructing an ethanol industry in 1933.

The IAA: Formal State Intervention in Sugar and Ethanol, 1933–1942

On June 6, 1933 with Decree no. 22.789, Getúlio Vargas and the provisional government created the Institute of Sugar and Alcohol (Instituto do Açúcar e do Álcool [IAA]).[33] The IAA, one of many autarkies President Vargas established for agricultural commodities, was a semiautonomous governmental body that was able to exert decisive and somewhat independent control over an agricultural industry. Joining the previously separated Commission for the Defense of Sugar Production (Commissão de Defesa da Produção do Açúcar [CDPA]) and the Commission of Studies on Alcohol-Motor (Comissão de Estudos sobre o Álcool-Motor), the IAA formalized the federal government's explicit role in sugar and ethanol policy planning.[34] It had two objectives: first, to eliminate overproduction and stabilize sugar prices and, second, to construct and/or equip distilleries for the production of anhydrous ethanol.[35] Over the course of its first decade, it successfully promoted the expansion of ethanol production by limiting sugar production, at times with contentious outcomes, and by incentivizing private producers to enter the ethanol market. São Paulo producers' redirection of these incentives toward private ethanol production shaped public–private collaboration in the ethanol industry that continues to this day.

Truda, as president of the IAA, and the executive commission guided federal sugar policy. With its headquarters in Rio de Janeiro, the IAA's executive commission allowed representatives from each state and various groups within the industry to influence sugar policy. They included the representatives from the Bank of Brazil and ministries along with nominated representatives for usineiros, planters, and suppliers.

In order to control sugar production, the IAA assigned quotas to each sugar producer based on his land and three previous harvest production cycles. In 1933, quotas were set for 200 modernized mills. Smaller, more traditional sugar production facilities did not have quotas until 1935, which complicated the IAA's work in instituting the sugar limitations overall.[36] Beyond setting production quotas, the IAA controlled the pricing of sugar products, from table sugar to ethanol, and handled the commercialization of these products.[37]

Sugar production objectives were connected to incentives for private producers to expand ethanol production. Ethanol for combustion addressed both of the IAA's objectives by potentially cutting petroleum imports and salvaging the dire situation of the northeastern-dominated sugar industry. By creating another domestic market for excess sugar production, ethanol would protect sugar producers, particularly northeastern producers, from the unstable global market and overproduction that plagued the industry.[38] Rather than dumping excess sugar, the policy attempted to redirect excess sugar into ethanol production for fuel.[39] This would ideally create a self-sufficient sugar industry in which sugar profits subsidized the alcohol distilleries, which would absorb excess sugar production to ideally reach a market-regulated equilibrium.[40]

The IAA created the Section on Alcohol-Motor within its government infrastructure to control all ethanol research, the delivery of ethanol from producers, preparation and delivery to distributors, and sales of the new product.[41] Although Vargas had already mandated a 5 percent mixture in 1932, the Section on Alcohol-Motor organized the supply and distribution of alcohol-motor on the basis of consumption. Each consumption zone received different alcohol-motor-mandated mixtures on the basis of access to distribution networks. The section set mandates of 20 percent alcohol and 80 percent gasoline for the majority of the country.[42] Thus, many areas consumed higher levels of ethanol than the 1932 mandate. Additionally, the institute was the sole supplier of anhydrous ethanol to gasoline distributors. In Rio de Janeiro, the IAA mixed the gasoline and distributed the new *álcool-motor* to the gas stations. In Santos, it delivered the mixture to gasoline importers, which they were obligated to purchase. The primary points of distribution, which were situated near the largest consumer and production markets in the country, were the city of São Paulo, Ponte Nova (MG), Recife (PE), and Campos (RJ).[43]

Consumers gave the new gasoline mixed reviews. The engineer Eduardo Sabino de Oliveira led research on the proper mixture levels in the IAA's technical section, confirming that anhydrous ethanol could reach as high as 25 percent without requiring adjustments in low compression motors. Problems were not related to actual car performance as much as to aesthetic perceptions. Distributors marketed the mixed fuel as *gazolina rosada* or pink gasoline because of its unique coloring, but consumers were wary of the new color and unsure of an engine's ability to run on it. The popularity of the mixture grew after distributors removed the color additive.[44]

Yet production and distribution fell far short of the mandated demand. Such shortcomings were not due to a lack of the raw material in these early years but rather to a shortage in production capacity and inadequate price incentives for producers. By 1936, production was not even half of the amount necessary to meet the nationally mandated mixture quota.[45] Production of ethanol in São Paulo state stood around 6.5 million liters, when the capital alone would need 7.2 million liters to meet the 10 percent mixture rate promoted by the IAA.[46] The failure to reach national production goals encouraged more direct action by Truda and the executive commission.

The IAA board established its own distilleries in an aggressive attempt to spur production. According to Article 4b of the original IAA Decree no. 22.789, the IAA encouraged anhydrous ethanol production "through the installation of central distilleries in locations most recommended" or by helping sugar cooperatives and syndicates "install distilleries individually or to improve their current installations."[47] As the prohibitive initial cost of ethanol distillation had limited early production, the IAA invested in building its own central distilleries in major production and consumption markets as well as offering substantial financing for additional private distilleries. The institute financed 50 percent of the installation costs for six different distilleries. It also completely financed two IAA-owned distilleries, one in Campos, Rio de Janeiro, opened in 1938 and another, located in Cidade do Cabo, Pernambuco, opened in 1940.[48] Given the IAA's role as the sole purchaser of sugar in the country, it directed excess sugar produced in the region by local sugar producers to these new central distilleries.

In contrast, São Paulo usineiros used a collective association, the Association of Sugar Mill Owners of São Paulo, to channel IAA-financing toward distribution and private firms. Their intermediary company, the Paulista Industrial Alcohol Company (Companhia Industrial Paulista de Álcool [CIPA]), exclusively controlled the state's ethanol distribution in association with the IAA. As the first paulista company to receive IAA financing for ethanol production, CIPA received 12,500,000 milreis (roughly US$101,500) for installation and equipment, which it used to equip tanks for transportation.[49] The associated sugar producers distributed their ethanol to CIPA, which then distributed the ethanol to gasoline distributors in the state. Their actions and interests ensured that São Paulo would not get a central distillery. Notably, this laid a foundation for greater private investment in ethanol production and distillery development that would transform São Paulo usineiros into leading ethanol producers by the 1970s.

In the initial years of the IAA, President Truda spent substantial time defending the IAA's limitation policy and convincing sugarcane producers in São Paulo and the Northeast to abide by it. At a São Paulo conference in January 1934, Truda addressed paulista producers' unhappiness with the limitations by stressing that the "solution to the [sugar] problem" lay in reconciling the "general conveniences" of excess sugar production with the "ultimate imperatives of the nation."[50] At the same time, he rallied support for ethanol production in the Northeast. He described ethanol to Pernambucan producers as "a product that greatly interests the national economy, for which we will have practically limitless application and will alleviate the country greatly from the cost that the urgent demands for our advancement in progress increase yearly."[51] Truda worked hard to ease the tensions between São Paulo producers, frustrated to have their production abilities limited despite a growing southern market, and those in the Northeast, who felt the expansion of paulista sugar production threatened their hold on the national market. Truda highlighted the IAA's efforts to address national interests as a whole.

The politics of the state-led ethanol intervention reflected growing regional conflicts between the Northeast and the Center-south. These have been chalked up to inequities in industrial investment, and to racial divisions embedded in economic divergence,[52] but the development of the sugar and ethanol industry contributed to these tensions. By the 1930s, the sugar industry would be an important platform on which the economic realities and social differences of the two regions would clash.

Notably, new sugar policies structurally favored northeastern producers. The IAA continued the sugar tax program initiated in 1931 under the CDPA, which taxed producers who did not store 10 percent of their sugar destined for the internal market.[53] Southeastern producers adamantly opposed this policy. As southeastern sugar refiners did not produce enough sugar to satisfy state demand, IAA production limitations kept São Paulo producers from expanding enough to independently supply consumers in the southeast. This aided northeasterners' hold on the sugar market, since the more industrialized southern producers already enjoyed cheaper production costs and, most importantly, lower transportation costs to the major markets in the southeast.

Still, paulista production grew in the south despite the IAA's efforts to balance regional production. The opportunities to supply the growing regional sugar market attracted many former and current coffee producers into the industry. Both crops thrived in São Paulo's semitropical environmental conditions. However, sugarcane made a particularly good follow-up to coffee because coffee trees draw their moisture from deep below the land, while the perennial cane is notoriously difficult to harvest with other plants because it draws moisture from soil at shallower levels.[54] In addition, coffee takes years to yield, while cane only takes months after planting.[55] Sugarcane's ability to grow in the exhausted lands of coffee trees drew in new producers, and sugar quickly established itself as an important part of the state's agricultural production in the 1930s. In the 1930/1931 harvest, São Paulo produced 1,108,510 sacks of sugar, and by 1936/1937 that number had doubled to 2,248,370 sacks.[56]

Many new sugar producers from this period would have an important impact on future sugar and ethanol production in São Paulo. The French firm, Société des Sucreries Brésiliennes, emerged as the state's largest sugar-producing firm after buying up many central engenhos (small sugar mills) between 1899 and 1907. Among other holdings, it owned three usinas concentrated in the first large sugar-producing region of São Paulo, Piracicaba, by the 1930s. The French firm also owned the first anhydrous ethanol distillery in the country, the Usina Piracicaba, which had produced 100,000 liters of anhydrous ethanol by 1933.[57]

Many descendants of immigrant families started domestic sugarcane firms in this period and would eventually own businesses that surpassed the larger international firm. Notably, Maurilio Biagi, the native Brazilian son of the Italian immigrant Pedro Biagi, purchased the Santa Elisa engenho in

1936 with his brothers, Baudílio and Gaudencio Biagi, and their partner João Pagano.[58] The Biagis' cousin, João Marchesi, was a major sugarcane producer in São Paulo as well.[59]

São Paulo producers quickly expanded ethanol production as well, taking advantage of federal incentives and their access to Brazil's largest consumer market. The usinas Itaiquara, Monte Alegre, Santa Barbara, Raffard, and Vassununga opened distilleries in 1935, producing a total of 37,500 liters of ethanol in that year alone.[60] By the 1934/1935 harvest, São Paulo was the third leading producer of ethanol in the country behind Pernambuco and Rio de Janeiro.[61] However, it transformed a larger percentage of sugarcane directly into ethanol (47.8%) than Pernambucano producers (40.8%). Considered a more efficient production path, this perhaps foreshadowed the state's ascendance as the eventual ethanol leader. By mid-1937, nine anhydrous ethanol distilleries were in operation in São Paulo and three more were under construction.

As the largest consumer market and the dominant car market, São Paulo was an important center of ethanol propaganda as well as production. Truda nominated the city of São Paulo to host "Alcohol-Motor Week" and the first Conference on Alcohol-Motor in October 1937. The week was marked by a series of public demonstrations, some of which were held on the popular Avenida Brasil, to commercialize the viability of alcohol-motor and the IAA's efforts in ethanol research and production. As Truda noted at the first conference, "In no other state . . . has the particular initiative been more active than in São Paulo; no region outweighs this region in the speed and efficiency of the [sugar] solution."[62] Within the state of São Paulo, Ribeirão Preto usineiros began investing in ethanol production too. The Usina Santa Elisa

Table 1.1 Anhydrous Ethanol Production by Major States (in liters), 1934–1940

State	1934	1936	1938	1940
São Paulo	481,400	4,052,248	4,443,053	15,192,588
Pernambuco	22,615	9,035,350	11,830,405	18,008,819
Alagoas	187,722	894,189	2,245,142	4,076,372
Rio de Janeiro	203,158	3,811,279	13,296,884	15,674,733
TOTAL	911,861	18,462,432	31,919,934	53,473,533

Source: De Melo, *A política do álcool-motor*, Appendix.

began producing ethanol in 1939, only three years after Maurilio and his brothers purchased it.[63]

The IAA consolidated sugar policy in the late 1930s, monitoring production quotas more closely thereafter. Political changes bolstered the power of the IAA. President Getúlio Vargas ended his constitutional presidency and began his dictatorship, known as the *Estado Novo*, on November 10, 1937. After the declaration of the Estado Novo, the IAA reported that "happily, for the well-being and prosperity of the laborious and honored sugar classes, the new constitution does not alter, but rather consolidates and increases the policy of the defense of sugar production."[64] The new IAA president Alexandre José de Barbosa Lima Sobrinho, a Pernambucan lawyer and journalist who was Trudá's handpicked successor, sought to limit the expansion of São Paulo production. Although he supported the declining national position of northeastern sugar production, the results were far from favorable to Pernambucan sugar producers. In 1939, the IAA started strongly enforcing limitations in the southeastern region and, in the early 1940s, it expanded into segmented quotas dictating from whom usineiros could purchase cane to mill and distill.

From the construction of its own central distilleries to financing for private distilleries and other incentives, the IAA successfully intervened in the sugar market to create an ethanol market in the first decade after its creation. There had previously been no anhydrous production, but, by 1940, eight distilleries were producing anhydrous ethanol in Pernambuco, including the IAA's Destilaria Central Presidente Vargas, three in Alagoas, nine in Rio de Janeiro, and twelve in São Paulo. Of these four states, São Paulo, with its private production led by private producers, emerged as the second largest ethanol producing state in the country behind Pernambuco.

The IAA and Paulista Influence, 1942–1950

When German submarines attacked Brazilian commercial vessels in 1942, Vargas declared war on the Axis Powers. The threat of additional attacks cut off transportation routes for shipping northeastern sugar to the southern market. Demand for ethanol grew, as gasoline imports into the country were limited. The sugar producer Maurilio Biagi took advantage of the wartime pressures on this industry to improve his production techniques and invest in ethanol production. These actions transformed the Usina Santa Elisa into a leading usina in the Ribeirão Preto region, as the government dropped earlier production restrictions and ethanol earned greater national importance.

Sugar shortages in the southeast, particularly São Paulo, forced IAA president Barbosa Lima and the executive commission to relax sugar quotas for regional producers, most notably those in São Paulo. Barbosa Lima authorized the construction of new usinas and dropped quotas, suspending restrictions for production of unrefined sugar and enabling the installation of small sugar plants in the "insufficiently supplied states" of São Paulo, Rio de Janeiro, and Minas Gerais.[65] As southeastern imports of northeastern sugar had secured the region's dominance of the sugar sector, the IAA tried to control the subsequent São Paulo expansion to protect northeastern producers. With Decree no. 49/43, the IAA limited authorization to new engenhos with only small production quotas of 400 sacks of sugar per year. Still, paulistas began to scramble to register production quotas after the initial release. While the IAA had used quotas to restrict entry into the sugar sector in the 1930s, the updated policy allowed new producers to break into the industry even as the expansion of paulista production slowed between 1940 and 1944.[66]

After Brazil entered the war on the Allied side, efforts to promote ethanol production expanded. To encourage production, the IAA established price parity between ethanol and sugar in 1942. The lower price previously offered for ethanol production had diminished producers' willingness to invest in sugar production. Parity provided an important incentive.

The IAA launched what the political scientist Maria de Castro Santos calls the "alcohol war package" to promote greater ethanol production, even as wartime needs drove the popularity of alternative fuel options. Limited imports, not just of petroleum, adversely affected ethanol's broader expansion. A shortage of benzol, a key dehydration ingredient in the production of anhydrous ethanol, hindered anhydrous ethanol's expansion from 1943. However, these policies ended up encouraging increased production of hydrated ethanol, which did not require the same dehydration process and was primarily used in industrial products.[67] The gasogene, an apparatus that attached to the back of an automobile and burned wood, charcoal, peat, and other combustibles for fuel, also became a popular alternative, particularly in larger markets such as Rio de Janeiro and São Paulo.[68] Nevertheless, government support remained firmly behind ethanol.

President Vargas and sugar policymakers refocused on ethanol production's political importance, as the wartime fuel shortages drew national security attention to ethanol for the first time. In late 1941, IAA president Barbosa Lima established the National Commission for Fuels and Lubricants with Decree no. 3.755 to "coordinate production and distribution policy" of fuels, including ethanol, in response to the wartime fuel shortage.[69] Under the leadership of the secretary general of the National Security Council, the commission explicitly connected the interests of the sugar, mining, petroleum, and gas sectors to national fueling priorities for the first time. This made ethanol production not just the solution to the sugar problem of the 1930s but also a part of national security concerns because of its role in the reduction of gasoline imports.[70]

The political transformations of the postwar period influenced sugar and ethanol policy as the country moved away from the interventionist policies of the Vargas era to a liberal economic model.[71] After the former war minister General Eurico Gaspar Dutra won the first democratic presidential elections in Brazil since 1930 and took office in 1946, his government embraced a return to high imports in a less restricted economy. In fact, these initial policies quickly drove the balance of payments back into a precarious situation, forcing the Dutra government to readjust its policies by 1948.[72]

With the war over, São Paulo sugar producers attacked the IAA and its protectionist policies, further asserting their growing dominance in the national sugar industry. São Paulo producers challenged the IAA president Barbosa Lima Sobrinho's continued efforts to restrict southeastern production and pushed for the abolishment of the IAA itself. The editors of the IAA's monthly magazine *Brasil Açucareiro* dedicated multiple articles to the defense of the IAA and its policies in 1945. Newspapers attacked the efficacy of the IAA and its leadership.[73] The debate over the IAA and its very existence reached the newly formed Senate, where the former São Paulo executive commission representative Paulo Nogueira was one of the many vehement supporters of the dissolution of the institute.[74] These battles continued through 1948, as the IAA executive commission repeatedly defended itself against efforts to replace the entity first with a rural bank under the Ministry of Finance and then under the Agricultural Ministry.[75]

Amidst these political battles, the IAA extended the more liberal wartime production policies by formally separating national quotas by state. This allowed São Paulo producers alone to expand capacity to provide for the largest consumer market in the country rather than sharing that market with numerous other states, most notably Pernambuco. Decree no. 9,827 of September 10, 1946 set production quota levels per state based on regional consumption rather than national quotas for a unified national market.[76] The decree effectively untethered paulista production from northeastern production. As the southern market expanded in response to higher sugar and ethanol consumption in the major consumer markets, the Northeast's hold on sugar production and influence in the IAA diminished.[77]

The shift toward São Paulo in the IAA reflects a broader national trend during this same period. As the Northeast's influence on sugar diminished and its primary economic engine lost steam, power tilted toward southern economic and political interests and enflamed enduring tensions. This exacerbated northeastern and southeastern producers' long-standing mutual disdain. In São Paulo, a steady stream of migrants to both rural regions and the city promoted a particularly negative image of northeasterners that was racially and economically driven. Paulistas' political dominance, connected to a growing population, its increasingly industrialized economy, and newly created identities of whiteness, bolstered the sugar and ethanol sector.

As the IAA loosened its regulation of sugar quotas, its control over ethanol production transformed as well. São Paulo producers worked to meet the large São Paulo demand, while also expanding their ethanol production capacity. The number of usinas in São Paulo grew from forty-two in 1946 to seventy-one in 1947 to more than ninety by 1956, while distillation capacity grew from 43,083,152 liters in 1946 to 51,172,271 liters in 1951.[78]

Nationally, hydrated ethanol production grew disproportionately in relation to the IAA's preferred fuel supplement, anhydrous ethanol.[79] This was partially related to the difficulty of importing the necessary dehydration components during the war, but the IAA continued to incentivize anhydrous ethanol through various promotional projects and legislation. The IAA executive commission financed another incentive program in 1945 for the construction of an usina and distillery similar to its 1931 distillery competition. Exclusively directed toward the construction of three usinas and attached distilleries in western São Paulo, the program required that the distillery have a production capacity of a minimum of 15 liters of ethanol per 60kg sack of sugar. To participate, producers had to have a requisite IAA sugar production quota of 30,000 sacks or more, which meant that minimum ethanol production capacity would be 450,000 liters per year. The quota requirement thus excluded many of the smaller new usinas, engenhos, and other sugar production mills and instead favored larger producers.[80]

Key legislation enabled a dramatic expansion in ethanol production. First, President Dutra's Decree no. 25,174A of July 3, 1948 reasserted ethanol's national importance, committing the IAA to increasing stocks of molasses and ethanol and improving transportation from regional producers to gasoline companies for mixing and distribution to consumers. These goals were not new to ethanol policy, but the decree also established price parity between sugar and direct ethanol (i.e., ethanol produced directly from the cane) and added additional bonuses for those mills that produced ethanol along with sugar.[81] Additionally, the IAA established the Anhydrous Alcohol Fund (Resolution no. 210/48), which funded the additional costs of production for the installation and maintenance of anhydrous facilities. Finally, the IAA established annual goals for anhydrous ethanol used in the fuel mixture, starting at 114 million liters in the 1948/1949 harvest.[82]

The expansion of the paulista sugar and ethanol industry during the war incentivized more entrepreneurs in the Ribeirão Preto region to invest in the sugar industry, which helped transform the region into a leading sugar and ethanol center by the 1970s. Take, for example, Antonio Paschoal, one of the first metallurgy business owners in Sertãozinho. A mechanic by trade, Paschoal worked in metallurgy offices in Ribeirão Preto and Piracicaba before taking over his father's company with his brother Braz in 1928, which they renamed B. Paschoal & Irmão. Working closely with the Engenho Central in Sertãozinho, Antonio focused on producing and fixing mill equipment such as boilers. In the 1940s, he won a license to produce gasogenes for alternative fuel use, and was hugely successful. Paschoal used these profits to build and invest in various new usinas in the region, including the Usina Santa Lúcia in 1947 and the Usina São Francisco in 1946.[83]

During this period, the Biagi's Usina Santa Elisa emerged as a leading usina in the region as well. Pedro Biagi gave his shares in the company to his three sons, Gaudencio, Baudílio, and Maurilio in 1941, because of fears that his status as an Italian immigrant might create problems during the war. Maurilio was the driving force behind the usina. The seventh of Pedro's twelve sons, Maurilio had studied accounting at the Salesiano High School in Campinas but had worked closely with his father and his brothers at their nearby usina in Serrana, the Usina da Pedra, before purchasing the Usina Santa Elisa in December 1936. He was deeply interested in technical experimentation to improve cane cultivation and in the use of sugarcane ethanol for combustion.

A self-directed student of agricultural technology, Maurilio closely read such journals as the IAA's *Brasil Açucareiro*, *Cultura dos Campos*, which compiled European publications for Brazilian agriculturalists, and *A Lavoura*, a publication by the National Society of Agriculture in Rio de Janeiro. He also followed agricultural research developed at the Agronomic Institute of Campinas (Instituto Agronômico de Campinas) and the Luiz de Queiroz College of Agriculture (Escola Superior de Agricultura "Luiz de Queiroz" [ESALQ]) in Piracicaba, centers of early research on sugarcane varieties, cultivation practices, and byproduct uses.[84]

Reforms unique to the Usina Santa Elisa in the late 1940s turned it into a leading "modern," industrialized usina. Biagi's son, Maurilio Biagi Filho recalled that his father "started to import new equipment and test the national prototypes, copied from foreigners. New cane varieties and planting techniques were introduced."[85] Biagi was a particular supporter of agricultural technology developed in the 1940s to overcome land quality issues in Ribeirão Preto. Although the region was famous for its fertile red earth (*terra roxa*), most sugarcane land had already been exhausted by extensive coffee production, and perennial agricultural production had stripped the land of its nutrients. Furthermore, the northeast of São Paulo included *cerrado* land, a savannah-like biome notable for its excessive acidity. In fact, after his son purchased the Usina Santa Elisa, Pedro Biagi warned, "You are going to keep losing, Maurilio, because on the Santa Elisa lands there are only green lizards."[86] Lowlands prone to flooding and gritty soil challenged his production of popular sugarcane varieties.

Biagi invested in new soil manipulation techniques under development in the 1940s and 1950s, particularly fertilizers, to compensate for these challenges. Brazil's obsession with fertilizers began in earnest in the 1940s with the creation of phosphate plants and intensified in 1950s with the petrochemical industry and increased potassium imports. In Ribeirão Preto, Biagi and other sugar producers used fertilizers to restore the land's productivity without having to leave it to lie fallow for two or three full years. After Lair Antonio de Souza, an accountant and former salesman of imported fertilizers, and an associate Arquimedes Barbieri opened a commercial fertilizer company in Ribeirão Preto in 1955, the regional sugar cooperative Copereste (the Cooperative of Mill Owners of Western São Paulo), of which Biagi was a founding member in 1953, was its largest client. In 1958, Solorrico opened the first plant for domestically produced fertilizer in Brazil, and Maurilio Biagi and his three siblings were the primary investors in it.[87]

Biagi utilized other innovative techniques to modernize the Usina Santa Elisa as well. He incorporated the use of tractors in 1945 and 1946. In the 1950s, Santa Elisa began burning cane to break it down and speed up cane collection, which still relied on manual laborers, mules, and wagons to transport cane from the fields to the usina. In 1948, after a destructive fire threatened the usina's harvest in 1947, the usineiro began using a mixed transportation system that utilized both trucks and wagons to deliver the harvested cane to the usina more efficiently. This also allowed for the incorporation of preharvest cane burning to break down the cane and speed up collection in the early 1950s. Although this controversial practice had previously been considered bad for cane's sucrose content, in 1946 the renowned sugar researcher Jaime Rocha de Almeida at the State of São Paulo's Sugar Experimental Station in Piracicaba published an article supporting the practice so long as no transportation bottlenecks prevented the movement of burned cane to the mill within 48 to 72 hours. Biagi's close attention to the work at ESALQ and particularly Rocha's research likely influenced his decision to lead the region in this controversial practice of preharvest burning.[88] Maurilio Biagi continued to import tractors and expand the mechanized transportation system, turning the usina into a model for its cultivation and transportation methods. Other usinas emulated Biagi's methods, improving mechanized production methods for numerous producers as a result.[89]

Maurilio Biagi invested not only in sugar and ethanol production but also in the agricultural equipment necessary for sugar production. In August 1950, he partnered with Ettore Zanini, a local mechanic, to found the Oficina Zanini Ltda, a metallurgy company that became the region's largest equipment company. Biagi started the business to compete with the Dedini metallurgy company, founded in Piracicaba in the 1920s, which was the only large producer of major industrial equipment for the Brazilian sugar industry.[90] Zanini transformed the Ribeirão Preto region into a center for cane equipment and technology. The close collaboration between the usina and the equipment company fostered more advanced distillation and cane cultivation methods, benefiting not only the Usina Santa Elisa but also neighboring usinas.[91]

These early technological improvements established the Usina Santa Elisa as a national leader in the modernization of the sugar industry and enabled it to define the direction of the sugar industry in the region.[92] First establishing its prominence in the region with new technology in its production process, the Biagis would use self-financed technological imports to later expand their hold on the market. Their early innovations in modernization techniques, domestic and foreign, were critical steps in industrializing sugarcane production.

Industrialization, Ethanol, and Automobiles, 1950–1959

Paulista sugar production expanded dramatically in the 1950s even as ethanol's importance as a contributor to the national fuel supply diminished. The IAA continued to support ethanol production, but a drop in international petroleum prices allowed the expanding car and steel industries to focus on oil consumption. Important changes in sugar and ethanol production and consumption that occurred in the 1950s were set against the broader political and economic transformations underway in Brazil.

President Dutra's economic policies in the late 1940s had encouraged a wave of industrialization in Brazil. His policies limited imports while simultaneously maintaining a high currency valuation. These conditions made investing in domestic industries more economically viable than relying on imported industrial goods.[93] This directly encouraged the expansion of agricultural and industrial companies such as Biagi's Zanini.

By the beginning of the 1950s, a developmentalist-nationalist ideology focused on aggressive domestic industrialization began to drive Brazilian economic policies and national politics, even though it had been present in government policies for the previous two decades. Vargas had created the IAA in support of an economic nationalist agenda focused on self-sufficiency in the 1930s, and his support for state-led industrialization as a form of economic nationalism was a key part of the Estado Novo. Import substitution policies followed Vargas's early initiatives. Theory followed policy in the 1940s, as economic theorists and public opinion alike fostered a growing sense that Brazil could only become an important power if it developed into a modern industrial economy.[94] This sentiment gained greater attention through Vargas's populist campaign for the presidency, run on the promise of the creation of a domestic oil industry. After his victory in 1951, Vargas created the new national oil company, Petrobras, which shifted all oil drilling and refining to the state-owned company monopoly.[95] Thus, petroleum became a symbol of national autonomy and security, displacing ethanol in importance.[96]

Following President Vargas's dramatic suicide in 1954, the next elected president Juscelino Kubitschek accelerated the petroleum-centered developmentalist-nationalist agenda and further diminished ethanol's place in the national energy and development scheme. The Minas Gerais native and former governor built his political career and eventually his presidency on "the idea of using the state to plan the development of the nation."[97] His presidential campaign, entitled "Fifty Years of Progress in Five," called for the rapid industrialization of the country. A centerpiece of this agenda was the establishment of Brazil's automotive industry, side by side with the construction of the new federal capital in Brasilia in the interior of the state of Goiás.[98]

For Kubitschek, like many Brazilians, the establishment of a domestic car industry was the key to a modern country and a source of nationalist pride. Volkswagen and Willys-Overland Motors began manufacturing trucks and cars in Brazil using an increasing amount of Brazilian manufactured inputs in 1954 and 1957, respectively. Brazilians connected these achievements with the idea of reaching a tangible level of development, but this modernization relied more on standard oil consumption rather than the alternative ethanol product that policymakers had supported so aggressively over the previous thirty years.[99]

The oil-based fuel economy expanded with the growth of the domestic steel company and car production. Brazil's Petrobras slowly replaced imported hydrocarbon products with those refined and distributed from domestic or imported crude. It was far slower to produce its own crude at a rate sufficient to meet the country's growing demand, so Brazil remained highly dependent on foreign oil even after Petrobras's founding.[100] The low international oil prices of the 1950s, officially cheaper than ethanol liter for liter, diminished demand for ethanol. In fact, the National Petroleum Council (Conselho Nacional do Petróleo [CNP]) reduced the national ethanol mixture rate from the previous 10 percent nationally between 1938 and 1940 to 5 percent in the 1950s. The government's diminished commitment to ethanol in favor of an oil-based fuel economy seemingly would have doomed the ethanol industry.[101]

Yet anticipated expansion of domestic sugar consumption with increased urbanization encouraged policymakers to promote agro-industrial growth within the sugar sector, which drove increased sugar and ethanol production. In anticipation of 6 percent consumption growth per harvest over the next five years, IAA president Fernando Pessoa de Queiroz and the executive commission increased the sugar production limit by over ten million sacks of sugar (from 23,220,794 sacks of sugar in the 1950/1951 harvest to 33,364,158 sacks in the 1956/1957 harvest) in Resolution no. 501 of February 1, 1951. Established and new usinas divided up the production of the additional 10,143,364 sacks (9,264,217 for old usinas and 879,147 for new usinas). Even when the commission lowered its expansion expectation to 4.87 percent per year, the expected domestic sugar consumption for the 1956/1957 harvest was still 30,331,053 sacks of sugar, less than 1 percent under the original figure.[102] Resolution no. 501, in turn, drove the creation of agro-industrial complexes across the paulista countryside to increase production capacity in the 1950s. Despite the IAA's attempts to contain paulista expansion, usineiros such as the Biagis with the Usina Santa Elisa consolidated the agricultural production of their sugarcane, the processing of that cane, and even the development of the equipment for processing into one large complex. Increasingly common amongst São Paulo's largest producers, these complexes took advantage of government incentives to process the sugarcane byproduct molasses into ethanol.

Despite its diminishing returns in the 1950s, the IAA continued to support ethanol production as an important part of sugar policy and regulation. It continued to expand quotas to reclaim control of sugar production that it had lost in the 1940s.[103] Following Resolution no. 501, paulista sugar and ethanol production dramatically increased. Nationally, sugar production expanded from 23.4 million sacks in 1950 to 55.2 million sacks of sugar in 1960. São Paulo alone produced 23.97 million sacks in the 1960/1961 harvest.[104] Even as sugar production grew in the country, Brazilian exports of this product were slow to expand. Not only had ethanol proven its worth during the wartime fuel shortages, but the fuel also still offered a practical alternative for excess sugarcane. As the IAA struggled to take control of the sugar policy, it continued to promote using excess sugar production for ethanol, among other regulated byproducts. Resolution no. 501 encouraged additional alternative fuel production by requiring all usinas to channel 10 percent of their overall sugar production to ethanol.[105] The legislation dictated that usinas independently finance distillery construction when possible, but northeastern producers quickly came to rely on IAA funds. The resolution also encouraged the production of other, cheaper byproducts but showed a clear preference by guaranteeing bonuses for anhydrous or hydrous ethanol. Such policies, in accordance with the IAA's continued guarantee of price parity for ethanol with sugar, expanded national production even as demand for ethanol declined.

São Paulo ethanol production in particular surged. In 1952, the state produced 64,447,332 liters of ethanol. By 1955, that amount had more than doubled, and the state's anhydrous ethanol production outstripped hydrous for the first time.[106] As the required buyer of ethanol, the IAA purchased and stored all of this excess. São Paulo surpassed Pernambuco as the leading producer of all ethanol types in 1954 after surpassing the northeastern leader in sugar production three years earlier.[107] The growing São Paulo anhydrous ethanol stock positioned paulista producers to quickly become major fuel producers under Proálcool in the 1970s.

Individual producers in São Paulo made great gains in sugar and ethanol production during this period. Industrialization efforts and business consolidations allowed Ribeirão Preto to emerge as a leading sugar- and ethanol-producing region in the growing São Paulo sugar industry. Exemplifying consolidation across the state, Maurilio Biagi and the Biagi Group began incorporating smaller usinas into the Usina Santa Elisa to expand its production capabilities, such as the Usina Santa Lúcia, formerly owned by the metallurgy businessman Antonio Paschoal.[108] In the 1950/1951 harvest, the Usina Santa Elisa produced 123,400 sacks of sugar but by the 1960/1961 harvest, it more than tripled production to 483,562 sacks of sugar. The Biagi-owned Usina da Pedra began producing anhydrous ethanol in 1953, while the Usina Santa Elisa's hydrous ethanol production expanded to 1,681,320 liters of ethanol in 1955.[109]

At the same time, the Biagis improved the Usina Santa Elisa's production methods. Its management participated in cane cultivation studies conducted by the Agronomic Institute of Campinas that contributed to the advancement of superior cane varieties for the various soil types across the state. Agronomists from the institute's sugarcane divisions set up experimental studies on cane varieties at six different usinas in the state, including the Usina Santa Elisa, in 1953.[110] Following Biagi's vision, the Usina Santa Elisa thus led early public–private collaboration in the technological development of the industry. However, unlike the equipment imports that characterized the Usina Santa Elisa's industrial growth, state intervention focused on the development of new agricultural technology.

Table 1.2 São Paulo State Compared with National Ethanol Production (in liters), 1950–1955

	1950/51	1951/52	1952/53	1953/54	1954/55
São Paulo	51,172,271	63,621,395	84,202,142	128,567,498	170,159,827
National	140,094,857	170,362,503	229,542,853	274,039,309	306,246,596
Percentage	36.5%	37.3%	36.7%	46.9%	55.6%
Anhydrous	4,947,962	5,117,200	12,613,402	50,011,200	80,658,684

Source: IAA, *Anuário Açucareiro*.

While sugar production technology expanded and the IAA's control of sugar limits diminished, regional producers founded early cooperatives to diminish collective commercial and distribution costs and to establish a stronger hold over the sugar sector's expansion. In 1953, fourteen usineiros in the Ribeirão Preto region formed Copereste (the Cooperative of Mill Owners of Western São Paulo) with Maurilio Biagi as a leading member. The cooperative's efforts focused on increasing industrial and agricultural production using technology and scientific information for increased efficiency.[111] Copereste standardized some of the research, the distribution of better cane seeds, and the use of machinery in agricultural processes that Biagi had already pioneered at the Usina Santa Elisa. The cooperative reinforced Biagi's important position in the industry as an innovator and businessman as these techniques spread through the region and eventually extended to a consolidated and influential state cooperative, Copersucar (The Central Cooperative of Producers of Sugar and Alcohol of São Paulo), in the 1960s.[112]

* * *

Unlike the manioc plan in 1944, following the government's plan and its money worked to the advantage of sugar producers who invested in ethanol production. Early ethanol production, aided by federal intervention in the sugar industry, created the producer-oriented incentives and national consumption mandates that later became the foundation of the Proálcool initiative. The IAA first imposed ethanol production in the 1930s as a way to limit sugar production and manage the impact of global price fluctuations. Increased energy demands and limited access to foreign and far-off domestic markets during World War II incentivized new sugar and ethanol policies in the 1940s and 1950s that continued to drive production as the industry shifted south from the Northeast.

The sugar and ethanol industry expanded in the Ribeirão Preto region, led by Maurilio Biagi. The connections to agricultural research centers and tighter business networks that they fostered allowed the Usina Santa Elisa to grow into an advanced sugar- and ethanol-producing complex by the end of the 1950s. As the Biagis led the region into a new era of sugar and ethanol development, IAA investment in the sector increased in response to new export opportunities on the world market and the military dictatorship's development agenda.

2

Sugar, Ethanol, and Development, 1959–1975

"The essential goal of my government can be summarized in one word: development."

President Emílio Garrastazu Médici (1970)

A year after President Médici announced his commitment to "development,"[1] the automaker Chrysler ran a half-page advertisement in the *Estado de São Paulo* for the Dodge pickup truck which celebrated the Usina Santa Elisa as "an authentic model usina." According to the advertisement, after Chrysler convinced the usina to use a Dodge 700 truck to collect cane, "That was enough. Today, the Usina Santa Elisa already bought 15 more . . . Follow the model of the Usina Santa Elisa: go see the Dodge 700."[2] The auto industry had been used to symbolize Brazilian development imagery since President Kubitschek established the domestic industry in the 1950s. In that same decade Biagi had been one of the first sugar producers to use trucks to rapidly transport cut cane to the mill for crushing. The advertisement implicitly highlights the usina's growing renown as the height of "modern" or industrialized sugar production, whose integration of technology and new equipment wed the São Paulo sugar industry to the idea of agro-industry as development.

This chapter explores how the government and individual usineiros such as the Biagis managed "modernization" efforts in the 1960s and 1970s to industrialize the sugar sector, while ethanol seemingly faded into the background. From the 1960s, new export opportunities increased the sugar industry's importance to the new military government's national development agendas. To capitalize on increasing international and domestic demand, the government's sugar organization, the IAA, implemented numerous initiatives focused on the expansion of industrial production capacity which

Sweet Fuel. Jennifer Eaglin, Oxford University Press. © Oxford University Press 2022.
DOI: 10.1093/oso/9780197510681.003.0003

encouraged large-scale consolidation of production in the process. Private financing, proximity to large domestic consumer markets in the southeast, and the construction of industrial sugar and ethanol complexes with superior, often imported agricultural and processing equipment enabled paulista sugar producers to take advantage of these new opportunities ahead of their rival northeastern producers. Ribeirão Preto producers such as the Biagis of the Usina Santa Elisa won particular fame as their concentrated industrial sugar production began to surpass that of other parts of the state.

Private sugar interests, rather than government officials, strategically positioned ethanol to become a future large-scale energy option in this frenzied period of sugar agro-industrialization. Policymakers focused on sugar exports, not ethanol production. However, even as ethanol production remained subordinate to sugar exports, entrepreneurial paulista producers continued to push support for ethanol for their own economic interests in the expansion of the sugar sector. By the early 1970s, newly consolidated large-scale producers used the federal incentive program, the IAA's Support Program for the Sugar Agro-Industry (Fundo para o Programa de Apoio à Agro-Indústria Açucareiro—Funproçúcar), to further expand their ethanol production capacity. As the newly restructured export-focused sugar industry transformed into a premier industrialized domestic agricultural sector, ethanol industrial production capacity expanded.

Exports and Brazilian Sugar in the Changing World Market, 1959–1964

Increased international and domestic sugar demand expanded with the rise of sugary packaged foods worldwide in the 1960s. New business opportunities drew new government financing for the sector by the end of the decade. This section examines the global sugar market and regional divisions between the Northeast and the growing São Paulo sugar sector that redefined the sugar and ethanol sector during this period. While ethanol did not drive sugar policy decisions, failed efforts to redirect excess sugar toward ethanol in the Northeast illustrate the growing dominance of the São Paulo sugar and ethanol industry.

The world sugar market was a highly competitive and, at the same time, closely protected industry by the mid-twentieth century. The largest sugar-consuming countries, led by the United States and followed by the United

Kingdom, France, and the Soviet Union, created protective blocks in which they favored "preferential" partners.[3] Having lost its place as an important sugar exporter earlier in the century, Brazil saw its access to these preferential export markets greatly expanded after US-Cuban relations collapsed. New export opportunities ultimately attracted the attention of the military government and, more importantly, financing for the sector by the end of the decade.

It was Cuba that first fed the Americans' intensifying sugar habit at mid-century. As of 1955, Cuba and to a far smaller degree the Philippines accounted for nearly 94 percent of all US sugar imports.[4] Brazilian sugar had struggled to compete with Caribbean competitors such as Cuba, whose closer proximity and economic ties to the United States had driven huge investment throughout much of the century. Despite limited exports to South American neighbors such as Argentina, Bolivia, Chile, and Uruguay and some European countries, Brazilian sugar policy in the early 1950s remained focused on domestic consumption and ethanol production, as it had since the 1930s. However, after the IAA relaxed domestic sugar production limits during World War II, usineiros again began to produce more sugar than domestic consumers could purchase. IAA officials, therefore, looked to expand exports as agro-industrial growth in the sector increased in line with the Kubitschek government's developmentalist-nationalist agenda. Despite small gains in the UK and Japanese markets, Brazil remained largely on the outside of the coveted US preferential market.[5]

The break in US-Cuban relations after Fidel Castro's successful revolution dramatically reshaped the world sugar market and profoundly affected Brazil's fortunes. US negotiations with the new Cuban Communist government collapsed in 1960 and, with it, so did the Cuban sugar quota. After the US Congress and President Dwight Eisenhower reduced Cuba's sugar quota to zero, they looked to other sugar producers in the western hemisphere to fill the large void.[6] Brazil won one-tenth of Cuba's former one million ton quota in 1960. In 1961, Congress added an amendment to the new Sugar Act further favoring western hemisphere countries that purchased US commodities. Thereafter, the two countries solidified their sugar relationship through Brazil's increased imports of US wheat.[7] In 1962, Brazil won a permanent protected 6.4 percent of the total US annual quota. Between 1961 and 1965, the United States quickly became the largest export market for Brazilian sugar by a significant margin. By 1967, Brazil exported just over 2 million tons of sugar a year worldwide.[8] The expanding export market triggered important changes in Brazilian sugar policy.

At the same time, increased consumption of new light industrial foods such as jellies, packaged treats, and especially sodas increased domestic sugar demand as well. The Biagi family led the growth of sodas, opening the first Coca-Cola factory as a shareholder in Refrescos Ipiranga in the 1960s.[9] São Paulo sugar producers' proximity to large consumer markets in São Paulo and Rio de Janeiro again positioned them for big gains compared with their northeastern domestic competition.

These massive changes on both the international and domestic levels created increased policy incentives to industrialize and consolidate Brazilian sugar production. In the process, government policy focus shifted away from ethanol as a secondary alternative to domestic sugar consumption and toward exports. President Jânio Quadros passed Provision no. 1/61 on April 7, 1961 to encourage the "centralization and coordination of export activities."[10] Two months later, to coordinate with this provision, the IAA president Edmundo Penna Barbosa da Silva and the executive commission created the export division within the IAA. The new division encouraged the export of sugar, molasses, and other sugar derivatives, with ethanol given less attention than more profitable derivatives. After 1961, supplying the booming export market became the IAA's primary objective. This export focus was even more evident when President Quadros made the IAA part of the Ministry of Industry and Commerce in 1962.[11]

To facilitate exports, the IAA financed extensive modernization projects, first in the Northeast as part of the IAA's ongoing efforts to revive the region's sugar industry. Northeastern producers had lost their hold on this market to São Paulo after the IAA relaxed state production quotas during the 1940s. The IAA also made low-interest credit available to usineiros, planters, and cooperatives to incentivize mechanizing the sugar production process with increased industrial equipment and expanding production capacity. In the postwar era, northeastern firms fell into cycles of debt in which producers took on credit to build ethanol distilleries to absorb excess sugar during the war, delayed repayment because of high production costs, took on more debt in anticipation of expanded sugar sales after the war, lost domestic sales to the more mechanized paulista firms, and continued to take on more debt from the IAA without improving efficiency or production.[12] By 1959, São Paulo had already become Brazil's largest sugar and ethanol producer. Meanwhile, the northeastern sugar industry had become increasingly dependent on government assistance to operate. The Northeast, primarily Recife, remained the primary port of embarkation for sugar exports because of its greater proximity to US and European markets. However, northeastern producers' distance from the growing domestic southern markets of São Paulo and Rio de Janeiro far outweighed this advantage.[13]

IAA officials turned to diversified ethanol use to support the northeastern industry. While the National Petroleum Council's policy maintained the low anhydrous ethanol mixture of 5 percent in the national fuel supply throughout the 1960s, the IAA still aggressively promoted the expansion of hydrated ethanol for industrial use. Producers in the Northeast, for example, briefly used ethanol as a prime material for synthetic rubber production. Notably, the IAA invested in the state-owned Pernambuco Synthetic Rubber Company (Companhia Pernambucana de Borracha Sintética), which sought to use an expensive process to convert ethanol into butadiene, a chemical more cheaply derived from petrochemicals, to then produce rubber. However, high production costs doomed the endeavor because other residual sugar products such as molasses were more profitable for export than high-cost, low-demand rubber. In the southern market with its proximity to growing urban centers, industrialists increasingly used hydrous ethanol in plastics, perfumes, pharmaceuticals, and other light industrial products. Although the IAA pursued opportunities to export ethanol, it never found a substantial international market, which led to a dramatic oversupply.[14]

IAA policymakers justified new incentive programs in the 1960s in order to support politically influential, yet struggling northeastern producers. Initiatives such as the Fund for the Recovery of the Sugar Industry created in August 1961 redirected funds earned from Brazilian exports to the United States to financial assistance and credit for northeastern sugar producers. Again cheap credit and lenient refinancing of mounting debt funded industrial equipment investments to improve northeastern production capacity and efficiency so that these producers could compete with the more industrialized southern producers, particularly in São Paulo. However, Northeast topography proved too hilly for new agricultural equipment developed in the São Paulo countryside, foreign equipment was too expensive to import, new cane varieties were less appealing than investment in industrial equipment, and competition from São Paulo was too steep.[15] Financial supports soon became inefficient profiteering endeavors for many northeastern producers.

Instead, São Paulo producers benefited from the IAA's centralization efforts as sugar prices soared. In 1962, the IAA established the "Plan for the Expansion of the National Sugar Industry." Setting the bold goal of producing 100 million sacks of sugar by the 1970/1971 harvest, the plan encouraged a massive restructuring of sugar production around large usinas with the economies of scale to reach the ambitious national production goal.[16] International sugar prices peaked at US$190/ton on the world market in 1963, which encouraged further growth of the sugar industry. Thereafter, the IAA executive commission passed Resolutions no. 1761 and no. 1762 on December 12, 1963, which increased São Paulo quotas and authorized the construction of fifty new usinas. Thus began another wave of industrial expansion in the sugar industry in early 1964.[17] The IAA continued to fund the expansion of usinas, but the largest proportion went to São Paulo and Paraná under the New Sugar Mills Commission formed in January 1964. Even as the IAA ostensibly targeted northeastern producers in the early 1960s, São Paulo producers won increased IAA funds.

Struggles in the once dominant coffee industry also incentivized expanded investments in sugar in São Paulo. Declining coffee prices on a saturated world market had long vexed São Paulo coffee producers. Coffee supports had initially focused on limiting production but beginning in the 1960s, policy shifted toward tree eradication to make coffee competitive again. After the president founded the Executive Group for the Rationalization of the Coffee Industry (Grupo Executivo de Racionalização da Cafeicultura) in 1961, the group worked with the Institute of Brazilian Coffee to transform old coffee plantations into cane fields and to build usinas to mill the new sugar yields.[18] Thereafter, reduced employer obligations, poor coffee harvests, and stiffer competition on the world coffee market further encouraged more paulista coffee planters to transition to sugar, particularly in 1962 and 1963.

Expanding sugar exports amid booming international sugar prices drove continued investment in the sugar sector and led to ethanol temporarily taking a backseat in the sector. Nonetheless, ethanol production expanded in this period as IAA support for broader industrialization sparked consistent overproduction of ethanol throughout much of the 1960s. All the while, this new export-oriented sugar policy positioned São Paulo producers more prominently in national politics as the new military dictatorship increasingly tied sugar to development by the late 1960s.

Sugar and the Brazilian Military Dictatorship, 1964–1970

In April 1964, a conservative faction of the Brazilian military installed a new dictatorship after a coup displaced the democratically elected president

Joao Goulart. Low coffee prices had exacerbated a deteriorating balance of payments after former President Kubitschek ran up the country's debt financing his development plan, which set off rising inflation.[19] While Brazilian coffers had benefited from the United States's embargo on Cuban sugar, Washington's fears of "another Cuba" heightened US support of Brazilian conservative landowning elites' attempts to suppress social unrest, particularly in the sugar sector, in the 1960s. São Paulo sugar producers were among the key supporters of the new regime and were rewarded handsomely for their fidelity in the years that followed. Sugarcane became a modernizing industry connected to the dictatorship's image of development, and São Paulo producers positioned themselves squarely in the center of this redefinition. Even as the military government encouraged the sugar industry's industrial growth, producers' efforts to consolidate production and marketing in São Paulo further advanced ethanol's place on a growing national sugar agenda during the early years of the dictatorship.

Military ideology drove an increased focus on industrialization and development during the dictatorship. The Superior War College (Escola Superior de Guerra), established in the postwar period with close American assistance, trained many young men in the 1950s and 1960s who became high-ranking officials within the Brazilian military and the federal government in the 1960s and 1970s. The school's "National Security and Development Doctrine" equated national security with a simultaneous focus on economic growth and the suppression of "all sources of cleavage and disunity within the country."[20] This ideology infused "military technocrats" in various government positions and industries.[21] The new military president General Carlos Castello Branco, a staff member at the Superior War College, unsurprisingly promoted a pro-development agenda with the support of foreign investment and close alliances with civilian technocrats and businessmen to encourage industrialization. Castello Branco's National Security Law, issued on March 13, 1967, became the backbone of the military's government's development ideology into the mid-1970s, which sought "national security and development" in a reworking of the Brazilian national motto of "order and progress." The military would fight the communist threat with capitalist economic development built on the expansion of foreign capital in private businesses and the repression of "subversives," who included an ambiguously broad base of people supporting popular politics.[22]

Castelo Branco's successors, Marshal Artur Costa e Silva (1967–1969) and General Emílio Garrastazu Médici (1969–1974), further advanced the regime's development strategy. Both favored military rule more than Castello Branco and intensified suppression of opposing social groups to achieve "progress." Costa e Silva's administration, led by Finance Minister Antônio Delfim Neto, shifted from Castello Branco's foreign investment development strategy to focus on agricultural exports to generate revenue and drive domestic industrial growth. By extending export incentives and making credit easily accessible at favorable rates, the national agriculture growth rate quickly jumped to 7.1 percent in 1967, a year when the total national GDP growth rate fell to 4.2 percent. General Emílio Garrastazu Médici's administration, led by the new Minister of Planning João Paulo dos Reis Velloso, extended these economic policies by reducing export taxes and providing credit incentives to encourage a sustainable export economy. Most importantly, both administrations focused on sugar rather than coffee as the means to expand agricultural export earnings.[23] These policies resulted in a period of unprecedented sustained growth known as the Brazilian "economic miracle," in which national GDP growth rates averaged above 10 percent per year from 1968 to 1974.

As the national government shifted its development focus, the sugar sector entered a new phase of overproduction cycles not seen since the 1930s. After international sugar prices reached US$190/ton in 1963, producers expected a continuing rise and expanded sugarcane planting in 1964. Instead, prices fell US$40/ton in the 1965/1966 harvest.[24] The sector's record yields, driven by new players in the São Paulo sugar market and expanded agro-industrial production, saturated the domestic market and depressed prices. After a brief period of stability, another year of overproduction in 1967 again threatened producers' bottom line.[25] While the IAA had pushed ethanol production to address overproduction in the 1930s, it was sugar producers who pushed ethanol in response to the overproduction crisis in the 1960s.

However, national fuel policy had shifted away from ethanol by then. While hydrous ethanol used for industrial purposes had a more diversified market, anhydrous ethanol was exclusively used for fuel mixture. The National Petroleum Council (CNP) and the IAA had contentiously shared control of ethanol pricing for fuel distributors for decades. However, as petroleum came to dominate Brazil's energy goals in the 1950s, the CNP, which set petroleum policy and prices, had campaigned to remove ethanol from the national fuel supply because petroleum was cheaper to import than ethanol was to produce. By 1966, the CNP gained full control of both ethanol and petroleum pricing. Its energy policies deliberately favored cheaper oil.[26]

Inconsistent international sugar prices drove many usineiros to ethanol production in the crisis years despite national ethanol fuel demand having dropped. Initially, anhydrous production significantly decreased in the early 1960s when sugar export opportunities opened up for the Brazilian industry and the Petrobras-focused fuel policy shifted away from the ethanol mixture. However, the overproduction crises in 1964, 1965, and 1967 encouraged increased ethanol production with limited places for the IAA to direct additional ethanol production because the CNP would not increase ethanol in the mandated fuel mixture. Between 1964 and 1965, São Paulo ethanol production increased by over 1.5 million liters to 352,568,838 liters of ethanol, that is, almost 2 million liters of anhydrous ethanol and a little over 1.5 million liters of hydrous ethanol.[27] While northeastern producers focused on hydrous ethanol production and began exporting molasses, a lack of alternative export options drove the acute increase in anhydrous ethanol production in São Paulo. Over 70 percent of all anhydrous ethanol produced in the country came from São Paulo in the 1965/1966 harvest, and the percentage kept rising in subsequent years.[28] Copersucar, a São Paulo-based sugar cooperative organization founded in 1959, pushed government officials to reconsider ethanol usage rates, given São Paulo production rates.

Copersucar (Cooperativa Central de Produtores do Açúcar e do Álcool do Estado de São Paulo [The Central Cooperative of Producers of Sugar and Alcohol of São Paulo]) combined two earlier cooperatives, Copereste (the Cooperative of Mill Owners of Western São Paulo) and Copira (the Cooperative of Mill Owners of Piracicaba), to become a lobbying cartel that heavily influenced and at times directed sugar and ethanol policy by the early 1970s. Copereste had already helped Ribeirão Preto emerge as a leading sugar-producing region in the state alongside Piracicaba, the state's first major sugar-producing region, through technical agreements with the Escola Superior de Agricultura "Luiz de Queiroz" (ESALQ) and investment in research stations and fertilizers to improve yields in the 1950s. Copersucar "blended agricultural, industrial, and commercial activities" to purchase and market processed sugar and ethanol products, represent producers with the IAA and local government, and provide credit and technical assistance, including its own united research experiments on cane varieties.[29] As researchers and technicians moved between positions at individual usinas, ESALQ, Copereste, Copersucar, and federal research institutes, São Paulo sugar producers built a research network and personal connections with policymakers that further advanced Copersucar's position.[30] The cooperative's network and research proved so successful for its members that the government even emulated the model on a national scale in the 1970s.

Led by Jorge Wolney Atalla, Copersucar played an important role in reasserting ethanol's importance in Brazilian sugar policy in the late 1960s. The son of a Lebanese immigrant coffee-producing family, Atalla earned a US engineering degree in oil technology from the University of Tulsa in the early 1950s before going to work as a technical assistant at Petrobras's President Bernardes Refinery from 1951 to 1958.[31] During his time at the refinery, he became an enthusiastic supporter of ethanol and "prepared the technical documents that ended up convincing the government of the need to invest more in the carburant mixture [ethanol and gasoline]."[32] Atalla entered the sugar industry after his family acquired the Usina Varjão in Brotas, São Paulo, in 1956. He became the secretary of Copersucar in 1966 and its director-president in 1968. While personal, economic, and political gains were likely part of Atalla's motivation, he was an ardent supporter of ethanol as a means of addressing the sugar crisis and often cited nationalist interests in expanding the sugar sector and reducing oil imports.[33] Copersucar allowed paulista producers greater influence over sugar policy just as the IAA's power over ethanol policy declined. By 1975, Copersucar's expanded membership represented 91 percent (56 million sacks) of all São Paulo sugar and 92 percent (377 million liters) of all ethanol production in the state. The cooperative alone could have serviced increased ethanol in the national fuel mixture for the large consumer-driven market of São Paulo.[34] Atalla's focus on ethanol as an industry solution helped turn government attention back toward ethanol as a fuel option.

Copersucar created a formidable bloc for São Paulo sugar interests, but the Biagis' industrial expansion shows how individual producers also invested in new technologies that enabled an increase in ethanol production capacity in the 1960s. Maurilio Biagi expanded the Usina Santa Elisa's production capacity by incorporating smaller sugar producers in the region first with the Usina Santa Lúcia in 1958 and later with the purchase of the old mill, Engenho Central, in 1964. On the industrial side, Biagi, Ettore Zanini, and Arnaldo Bonini incorporated the Zanini company in 1957 and turned the regional rum- and sugar mill-focused company into a national custom agro-industrial equipment company in the following decade. In 1970, Biagi and the other shareholders restructured the company into a public enterprise, Zanini S.A. Equipamentos Pesados, which sought out international partnerships to acquire more foreign technology to expand its industrial reach beyond the sugar sector in Brazil.[35]

Over the course of the 1960s, Maurilio Biagi also brought his sons, both of whom became enthusiastic ethanol supporters, into the management teams of the two companies. His elder son, Maurilio Biagi Filho, joined him at the Usina Santa Elisa, first as an agricultural manager at the age of 20 in 1962 and later as superintendent. Biagi Filho, who grew up working at the usina and studied business in Ribeirão Preto, stated that after he moved into the position of superintendent, Biagi Sr. "never hired anyone without talking with me beforehand."[36] Biagi's second son, Luiz Lacerda Biagi, worked in the family's equipment production company, Zanini. Trained in economics at the Mackenzie University in São Paulo, Lacerda Biagi set up the Zanini office in the capital city in the 1960s. He became the commercial director of Zanini and sold Zanini products, generated orders, and built connections with international firms. He became the public face of the company after his father stepped down in 1975.[37] Biagi Filho and Lacerda Biagi's commitment to improving equipment and production for sugar and ethanol, along with their father's commitment to improved production techniques, positioned the Usina Santa Elisa as a premier industrial usina by the early 1970s.

Military, technocrats', and private businessmen's interests aligned to drive industrial expansion in the sugar industry by the late 1960s. A clear model of new sugar development emerged in which the government financed industrial development with domestic resources while expanding exports. In this export-oriented frenzy, individual sugar producers and cooperatives became central drivers of ethanol's expansion to counteract periodic overproduction cycles. This trend only continued as international sugar prices skyrocketed in the early 1970s.

Sugar Booms, the Oil Shock, and Deeper Investment, 1970–1974

At the peak of Brazil's "economic miracle," sugar prices surged to make sugar exports the top Brazilian export for the first time in a century, until they again collapsed. While prices began at US$61.20 per short ton in January 1970, thanks to failed crops in other sugar markets prices spiked to US$1122.80 in November 1974.[38] Médici's administration accelerated the new sugar development model of agro-industrialization. The newly appointed IAA president

Major General Álvaro Tavares Carmo, who had no previous experience in the sugar industry, efficiently executed the Médici administration's agro-industrial development agenda. Through a series of "modernization programs" in the early 1970s, the IAA explicitly focused on measures intended to consolidate production, quotas, and land for larger production capabilities concentrated in the hands of fewer large-scale producers.[39] When oil prices tripled in late 1973 and sugar prices collapsed in late 1974, the government had already invested so much money in the sugar sector that a large-scale ethanol program became a viable alternative to fossil fuel. As owners of both the Usina Santa Elisa and Zanini S.A., the Biagis were prominent among paulista producers who utilized government investments in sugar exports to position ethanol as a significant alternative energy option during the sugar boom. Their efforts enabled and virtually guaranteed some form of a national ethanol initiative by the mid-1970s.

The Usina Santa Elisa already had become a leading usina in Ribeirão Preto, but the government's sugar modernization program of the early 1970s streamlined additional financial support for major usineiros such as the Biagis to consolidate and expand agro-industrial production. Decree no. 1.186 of 1971, which enacted the Program for the Rationalization of the Sugar Agro-Industry (Programa de racionalização da agroindústria açúcareira) and Decree no. 1.266 on March 26, 1973 formalized the modernization efforts in this period.[40] Decree no. 1.186 stipulated that only usinas with quotas above 400,000 sacks of cane per harvest could absorb quotas transferred from smaller producers and could relocate usinas to more favorable land at the discretion of the usineiros. Decree no.1.266 and Act 19 of April 4, 1973 officially renamed the program the Support Program for the Sugar Agroindustry (Fundo para o Programa de Apoio à Agro-Indústria Açucareiro [Funproçúcar/Proçúcar]), which aimed to maximize large-scale productivity. The program formally financed the fusion, incorporation, and relocation of industrial units and planter quotas; the reduction of capital costs to finance the sugarcane subsector (such as ethanol); the rationalization of industrial sugar complexes; the acquisition of agricultural machines, vehicles, and other goods; and the development and promotion of better-quality cane varieties through a new sugarcane research program, Planalsucar.[41]

Funding for Funproçúcar came from the IAA's Special Export Fund, which illustrates sugar's importance to the dictatorship. First created in December 1965, the Special Export Fund consisted of the profits generated from the difference between prices paid to domestic producers for sugarcane and the prices collected in sugar exports. It did not have a positive balance until 1968, but as international prices began to rise, the fund accumulated a great deal of money, which officials then redistributed to the sugar industry to finance development and support for producers and workers.[42] Thus, sugar exports generated by large exports financed the policies that favored major usineiros, to the detriment of smaller and medium-sized producers. Thus, sugar exports became the goal and the creator of financing possibilities in a sector no longer focused on domestic production.

Agricultural industrial development accelerated by Funproçúcar allowed the sugar sector to diverge from the three-pronged industrial development model of the era. The theorist Peter Evans famously critiqued the Brazilian development model of the 1970s for its heavy dependence on multinational investment and foreign goods to support Brazilian intermediate industrialization. He argued that foreign multinational firms dominated more capital-intensive, technologically based production, such as transportation, rubber, and chemicals, while local capital became "increasingly marginalized" in smaller, less capital-intensive and technical industries such as textiles, food and beverages, wood, and some metal production.[43] However, the sugar industry did not follow this exact model. Domestic sugar producers maintained control of production and expanded their own industrial equipment industries such as the Biagis' Zanini by importing foreign technology with local and national funding in the early 1970s and adapting it to the domestic industry's needs.[44] Zanini manufactured its first full sugar usina for sale in 1965. Other major products included steam turbines, industrial boilers, equipment for construction, cement, and steel plants, and kilns for paper and trash industries by 1973. Zanini signed "know-how" contracts with foreign companies to import and adapt products such as the Denmark-based Atlas steam turbine for the sugar industry.[45] Their establishment of specialized domestic equipment production secured domestic producers' hold on the industrializing sector and made larger-scale national ethanol production possible.

Funproçúcar and the Usina Santa Elisa

The Biagis emerged as sugar and ethanol industry leaders outside of the umbrella of Jorge Wolney Atalla and Copersucar in the 1970s. Not all usineiros were enamored of Copersucar's leadership, and the Usina Santa Elisa was the largest to break from the cooperative in 1973.[46] Leaving Copersucar's preferential access, the Biagis built their own direct connections to the military in order to secure government support for their agro-industrial investments. The Biagis brought together government sugar supports, private investment, multinational technology, and domestic interests to expand their agro-industrial sugar empire.

The Biagis fostered their government links by hiring as director of the Usina Santa Elisa Colonel Milton Camara Senna, a Rio de Janeiro native who served as the former chief of the 7th Military Region and the superintendent of the Amazonian development program. For that program, he had been tasked with recruiting southern businessmen to invest in development programs in the Amazon region.[47] This experience tying government programs and private businessmen together made Senna invaluable in the development of the Biagi empire. It was no coincidence that Senna joined the usina in 1974, only a year after the Biagis broke from Copersucar and the same year that they applied for Funproçúcar financing.[48] As a member of the military during the dictatorship, Senna likely helped ensure the success of the Biagis' funding applications in the face of notoriously difficult Brazilian bureaucracy.

Fig 2.1 The Usina Santa Elisa Directorship in 1996. Pictured in the middle and to the center-right are Edilah Lacerda Biagi, wife of patriach Maurilio Biagi Sr. (pictured in the framed photograph), and Maurilio Biagi Filho. After the sudden death of Biagi Sr. in February 1978, she became the acting president.
Source: *A Revista Santa Elisa*, 27. APHRP Caixa 140.

Biagi Sr. and Biagi Filho applied for Funproçúcar financing only months after the program began and before the oil crisis started. Project approval involved an extensive review of both the usina's financial situation over the previous three years and that of its board of directors in order to assess its ability to repay the Funproçúcar loans. The stipulation, which was logical for the Bank of Brazil as an investor, would have been a key step in weeding out smaller usinas that were less financially capable of repaying such large loans.

On April 4, 1974, the IAA president General Tavares Carmo approved Santa Elisa's application for Funproçúcar funding, offering Cr$18,501,100 (US$2,720,750 in 1974 terms) to improve industrial capacity with the "acquisition of industrial equipment, installations, consignments, and civil projects."[49] As with all the projects, Funproçúcar did not finance 100 percent of the project; rather, the respective usina directorate was also expected to incur some modernization costs itself. In the case of the Usina Santa Elisa, the IAA expected less than 5 percent of the funding to come from the owners themselves.[50] The government's financial assistance solidified the Usina Santa Elisa's position as a leading usina in the country.

The Bank of Brazil, the financial institution through which the IAA distributed government funds and the primary arm of the federal government's agenda for agricultural development, provided the credit for a 10-year repayment plan. Federal financing provided was well below the market rates of other regional banks. Funproçúcar provided interest rates fixed at 12 percent in the Center-south and 10 percent in the North and Northeast. By comparison, small and medium-sized companies received loans with a 22 percent interest rate.[51] Given Brazil's history of high inflation, the guaranteed 12 percent interest rate with no monetary correction for inflation was a steal. In a presentation to the Federal Senate on October 25, 1973, the IAA president General Álvaro Tavares Carmo stated in regard to the financial conditions of the program, "I believe that no other credit establishment could offer financing under these conditions."[52] The Usina Santa Elisa had outstanding loans with other regional banks, but the preferential rates offered by the Bank of Brazil were a great incentive for any producer to participate in the national program.[53]

Funproçúcar favored contracts with domestic companies to drive domestic industrial growth, which the Biagis strategically used to expand their ethanol production capacity. The Biagis doubly benefited from the program because they were able to purchase the majority of the new industrial equipment for the Usina Santa Elisa from their own company, Zanini S.A.[54] Although they had already begun expanding the Usina Santa Elisa in close association with Zanini in 1970, under Funproçúcar they were able to purchase rollers and electric winches for cane processing, a cane feeder table, a rotating filter, evaporation boxes, centrifuges for sugar processing, multi-jet vacuums, turbogenerators, regulators, and water boilers, among other equipment from their own firm. Through other companies, the IAA financed buildings for cane storage, a warehouse, offices, garages, the expansion of the boiler room, the transformation of old cane crushing buildings into sugar depositories, and the distillery. However, the largest single piece of equipment that the Biagis' purchased with Funproçúcar financing went to the usina's distillery. Contracted with the Piracicaba-based Metalúrgica Conger S.A., Funproçúcar financed a distillation, rectification, and dehydration apparatus that would produce 70,000 liters per day.[55]

Zanini's growth alongside the Usina Santa Elisa captures the way domestic producers were able to maintain control of the sugar industry while multinational firms won control in other industries. Export profits fueled interest in Funproçúcar and financed approved projects. Through Funproçúcar, the government redirected these funds via large-scale sugar producers into domestic equipment companies such as Zanini to industrialize the sugar industry in the early 1970s. This domestic industrial investment increased the very capital-intensive, technology-based production that Evans claimed was absent.[56] While multinational investment drove other industries' development, President Médici's sugar development agenda was largely driven by domestic funds and domestic industries. Thus, as Zanini S.A. won numerous contracts through the program beyond those supplied by the Usina Santa Elisa's projects, Funproçúcar financed not only the expansion of usinas in Ribeirão Preto but also the region's transformation into an agro-industrial capital.[57]

The Usina Santa Elisa drew particular attention for its IAA-financed remodeling. In a letter to Santa Elisa's director-president, the Funproçúcar administrators requested that the usina clearly display a placard indicating the usina's part in the program.[58] While only a simple identifier, it highlights the important role of public visibility in the program's execution. The sugar sector's modernization was not solely about efficiency but was also a show of greater technical prowess, just as the *Estado de São Paulo* had asserted in 1971. Funproçúcar's commitment to extensive mechanization, international competition, and efficiency in order to build industrial capacity in the

Brazilian countryside captured the essence of President Médici's nebulous goal to simply "develop."[59] At the same time, this visibility reflected exclusivity. With a required minimum production quota of 400,000 sacks of sugar a year, many usinas were not eligible for program financing. Only 116 usinas received funding under the program across the country in total by May 1975.[60] Entry into this small group of producers opened up access to greater expansion and tagged the usina for greater government investment under the next sugar-related development program, Proálcool in 1975.

The Oil Shock and the Usina Santa Elisa

Not long after the IAA set up Funproçúcar, major changes in the global oil market drew the attention of sugar producers, along with the rest of the world. In October 1973, the Organization of Petroleum Exporting Countries (OPEC) placed an embargo on oil to the United States and allied countries in retaliation for America's military support for Israel in the Arab-Israeli War. This sparked an oil shock that quadrupled global petroleum prices between November 1973 and January 1974.[61] The new spike in oil prices instantly made ethanol production appear more economical. Funproçúcar-financing made investments in larger ethanol production capacity possible and worthwhile for savvy large-scale sugar industrialists such as the Biagis, even as government policy explicitly promoted increasing sugar production capacity.

The oil shock had a latent effect on Brazil's economic outlook. Unlike in the United States and many other countries, the 1973 oil shock did not immediately devastate Brazil's economy because of the country's more protected oil production structure. Following the creation of Petrobras in 1953, Brazilian oil production was significantly more expensive than in other countries because its infrastructure and employee training lagged behind other oil-producing and oil-refining countries. Between 1954 and 1973, Brazil actually paid US$3.7 billion more for its domestic oil than it would have for imports because of bureaucratic red tape and the high cost of inexperience. Thus, while the 1973–1974 oil price increases did not adversely affect the country, they had a stark impact on the country's balance of payments. In a single year, the current accounts deficit grew by 320 percent, from US$1.7 billion in 1973 to US$7.1 billion dollars.[62] To rebalance the account, the country needed to offset the more expensive oil imports by increasing exports such as sugar to compensate for petroleum's higher cost or reducing imports of foreign fuel.

The oil shock quickly exerted pressure to change national ethanol policy. The Minister of Industry and Commerce Marcus Vinícius Pratini de Moraes first called for increased ethanol in the fuel mixture in December 1973 as international petroleum prices jumped. He even approved an increase in cane planting in January 1974 in order to support this objective.[63] Within the sugar sector, Biagi Sr. and Biagi Filho were very vocal about their interest in expanding ethanol production to decrease dependence on oil imports. In fact, Maurilio Biagi Sr. contributed to an April 1974 anonymous report proposing a large-scale ethanol program to the National Petroleum Council, which drove concurrent debates in public forums.[64] As Biagi Filho revealed in an interview:

> In 1974, we [Biagi Filho, his father, and other specialists in the industry] sent a report to the President of the Republic, during the General Geisel era, which was titled "Photosynthesis as Energy." The report [proposed] subsidies for the government to create the "National Ethanol Program" or "Proálcool." When the agent delivered the report to the government, [it] was coordinated by Dr. Lamartine Navarro Junior, then vice president of Associgas, a gas association.Thus it was an oil man that made the ethanol [program] work . . . with the collaboration of my father, Maurilio Biagi.[65]

Indeed, the 1974 report directly influenced subsequent policy by proposing different programs that would promote the expansion of ethanol production in São Paulo and the country. One program supported financing the construction of autonomous distilleries for direct ethanol production and expanding the idle capacity of annexed distilleries like that at the Usina Santa Elisa. This proposed model quickly became policy when the IAA president Tavares Carmo and the deliberative council of the IAA approved the construction of new autonomous distilleries to produce ethanol for fuel under restrictive conditions in May 1974.[66]

As the Biagis led outside efforts to promote greater ethanol production on the national level, they also attempted to shift the focus of their Funproçúcar financing. Although they had already secured approval for the initial financing, Maurilio Biagi Filho amended the financial request not long after its approval in anticipation of new ethanol interests after the oil shock. In June 1974, Maurilio Biagi Filho, the superintendent director of the usina and adviser to the usina's transportation section, submitted a request to the IAA president Tavares Carmo to restructure the usina's

Funproçúcar financing.[67] In particular, he proposed changes to the allocated Zanini equipment:

> With the evolution of the approved plan's application, there arose, as is normal, more convenient alternatives, not only for more modern and more consistent equipment quality with the purpose [of Funproçúcar] in mind, but also the said equipment will be more adequate for the projected systems, better attending to the focus on economy.[68]

These cost-saving changes included a reduction in turbogenerators and Zanini and Woodward speed regulators for the turbines, which were part of the electric energy equipment outfit, and a complete replacement of the cane feeding equipment for a new unloading system. Additionally, Biagi Filho requested the expansion of the "sulfitation ensemble" (which included new ovens, compressors, and other accessories for cane processing) based on the outcome of the 1973/1974 harvest.[69]

The distillery seems to have been Biagi's primary reason for requesting these changes. Biagi Filho proposed that the IAA redirect the unused funds to the expansion of the approved distillery. Originally, the distillery had an allotted production capacity of 70,000 liters per day, but Biagi Filho proposed a new distillery with a production capacity of 240,000 liters per day.[70] Biagi Filho explained, "Given the global oil crisis, the Usina Santa Elisa believes that the production of ANHYRDROUS ETHANOL [*sic*] will be of great importance for the national economy."[71] The application's mention of ethanol's connection to the national economy reflected broader thinking on the importance of ethanol within the sector and even within the government during this period.

The Usina Santa Elisa was not the only usina to use Funproçúcar funding to enhance its ethanol production capacity. The Usina Santa Lydia, a prominent usina in Ribeirão Preto owned by Arnaldo Ribeiro Pinto, began as a cachaça distillery and transitioned to a fully equipped sugarcane and anhydrous ethanol usina in 1946.[72] Between the 1969 and 1972 harvests, it increased its ethanol production from 2,976,000 liters to 3,291,000 liters, while its sugar production decreased from 391,000 sacks of crystallized sugar (processed) to 363,000 sacks. In the Usina Santa Lydia's original bid for Funproçúcar funding, Funproçúcar administrators only approved financing for crystallized sugar equipment. However, upon reassessment in July 1974, the committee approved additional financing for a new distillery apparatus, new ethanol storage tanks, and the construction of a building to house the distillery much like that of the Usina Santa Elisa.[73] Santa Lydia's financing highlights the important role increased ethanol production held in the IAA's modernization efforts for other regional producers.

In the case of the Usina Santa Elisa, the IAA president Tavares Carmo denied Maurilio Biagi Filho's request to redirect funds and streamline the bureaucratic process. He accepted the requested changes to the equipment, replacing the two turbines with the one Stork-Toshiba turbine and canceling the cane-crushing table. However, the IAA denied his request to replace previously approved equipment on the basis of the program's financial limitations. Instead, GECEP informed the Usina Santa Elisa that the Bank of Brazil, the financier of the projects, would take back the funds that had been distributed to Zanini for those pieces of equipment. Furthermore, the Usina Santa Elisa would have to cover the additional costs of the new imported Stork-Toshiba turbine, which exceeded the cost of the previously approved domestically produced one.[74]

While the IAA would not comply with Biagi Filho's request, it did approve the Usina Santa Elisa's own financing of the requested expansion. As such, the usina benefited from the Funproçucar program but was able to execute its own agenda, namely, the expansion of its distillery, beyond the federal path laid out by the program. Biagi Filho's ability to move ahead despite the resistance of administrators in the IAA allowed the Biagi family to shape future ethanol production initiatives in the region and the country.

Independent Ethanol Expansion and Sugar Busts, 1975

As Brazilian sugar won a larger share of the US sugar market in the early 1960s, the federal government invested billions of dollars in the sugar sector to promote exports. The launch of programs such as Funproçúcar only intensified the amount of federal capital tied up in the sugar sector by 1974. However, sugar prices peaked in November 1974 at US$63.76 before falling in 1975. This put pressure on government officials as powerful sugar producers pushed for increased financial assistance to avoid insolvency. Ethanol again became an outlet for government support, and the Biagis had already positioned themselves to reap broader windfalls from increased national ethanol consumption.

By 1975, the IAA had granted nearly Cr$3.5 billion (US$432,098,765) in funding to 111 usinas through the Funproçúcar program. The program benefited São Paulo more than any other other state, but Ribeirão Preto usineiros specially benefited. Of the 111 projects approved, São Paulo received nearly half of the projects (52), of which 12 were located in the Greater Ribeirão Preto region.[75] Adding the creation of sugar experiment stations with Planalsucar, government investment in the sugar sector reached Cr$10 billion (almost US$1.5 billion) by 1975. The producers such as the Biagis who directly benefited from the program to modernizetheir agro-industrial outfits were able to make riskier investments at that point.

After the Usina Santa Elisa completed its Funproçúcar construction, the Biagis looked to further expand the usina's distillery capacity. On February 21, Biagi Filho received approval from the IAA for the expansion of its distillery to 180,000 liters per day, which the business would have to finance itself. Thus, in addition to the new 60,000 liters per day distillery financed by Funproçúcar, the Usina Santa Elisa built a second distillery with a capacity of 120,000 liters per day.[76] The Biagis expanded in anticipation of larger ethanol consumption on the national level. In his Proálcool application for the Usina Santa Elisa submitted in 1976, Biagi Filho even asserted, "We were certain, us and the IAA, even in 1974, of the opportunity for the increase in national production of ethanol to contribute."[77]

Renewed international competition drove sugar prices down in 1975. Since the 1930s, international sugar quotas had allowed major sugar-importing countries such as the United States and the United Kingdom to give preferential sugar quotas to preferred trade partners, but in late 1973, contentious negotiations over new international export quotas led to the collapse of the International Sugar Agreement. At the same time, many countries invested in sugar alternatives that depressed sugar demand. The Soviet Union increased its refined beet sugar production, which allowed the country to only rely on its longstanding contract with Cuba to supply its sugar needs and removed a major sugar importer from the world scene. American high-fructose corn syrup production increased to replace sugar in soft drinks and other manufactured foods, which drove per capita sugar consumption down from 48 kg to 30 kg over the next few years. Yet global sugar production and sales, including cane, beet sugar, and high-fructose corn syrup, continued to grow and sugar prices kept falling. While world market prices began at US$38.31 per lb. (US$766.20 per ton) in January 1975, they dropped to US$13.65 per lb. (US$273 per ton) by June. Sugar prices would not recover from this market depression until 1979.[78]

In addition, droughts and severe cold spells in São Paulo hurt Brazilian production. In July 1974, the worst frost in thirty years hit São Paulo, Minas Gerais, Rio de Janeiro, and Paraná. Much of São Paulo's coffee harvest was lost, and sugar harvests in the Ribeirão Preto region did not fare much better.[79] The unusually cold and dry winter pushed many sugar producers in the state to the brink of financial collapse. By September 1975, the Biagis' holdings reported they were producing about half the sugarcane per hectare (62,589 tons) than they had a year earlier.[80] Due to these "adverse conditions," São Paulo produced only 47.2 million sacks of sugar of the anticipated 60 million in 1975.[81] With this poor harvest and the declining world sugar prices, already reduced to a paltry US$18.61 per lb., the Biagis and many other sugar producers in the southern region were forced to turn to the IAA for assistance.

The government responded by reinforcing its heavy sugar investments. Of the affected states, São Paulo received the greatest amount of financial assistance from the IAA. At Santa Elisa, this meant that, after receiving the remainder of its Cr$18,501,000 in Funproçúcar financing in April 1975, the Funproçúcar coordinator Augusto Cezar da Fonseca and the IAA president Tavares Carmo deferred the interest payments for the Usina Santa Elisa, along with nine other usinas (including another Biagi holding, the Usina da Pedra) in November 1975.[82] Upon deferring the payments, the IAA explicitly noted that they would not accrue additional interest nor should the delayed payments be subject to any monetary correction for inflation. Given the rising inflation rate (an average of 29.4% in 1975), with no monetary adjustment and in real terms, the required payments were progressively cheaper each year for additional financial support.[83] Ultimately, the IAA used the Special Export Fund to extend credit via the suspension of interest payments to the tune of over Cr$51,500,000 (US$6,296,296) to usineiros in the state of São Paulo throughout 1975.[84]

At these levels, the military government's already massive investment in the sugar industry grew to potentially "too big to fail" levels. The Médici administration had already banked on sugar exports as a central part of its development agenda that had been so successful until 1974. The staggering investments in the sugar sector in the 1970s have led many historians of the program call the future national ethanol initiative a sugar bailout initiative.[85] The government had invested so much money in the sugar industry that finding a place for excess sugar on a depressed international market drove government officials back to that particularly twentieth-century Brazilian solution: ethanol. Special interest groups such as Copersucar and producers such as the Biagis had urged the government to reconsider ethanol for years before the 1975 sugar bust. Their early support of ethanol as a sugar solution, redirection of government financing, and individual investment in ethanol production capacity alongside the massive industrial investments of the previous fifteen years made ethanol a viable economic option to support the sugar industry and address the oil shock's persistent economic effects.

Biagi Filho anticipated and shaped the solution for salvaging the energy sector. With Biagi Sr.'s participation in early ethanol expansion proposals and the self-financed expansion of the Usina Santa Elisa, the Biagis positioned the Usina Santa Elisa a step ahead of many other usinas in ethanol production. Despite the IAA's hesitance, other indicators, particularly the 1973 oil shock and some early policies supporting increased ethanol mixtures in the fuel source, encouraged the Biagis to risk investing in ethanol's expansion so early. The collapse of the price of sugar was not the sole force driving increased use of ethanol as a fuel option. As a result, the Biagis were set to lead the ethanol industry for the rest of the decade and beyond beginning with Proálcool in 1976.

3

Proálcool, 1975–1985

"The ethanol is ours."

Maurilio Biagi Filho (1983)

In 1953, President Vargas championed the creation of the state-owned oil refining company Petrobras under the populist campaign motto, "O petroleo é nosso (The oil is ours)." The campaign claimed Brazil's oil was the property of its people and therefore foreign corporations should be prohibited from extracting, refining, and distributing a resource so crucial to national development. Thirty years later, Maurilio Biagi Filho tried to summon similar nationalist sentiments about the National Ethanol Program, Proálcool (Programa Nacional do Álcool), when he proclaimed, "O álcool é nosso (The ethanol is ours)."[1] Created in November 1975 ostensibly to diminish the country's dependence on foreign oil amid a global energy crisis, the national program was initially more an ambitious idea than a formulated plan. However, over the years that followed, various actors, from sugar producers such as Biagi to government officials, automotive executives, and researchers, molded the program into an initiative deserving of comparison with the previous nationalist petroleum campaign. With their help, Proálcool successfully coordinated the expansion of an ethanol industry owned and operated by the private sector.

This chapter examines Proálcool's creation and the initial expansion of this new national alternative fuel option. With the new ethanol car, private interests tied Proálcool to long-held visions of modern Brazilian independence and ingenuity and transformed ethanol into a central part of the Brazilian energy infrastructure by 1985. The consolidation of a nationalist ethanol agenda was rocky but rapid. Politicians and producers aggressively protected domestic control of production and technological innovation at a time when foreign capital and ownership pervaded other industries.[2] The development of the ethanol-fueled car spearheaded the program's expansion

Sweet Fuel. Jennifer Eaglin, Oxford University Press. © Oxford University Press 2022.
DOI: 10.1093/oso/9780197510681.003.0004

in 1979. By focusing on the expansion of the Biagis' holdings through the program, this chapter shows how private producers strategically used the government's agro-industrial agenda to define and refine the contours of a national ethanol agenda to their interests. Even as foreign capital entered some parts of Proálcool, program development and marketing remained focused on domestic private production and domestically developed ethanol-fueled engines.

The Creation of Proálcool

A superficial look at the National Ethanol Program would suggest that the 1973 oil shock was the sole factor that led to the program's creation. The country relied on petroleum imports for over 80 percent of its oil consumption, more than doubling Brazil's total import bill between 1973 and 1974 (US$6.2 billion to US$12.6 billion).[3] Given the high growth rates that had established Brazil's "economic miracle" and the military government's commitment to development with continued economic growth, the oil shock presented a serious threat to future policymaking. However, the collapse of international sugar prices also drove concerted efforts to encourage increased domestic consumption of sugar products, principally by the powerful sugar lobby in São Paulo, beginning in 1975. Moreover, the new domestic development of an ethanol-fueled car added an additional impetus to expand ethanol production and consumption in line with national development interests. These factors combined to turn a national program into a reality in less than a year.

The most important actor in the propagation of the National Ethanol Program was President Ernesto Geisel. Originally from Rio Grande do Sul, Geisel attended the influential General Staff School (*Escola de Comando e Estado Maior do Exército*) and was later a permanent staff member at the influential Superior War College before moving into political administration. Geisel gained experience in the energy sector first as superintendent at Petrobras's President Bernardes refinery from 1955 to 1956 and then as president of Petrobras from 1969 to 1973. During his time at the refinery, he built a close relationship with the ethanol enthusiast Jorge Wolney Atalla, which put the alternative fuel on his radar long before he became president. After receiving the presidential nomination in 1973, Geisel faced the challenge of continuing the high economic growth rates of the previous six years amid the new economic reality of the oil shock, rising inflation, and the recent collapse of the international Bretton-Woods monetary system.[4]

In September 1974, Geisel issued his new national development plan, the Second National Development Plan (Segundo Plano Nacional de Desenvolvimento [II PND]), which had energy alternatives at its center. He advocated expanding "new sources of energy" with a "realistic policy of import substitution, favored by the availability of resources and by the new levels of international prices," which made the investment in alternative fuels economically competitive.[5] II PND focused first and foremost on the oil shortage. Only brief mention was made of the ethanol mixture as one of many ways to reduce petroleum consumption; more attention was paid to increased state investment in hydroelectricity and nuclear energy. This makes sense, since sugar exports were still booming in 1974. II PND states that the Geisel administration would promote the "expansion of agro-industry (particularly sugar and other tropical products), taking into account its role as a center for the diffusion of new technologies in agricultural production."[6] Sugar remained an important industry and ethanol a part of a diversified national response, but a national ethanol program was not yet on the horizon.

Advanced domestic development of technology to run engines exclusively on ethanol soon changed President Geisel's outlook. Brazilian scientists had been working on an ethanol-fueled engine since the 1950s at the Aeronautical Technology Institute, an aviation engineering school in São José do Campos in the interior of São Paulo. Urbano Ernesto Stumpf, a native of Rio Grande do Sul and a student in the first class of the institute, began publishing early results of his research on ethanol-driven motors in 1952 in various journals and magazines, including the Institute of Sugar and Alcohol's *Brasil Açucareiro*. Stumpf served as a professor at the Aeronautical Technology Institute, the University of São Paulo-São Carlos, and the University of Brasília before moving to the Aeronautical Technology Center (Centro Tecnológico de Aeronáutica [CTA]) to direct research on the adoption of ethanol as a combustible fuel source in 1972.[7]

Geisel first learned of Stumpf's work on an internal combustion engine propelled by ethanol during a ceremonial visit to the CTA on June 28, 1975.[8] While the CTA was best known for its work on air travel, Stumpf introduced the president to the work he and his team of engineers were conducting to run an engine exclusively on ethanol. Notably, they found that an engine run on ethanol at a higher compression ratio was as efficient as a gasoline engine. With his extensive background in the energy sector, Geisel quickly saw the possibilities of a domestically developed ethanol-fueled car and grilled Stumpf on the technical aspects of the engine and potential fuel production. According to a report in the *Estado de São Paulo*, Geisel worried about the use of sugar as the energy source because of the high export price that it still earned on the international market.[9] Stumpf and his team responded that other sources such as manioc were just as viable. The president ended up staying at the center hours longer than planned for the ceremonial visit.[10]

São Paulo politicians and private interests held sway as Geisel pondered the formation of an ethanol initiative. Within the government, important paulista officials had the president's ear. For example, another important attendee at this CTA visit was the current Governor of São Paulo and former Minister of Industry and Commerce, Paulo Egydio Martins.[11] The São Paulo native had held the ministerial position from 1966 to 1967, during the intense sugar overproduction crisis, before Geisel appointed him governor in 1974. In the private sector, President Geisel already had a close relationship

Fig 3.1 Federal, state, and private interests align. Pictured (from left to right): Governor Egydio Martins, President Ernesto Geisel, and the Anfavea (Associação Nacional dos Fabricantes de Veículos Automotores [National Car Producers' Association]) president, Mário Garnero (driving).
Source: Salão de Automóvel, São Paulo, BR. November 17, 1978.

with Jorge Wolney Atalla.[12] Martins and Atalla's close ties to President Geisel and particular connections to paulista sugar and ethanol interests gave them access to the most powerful to advocate for a national ethanol program.

The selection of sugarcane as the material base for expanded ethanol production illustrates the influence paulistas had on the new program. Stumpf and his engineers highlighted that sugarcane was but one possible raw material source for the ethanol-fueled engine. Many within the government were more enthused about using manioc because sugar is a seasonal crop while manioc can be grown all year.[13] Yet sugarcane won the vast majority of the attention, and officials quickly dismissed most other options. Policymakers ultimately favored this crop because the national sugar industry already had a well-developed infrastructure, first built under the IAA in the 1930s and enhanced in the 1960s and early 1970s. Certainly, sugar's many influential advocates such as Copersucar and paulista government officials like Martins were able to attest to the benefits of a sugar-focused ethanol program.

Only months after his visit to the CTA, President Geisel announced the program along with a series of other measures to diversify energy options. On October 9, 1975, he committed the country to a 20 percent mandated ethanol mixture in the national fuel supply. Stumpf and his team had proven that this percentage was the outer limit at which traditional gasoline engines could run on fuel mixed with anhydrous ethanol without any engine adaptation.[14] Later that year, Geisel also created the Department of Industrial Technology (Secretaria de Tecnologia Industrial [STI]), which came under the Ministry of Industry and Commerce, "almost exclusively for the research of ethanol as an energy source."[15] The STI's focus was to support Stumpf and the CTA with the perfection of the ethanol engine in order to phase in an ethanol car for the commercial market. Creating an ethanol engine quickly moved from a small research project to a central technological agenda.

Following Geisel's announcement, debate ensued over the structure, direction, and control of the program. The IAA, which was the driving force in sugar policy, the Ministry of Industry and Commerce, which oversaw the CTA, and the Ministry of Mines and Energy, with its ties to Petrobras, all vied to control the forthcoming national ethanol program but each had different visions of what the program would become. The IAA president Tavares Carmo, still focused on sugar exports, proposed that the government invest in standalone or autonomous distilleries in different areas than the most dominant sugar-producing regions so as not to interfere with the existing sugar agro-industrial complexes.[16] The Ministry of Industry and Commerce pushed the national technology agenda. As Minister Severo Gomes asserted a year into the program's development, ethanol was a "high priority" project that would ensure that Brazil be "an independent nation."[17] The Ministry of Mines and Energy, led by Minister Shigeaki Ueki, proposed a less ambitious program.[18] Prior to his appointment as minister, Ueki had served as the commercial and financial director of Petrobras under Geisel at the state oil company, where he had pushed to replace the common gasoline additive, lead, with ethanol.[19] On the basis of his experience at Petrobras, Minister Ueki wanted Proálcool to promote ethanol as a petrochemical replacement rather than large-scale substitution or fuel replacement.[20]

The ongoing dispute between these factions became very public as private business interests inserted themselves into the debate.[21] After a draft of the forthcoming decree leaked to the press on October 31, Atalla used Copersucar to remain a vocal and aggressive lobbyist for the private sector in the formation of the ethanol initiative. He objected to the IAA's proposal to disaggregate ethanol distilleries from the existing sugar-ethanol complexes since their connection favored the concentrated number of large-scale sugar producers in São Paulo, many of whom already had ethanol distillation capacity. He openly criticized government action by placing Proálcool at the center of a growing debate on the presence of the state in Brazilian development. Atalla argued that it was "incomprehensible psychology" to tell the sugar-ethanol agro-industry "go to battle, but you will win none of the spoils for yourselves" in the national emergency of the energy crisis.[22] While the Brazilian state had intervened in the steel and mining industries when the product was beyond a producer's individual interests,[23] private producers had already spent years building up ethanol production capacity for excess sugar and had increased ethanol use in the national fuel supply. Thus, Atalla pushed for increased state financing rather than a state-owned endeavor. He claimed that government monopolization of ethanol production would be a "confiscation against business, businessmen, and agricultural workers—genuinely national—to which the country owes a substantial part of its incredible export figures."[24] Self-interested equipment producers, including Zanini, supported Atalla's position on the dangers of nationalization of the program.[25] By structuring their argument around the need to support private–public collaboration to reward national businesses, private interests deterred government officials from creating a nationalized Proálcool.

President Geisel ultimately instituted the National Ethanol Program (Programa Nacional do Álcool [PNA or Proálcool]) with Decree no. 76.593

on November 14, 1975. Although it supported the use of manioc as well, the program focused on the expansion of sugarcane. As one of several alternative fuel efforts to reduce petroleum dependence, the new ethanol program would attend to "the necessities of the internal and external market and to the policy of automotive gasoline."[26] The program's goals were to save foreign currency through the substitution of imports of fuels and primary materials derived from petroleum; reduce regional and individual income disparities; increase internal income through the expansion of domestic jobs; and expand the production of capital goods through "highly nationalized" equipment contracts for the expansion, modernization, and installation of distilleries.[27]

In practice, Proálcool financed industrial and agricultural investments. Unlike other investment programs developed under II PND that received support as formal state enterprises or through the National Economic Development Bank (BNDE), financing for Proálcool came from the Central Bank. These funds were allocated through a series of government-related banks, but the Bank of Brazil dominated.[28] Proálcool offered financing at an interest rate of 17 percent over a twelve-year period with a three-year grace period for industrial equipment. This included the physical installation of distilleries and the necessary equipment involved in the establishment of the distillery.[29] For agricultural equipment, the interest rate was 7 percent with a maximum time frame of five years to repay and a two-year grace period.[30] By comparison, Funproçúcar, the previous IAA sugar program, had offered producers financing with an interest rate of 12 percent in São Paulo (and the rest of the Center-south) and 10 percent in the North and Northeast. With rates on most loans hovering above 40 percent, the government offered favorable financing to the sugar sector in the 1970s through Proálcool.[31] Such incentives encouraged producers who might have previously been discouraged from investing in the ethanol industry to enter the market.

In the end, numerous entities split control of the new program's administration. President Geisel created an interministerial commission, the National Ethanol Commission (Commissão Nacional de Álcool [CNAl]), to administer the program.[32] Representatives from the Ministry of the Interior, Agriculture, Mines and Energy, Industry and Commerce, the Interior, and the Department of Planning made up the new entity, over which the General Secretary of the Ministry of Industry and Commerce Paulo Vieira Belotti presided. The commission defined the roles of each government entity involved. In the process, the National Petroleum Council (Conselho Nacional do Petróleo [CNP]), the petroleum policy-setting entity, again continued to beat out the IAA for more control of ethanol policy, as it had since the 1960s. The CNP controlled the ethanol-gasoline mixture quota for fuel distribution companies and the amount of ethanol substituted for petroleum sent to chemical industries. In effect, the CNP set ethanol pricing.[33] Producers submitted program applications to the IAA for economic and agricultural review. Like Funproçúcar before it, Proálcool financed private rather than state-owned projects.

In its initial phase from 1975 to 1979, the government set the conservative goal of producing 3 billion liters of ethanol by 1980.[34] The requisite distillery capacity to meet this goal was well within reach, given the extensive excess capacity available in paulista distilleries alone. However, specialists and government officials questioned whether the country could expand the agricultural production of sugarcane fast enough to meet ethanol expansion goals. The IAA president Tavares Carmo pessimistically noted that the country's primary method of producing ethanol at the time, via processed sugar rather than directly from sugarcane, would never alone be sufficient to meet the 1980 production goals.[35] Given such doubts, private producers' responses and visions for the program were critical to its successful execution.

Phase I and the Usina Santa Elisa

The Usina Santa Elisa was the first annexed (or attached to a sugar mill) project approved and completed in the new national program.[36] This was no surprise, given that the Biagis had already established the Usina Santa Elisa as a premier sugar and ethanol producer with established agro-industrial production capacity. As São Paulo consumed the vast majority of Brazilian fuel, the Ribeirão Preto region's relative proximity to the large paulista market drove down transportation costs for a risky experimental project. Pre-existing producers in the region with established sugar and ethanol capacity were a safer bet. However, the program's success was far from guaranteed. A complicated bureaucratic process and slow buy-in from various sectors threatened the program. The Usina Santa Elisa's early Proálcool expansion reveals the tensions of the program's first phase and how private producers influenced its development.

The National Ethanol Commission (CNAl) defined the steps for project approval and distribution of funds in Resolution no. 3/76 of January 27, 1976,

Fig 3.2 The Usina Santa Elisa in 1976
Source: BR RJANRIO IY (A6.16 Caixa 443).

and Maurilio Biagi Filho, superintendent director of the Usina Santa Elisa, submitted an application for the expansion of the 's distillery capacity to the IAA just over two weeks later.[37] Biagi Filho requested a two-step expansion of the 's distillery capacity. First, he requested the addition of another distillery to produce 120,000 liters per day. Together with the Funproçúcar-financed distillery producing 60,000 liters per day and the self-financed distillery producing 120,000 liters per day still under construction, the Proálcool expansion would increase the 's total ethanol production capacity to 300,000 liters per day. This included a request for an expanded sugar quota to be able to produce 1,500,000 sacks of sugar (9,9208 tons) and 294,500 liters of ethanol per day over a 150-day harvest schedule.[38] Rather than cutting into their sugar production to accommodate expanded ethanol production, as many critics of the program feared, the application proposed to expand both.

For many applicants, securing financing was difficult. According to the commission's resolution, had 180 days from the day of the submission of a proposal to secure a contract with a financial agency with a strict 90-day deadline for dispersal of the loan to the respective companies thereafter or a project would be cancelled.[39] Financial institutions used delaying tactics in the approval process to express their concerns about the risk investors incurred through the program.[40] New Proálcool loans required a substantial financial commitment to the program with little guarantee that businesses would be able to repay the loan if the program was unsuccessful. Furthermore, the Bank of Brazil had already served as the primary financial investor in the sugar industry's big-budget program, Funproçúcar. Many of these rather large loans remained outstanding at the beginning of Proálcool, including one to the Usina Santa Elisa. In response, the Central Bank purposely delayed the release of funds, and the Bank of Brazil created "difficulties for financing approval" until President Geisel recommended that the bank ease the loan guarantees (collateral requirements) demanded of interested businessmen. This finally accelerated financing approval in late 1976.[41] Despite the commission's 180-day requirement, in practice it took an average of seven to twelve months for a project reach signature of a contract with a financial agency after receiving project approval.[42]

In the case of the Usina Santa Elisa, the IAA went to great lengths to push project financing forward even as the Bank of Brazil dragged its feet. The commission approved the Usina Santa Elisa's application on March 31, only a month and a half after the Biagis submitted their application.[43] Approval included an initial loan of Cr$119,075,000 (approximately US$11,128,505), of which Cr$116,023,000 was spent directly on distillery equipment. The would put up Cr$56,586,000 (US$5,288,411) of its own resources and generate Cr$42,250,000 in third-party investments.[44] Upon receiving project approval, Biagi Filho requested to move the outstanding Funproçúcar loan provided by the Bank of Brazil to a second lien behind a Proálcool loan from the Bank of Brazil and third-party lenders such as the Antonio Queiroz Bank. This meant that the Proálcool loan would take repayment precedence over Funproçúcar funds.[45] The IAA overrode the Bank of Brazil's preference for keeping Proálcool funds separate and subordinate to the original Funproçúcar funding. Specifically, the IAA President Tavares Carmo authorized the Bank of Brazil to suspend the collection of Funproçúcar interest due on the 1976 to 1977 harvest, and even required the Bank of Brazil to return previous interest payments made by the on that loan.[46]

Inflation had devalued the currency so much that the value of the money borrowed was more than the value of the interest accumulated for repayment.[47] Thus, in practice, lenders essentially transferred money to borrowers through loans.[48] At the same time, an inflation rate of 41 percent or higher at the time virtually guaranteed that initial loans, devalued by rising inflation, were insufficient to actually complete project construction and installation. The government even corrected for inflation on financing to address the issue by 1977.[49] Projects, including that of the Usina Santa Elisa, often needed increased financing to account for the economy's inflationary realities, but winning project financing was a direct economic boon.

The Biagis' connections likely enabled them to overcome the difficult bureaucratic process to speed up project approval, financing, and completion. The family had relied on direct ties to the military government through their director, Colonel Senna, since 1974. Senna signed off on all of the Usina Santa Elisa's first Proálcool applications in 1976.[50] The Biagis accelerated application and approval process had direct financial benefits. According to the policymaker Confúcio Pamplona, Proálcool financed 100 percent of total industrial investments until 1977, a percentage that dropped to 70 percent for annexed distilleries such as Santa Elisa and 80 percent for autonomous, stand-alone distilleries.[51] The Usina Santa Elisa benefited, since it received additional funds for construction months after project approval, although later application rules explicitly noted that readjustment costs would not be financed.[52]

As institutions remained wary of an unproven program that carried financial risk, private businessmen were able to shape the program and build the sugar sector's industrial infrastructure through it. The Usina Santa Elisa's largest Proálcool contracts went to the Piracicaba-based metallurgy company, Conger, and the Biagi-owned, Zanini S.A. At the beginning of Proálcool, Zanini still did not have the technology to construct its own distilleries. Thus, "Zanini, the mill and boiler manufacturer, proposed to absorb Conger, the distillery manufacturer."[53] Though short-lived, the partnership allowed Zanini to enter the distillery market, after which the company would begin producing its own distillation equipment. The two domestic companies combined to compete with the larger Dedini-CODISTIL distillery production company. The Usina Santa Elisa also contracted Brazilian companies such as Arno S.A., KSB S.A., and Siemens S.A. for hydraulic tanks, ventilators, pumps, electric motors, and other necessary industrial equipment. Many of these were domestic companies built through multinational investment or joint-venture agreements with international companies to purchase new technology. Yet these companies did not penetrate the actual sugar mills and distillery ownership, so that foreign interests remained outside the center of the sugar industry, unlike in other industries.[54] At the same time, Proálcool did not fund imported goods and instead favored domestic industrial suppliers. For the Santa Elisa project, imported equipment accounted for less than 1 percent of the entire budget.[55] Proálcool maintained this separation as the equipment companies such as Zanini which did allow some degree of foreign penetration grew around the sugar mills and distilleries.

The Biagis were able to quickly get their new Proálcool distillery up and running despite the program's notorious delays. Construction began in April 1976, and the new distillery was operational by June 1977.[56] The new Minister of Industry and Commerce Dr. Ángelo Calmon de Sá and the IAA president Tavares Carmo attended the inauguration. In a letter to Carmo, Biagi Filho noted the significant impact that Proálcool-financing had on the 's position in the country:

> As a result of this support, we already produced, in the 1977 harvest, 50,007,000 liters of ethanol, which, compared with 8,712,000 liters in 1976, truly represents a significant increase and positions us as the third largest producer of ethanol in the country and the first in relation to sugar/ethanol.[57]

These impressive statistics highlight the leading position the Biagi family and the Usina Santa Elisa held in ethanol production by 1978. Even when the bureaucratic process was unclear, the Biagis enthusiastically embraced Proálcool and quickly reaped its benefits.

Nevertheless, media attention mostly focused on the program's slow progress in its first years. Some openly criticized the program's speed. The Paraná Secretary of Industry and Commerce Luiz Gonzaga Pinto claimed that the delays "create at the same time a climate of distrust and concern on the part of investors whose projects were not approved and [those who] are in power on the National Ethanol Commission."[58] In response, the National Ethanol Commission president Lycio de Faria affirmed that the government was acting "not slowly, but cautiously, since it cannot risk hasty decisions."[59] By the end of 1977, the Copersucar president Jorge Wolney Atalla was calling for the "debureaucratization of Proálcool," while government officials knew they needed to create a way for the country to have more "enthusiasm" for the program.[60]

Confusion abounded as ethanol distribution problems also damaged public opinion about the program. The CNP set mixture quotas and pricing, while the IAA coordinated ethanol producers' shipments of anhydrous ethanol via fuel tank trucks directly to distributors to mix in the national fuel supply. For example, the CNP mandated distribution of fuel with a 20 percent mixture began in metropolitan São Paulo in June 1977, but even a week earlier distributors still lacked the necessary information about when the mixture requirement would officially come into effect. Some complied, such as Bruno Iughetti, the São Paulo operations coordinator of the fuel company Esso, who had all his resellers drain their reserves in late May in order to begin mixing the highly refined ethanol by the June deadline. Other distributors, still unclear about the government's plan, made no moves to prepare to add ethanol at the requisite levels.[61] IAA delegates in São Paulo announced that distributors started receiving ethanol on May 18 to build the required 10,000 liter stores of ethanol to mix in the fuel, but, as of May 24, distributors such as Esso and Petrobras reported that they had yet to receive any.[62] Criticisms continued in 1978 even as ethanol production surpassed the 1980 goal and most major markets had reached a 20 percent ethanol mixture rate in the fuel supply.[63] However, enthusiasm for the program grew as domestic engine developments and global events propelled a reorganization of the program and its objectives later that year.

Restructuring Proálcool and the Introduction of the Ethanol-Fueled Car

Even as the media criticized the program's early implementation, buzz about a Brazilian-developed ethanol car grew. Stumpf and his team of engineers regularly spoke to the media about their ethanol engine research. While meeting the ethanol mixture rate was important, Stumpf asserted at the 1977 National Sugar Producers' Meeting that "The medium- and long-term solution [to the fuel crisis] is the adoption of motors powered only by ethanol, a technology that is being developed quite successfully by Brazilian scientists."[64] The pressure to complete this project only intensified when a second oil crisis triggered a larger Proálcool commitment to full fuel replacement rather than simply mixing ethanol into national fuel supplies. Bringing the ethanol car to market boosted Proálcool from an ambitious experiment to a central piece in the country's national fuel strategy, while the pride generated by the engine's development transformed the program into a national treasure.

Efforts to produce ethanol-fueled cars in Brazil began quickly after Proálcool became official. Geisel tasked the Department of Industrial Technology (STI), led by its first secretary José Walter Bautista Vidal, with accelerating the completion of the CTA's ethanol engine in 1974.[65] Within two years, the CTA was publicly testing ethanol vehicles. The First Circuit of National Integration for Ethanol Vehicles showcased the CTA-developed ethanol engines in a twenty-three-day, 8,000 km rally from the CTA in São Jose dos Campos, São Paulo, to Manaus, Amazonas in the north of the country and back. Fitted in three vehicles, the Dodge Polara, the Volkswagen 1300 (the Beetle), and the Brazilian Gurgel utility truck, the Xavante, the hydrous-ethanol engines outperformed their gasoline-engine counterparts. Stops on the rally regularly drew crowds of "scientists, technocrats, drivers, and the curious," who asked questions of the CTA team about the vehicles. During the event, Stumpf proclaimed, "What we intend to show to the Brazilian public, by doing this integration circuit, is the economic viability of the project, and we seek to alert the country's authorities of its importance and immediate execution."[66] At the end of the popular circuit, a subsidiary of Dedini, the sugar equipment company based in Piracicaba, placed an advertisement in the *Estado de São Paulo* thanking the team for their work. One of the outcomes of their success, the advertisement noted, was the President's mandated acceleration of Proálcool and STI secretary Bautista Vidal's declaration that "The true solution is to adopt ethanol as an automotive fuel."[67]

As the viability of ethanol engines became more certain, automakers entered into the race to develop the ethanol car. Beginning in 1976, Bautista Vidal and the STI coordinated a joint research agreement with Volkswagen to develop ethanol-fueled cars. Researchers at the German company were already developing a coal- or wood-based methanol engine, while Brazilian scientists had focused on ethanol. However, according a report in the *Estado de São Paulo*, "Bautista Vidal convinced Volkswagen's global president to perform research in the ethanol field, which made the integration of the technological development projects in the two countries possible."[68] Volkswagen's team found that the high-compression ethanol engine, as Stumpf and his team had already identified, required numerous adaptations to the standard carburetor, fuel line, gasket parts, fuel tank, and fuel delivery system for an ethanol vehicle. They began testing their own ethanol cars, developed in tandem with Volkswagen do Brasil, around the same time as the CTA rally. All the while, German members of the Volkswagen team bristled at the Brazilians' "fierce nationalism" regarding ethanol and the ethanol car.[69]

As CTA director Colonel Sergio dos Reis Vale affirmed when asked about importing foreign technology to produce ethanol motors, "It is prohibited to think of the importation of technology at this point in the game."[70]

Other car manufacturers saw the ethanol car as an opportunity to build their share of the Brazilian market. Until the 1970s, American and European brands, particularly the market-leading Volkswagen Beetle or *fusca*, dominated the Brazilian car market. The Italian manufacturer Fiat had had little success in breaking into the market. However, in 1973, the Governor of Minas Gerais Rondon Pacheco worked with Fiat to set up a factory in Betim, MG, north of São Paulo and west of Rio de Janeiro, by offering direct concessions from the state to the company. In the midst of the oil crisis, the new plant was to focus on "small, energy-efficient passenger cars." The company strategically embraced the country's growing interest in ethanol cars.[71] At the opening of the plant in July 1976, the company gifted President Geisel with a prototype of an ethanol version of its Fiat 147. Led by the engineer Paulo Penido Filho, Fiat continued to revise the ethanol model to address similar issues experienced by other manufacturers, such as corrosive carburetors, the cold-start system, and ethanol's higher rate of evaporation, while the gasoline-powered 147 won a small share of the market over the next few years.[72]

Ethanol cars began appearing on Brazilian roads in 1977. The São Paulo State Telephone Company, Telesp, became the first company in Brazil to adapt their Volkswagen service vehicles to ethanol cars over the summer of 1977.[73] After the CTA's successful rally in 1976, Telesp officials reached out to the CTA to incorporate ethanol vehicles into their fleet. CTA officials directed the company to Motorit, a São Paulo-based maintenance company, to convert their vehicles with technology developed at the CTA.[74] At the 1977 Sugar Producers' Meeting held just months after Telesp committed to the program, Stumpf notably announced that the CTA had already started the process of technology transfers to a private initiative, presumably referencing Motorit. Furthermore, Stumpf announced that the CTA would begin producing kits to allow the well-developed Brazilian auto parts industry to begin converting current gasoline cars to ethanol that year.[75]

Although some industry buy-in to the ethanol car began in 1977, no single event solidified the government's commitment to the national ethanol program and consumers' interest in expanded ethanol consumption more than the second oil shock of 1979. The beginning of the Iranian Revolution in December 1978 sparked a 14.5 percent increase in OPEC prices. Conflict in

Iran, the second largest supplier of oil to Brazil, left the country particularly vulnerable to the new crisis.[76] The new Iranian government cut oil production by 2.7 million barrels a day, after which oil prices nearly doubled from around US$12.85 in October 1978 to US$24 by the end of 1979.[77] While the first oil shock had justifiably caused alarm, the second shock established a new reality in which consumers knew they could no longer count on low fuel prices. The fragile balance of payments, which had recovered from the last oil shock in 1973, quickly crumbled, and the Brazilian government found itself mired in crisis.

The second oil shock became a central feature of the administration of the new military president General João Batista de Oliveira Figueiredo, installed in March 1979. Born to a military family, Figueiredo had been a key conspirator in the 1964 coup and later served in both the Médici and Geisel administrations.[78] A month before the Iranian Revolution began, Geisel nominated Figueiredo as his successor. Figueiredo made accelerating Proálcool a major piece of his strategy to address the energy crisis in his National Development Plan.[79] In June, he echoed nationalist sentiments already circulating around the ethanol car when he told the *Veja* reporter Paulo Sotero, "Ethanol is the Brazilian response to the energy crisis. More than a solution for external contingencies, [the crisis] is the great challenge of the 1980s that the entire nation—the people and the government—will have to confront and overcome."[80] By July, President Figueiredo and the Economic Development Council had raised the production target for the ethanol program to 10.7 billion liters by 1985. A second phase of Proálcool focused on bringing ethanol cars to the commercial market drove Figueiredo's new energy agenda. The Ministry of Mines' 1979 Energy Report made this particularly clear, as it marked 6.1 billion liters of the projected 10.7 billion liters of ethanol to be produced by 1985 as hydrous ethanol for ethanol cars compared with just 3.1 billion anhydrous ethanol for the ethanol-gasoline mixture and 1.5 billion liters for industrial use.[81]

Such significant program expansion required resolving the nagging administrative and logistical problems from Proálcool's early implementation.[82] While the interministerial National Ethanol Commission had allowed competing interests to vie for control of the program since Proálcool's formation, Figueiredo instead created a new National Energy Commission that reported directly to him and integrated ministers with Petrobras representatives and select civilians to address bigger energy policy questions.[83] The IAA was notably not part of the new energy commission. To resolve

Proálcool's administrative bottlenecks, Figueiredo created the National Ethanol Council (Conselho Nacional do Álcool) and the National Executive Ethanol Commission (Commissão Executivo Nacional de Álcool [CENAL]) to replace the original National Ethanol Commission. The new entities simplified the application process to allow for quicker new project approvals and to streamline the program's administration.[84] Capturing the sentiment of the restructuring, the new Minister of Industry and Commerce João Camila Penna said:

> The success of Proálcool is linked to the national effort. It depends on the action of the new National Ethanol Council, on the government as one united entity, on the businessmen who want to take part in the program, on the automobile industry, on Petrobras, on the National Congress, on all Brazilians, in total. And the government is committed.[85]

The potential large-scale commercial sale of ethanol cars also required implementing a reliable ethanol distribution infrastructure in the second phase. Telesp set up the first hydrous ethanol pumps to service their ethanol vehicles at their service stations in May 1977, but ethanol cars would require accessible hydrous ethanol at local fueling stations nationwide.[86] However, on a national scale, the disorganization that had hindered anhydrous distribution in the early phase caused concern for automakers whose cars would rely on hydrous ethanol distribution. The plan was to replace pumps with *gasolina azul*, a premium fuel, with those for hydrous ethanol.[87] General Oziel Almeida Costa, President of the National Petroleum Council (CNP), pledged the quick adaptation of pumps when demand was in place, stating: "On the day that the National Ethanol Commission says that there is enough ethanol and cars for the use of the fuel, we will be quick to activate the distribution system, which is pretty easy."[88]

Yet building demand for ethanol fuel with commercial ethanol car production required buy-in from Brazil's dominant multinational car producers. Fiat was the first to commit. After Fiat's ethanol-powered 147 won the First International Brazilian Rally in June 1979, the STI approved its ethanol motor to make it the first brand to reach large-scale production. The ethanol car tests were so successful that the Governor of São Paulo Paulo Maluf ordered the state's fleet of government cars be replaced with ethanol vehicles in July 1979, after which Telesp ordered 517 new ethanol powered 147s to expand their fleet.[89] Brazil's major manufacturers, Volkswagen, GM, and

Ford, were more hesitant. As the second oil crisis intensified, the Minister of Industry and Commerce Camila Penna stressed to manufacturers that their insistence on gasoline cars would result in "fuel rationing and the establishment of ever lower quotas for car production."[90] Nevertheless, manufacturers were wary to commit to launching a car exclusive to the Brazilian market with such an uncertain fuel source.

In the end, backdoor agreements between the government, the auto industry, and Petrobras resolved the fuel distribution problem and secured the industry's ethanol car production at the same time. Mário Garnero, director of Volkswagen do Brasil, president of the National Car Producers' Association (Associação Nacional dos Fabricantes de Veículos Automotores [Anfavea]), and the only civilian businessman sitting on the National Energy Commission, negotiated the car industry's participation.[91] Known as the "godfather of ethanol," he recalls, "We [car producers] had a choice, which was rationing [gasoline] or creating something new, and from this choice arose, objectively, our work to coordinate with the car industry, the government, and with producers and distributors, in this case Petrobras."[92] Garnero struck a deal with the Minister of Finance Mário Henrique Simonsen, his close friend, and Paulo Vieira Belotti, vice president of Petrobras, at a dinner at Simonsen's house in August 1979. The auto industry would produce 600,000 ethanol cars, Petrobras would distribute the new alternative fuel at sufficient levels to guarantee the ethanol car's viability, and the government would provide incentives for ethanol cars.[93]

The details were ironed out in September. In the original dinner agreement, the three men committed to supporting 600,000 ethanol cars, but the Minister of Mines and Energy Cesar Cals ultimately approved the production of only 250,000 ethanol cars in the first year.[94] Each manufacturer would produce its share of the quota of ethanol cars in proportion to each manufacturer's share of the market. Thus, Volkswagen would produce the largest share, starting with their popular fuscas. In addition to offering tax incentives to encourage car sales, the government would allow Petrobras to sell the fuel on the weekends and on holidays but ban gasoline sales on such days. As Garnero later pointed out, he anticipated some gasoline car owners would buy a second car run on ethanol just to guarantee the ability to travel on the weekends and over holidays.[95] Petrobras acquired primary control of ethanol distribution in the restructured second phase, a victory that would prove costly by the late 1980s. The state company adapted refinery tanks, pipelines, and maritime terminals to receive ethanol via coastal shipping to directly pump ethanol to the bases of its distribution companies.[96] Resolving the fuel distribution problem and securing the car industry's buy-in ensured the ethanol-fueled car's commercial debut.[97] In fact, Volkswagen had already set its target rollout for November 1979 back in February when the new government made its commitment to Proálcool clear.[98]

With the rollout set, winning the royalties on the ethanol-fueled engine transformed the ethanol car into a Brazilian national treasure. Brazilian researchers at the CTA had conducted ethanol-fueled engine research long before Proálcool began. Upon the commitment of the car industries, foreign companies filed for royalties on their own engines that they claimed to have privately developed. The CTA strongly opposed this position. Lieutenant Colonel Sergio Ferolla, director of the Institute of Research and Development at the CTA, noted that Brazil already had the ethanol motor patented and claimed that the country "will talk on an equal footing with international manufacturers."[99] Furthermore, the CTA's required approval and input on each model further validated its claims. Ultimately, the foreign companies gave Brazil full rights to the ethanol-fueled engine. Brazilian ownership of the new technology contravened development in other areas of the economy.[100] For Brazilians, the royalties established the country's place in modern automotive technological development, and the ethanol car became a source of pride for the modern Brazilian nation.[101] Although the automobile remained a luxury many Brazilians could not afford under the dictatorship, Proálcool's ability to connect energy, technology, the economy, and the car represented a type of modernity that government officials, private businessmen, and the military victoriously attached to ideas of a modern Brazilian national identity.

Phase II and the Usina Santa Elisa

In the second phase, the ethanol car became the new symbol of Proálcool. While Garnero's agreement cleared the path for ethanol's large-scale rollout in late 1979, getting consumers to buy the new car proved to be a bit more challenging in the early 1980s. To win over consumers, the government repeatedly had to offer larger, more expensive incentives on the fuel and the car. At the same time, project delays continued. Brazil's expanding national debt incited public debate about bringing foreign investment into the program. Amidst these challenges, the Biagi brothers, newly in charge of the family's sugar and ethanol interests after the death of their father, Maurilio Biagi Sr., in 1978, embraced the new car technology and continually reasserted the program's nationalist implications to rally public support. Their promotion of the program in the 1980s was critical to the program's success within a few years.[102]

Ethanol car sales got off to a difficult start as steelworkers' strikes affected the ethanol car's rollout. The dictatorship had suppressed union activities and wages in the economic recovery of the "Brazilian miracle," but new union leaders emerged to challenge the military government in the late 1970s. Among them, Luiz Inácio "Lula" da Silva, a Volkswagen metalworker, was the most prominent. Workers in the industrial corridor of São Paulo's suburban municipalities, known as the ABC (Santo André, São Bernardo, and São Caetano), mobilized around the government's systematic underadjustment of minimum salaries in the face of growing inflation. In May 1978, some 500,000 workers successfully led their first twelve-day sit-in strike in the auto industry. After direct bargaining with the auto firms, the strikers won limited pay increases. Lula, the president of the Metalworkers' Union of São Bernardo, won national attention for the successful strike and founded the Worker's Party (Partido do Trabalhador) in 1979. Public support for workers grew as strikes expanded in 1979 and 1980. These strikes quickly conflicted with the launch of the ethanol car. Some Proálcool supporters argued that the ethanol car would buoy car production and thus steelworkers' jobs in the growing economic crisis. However, a forty-one-day strike in April and May 1980 pushed officials to reduce the target for ethanol car production by 50,000 units.[103]

Consumer opinion of the new cars was more damaging. Early models of the new ethanol-fueled car faced myriad problems. Maurilio Biagi Filho recalled, "[The] first generation of motors was awful, the second awful, the third, bad, the fourth good."[104] Technical difficulties with the car affected public support. As one report noted, "The brave little [Volkswagen] Beetle, for example, for so many years the most reliable national car, gave the greatest problems. Its motor, designed basically half a century ago, did not work with the new fuel."[105] Engine corrosion, a faster burn rate than gasoline, and failure to start in cool temperatures (below 60 degrees Fahrenheit) most vexed consumers. These technical problems quickly affected sales in the second year of mass production.[106]

Nevertheless, ethanol producers' promotional efforts combined with continued fears of increased oil shortages and gasoline rationing initially boosted sales. Biagi Filho and Lacerda Biagi promoted the program by purchasing the first ethanol-driven car, the Fiat 147, despite Biagi Filho's recollection of how bad the early models were. They promoted the program to local businesses, as well as consumers in the Ribeirão Preto region. The brothers "distributed caps and T-shirts with the national motto 'See this T-shirt. Choose ethanol.' "[107] After the Iran-Iraq War began in September 1980, sales exceeded expectations over the next six months, hitting 240,643 new cars in 1980 alone.[108]

Yet sales dropped by almost 100,000 cars in 1981as the program's financial struggles were made public.[109] Proálcool's second phase as a fuel replacement program required an extensive and expensive expansion from its initial more conservative fuel supplement focus. Some government officials suggested using foreign financing to support the program, beginning with former Minister of Mines and Energy Shigeaki Ueki in 1979. Ueki's proposal followed the era's common development strategy of combining foreign capital and private domestic interests with state direction, in this case through a state-led ethanol subsidiary of Petrobras, to expand sugarcane and manioc production, ethanol distilleries, and storage and distribution facilities. The Ministry of Industry and Commerce, along with private business owners, including the vocal Zanini vice president Lacerda Biagi, vehemently opposed the proposition. Although the Minister of Mines and Energy Cesar Cals ultimately vetoed the suggestion, debate about the role of foreign interests in the program continued.[110]

Military officials and private citizens publicly spoke out about foreign financing. Supporters claimed that the exclusion of foreign capital was not worth the failure of the entire program.[111] However, opponents played to Proálcool's nationalist leanings. General Ernani Ayrosa, Chief of the General Staff of the Army, claimed, "Prudence shows that the energy problems ought to be solved within our own country, without foreign dependence."[112] General Antonio Carlos de Andrada Serpa, Chief of the Military Personnel Department, compared potential foreign entry to what happened in the Brazilian pharmaceutical industry, where, he claimed, "Wild capitalism developed in the country."[113] Still other private businessmen, such as Anfavea president Garnero, toed the line by supporting foreign financing so long as domestic capital outweighed foreign capital interests.[114] While the military officials' opinions reasserted the program's national security implications, all sides expressed deeper doubts about the standard development model of the era. Opponents wanted to avoid such foreign control entirely, while supporters wanted to limit it if possible.

Meanwhile, program expansion continued to stretch the program's budget in 1980. For example, after significantly expanding their land holdings to enable larger cane production capacity in the program's first five years, the Usina Santa Elisa applied for Proálcool assistance to expand its annexed distillery from 300,000 liters a day to 540,000 liters a day in September 1980.[115] Proálcool financing would support the addition of two more 120,000 distilleries to the four already in place. The additional distilleries, estimated to cost Cr$647,945,900 (US$12,807,323), would both be for hydrous ethanol production to support ethanol car fuel demand. According to the application, ethanol production at the Usina Santa Elisa would increase from 71,001,100 liters of ethanol in the 1979/1980 harvest to 81,000,000 liters in the 1981/1982 harvest.[116] CENAL approved the Usina Santa Elisa expansion project on November 19, 1980.[117]

Financial issues brought broader new and expansion project approvals to a complete halt in mid-1981.[118] While sugar exports, federal budget allocations, and the sale of ethanol-gasoline had supported the program until 1979, these financial bases had been stretched thin by 1980. Furthermore, the government's other alternative fuel initiatives, including nuclear and hydroenergy, began to draw from the same federal budget in 1980, further reducing available capital for ethanol.[119] The Minister of Planning Delfim Neto, known for his focus on controlling inflation, focused his economic campaign on Proálcool in late 1980 and adamantly supported foreign financing.[120] He connected Proálcool to the rising inflation rate, because the program cut into agricultural exports without reducing actual fuel consumption, instead only exchanging one fuel for another.[121] Neto suspended program approvals in June 1981. For Proálcool to continue as a fuel replacement program, an infusion of foreign capital became the only option to support expansion.

The World Bank controversially entered program financing in 1981, but private domestic producers continued to control the program. The government approved the World Bank's US$250 million financial incorporation into Proálcool under very stringent conditions. The contract required that the World Bank support international bidding for distillery equipment; a reduction and eventual elimination of interest rate subsidies on Proálcool loans that had long been so advantageous for producers; and a revised ethanol pricing policy that would constantly adjust to the rising inflation.[122] However, the National Executive Ethanol Commission (CENAL) maintained control of project approvals, and domestic producers received a 15 percent preferential margin in project bidding prices. Domestic industries won all the bids. In fact, the Biagis' Zanini S.A. won the largest share of projects after the World Bank's entry by cutting prices even further below CENAL's requirements to outbid potential competitors.[123] Thus, the restrictive financial restructuring was able to appease both sides of the foreign entry debate by keeping the level of international influence that slowly eroded domestic presence in such capital-intensive industries as pharmaceuticals and steel out of Proálcool.

The government removed the freeze on program expansion in August 1981, but public confidence and support required more coaxing.[124] The government offered additional incentives in the form of subsidized fuel prices and various reduced car taxes to attract consumers back to ethanol cars. The new hydrous fuel initially arrived at the fuel pumps at 65 percent the price of gasoline. However, after the car's struggles became apparent, interest groups such as Anfavea pressed for more government support. In 1982, President Figueiredo and the National Energy Commission responded by passing a series of additional ethanol car incentives. These included: lowering the standard ethanol price to 59 percent that of gasoline per liter; lowering the IPI (Industrial Product Tax) for ethanol cars to 28 percent (from 32%) while increasing the IPI on gasoline cars to 33 percent (from 32%); a reduction in the price of the ethanol car to 2% below that of the gasoline car, despite the fact that its production costs exceeded those of the gasoline car; cutting the car's Road Tax (the TRU, Taxa Rodovíaria Única) in half; and offering longer lease terms for new ethanol cars.[125]

At the same time, producers led promotional efforts to build confidence in the fuel and the ethanol car. Notably, Maurilio Biagi Filho continued to place the Usina Santa Elisa at the forefront of expanded ethanol use to promote the program. In 1981, all of the trucks used at the were ethanol-fueled.[126] This was generally unheard of at the time, as less than twenty-five of these trucks had been produced in the country prior to 1981. In fact, in 1981, the industry only produced 1,126 ethanol-fueled trucks, of which the Biagis purchased 300 for use at the . As ethanol-driven agricultural equipment, particularly tractors, became available, the Usina Santa Elisa would be one of the first to use this equipment as well.[127]

The Biagis promoted Proálcool with words as well as action.[128] Luiz Lacerda Biagi regularly promoted foreign competition in Proálcool, asserting private producers were up to the challenge.[129] Biagi Filho promoted the program by publishing articles in various newspapers that continually asserted Proálcool's importance and the need for support from the Brazilian public.

In a 1983 article, "The Ethanol is Ours," he argued that Brazilians "ought to, indeed, defend our nationalist interests. The technology and labor are ours. We do not pay royalties. On the contrary, we have an international market importing our technology."[130] By embracing the nationalist meaning of the program and the ethanol car, Biagi Filho's promotion appealed to consumers' hearts and minds. As he later recalled, the Santa Elisa's inclusion as an early Proálcool project "was the beginning of the Usina Santa Elisa [as a] leader not only in production but principally in intellectual leadership . . . in the conduct of the program."[131] The Biagis, who had long pushed for the program's creation, built the infrastructure for their ethanol empire through Proálcool. Their Usina Santa Elisa was the first to receive approved Proálcool financing, and their sugar equipment company, Zanini S.A., became one of the largest distillery manufacturers under the program. The Biagis' promotion of the fuel directly influenced the program's creation, implementation, and expansion and made them unequivocal leaders in the industry by 1984.

Ultimately, government intervention, foreign financing, and private producers all were essential to Proálcool's success in the second phase. Government intervention, in the form of market manipulation and incentives, salvaged Proálcool's most visible metric, ethanol car sales. Ethanol car sales peaked in 1986 at 699,183 units, compared with 219,347 gasoline cars, and between 1983 and 1989, they accounted for 90 percent of the cars sold in Brazil.[132] Foreign financing buoyed program expansion. However, private producers shaped these efforts by embracing the program's nationalist meanings, particularly for domestic ethanol car development, to assert their preeminence amid the three contributing sectors in ways that diverged from other typical Brazilian development efforts of the era. Proálcool remained fundamentally Brazilian and the ethanol car its shining example.

4

Lakes of Sacrifice

Ethanol and Water Pollution

Ethanol distilleries are actually vinasse factories that eventually produce ethanol.

Common Brazilian Saying

Proálcool rapidly shifted car fuel consumption away from oil to address the fuel crisis by the mid-1980s. Booming ethanol car sales seemed to declare the program a resounding triumph by the mid-1980s.[1] Yet, despite the program's success, the expanding ethanol industry brought with it destructive water pollution.[2] Sugar production generates a great deal of waste, some of which is repurposed into additional products such as bagasse (the woody sugarcane stalk), ethanol, and drinking alcohol.[3] However, ethanol production, whether as a means of dealing with waste or as an end in itself, also produces a wasteful byproduct: vinasse. This liquid byproduct of ethanol distillation is produced at a rate of ten to sixteen liters for every liter of ethanol created. Producers generally have disposed of it in local waterways, where the acidic liquid absorbs oxygen in the water, decimating aquatic flora and fauna and causing other public health issues. Such environmental destruction is also entirely contradictory to the image of the environmentally beneficial industry that Proálcool promoted well into the twenty-first century.

This chapter focuses on how producers' detrimental disposal of vinasse turned the ethanol industry into one of Brazil's most polluting industries and the inadequacy of government and private enterprise in dealing with this byproduct. Vinasse was initially a problem known only to locals in sugar-producing regions, but government support of ethanol production transformed it into a national problem as the waste's impact on waterways drew increased attention. Legislation, the promotion of alternative uses, and the inconsistent enforcement of banned dumping allowed government officials and

Sweet Fuel. Jennifer Eaglin, Oxford University Press. © Oxford University Press 2022.
DOI: 10.1093/oso/9780197510681.003.0005

producers to continually claim that the vinasse problem was solved. Yet these solutions, which included retention sites known as "areas of sacrifice" and "lakes of accumulation" to hold vinasse at a limited distance from local waterways, remained only a partial fix as ethanol production exponentially increased under Proálcool.[4] By the 1980s, ethanol was commonly linked to water pollution, and local communities bore the brunt of the environmental costs of this alternative fuel.

Despite the community outrage vinasse provoked in São Paulo from the 1930s through the 1980s, government response on the local, state, and national level to the vinasse problem remained limited. The sugar industry's contribution to water pollution received a multilayered response from public, private, and government entities beginning in the 1930s as ethanol and aguardente (drinking alcohol) production expanded in São Paulo. By the 1950s, vinasse dumping had created a crisis in the large sugar-producing region of Piracicaba. Public outcry about vinasse's health implications pressured the government to intervene, but officials often attributed the problem to another source rather than resolving it. Brazilian agronomists and industry specialists repeatedly promoted repurposing the product and declared the vinasse problem solved. However, limited government enforcement never led to full compliance, and the problem continued to grow as Ribeirão Preto emerged as the leading ethanol-producing region. By examining early community environmental demands to limit vinasse dumping and the innovative but ultimately inadequate responses by government and private producers, this chapter reveals how piecemeal solutions sacrificed the water quality of residents as ethanol became an increasingly important industry in the state.

Vinasse: A Byproduct of Destruction

Vinasse production had accompanied the sugar industry as a byproduct of the distillation of drinking alcohol for centuries. Producers, always in need of a disposal site for the toxic byproduct, dumped it in local waterways. The Brazilian sociologist Gilberto Freyre best described the practice in his 1937 book, *Nordeste*, where he said the monocultural production of sugar:

> turned the water of the rivers into a urinal, a urinal of the smelly caldas [vinasse] of the sugar mills. And the smelly caldas kill the fish. They poison

> "the fisheries." They dirty the riverbanks. The caldas that the sugar mills throw in the rivers every harvest sacrifices a considerable part of the fish production in the Northeast at the end of every year.[5]

The byproduct's broader connections to public health concerns would only emerge as the scale of vinasse production increased in tandem with the ethanol industry beginning in the 1930s.

To understand why and how the product's damage increased with the government's formal support of ethanol production requires a basic understanding of the composition of vinasse and its impact on water. A dark brown, thick, pulpy, smelly liquid, vinasse has a biochemical composition that makes its disposal a challenge for large-scale producers. The product is highly acidic, reaching pH levels as low as 4.5.[6] Vinasse is mostly made of water (over 90%) and organic material (around 5%) including nitrogen, phosphorous, calcium, and potassium.[7] When dumped in the water at concentrated levels, these organic materials produce bacteria that create what are commonly called algae blooms. Vinasse spurs algae growth that kills the protozoa and aerobic bacteria along with the flora and fauna of the waterway. Large amounts of carbon dioxide are also created, which decrease the water's pH levels.

The product's biochemical content presents an important option for alternative use: fertilizer. Excessive agricultural production, particularly of monocultural crops such as sugarcane, notoriously strips the soil of nutrients. Vinasse's relatively high nitrogen, phosphorous, and potassium content make it a viable fertilizer alternative when recycled for other agricultural uses. In the 1930s, producers and researchers began experimenting to figure out what quantity of vinasse would be beneficial as a soil supplement. Too much would decrease the sugar content and the purity of the juice of the sugarcane.[8] Depending on the soil's pre-existing pH, the ideal application ranged from 500,000 to 1,000,000 unprocessed liters per hectare when applied directly and more when sprayed.[9]

Yet the amount of vinasse applied to the harvest has never offset the amount produced. An usina that produced 100,000 liters of ethanol per day and worked 150 days per harvest would produce a minimum of 150,000,000 liters of vinasse per harvest. By 1980, each ton of cane produced an average of 70–80 liters of ethanol and 800–910 liters of vinasse.[10] Small mills (engenhos) and later autonomous distilleries tended to produce more vinasse than annexed distilleries at sugar mills. While researchers genetically manipulated sugarcane varieties to increase yields per hectare, the harvest produced an average of 38 tons of cane per hectare in 1951.[11] By the 1970s, this rate expanded to about 70 tons per hectare in São Paulo.[12] Each hectare of sugarcane harvested produced between 34,580 and 63,700 liters of vinasse per hectare. This is less than the suggested application rate per hectare, so technically the vinasse produced could all be used as a fertilizer replacement. However, many producers did not apply the product at the same suggested rate, if they applied it at all. Most importantly, producers purchased sugarcane from *fornecedores* (growers) in addition to the sugarcane produced on their own land, so they produced far more vinasse than they could reuse on their own land.

Unlike popular organic fertilizers of the time, such as guano, vinasse's acidity deterred producers from repurposing the product.[13] Most producers originally deemed vinasse to be "completely unusable" and indeed "dangerous to the soil" because they assumed it would make the soil acidic and harm the harvest. Rather than use it as a fertilizer, producers instead often threw the acidic waste into nearby rivers and streams.[14] As the algae and organic material decompose, they create large amounts of carbon dioxide, which decrease the water's pH levels.[15] In this acidic state, the water becomes undrinkable and further endangers aquatic flora and fauna. Given that the sugar harvest occurs in the dry season, producers tended to dump large quantities of the product in low-volume waterways, which accelerated this process so that at times it was completed in a matter of days. Not only did vinasse dumping destroy fish, frogs, and crustaceans, but the acidic vinasse water became a place where large mosquito populations festered.

Vinasse dumping also created significant public health problems. Most of the exposed waterways supported drinking supplies for local communities. The polluted water acquired a nauseating smell, an abnormal color, and a disagreeable taste and could turn toxic. The subsequent infestations of mosquitos as freshwater fish disappeared increased the threat of the spread of malaria and other endemic diseases linked to amoebic dysentery and schistosomiasis.[16]

Growing Tension over Deteriorating Waters

As the ethanol industry expanded in the 1930s, vinasse increasingly threatened the state of São Paulo's waterways over the next two decades, compelling the government, academics, and the public alike to pay attention to the grave problem. However, potential solutions proposed from within the industry, including the use of vinasse as a fertilizer, proved either unpopular or unviable. In the 1930s and 1940s, federal legislation occasionally addressed vinasse dumping, but producers mostly continued to dump vinasse despite increased public attention. Some producers adapted their vinasse practices as other entities such as the Institute of Sugar and Ethanol (IAA) and research institutions promoted alternative uses. However, the enforcement of legislation remained weak and the solutions inadequate to address the expanding problem.

Vinasse was certainly not the only waste dumped into Brazilian waters, and water pollution generally drew increased federal government attention in the 1930s. As President Vargas sought to centralize power with the new Constitution of 1934, the government passed groundbreaking legislation claiming ownership of all domestic waters, declaring them public rather than private domain. The law explicitly noted that those who polluted the water were criminally responsible for the losses and damages done to it. It even included a specific article stating that agricultural or industrial companies that used the water were explicitly required to put it through a purifying treatment before it was returned to its natural source.[17] As vinasse was an agricultural byproduct, the law technically covered vinasse dumping, but it was not explicitly mentioned. The Fishing Code of 1934, later revised in 1938, also set fines for companies that polluted the waterways. It explicitly prohibited dumping oil into domestic waters and more vaguely stated that the Hunting and Fishing Division would control the discharge of "solid waste and toxic effluents" into domestic waterways.[18] Vinasse was not specifically mentioned, but the laws set the parameters to hold sugar and ethanol producers accountable.

Vinasse's destructive impact on local waterways formally drew federal intervention in 1943. The Director of the Hunting and Fishing Division of the Ministry of Agriculture issued Ordinance no. 69 on March 3, 1943, which recognized vinasse's connection "to pollution of waters destined for the use of riverside populations" and made dumping vinasse from distilleries into local waterways illegal.[19] Taking into account early research and the practices of some producers, the law acknowledged alternative uses of the byproduct, particularly as a fertilizer or a fuel, as legal. The law called for the complete prohibition of vinasse dumping in waterways a year later in March 1944. The delay gave distillery owners a year to invest in the equipment to process the removal of the organic material from vinasse before returning the water to the riverways or to repurpose the product, which included necessary storage of vinasse until use.

The ruling directly linked vinasse dumping to the 1938 Fishing Code's financial penalties. If producers violated the ruling, they were required to pay a fine of 100,000 to 500,000 contos de réis (roughly US$6,000 to US$30,000 at that time) to the Minister of Agriculture.[20] However, ordinances were low-level rulings and did not have the same weight as full-fledged laws, which left enforcement responsibilities somewhat unclear.[21] The Water Code, the Fishing Code, and Ordinance no. 69 opened the door for criminal action against producers who threw vinasse in local waterways.

The Ministry of Agriculture's Hunting and Fishing Division proved poorly equipped to oversee and enforce the vinasse ban. The 1934 Fishing Code had tasked the states and municipalities with organizing the oversight services to enforce the code, but when this failed, the 1938 code moved that responsibility to the division.[22] Although the division created the Hydrobiology Section to test the water, between 1938 and 1959, the section never received any "material from the State [of São Paulo]. The federal government sent it only 400 vials for dissolved oxygen [samples], a refrigerator, four thermal boxes and an incubator, which never worked."[23] Woefully underfunded, government enforcement was so weak that producers had little incentive to comply with the new laws.

Nevertheless, the media amplified public frustration with increasing vinasse pollution. Reports of strange fish population collapses in sugar-producing regions began popping up in the *Estado de São Paulo* throughout the 1930s during the harvest season. Accounts of large-scale "decimation" of fish "asphyxiated," with a "bad smell," and/or dying of an "unknown disease" in sugar-producing regions appeared in regional news reports in July from 1931 through 1938.[24] By specifically noting the impact it had on children and fishermen in addition to the general public, the reports attempted to provoke government action. As one report noted in 1933:

> It is clear that, on several occasions, the local and city newspapers have not only attracted the attention of the authorities, but also pointed out the drawbacks to the Directorate of the Animal Industry, which is the one which could do something more closely for the benefit of the municipality's aquatic fauna.[25]

The timing of the pieces was no accident. July, two months after São Paulo's sugar harvest season began and when cane crushing would have been completed and distillation well underway, was exactly when producers were keen to dispose of excess residues in the sugar ethanol distillation process. Even though these reports made no explicit mention of vinasse, the timing and location suggest these incidents were linked to the sugar industry and the expansion of ethanol production.

Some reports explicitly tied the pollution to the sugar industry and tried to demand enforcement of the Fishing Code's ban, but their complaints tended not to bring action. For example, a 1938 news report accused the Usina Tamoio, the largest ethanol producer in the state of São Paulo the following year, of dumping "its residues" in the local Chibarro River.[26] The report claimed that these effluents, likely including both vinasse and water to wash cane, caused the "decimation, on a large scale, of the fish of the river, which are seen dead, floating, in a truly impressive quantity."[27] In line with the 1938 Fishing Code, the report called for an investigation by the Hunting and Fishing Division, which sent a hydrobiologist to study the topic and the water.[28] However, given the limited budgets of the Hydrobiology Section and the Hunting and Fishing Division, large-scale enforcement could not keep up with the growing vinasse dumping problem. For every report issued, many more cases of vinasse dumping were likely left unaccounted for or had no action taken to stop them.

Even as federal, state, and municipal enforcement faltered, the IAA promoted alternative uses of vinasse to incentivize some producers to change their disposal methods as part of its broader efforts to distribute information on best practices for sugar producers across the nation. Because of vinasse's acidity, many producers believed the byproduct had to be processed before being applied to the harvest. Research also supported using processed vinasse as a liquid fuel to substitute for firewood.[29] The IAA financially supported some prominent northeastern mills' construction of plants to process vinasse into a fertilizer as early as 1935.[30] After the Ministry of Agriculture passed the new vinasse law in 1943, the IAA published advertisements for new evaporation equipment which concentrated and incinerated vinasse in compliance with the law.[31] However, such processing equipment was costly and not available to most producers.

Some producers embraced vinasse's fertilizing potential, but many did not. In Ribeirão Preto, Maurilio Biagi was among the earliest adoptors of vinasse as a fertilizer. He required that the Usina Santa Elisa begin using vinasse as a fertilizer in 1938, long before most others in the state employed the practice.[32] Still, agriculturalists feared vinasse's impact on the land. Urgel de Almeida Lima, an agronomic specialist of this period, acknowledged that well into the 1940s, "It was tacitly accepted that vinasse, a product of strong acidic reaction, would contribute to harming the cane harvest severely, making it unviable for the cultivation of sugarcane."[33] Such fears further promoted dumping vinasse in local waterways.

The Ministry of Agriculture's 1943 vinasse legislation dissuaded some producers from dumping the acidic product in local waterways and encouraged problematic storage practices instead. To avoid fines, two popular forms of storage emerged: above-ground storage containers and ground-level storage pits. Large above-ground tanks were expensive and prone to erosion because of vinasse's acidic nature. The cheaper ground pits required tracks of land exclusively for vinasse storage, which exacerbated the environmental problems created by vinasse. According to researchers, the accumulated vinasse, regardless of its distance from waterways, increased "the possibility of anaerobic fermentation, with consequent putrefaction and production of putrid gases, smelly or even toxic, contamination and pollution of groundwater, pollution of the air," and permanently attracted mosquitoes to the region.[34] These nasty effects surely reinforced producers' fears that using the unprocessed byproduct on their harvests would damage their fields.

More formal research on vinasse was conducted at the University of São Paulo's Luiz de Queiroz College of Agriculture (Escola Superior de Agricultura "Luiz de Queiroz" [ESALQ]) in the 1940s. Located in Piracicaba, the state's first sugar-producing hub, the school carried out important research into and development of cane varieties. When an above-ground vinasse tank collapsed in 1946 and inundated an entire cane harvest at a major usina in Piracicaba, sugar industrialists approached Professor Jayme Rocha de Almeida, the director of the Zimotécnico Institute at ESALQ, on how to resolve the problem.[35] Thereafter, Rocha spent several years conducting specialized research on vinasse.

Rocha's work definitively proved that the byproduct could be productive in the harvest and not just a water pollutant, a finding critical to transforming ideas about vinasse use in the 1950s. He proved that the product in pure, unfiltered form was useful for neutralizing previously acidic soil. He also showed that it could be used on any agricultural product, not just sugarcane. Finally, he showed that, when applied properly, the organic material in vinasse restored productivity to land that had been exhausted by agricultural production.[36] However, initial promotion of these findings was limited.

Although many Brazilian agricultural researchers claimed that vinasse did not become a real problem until the 1950s or even the 1970s, the sugar and ethanol industry's connection to water pollution had been widely discussed in public forums by the end of the 1940s. A 1948 report on fisheries in São Paulo State specifically identified the ethanol industry as one of the key contributors to water pollution because of its "high doses of acids, salts, and alcoholic residues" and more broadly identified water pollution as "the most important cause of fish depopulation in the waterway systems or lakes."[37] Despite the progressive national legislation and some forward-thinking owners, most sugar producers systematically ignored the law in the sugar-growing regions and continued discarding vinasse in local waterways. Government intervention, public outcry, and producers' adjustments were ineffective until the 1950s, when an environmental crisis emerged in the first major sugar-producing region of the state, Piracicaba.

Piracicaba: The First Crisis

Vinasse dumping reached its first breaking point in the 1950s. Given the inadequate efforts to limit vinasse dumping over the previous two decades, the health of the Piracicaba River had deteriorated as vinasse production accelerated with the increased distillation of drinking alcohol and ethanol. Outraged over the state of the waterways, rural and middle-class citizens, fishermen, and specialists promoted alternative vinasse disposal techniques throughout the state, as well as a major public health campaign and legal intervention on the municipal, state, and national levels between 1953 and 1956. The Piracicaba case presents a rare example of local pressure yielding some success. These efforts, mostly through legal institutions, represent early environmental activism focused on limiting producers' negligence at a time when industry mostly dominated.[38]

By the 1950s, Piracicaba was the state's first sugar hub and the site of the country's first anhydrous ethanol distillery, the Usina Piracicaba. When the state lifted production quotas during World War II, engenhos (small mills) for aguardente (drinking alcohol) and/or ethanol production had expanded dramatically in Piracicaba. In 1953, there were over 100 engenhos there.[39] The greater basin of the Piracicaba River supported numerous other sugar-producing regions, all of which dumped their vinasse into streams that ran into the river, with catastrophic ecological effects.

The concentrated levels of vinasse in the Piracicaba River decimated the region's fishing industry. Reports on the collapse of fish populations regularly made statewide news in the *Estado de São Paulo* newspaper. Freshwater fish native to the rivers were dying off by the ton.[40] The agronomic engineer Felisberto Pinto Monteiro noted that the Piracicaba River was so bad during the harvest that when producers would dump vinasse, "a fisherman who threw his line in [the river], would see it wrapped in organic material in minutes."[41] As the river's native freshwater fish died off by the ton, "dense clouds" of mosquitos spread in Piracicaba.[42]

According to a November 1953 public health report, vinasse's excessive presence in the Piracicaba river made local water "corrupted," "severely polluted," "inappropriate for consumption," and "extremely dangerous to health" for humans.[43] A team of four local doctors and professors conducted rigorous physical, chemical, toxicological, microscopic, and bacteriological exams on filtered, thrice-distilled tap water in Piracicaba for a case against usineiros brought by the city's public prosecutor. Even after treatment, they found high levels of cane wax, restyl, chlorophenol, and benzene hexachloride (BHC) from the benzene used to distill ethanol in the "bread, beans, cooked rice, pasta, baked goods, sweets, ice creams, sodas, pastries, and crackers" made in the city with local filtered water. Even the coffee, noted the report, had a harsh taste "like carbolic acid" because of how polluted the water was even after filtering.[44] Clothing washed in local filtered water was covered in the substance. The report found that "the human skin, after a bath, conserves harmful components of restyl [vinasse], constituting itself in irritant agents, annoying and harmful, principally for children." Ultimately, the expert report asserted that Piracicaba's water was "not fit" even to bathe in, let alone consume directly.[45] Assessments were done of urban dwellers with access to local filtered water, which means that the families in rural areas would have experienced even more extreme exposure.

The Piracicaba River's biochemical oxygen demand (BOD) rating further illustrates the water's degradation. A test to assess water pollution and sewage regulation, BOD estimates how much dissolved oxygen in water is absorbed over a certain distance before the water filters the organic material and returns to its original dissolved oxygen levels.[46] North American legislation considers anything over a 4 BOD rating polluted and inappropriate for food; in Brazilian law, the limit is 5 BOD. In 1953, a reporter noted that the Piracicaba River, which received millions of liters of vinasse from ethanol production in the region, had reached an average level of 26 BOD by the late 1940s.[47] The same year a report indicated that the Piracicaba River was "twice as polluted as the Tiete River, which carries the waste of São Paulo, the largest industrial city in Latin America."[48]

Public outrage over the severe pollution of the waterways reached breaking point in the sugar-producing region of Piracicaba in 1953. The local newspaper, *Jornal de Piracicaba*, published explicit denunciations of vinasse dumping, while specialists such as Dr. Francisco Bergamin, a sanitation doctor and head of the Hydrobiology Division in the State of São Paulo's Department of Agriculture, published on the topic in larger news sources, such as the *Estado de São Paulo*.[49] Piracicaba's public prosecutor, Dr. Neto Armando, brought criminal charges against usineiros for illegally contaminating the waters before he was forced out of office in December 1953.[50]

Rural citizens also found ways to protest vinasse dumping. Some agricultural workers and local citizens considered "vandalizing usinas and burning cane fields" to stop the dumping. Historically, workers in sugar communities and activists in Brazil and Cuba used field burning to demand various labor rights.[51] Here, citizens used field burning to demand their right to clean water, providing early examples of fights for environmental justice, even if protestors did not reference it as such.[52]

Government Action

Despite the various regulatory bodies and laws in place, federal and statewide attention to the problem of vinasse pollution was lacking. To help execute 1934 federal water legislation in the State of São Paulo, in December 1951, the State of São Paulo created the Department of Water and Electrical Energy (Departamento de Águas e Energia Elétrica [DAEE]), which came under the Department of Travel and Public Works (Secretaria de Viação e Obras Públicas).[53] In theory, the department was meant to manage water issues related to hydro-energy, agronomy, and public health. In practice, the entity focused more on hydroelectricity than on regulating the ethanol industry's industrial waste disposal.

Recognizing that the problem was greater than a single region, State Decree no. 2.182 of July 23, 1953 was passed to extend the scope of water protection to the entire state. The decree legislated a fine of 5,000 to 100,000 cruzeiros (approximately US$265 to US$5,319) for any producers who contaminated or polluted the waters of the state, although it did not identify vinasse as a particular source of pollution. Furthermore, the law allowed for continued dumping of either treated or untreated residues in the waters so long as the waters do not "become polluted" after dumping the product in the water.[54]

With so little state or federal leadership, it fell on the municipalities that suffered the greatest damage from vinasse dumping to be more aggressive in regulation and enforcement. Piracicaba led the charge. In September 1953, the Piracicaba city councilman Salgot Castillion proposed Municipal Law 393 (known as the Salgot law), which gave the Municipal Executive the right to revoke the license and operation of industries that threw vinasse in the Piracicaba River and its tributaries and charged the municipal police with enforcing it.[55] In addition to the right to revoke an usina or distillery's license for dumping, the law reinforced the existing but poorly enforced 1943 law's 5,000 to 100,000 cruzeiro fine on producers found guilty of dumping vinasse in local waterways.[56]

State and municipal action aligned as complaints about water pollution mounted. Importantly, Decree no. 2.182 created the State Council on the Control of Water Pollution (Conselho Estadual de Controle da Poluição das Águas) to set standards for water protection, regulation, and enforcement of the new state law.[57] When the State Council for the Control of Water Pollution officially started operating in December 1953, its first order of business was the vinasse problem in Piracicaba. Among its first acts in January 1954 was a law that prohibited the throwing of vinasse specifically in the Piracicaba basin.[58]

Response to the New Regulations

The municipal law and the council were able to effect some quick improvements. A news report in November 1954 claimed that tighter regulation and better enforcement of antidumping legislation had directly prevented 200 million liters of vinasse from being thrown in Piracicaba's waterways in 1953 and at least 400 million liters in 1954. The report credited Municipal Law 393, along with the newspaper campaign denouncing dumping and articles by specialists, community round tables, and local lawyers, with offsetting the "great apathy" of the authorities.[59]

In response, some producers became increasingly creative in their evasion of the antidumping laws. As the law required that producers store vinasse rather than dump the byproduct, producers waited until rainstorms began and then dumped vinasse in local waterways so no one could prove the exact source of the vinasse dumping. Thus, assigning blame turned out to be a far more difficult task because officials had to demonstrate that the usina had intentionally dumped the product in the waterways in order to levy the penalties. This allowed producers to evade fines and the cost of vinasse storage, rendering the law at times ineffective.[60]

Private citizens occasionally were successful in holding producers accountable for their water pollution when legislation failed. Most of the public remained skeptical that the new state council would effectively prevent producers from dumping vinasse in the rivers, given the water's continued deterioration and the government's weak record on enforcement.[61] Public prosecutors continued to file criminal charges against usineiros, which were listed publicly in local and statewide news sources. For example, the Piracicaba-based lawyer and activist Jacob Diehl Neto led a public fight against ethanol producers in 1955. On January 6, a major storm hit Piracicaba and allegedly damaged one of the Usina Costa Pinto's vinasse storage units. The usina's reserve of 500,000 liters of vinasse situated on the bank of the Rio Corumbataí, a local riverway in Piracicaba, spilled directly into the water. As the harvest season had already ended, the usina was not technically held responsible for the spill according to municipal law. Nonetheless Neto sued the usina for damages after the catastrophic spill killed over thirty tons of fish across over 150 km of the Piracicaba River in just a few days. The spill also polluted the city of São Paulo's major water source, the Tiete River. Neto argued that the Usina Costa Pinto should be held accountable because it built its vinasse storage units on the edge of the riverway, which knowingly exposed the public to the threat of a potential spill. Neto won.[62]

The Piracicaba situation also encouraged the IAA to do more to promote vinasse as a fertilizer. The IAA granted Rocha and a small team of researchers at the Zimotécnico Institute $150,000 cruzeiros (about US$8000) to expand their experiments in the state of São Paulo.[63] The IAA also published Rocha's findings in pamphlet form for broader distribution in 1955. Entitled "O problema da vinhaça" ("The Vinhaça Problem"), his study portrayed the vinasse problem as a larger public health crisis that science could solve.

Rocha explained how the direct application of fertilizer to the harvest would dramatically improve sugar yields while also reducing the oxygen decomposition in the water, the smell, air pollution, and the contamination of subterranean waters that accompanied vinasse dumping.[64]

Piracicaba's new legislation also drove increased antidumping legislation in neighboring sugar and ethanol producing regions around the state. The state council passed Ordinance no. 4 in June 1955 that banned all vinasse dumping in other large sugar- and ethanol-producing regions, including Araraquara, Descalvado, São Carlos, and Ibaté within the state of São Paulo. In 1956, Ordinance no. 10 prohibited the disposal of vinasse in all of the state's waterways.[65] The progressive expansion of anti-vinasse legislation throughout the state, even if some of it overlapped, asserted government commitment to enforcing antidumping legislation and paying increased attention to ethanol's contribution to São Paulo's growing water problems.

The multilayered response to the Piracicaba crisis allowed many specialists to claim that the vinasse problem was solved. Forcing producers to stop dumping vinasse and start storing it for use as a fertilizer became the chosen solution. Public pressure demanded environmental justice from private producers. When producers continued to resist, victories like Neto's illustrated how the public also pressured producers to comply. However, using vinasse as a fertilizer by no means fully solved the ethanol problem, and state action on water pollution remained inadequate.

Environmental Degradation in the New Sugar Economy

Despite extensive legislative efforts to prohibit vinasse dumping in the 1950s and pronouncements that the vinasse problem was solved, the state's waterways continued to deteriorate as sugar and ethanol production expanded over the next two decades. As Ribeirão Preto emerged as the leading sugar- and ethanol-producing region, attention turned to the deteriorating waterways of the Mogi-Guaçu basin in the 1960s and early 1970s. Many producers in the new sugar and ethanol region continued dumping vinasse at high levels. The political-economic focus on agro-industrial growth led to ongoing environmental negligence, but media attention given to the problem continued to pressure producers to improve their vinasse reuse practices.

Acronyms of Confusion

Water pollution increased even as government infrastructure to address it expanded from the mid-1950s through the early 1970s. A 1965 exposé succinctly explained the problem: "the multiplicity of technical organs charged with combating and controling the pollution of the waters, the absence of adequate laws, and the complete lack of resources for the oversight of offenders" complicated and slowed down government enforcement and actually limited the improvement of water quality. The author aptly called the complex oversight infrastructure in which all these new administrative organizations existed the "acronyms of confusion."[66] While demand for increased environmental attention eventually led to the streamlining of organizations, in the meantime, brief advances made during the first vinasse crisis were lost and producers were able to keep dumping vinasse with little punishment.

Water pollution management remained largely the responsibility of state entities until the 1970s. Following the establishment of President Castelo Branco's administration in the new military dictatorship, the federal government expanded its internal infrastructure to incorporate water management. In December 1965, the federal government created the National Department of Water and Energy (Departamento Nacional das Águas e Energia, later renamed the National Department of Water and Electric Energy).[67] The earlier National Council of Water and Hydroelectricity (created in 1939) and the new National Department of Water and Energy shortly coexisted before the latter absorbed the former in 1969. Despite the infrastructural expansion, the new department, which came under the Ministry of Mines and Energy, was far more focused on expanding hydroelectric energy than basic health management in the 1960s. Thus, federal regulation and the enforcement of measures to combat vinasse dumping remained absent even as the language of the department indicated that the elimination of such pollution would be part of its enforcement objectives.

The São Paulo state government's administration of the 1953 antidumping law, later upheld as a decree in 1955, fell apart in the late 1950s. Eight different state organizations and entities gained some responsibility for policing vinasse dumping, but they never coordinated their efforts. Many of the state entities focused exclusively on the metropolitan city of São Paulo, like the earlier state-level efforts. Of those eight, much of the responsibility for limiting vinasse dumping fell to city governments, which failed to enforce accountability. Article 6 of the decree, which linked operating licenses to waste treatment plans, went unheeded. Instead, many offered "concessions and tax breaks to attract new industries."[68]

Those entities that tried to enforce water pollution standards often did not have the resources to follow through. The Hunting and Fishing Division did not have the authority to combat an industry or a municipal government, so they could only "advise and threaten, but amicably," to very limited success. The Hydrobiology Section employed four or five inspectors to cover the entire state and remained so underfunded in the 1960s that it could not buy the mobile units and equipment technically budgeted by state funds. The State Council on Water Pollution Control formed in 1953, whose actions had been critical to reducing dumping in Piracicaba in 1954, ceased operating in 1960 and was only revived again in 1965.[69] Where infrastructure had previously been inadequately sparse, the state apparatus expanded administrative control over the waterways so extensively that it hindered effective oversight.

The state of São Paulo finally began consolidating its government infrastructure to monitor water and broader environmental threats in the late 1960s. In 1968, the state government created São Paulo's Technological Center for Basic Sanitation (Centro Tecnológico de Saneamento Básico [CETESB]) under Decree no. 50.079, which consolidated various research institutions working on combating water pollution in the state.[70] The state government followed this with the creation of the State Promotion of Basic Sanitation (Fomento Estadual de Saneamento Básico [FESB]) agency in 1969. The decree of February 19, 1970, the first state law on water protection since 1955, more clearly banned the dumping of any harmful "effluents from sewage networks, liquid residues from industries, and solid domestic or industrial residues" in the waterways. The new law also gave FESB the authority to financially punish, in line with the level of contamination, any industry that failed to comply with antidumping laws. Thus, fines could exceed the levels previously mandated in the 1953 law.[71]

Brazilian environmental legislation expanded dramatically in the 1970s, a pivotal point in global environmental awareness. While green politics and environmental consciousness began in the United States in the 1960s, sparked by popular books such as Rachel Carson's *Silent Spring*, they have been credited with inspiring international changes in environmental protection. Brazil came under particular pressure after the United Nation's Conference on the Human Environment in Stockholm, Sweden, in June

1972 when the Minister of the Interior General José Costa Cavalcanti memorably resisted international calls to increase environmental protection, claiming this was detrimental to the military dictatorship's focus on industrialization.[72] Brazilian specialists also pointed to the Stockholm Conference as a turning point for government policy on socio-environmental issues.[73] However, as the state and municipal efforts to limit vinasse dumping in the 1950s show, domestic interest in conservation and environmental protection existed long before the international pressures of the 1970s.[74]

Government administration against pollution was significantly streamlined in the 1970s. On the national level, a new cadre of environmental leaders emerged as federal environmental organizations were set up. A year after the Stockholm Conference, General Médici and the federal government created the Special Department of the Environment (Secretaria Especial do Meio Ambiente [SEMA]), which was was tasked with setting national norms and standards on pollution.

CETESB's authority as the State of São Paulo's central environmental agency was also consolidated in 1973. On June 29, the governor passed Law no. 118, which gave CETESB, newly named the State Company of Basic Sanitation Technology and Water Pollution Control (Companhia Estadual de Tecnologia de Saneamento Básico e de Controle de Poluição das Aguas), broader administrative responsibilities. This specifically included the charge "to lead studies, research, training and the improvement of personnel and to provide specialized technical assistance for the operation and maintaining of the systems of water and sewage and industrial residues."[75] FESB technically brought other entities under the umbrella of the state's water and waste management agency, Sabesp (Companhia de Saneamento Básico do Estado de São Paulo), but all its environmental oversight authority passed to CETESB. With a new bigger state budget, the growing CETESB tied together the agency's original research focus with new enforcement authority over pollution in all of the state's waters. This resolved many of the assessment issues of the late 1950s and 1960s.

As CETESB's regulatory reach grew, it extended its attention from the metropolitan area to the rest of the state's waters and broader pollution issues. In April 1975, the state government gave the entity responsibility for dealing with soil and air pollution in addition to water pollution. The larger CETESB received final approval over numerous protected areas and environmental legislation in the state just as Proálcool was being set up in late 1975.[76] Nonetheless, vinasse dumping continued.

Degradation of the Mogi-Guaçu

Despite the expansion of federal and state infrastructure for water management, enforcement at the federal and state level remained inadequate. As a result, the water quality of the Mogi-Guaçu River in the Ribeirão Preto region deteriorated between the 1950s and 1975. Still, the media continued to publicize growing water pollution problems and demanded better regulation.

Ribeirão Preto had largely been left out of the vinasse debates of the 1950s because the conditions in Piracicaba had been far worse. In the *Estado de São Paulo*'s 1953 multipart series on pollution and rivers in São Paulo, Francisco Bergamin, the chief of the Hydrobiology Section at the Department of Agriculture, asserted that the Mogi-Guaçu River could be considered "free" of water pollution. This is largely because Piracicaba had a far more concentrated number of sugar, ethanol, and aguardente (drinking alcohol) producers in a small area than Ribeirão Preto did at the time. Thus, Ribeirão Preto was a region where "the volume of residues is large but the river suffers little—because of its large size in relation to the waste." When listing the "special problem" of vinasse pollution in the sugar-producing regions of the state, Bergamin did not include Ribeirão Preto.[77]

However, as Ribeirão Preto surpassed Piracicaba as the top sugar and alcohol-producing region in the 1960s, its water pollution problems also earned more attention. Initially, the improving conditions in the Piracicaba water basin were compared with the declining conditions in the Mogi-Guaçu region. For example, while explaining the cause of fish deaths in the Piracicaba region in early November 1966, Bergamin noted, "Pollution rarely provokes the massive death of fish, except when a toxic residue is dumped. Pollution provokes the progressive depopulation of the waterways. This is what is happening currently in the Mogi-Guaçu River, which, according to a member of the government, is not polluted."[78]

Newspaper reports increasingly contradicted government claims that the Mogi-Guaçu basin was clean. In October 1968, a report in the *Estado de São Paulo* addressed the basin's growing water pollution problem. According to Manoel da Costa, a fisherman who had worked on the river for thirty-five years, the problem barely existed outside of the sugar-producing region. Key pockets of degradation aligned with the most intense parts of the sugar- and ethanol-producing region of Ribeirão Preto between Pitangueiras and Guariba, located about 44 km south. The report specifically identified the Usina São Martinho in the municipality of Guariba as a major polluter of the

Mogi-Guaçu. According to the report, the distillation residue and acids used to clean machines during the harvest season flowed into the river through local streams and caused massive deaths of "several tons of fish." The floating dead fish were so numerous they even clogged the wheel of a local tannery on the river.[79]

As a major sugar and ethanol producer in the region, the Usina São Martinho quickly responded to these accusations of vinasse dumping to protect its public image. The usina's managing director called for the paper to

Fig 4.1 Map of the Mogi-Guaçu and Pardo Rivers and major cities within the basins
Source: Map by Bill Nelson

retract the story a month later. He claimed that the reporter was totally ignorant "either about the vinasse problem or about the polluted waters" and "distorted the facts and unjustly and criminally compromised the industry before public opinion." Contradicting the report, the managing director noted that the Usina São Martinho had been renowned for its application of vinasse as a fertilizer since the 1930s. The usina, which was one of the largest in the country and produced over 1.5 million sacks of sugar per year, drew researchers to the region to study and imitate their practices from as far away as Japan.[80]

The director further mentioned the praise the Usina São Martinho had received for its efficient vinasse use in recent years. Specifically, the specialist Jorge Bierrenbach de Castro, the director of the agricultural supplement of the *Estado de São Paulo*, had pointed out the mill's efficient use of "land tanks" to store vinasse.[81] Producers used these land tanks to redirect vinasse to the various seed beds during the harvest. Either the usina's practices had changed or the land tanks were in fact contributing to water deterioration.

The 1968 report on São Martinho's connection to water pollution reflected the public's growing distrust of government and usineiro claims regarding the quality of the Mogi-Guaçu. The editor of the *Estado de São Paulo* responded to the Usina São Martinho's request to retract the report by highlighting the meticulous research conducted by the reporter to corroborate the fishermen's claims. The reporter sought out various authorities on the subject, including Angelo Parachinim, an official of the state's Hunting and Fishing Division based in Ribeirão Preto, to confirm that the São Martinho and São Francisco mills were the primary polluters. Furthermore, the editor noted, "The purpose of the report was to point out the damage to fishing caused by the pollution of the rivers, which ceased completely with the paralysis of the mills," not to address the improved uses of vinasse touted in the managing director's response.[82] Good harvest practices and efforts to reuse vinasse did not preclude these large usinas from being major polluters as well. The editor's effort to disaggregate the two highlights how such techniques had likely been used to effectively divert negative attention from usinas in the past.

Even as CETESB established itself as the state's central environmental agency, it failed to publicly address the growing vinasse issue in the Mogi-Guaçu basin. Initially, CETESB focused almost exclusively on water pollution issues in the greater metropolitan area of the city of São Paulo. When the state consolidated the agency's power in 1973, it began to direct more attention to the waters around the state outside the greater São Paulo metropolitan region. CETESB's predecessor, FESP, had already claimed the Mogi-Guaçu's biological condition was "alarming" in 1969. Four years later, after more industries had moved into the river basin, however, a CETESB report noted that the Mogi-Guaçu River presented "relatively acceptable quality levels" in terms of the dissolved oxygen and the biochemical oxygen demand (BOD). Instead, the report blamed domestic effluents discharged into the water near populous municipalities for the high levels of "discoloration detected in certain stretches" of the river. The "ever optimistic" CETESB report played down the seriousness of water pollution in the interior.[83]

Meanwhile, the *Estado de São Paulo* continued naming regular polluters in its pages. In 1973, the newspaper reported on potential evasion of CETESB dumping regulations at the Usina Açúcar e Álcool São Luiz in Pirassununga, in the Piracicaba region near the Emas Falls tourist attraction. The analyst Nelson Rodrigues claimed that, during one month in which the mill stopped production, the level of pollution in the Mogi-Guaçu tested near the falls decreased. He argued that this proved the usina was dumping vinasse in the river. However, the general manager Luiz Nilson Fontanari rebutted this argument by stating that the machines had not stopped "for even a week," although they had slowed at the time. Instead, he affirmed that the usina used its vinasse for fertilizer on the company's own lands, complying with the CETESB restrictions that prohibited dumping in waterways. As the usina satisfied CETESB regulations the analyst's claims were dismissed.[84]

The local demands for vinasse restrictions in the 1950s and 1960s gathered steam in the 1970s as growing media attention paid to the environment and pollution on the national and state level increased government enforcement. Public attention challenged usinas' claims of innocence and linked water contamination to ethanol production even before Proálcool began in 1975. Reports like the 1973 story about Emas Falls showed that CETESB regulations were inadequate for protecting local waters and fisheries. Just how inadequate the agency's regulations were became clearer after the creation of Proálcool.

Proálcool: The Second Crisis

The creation of Proálcool in November 1975 put immediate pressure on producers and government officials to address the exponentially worsening vinasse problem. Specialists had claimed that the vinasse problem had been solved as early as the 1950s because of the option to use the byproduct as a fertilizer alternative.[85] Even if antidumping had been well enforced between the 1950s and 1975, which it had not been, ethanol production had undergone a more than tenfold expansion in a single decade and created more vinasse than producers were prepared to use as fertilizer. Despite the sugar industry's ongoing resistance to vinasse as a fertilizer and evidence that its deployment as such could not fully address the problems of disposal, Proálcool advocates kept repeating that this was the answer to the pollution problem.

As ethanol production intensified across the state and the country, vinasse production spiraled in the first five years of Proálcool. Nationally, production jumped from 740 million liters of ethanol and 9.62 billion liters of vinasse in the 1975/1976 harvest to 1.47 billion liters of ethanol and 19.11 billion liters of vinasse in the 1977/1978 harvest only two years later.[86] In São Paulo, the leading sugar- and ethanol-producing state in the country, ethanol production soared from 355 million liters of ethanol in the 1975/1976 harvest to over 2.3 billion liters of ethanol in the 1979/1980 harvest. Assuming a conservative estimate of 13 liters of vinasse produced per liter, the state alone produced a minimum of 29.3 billion liters of vinasse in the 1979/1980 harvest, more than the entire country produced in the 1977/1978 harvest. This conservative estimate is low, given that independent ethanol distilleries not linked to sugar mills tended to produce higher average amounts of vinasse.[87]

Even industry specialists had to acknowledge the public health problems being caused by vinasse, particularly in São Paulo. As the state of São Paulo was the largest recipient of Proálcool financing and Ribeirão Preto was the largest region in the state to receive financing from the program, the environmental burden fell heavily on the Mogi-Guaçu basin. A 1976 report showed that the Piracicaba, Mogi-Guaçu, and Pardo rivers, which flow through Piracicaba and the Ribeirão Preto region, had all experienced precipitous collapses in their fish populations over the previous thirty years.[88] In 1977, one specialist claimed that, if left unaddressed, vinasse production would soon be "unbearable."[89] Another report claimed in 1980 that it would be the cause of "the gravest ecological disaster in the state of São Paulo."[90]

In the mid-1970s, vinasse processing became the leading market solution to the overproduction problem. Processed liquid vinasse can be used to create other versatile products, including proteins for animal feed, concentrated vinasse, and methane. For example, vinasse naturally produces a fair amount of yeast. After the industrial process of separation, filtration, and drying, the yeast from the fungus produced from vinasse yields protein substances for animal feed. Or, by using evaporators, vinasse can be transformed into a purer source of nitrogen and organic materials; the concentrated vinasse can be used directly in the harvest in lower amounts than vinasse *in natura* or, if treated with additional inputs such as sulfuric acid, it can be used as a potassium fertilizer.[91] Finally, vinasse can be used as a fuel to power mills through anaerobic fermentation to produce methane.[92] Some researchers advocated the use of concentrated vinasse as a fuel substitute as early as the 1930s, but this did not catch on because of its associated costs. However, as vinasse production exponentially expanded, industry specialists devoted more attention to these processed concentrate alternatives, which were cheaper to store than the heavy water-laden vinasse *in natura* used as a fertilizer.

The Biagis were among the earliest producers to invest in the vinasse concentrate technology under Proálcool. Biagi Filho submitted a request to finance the installation of an additional treatment unit to process vinasse with the 1976 Proálcool application for financing the expansion of the Usina Santa Elisa's distillery capacity. This would cover a building for the vinasse concentration unit and storage tanks for 11.6 million liters of ethanol and 4 million liters of concentrated vinasse. After this project was completed in 1977, the Usina Santa Elisa boasted one of the first vinasse processing plants in the country.[93]

The Biagi's investment in the vinasse concentration plant became critical to marketing the mill as a progressive and modern "miracle."[94] While it was ultimately just over 1 percent of the cost of the initial Usina Santa Elisa project, the additional storage and processing of vinasse had important environmental implications. The new processing plant transformed 1.6 million liters of diluted vinasse into 110,000 kilos of concentrated vinasse, which could be used in the harvest as a fertilizer replacement or a ration complement for animals.[95] As the Usina Santa Elisa's daily production capacity expanded first from 180,000 in 1975 to 300,000 liters in 1977 and then to 540,000 liters of ethanol in 1980, the usina was able to redirect millions of liters of vinasse to alternative markets. The rare concentrate plant connected to the distillery allowed the Biagis to more easily store the dehydrated fertilizer for later use and to sell it to other buyers while protecting their own waterways. The new concentrate center placed the firm at the forefront of agro-industrial technological advances in the sugar sector, subsidized by government financing.[96]

Concentrated vinasse also opened up a new market for the byproduct as a viable animal feed for export. Luiz Lacerda Biagi, leader of the Biagi empire alongside his brother Maurilio, had become by 1980 an outspoken supporter of the sale of concentrated vinasse abroad as an animal feed supplement. The Netherlands, Belgium, and France all imported the product to help animals gain weight. This byproduct market provided a potential incentive to invest in the expensive concentrate equipment necessary to commercialize a new product that could help Brazil's balance of trade.[97]

New export opportunities were appealing, but vinasse's properties as a fertilizer alternative, in concentrate and natural form, remained a major domestic boon. Given the program's early focus on economic savings due to lower petroleum imports, the transformation of vinasse into a viable fertilizer alternative presented an equally valuable opportunity to reduce fertilizer imports. For example, as one advertisement stated, "Based on this technology, this set of activities at Santa Elisa represents the creation of domestic wealth, immediately generating currency savings and fewer imports of petroleum and fertilizers." Large-scale agricultural production relied ever more on fertilizers to boost production capacity of sugarcane and other agricultural products as well, which made Brazil one of the largest fertilizer importers in the world by the late 1970s.[98] Thus, vinasse as a fertilizer alternative was just as marketable as ethanol's reduction of petroleum imports.

However, problems with the distribution of vinasse as a fertilizer deterred compliance. Early vinasse storage and distribution units were inadequate in size and made of an unsuitable material for storing the highly acidic product. As legislation tightened, usineiros blamed unintended spills on tanks and valves that commonly eroded. Some usineiros even blamed truck drivers, who, they claimed, intentionally dumped the vinasse in rivers.[99] According to a 1981 Copersucar study, the direct application of vinasse *in natura* was only economically viable in a 10 km radius, depending on fuel prices, after which the associated storage and distribution costs were not economically worthwhile. Given the high price of fuel that incentivized the creation of Proálcool in the first place and the expansion of the program after the oil shocks of 1973 and 1979, this further incentivized producers and distributors to dump vinasse rather than store it or deliver it to other producers.[100]

Some sugar producers also continued to resist using vinasse because of the particular demands involved in its application. While using too much vinasse could harm the soil, if appropriately applied, vinasse reduced the amount of sucrose produced during harvest.[101] Those usineiros who used vinasse preferred to apply it by spraying rather than through irrigation to deposit the liquid evenly at controlled amounts and not adversely inundate the cane; this required additional investment in distribution machinery. Many

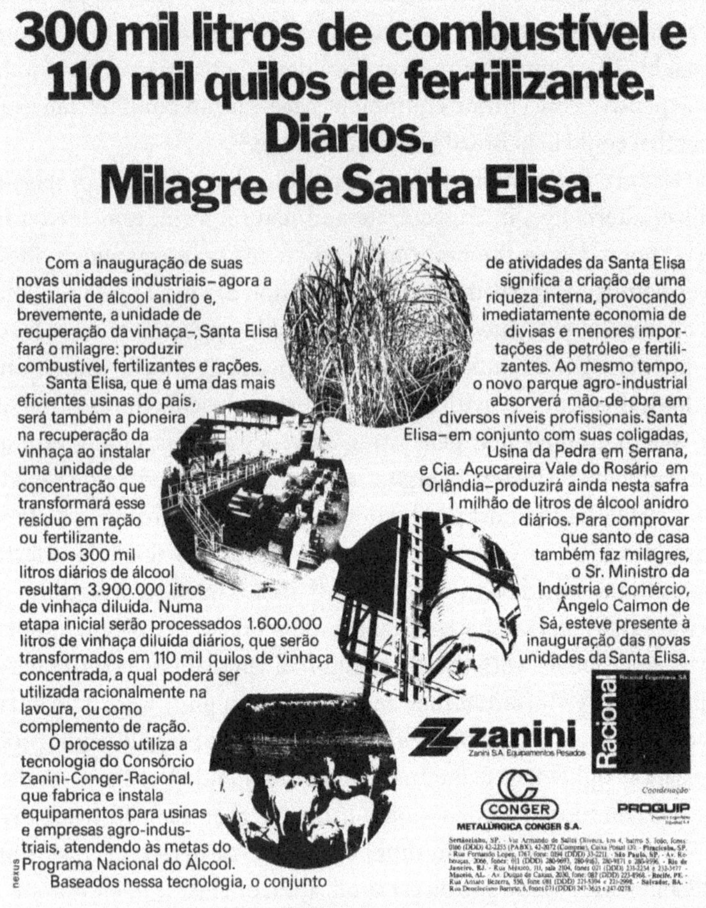

Fig 4.2 Advertisement for Santa Elisa vinasse concentrate center: "300,000 liters of fuel and 110,000 kg of fertilizer."
Source: Conger, Zanini, Racional advertisement, n.d. APHRP Caixa 193.

usineiros still preferred mineral fertilizers because of vinasse's adverse effects if the proper application technique was not employed.

Innovations in storage and distribution equipment improved vinasse's viability as a long-term fertilizer alternative in the early years of Proálcool. Luis Antonio Ribeiro Pinto, a Ribeirão Preto-based ethanol producer and owner of Santal S.A., a sugarcane equipment manufacturer, developed trucks specifically for vinasse distribution. These vehicles, known as vinasse transport vehicles (veículos de transporte do vinhaça- VTVs) were equipped with antioxidant, stainless steel tanks and pumps and distribution wings to safely store and distribute the highly acidic vinasse without eroding on both plowed and unplowed land.[102] Santal, which held shares of more than 50 percent of the loading equipment and 80 percent of the cane-cutting equipment in the sugar production market, quickly sold the new VTVs to mills across the country. Improved distribution trucks proved to be an important part of spreading vinasse use.

As vinasse storage and distribution techniques improved, the media praised the new technology for producing vinasse concentrate alongside its traditional support for vinasse as a fertilizer alternative. While the fertilizer option had been the first major step to reducing vinasse dumping in the waterways, the concentrate option seemed a more viable solution, given that it required less expensive storage than the heavier liquid form. Scientists and specialists positively promoted the byproduct as a cost-effective input in cane production through the media. For example, one advertisement shows piles of asphyxiated dead fish and proclaims that the same product could have positive outcomes: "Vinasse: the problem that engineering transforms

Fig 4.3 Usina Santa Elisa's application of vinasse, 1976
Source: BR RJANRIO IY (A6.16 Caixa 443).

into a benefit." At times, such attention ignored the promotion of vinasse as a fertilizer over the past three decades. On the one hand, this presumably sought to change the behavior of usineiros who still resisted using vinasse productively and instead dumped the product in the waterways.[103] On the other, marketing aimed at the burgeoning environmental consciousness of the 1970s allowed the industry to repackage vinasse-based fertilizer as a new solution to a new problem under Proálcool, giving it a new spin that might make the public forget the industry's problematic history.

Support for vinasse processing projects slowly ramped up after Proálcool began in November 1975. While boosters claimed that this new innovation would solve the vinasse problem in the 1980s, the high cost of processing equipment kept it from being available to all distillers.[104] Those who won the most government financing, like the Biagis, had the ability to adopt these new technologies. However, many ethanol producers continued with outdated production practices, especially at the beginning of the program, adding to the ever-growing problem.

Lakes of Sacrifice: Formalizing Waste

Despite the marketing campaign and the diversification of its uses under Proálcool, the vinasse problem increased in the late 1970s and throughout the 1980s as the ethanol car market expanded. Federal enforcement stepped up its efforts to protect the environment. By the end of the 1970s, national legislation finally standardized states' varied anti-vinasse legislation.

In November 1978, the Minister of the Interior, Mauricio Rangel Reis, introduced Ordinance no. 323, explicitly prohibiting ethanol distilleries from the direct or indirect disposal of vinasse in any body of water from the 1979/80 harvest onward.[105] The law required that distilleries, both new and established, present proposals for the treatment and/or use of vinasse and contaminated cane cleaning water within the following three months to state environmental agencies such as CETESB in São Paulo.[106] These agencies would then send the proposals to the Special Department of the Environment (SEMA) for approval, after which the state entities would oversee the execution of the project. Usinas that failed to comply would then be reported to SEMA and up the chain to the National Ethanol Commission (CNAl), the IAA, and any governmental financial institutions supporting their Proálcool financing, which would revoke project approval and financing.[107] While the Usina Santa Elisa had already independently established a vinasse-processing

Fig 4.4 Advertisement marketing solutions to the vinasse problem: "Vinasse: the pollution that engineering transforms into a benefit."
Source: Internacional de Engenharia S.A. ad, *Petro & Química* 2, no. 8 (1979): 7. APHRP Caixa 192.

infrastructure, thereafter all Proálcool funding applications required such information in their paperwork.[108]

The new ruling extended state agencies' enforcement abilities by incorporating agency approval into the federal program financing. Like the municipal legislation in Piracicaba in the 1950s, the new legislation directly tied producers' behavior to restrictions on operations. However, Proálcool's unique position as a federal program gave it even greater punitive financial control of vinasse dumping and empowered state environmental agencies as well. Proof of vinasse management plans and approval from these agencies were required for producers to access Proálcool's heavily subsidized financing.

The legislation initially won praise in São Paulo. The author of an editorial in *Estado de São Paulo* praised its simple, concrete measures at accountability that would allow "the evil [of enduring pollution of Brazilian rivers] to be cut at the root."[109] Supporters hoped that the SEMA infrastructure and its connection to Proálcool's intricate administration would finally create the necessary changes nationally rather than just municipality by municipality, or state by state, as previous government interventions had done.

However, the legislation still allowed land storage methods that reduced the law's environmental effectiveness. In addition to above-ground storage tanks, producers commonly used surface-level vinasse "pits" and later "land tanks," "retention tanks," or "vinasse containment basins."[110] From these land tanks, which were often lined with plastic and other materials to contain the liquid, producers would construct canals or pipes to distribute the product as evenly as possible throughout the fields to avoid inundating the cane.

In practice, the land used to store vinasse became a sacrificial wasteland. Lakes of accumulation, also known as "areas of sacrifice" or "basins of accumulation," served as legally approved dumping sites. One specialist described them as "swamps," and they were sometimes larger than 100 hectares in size. In 1979, one specialist estimated more than 90 percent of vinasse was either applied to the cane harvest or stored in these lakes and thus only 10 percent was diverted to vinasse's various concentrated uses.[111]

Fig 4.5 Vinasse surface tank: lakes of accumulation
Source: Carlos Alberto Nonino, "Vinhoto: de problema a solução," *ESP* (January 7, 1987), 47.

These lakes of sacrifice produced many of the same environmental problems they were meant to prevent. While the land tanks were supposed to prevent vinasse from seeping into the subsoil and overflowing into the harvest, leaks and inundation remained common.[112] In 1980, SEMA legislation eventually mandated that storage places for vinasse and other water pollutants had to be placed at a minimum of 200 meters away from any water source, but that did not alleviate the runoff situation much.[113] In fact, specialists in Ribeirão Preto had long complained that these "decantation lakes" contaminated the region's water table. While cheaper for usineiros than other alternative treatment methods, they directly affected the region's groundwater.[114]

Even though Brazilian legislation against vinasse dumping advanced during the first several years of Proálcool, practice did not always follow. New laws and enforcement agencies successfully pushed producers to account for their environmental waste in ways early legislation could not. In 1981, the National Environment Law (no. 6.938) further enhanced SEMA's size and presence. Technically, Brazilian environmental legislation was some of the most advanced in the world, but authority and enforcement remained precarious and dubious. SEMA was often a member of government councils that approved national development projects but had no real say in them, even as legislation sought to push environmental protection forward.[115]

Instead, despite marketing to the contrary and stricter legislation to limit their actions, producers continued to dispose of vinasse in local waterways in the 1980s. As a result, increasingly devastating catastrophes across the country continued to draw national attention in the 1980s. In 1981, the *Estado de São Paulo* reported that, according to a CETESB study, fifty-three of São Paulo's seventy-seven ethanol producers accounted for 90 percent of the state's water pollution.[116] Beyond São Paulo, the problem deepened as reports of massive spills across the country regularly appeared in the news even as producers claimed the issue solved.[117] Rather, as the agronomic engineer Joalito de Oliveira Rezende observed in 1984, given the economic clout of national sugar and ethanol producers in states such as São Paulo, Rio de Janeiro, Alagoas, and Pernambuco, environmental institutions' pressures and penalties were "too small a solution to the problem."[118] Indeed, the lakes of sacrifice illustrate how producers still evaded more costly but environmentally sound alternative uses of vinasse with the tacit approval of government legislation.

***

The history of vinasse illustrates how the ethanol industry brought Brazil increased energy self-sufficiency but at a high ecological cost. The focus of nationalist political and private economic interests on an alternative fuel for national consumption created extensive water pollution that tormented residents in sugar- and ethanol-producing regions. As vinasse disposal in local waterways exponentially increased during the twentieth century, local residents pushed, often unsuccessfully, government oversight to limit the waste that accompanied the polluting industry's expansion.

The incomplete solutions that the government promoted and then weakly enforced, like lakes of sacrifice, are not peculiar to Brazil. Across the globe, humans have searched for the perfect sink to dispose of industrial waste since the Industrial Revolution, and local waterways have been primary targets.[119] Similar stories abound of local populations that have demanded government intervention to address water pollution linked to urban industrial refuse, including sewage and chemical and nuclear waste. The journalist Steve Lerner named these places of refuse "sacrifice zones," where disenfranchised, often low-income residents have struggled to get city governments to provide protection from neighboring polluting companies.[120] Stories abound of extensive logging and timber waste that have wreaked havoc on waterways and countrysides alike. The historian José Augusto Pádua even equated an entire biome in Brazil with a sacrificial zone as deforestation has accelerated to accommodate unfettered agro-industrial expansion.[121] Still, although reforms were slow and incomplete, community resistance to vinasse dumping won limited success and the resulting legislation incentivized industry innovation for new uses of the byproduct.

Proálcool's scale both amplified a pre-existing problem and intensified attention on industry behavior. As legislation increased and dumping continued, residents questioned the government's real commitment to limiting vinasse's environmental impact in the face of the sugar and ethanol industry's sizable economic power. As ongoing dumping spread public discontent about the industry's environmental impact, critical questions about the program's social impact also entered the national debate in the 1980s.

5

Proálcool, Caneworkers, and the Guariba Strikes of 1984

> "The reasons [for the Guariba strikes] are so clear, so well known, that this explosion is only surprising for not having happened earlier."
>
> José Murilo de Carvalho (1984)

On May 15, 1984, over 5,000 workers from sugar mills in and around the small town of Guariba, an "island of cane," and usinas within the region of Ribeirão Preto went on strike. Protesters formed picket lines blocking the entrances and exits to the city to stop the trucks that transported workers to the fields daily to cut cane at dawn and marched to the city's small central plaza. They looted the city's largest supermarket, destroyed two floors of the São Paulo State Basic Sanitation (Sabesp) building, and burned a few vehicles. They protested extended workdays, miserable work conditions, low wages, and poor transportation services. These workers, derogatively known as bóias-frias, or "cold sandwiches," in a reference to the cold lunches eaten in the sugarcane fields during their long workdays, dominated the agricultural labor market in the Ribeirão Preto region, which produced over a third of national ethanol output and a fourth of national sugar production.[1] Their strike threatened to bring the industry to a standstill and brought national attention to the sugar industry's terrible working conditions. Through the strike, workers won the first collective bargaining agreement between usineiros and salaried workers in the region. The workers' efforts exposed the contradictions between Proálcool's rhetoric about job creation and the realities of employment conditions amidst mounting criticism of the ethanol program.[2]

This chapter explores the history of the Guariba strikes and their impact on Proálcool. Legal and social changes in the sugar industry in the

Sweet Fuel. Jennifer Eaglin, Oxford University Press. © Oxford University Press 2022.
DOI: 10.1093/oso/9780197510681.003.0006

mid-twentieth century led to increased dependence on temporary, salaried rural workers who later organized against common exploitative labor practices intensified by Proálcool's demands on sugar production in the 1980s. Beginning with the connections between sugar production, labor, and demands for agrarian reform in the 1960s, it considers how larger shifts in national labor policy ensured that temporary workers provided the labor for the massive expansion of the sugar industry in the 1970s and 1980s. Government officials and private producers such as Maurilio Biagi Filho boasted how many jobs ethanol's expansion created at a time of economic crisis but ignored their low quality and the low pay given to these workers. By 1984, the divergence between rhetoric and reality had become clear as the Guariba strikes tied the realities of sugarcane workers' labor conditions to public critiques of the program's social impact.

Labor, like the environment, remained largely at the periphery of the attention paid nationally to the growth of the ethanol industry. What the literary scholar Rob Nixon calls the "slow violence" of dangerous work and transportation conditions, precarious housing with limited access to clean water, constant exposure to poor air quality, unstable job access, ever expanding labor demands, and inadequate pay slowly drove workers to protest.[3] While the problematic relationship between the sugar industry and labor exploitation has been the subject of scholarship, few have focused on the ways workers' actions affected national discourse about the ethanol program.[4] By explicitly connecting the rise of temporary, salaried rural workers, Proálcool, and rural labor protest to growing critiques of the program's impact, this chapter asserts that rural laborers too played a role in the ethanol industry's changing trajectory in the mid-1980s.

Making the Modern Sugar Worker: From Permanent to Temporary Laborers

In the 1950s, rural laborers pushed for expanded labor rights as the region's political economy shifted from coffee to sugar. However, new government legislation allowed employers to shift the rural workforce toward temporary labor to accommodate the emerging agro-industrial model. Producers' slow erosion of rural labor rights backed by increasing government support during the military dictatorship transformed the sugar and ethanol industry into one heavily dependent on temporary rural labor under Proálcool.

In the early twentieth century, a family-based debt peonage system called the *colonato* dominated the agricultural, predominantly coffee-producing sector whereby plantation owners contracted free, mostly immigrant laborers (*colonos*), to work off their family's debts in the fields. This process reshaped the country as millions of Italians and other immigrant groups moved to the region. Intact until the 1950s, the colonato system slowly collapsed after coffee profits fell and sugar production expanded.[5] In its stead, large "modern" agricultural complexes bolstered by extensive mechanization and agricultural technology began to emerge, and short-term contract workers were hired to replace the colonos' labor. The shift from coffee to sugarcane coincided with and contributed to lower wages, reduced investment in community development, and a shift from permanent labor to temporary seasonal work.[6]

This fundamental transition led to the growth of rural labor mobilization in the 1940s and 1950s. While urban laborers were given the right to unionize and won minimum wage guarantees through the Consolidated Labor Laws of 1945 after decades of protest, rural workers did not.[7] The Brazilian Communist Party (Partido Comunista Brasileiro [PCB]), briefly legalized between 1945 and 1947, began organizing peasant leagues in the countryside "to build support for the improvement of agricultural working conditions and living standards."[8] Leaders such as the agricultural worker Irineu Luís de Moraes, who helped form the Dumont Peasant Leagues (*Ligas Camponesas de Dumont*), mobilized rural coffee and sugarcane laborers in the Ribeirão Preto region to successfully influence elections in the region and protest for agrarian reform and labor rights.[9]

Thereafter, the rural labor movement expanded rapidly. Rural workers across the country, notably sugarcane workers in the Peasant Leagues of the Northeast, used protests and organized strikes to push for rural labor rights and large-scale land reform.[10] Their contentious ongoing protests triggered broader Cold War-driven fears of a communist revolt among Brazilian elites, particularly conservative agricultural elites and military officials. However, demands for rural unions slowly won popular support in the 1950s and early 1960s, In response, conservative groups such as the Catholic Church and leftists such as the Brazilian Communist Party sought to control the impending creation of rural unions and agrarian reform with assistance from the United States.[11]

Rural laborers won the right to unionize in the 1960s, which completely reshaped the labor market. President João Goulart, the former Minister of

Labor who was closely affiliated with the broader labor movements, passed the Rural Worker Statute (Estatuto do Trabalhador Rural [ETR]) in March 1963. With this statute, full-time rural workers gained the right to worker registration cards that confirmed employment and required employers provide benefits including healthcare, social security, legal assistance, holidays, a paid weekly rest day, unionization, job stability after ten years of work, and a minimum salary.[12]

However, the military quickly cut down rural laborers' gains after the coup of 1964 as both the military and police quickly and violently repressed leftist union leaders as political "subversives."[13] After the coup, the new military government more explicitly pursued an agro-industrial development model with policies that promoted expanded agricultural exports, concentrated landownership, and large-scale producers' control of low-cost rural workers. The 1964 land reform law, the Land Statute (Estatuto da Terra), promoted the consolidation of smaller land holdings using land taxes, zoning, and rural land registry. Thereafter, tax breaks to support agricultural mechanization disproportionately favored large landholders as part of a national economic plan driven by easy credit.[14] Policies favoring employers' hiring of temporary agricultural workers to keep labor costs low were essential to the relatively cheap agro-industrial expansion of the sugar sector throughout Proálcool. Decree no. 6.019 in 1978, for example, deemed all workers employed for less than 90 days and those contracted by an intermediary as temporary workers ineligible for legal labor benefits.[15]

Government-subsidized coffee eradication programs in the 1960s created large-scale rural labor unemployment and incentivized temporary workers to migrate to towns in agricultural regions of São Paulo, like Ribeirão Preto. The ETR legally allowed employers to skirt previously established obligations for subsistence provisions when hiring seasonal wage laborers. Moreover, women and children who had worked the lands collectively with husbands and fathers under the colono system then became available as temporary workers. Landowners fired droves of permanent workers, removed them from their land where they had previously provided housing, and replaced them with newly available wage laborers who commuted from the towns. At the same time, landowners exploited the legal parameters of the ETR by employing labor contractors, known as *empreiteiros* or *gatos*, to recruit contract rural laborers from neighboring parts of São Paulo and Minas Gerais during peak seasons.[16]

Contractors' recruitment practices exploited workers through propaganda and coercion. With promises of better working conditions, they often trapped workers by demanding exorbitant charges for cheap transportation from their native regions to the town of the employer, housing, and work materials that exceeded their expected pay for the season. Thus, many workers were forced to stay in their migrant cities rather than returning to their native regions during the off-season.[17] These intermediaries took around 20 percent of the salary destined for the cane cutter and failed to follow labor laws, forcing laborers into poor working situations and conditions of dependency.[18]

The overlapping sugarcane and citrus harvests created increased competition for migrant labor in the Ribeirão Preto region at the peak of the season and left excess, available wage labor the rest of the year. Despite the efforts of rural labor unions in the region, the number of permanent rural workers in the greater Ribeirão Preto region fell by 65 percent between 1950 and 1970, while the number of temporary workers, who commuted daily from the city to the countryside, increased by 15 percent during the same period. The creation of Proálcool accelerated migration to Ribeirão Preto as the availability of cane-cutting jobs exploded in the region during the 1970s and 1980s. However, this agro-industrial expansion of the sugar sector disproportionately depended on migrant temporary laborers suffering under an exploitative labor system.[19]

The Everyday Violence of Proálcool

"It is a life from hell" is how the temporary worker José Gonzaga Medeiros described working cane fields in 1984.[20] He and others like him woke before dawn to get to the company pick-up points around 4 a.m. with a packed lunch, a machete, and a long file to cut cane all day. After a nearly two-hour ride to the cane fields, the cane cutters worked until 4:30 p.m., with two brief breaks to eat. After hours in the baking sun, workers collected their tools and returned on a two-hour bus ride back to the towns where they lived, preparing to do it all again the next day. Medeiros was one of at least 10,000 other wage laborers in Guariba and over 100,000 temporary workers in cane fields throughout São Paulo who eked out this daily existence, as the cane they cut went on to fuel millions of cars across the country.[21] Understanding the everyday conditions of workers and the new labor policy illuminates the desperation that drove workers to strike in 1984.

José Gonzaga Medeiros had worked in Guariba's cane fields for three years by 1984. He, like the largest percentage of interstate permanent and temporary migrant workers arriving in Ribeirão Preto during the 1970s and 1980s, was originally from Minas Gerais. Medeiros then moved to Paraná, another agricultural migrant labor hub, before eventually ending up in São Paulo's cane fields. A smaller percentage came from the Northeast, like Pedro Ulisses de Lima, who moved from Pernambuco to Guariba.[22] Northeasterners often met racialized and regional hostility from paulista residents, who stereotyped these often poor darker-skinned migrant workers as violent foreigners from the "countries of the north."[23] However, demand for sugarcane-related labor pushed job growth in the interior of São Paulo higher than that of the metropolitan area in this period.[24] At the height of Proálcool, between 1980 and 1991, the greater Ribeirão Preto region had the fastest-growing population in the entire country.[25] Migration from the city, often of Brazilians who came from the Northeast to the city of São Paulo and then to the countryside in search of work, increased as Proálcool expanded in the early 1980s and the industrial economy contracted.[26]

The recessionary economic conditions of the early 1980s pushed workers out of other industries toward rural labor. Take, for example, José Miguel da Silva, a 23-year-old bóia-fria, who had been a metallurgical worker at the Volkswagen plant in São Bernardo do Campo but turned to cane-cutting as a temporary laborer in February 1984 when he lost his job.[27] Increased competition among laborers for these jobs allowed employers to maintain a high turnover of temporary workers with even less focus on workers' rights. Despite the exploitative realities of these jobs, workers had few options and still flocked to labor in the fields of the Ribeirão Preto region as the nation's economic struggles grew in the 1980s.

Employers traditionally used the established five-row policy, in which they paid workers either per ton (permanent workers) or per meter (temporary workers) for an expected five rows of cut cane per day. The average cane worker cut five tons of cane over the course of eight- to ten-hour workdays during the harvest months. A complicated wage system determined pay, but various reports estimated that workers made an average of Cr$1,200 per ton, which came to around Cr$6,000 (a little over US$3 in 1984) per day. Women, the elderly, and children who worked in the field were paid even less. Some workers were able to cut up to ten tons individually, often with the assistance of family members, to make Cr$10,000 a day, but this was not the average. A 1984 report estimated that workers earned, on average, Cr$130,000 to Cr$150,000 (around US$70–80 in 1984 terms) a month. Other reports indicated this average income was nearly half that, at closer to Cr$60,000 a month. Rainy days, injury, and illness surely affected workers' ability to reach this monthly estimated income.[28]

Although mechanization was introduced into various steps of production, sugarcane cutting remained a manual labor-intensive job in this period. To put it simply, temporary salaried workers still were cheaper than mechanized sugarcane collection. Specifically, temporary manual workers remained far cheaper than the cost of gasoline to fuel mechanical collection.[29] Thus, usineiros mechanized large tasks with more heavy equipment such as tractors, trucks, and fertilizer to expand production at a faster rate but still depended on manual labor to cut the cane. According to the cane cutter Expedita Rosa from the Usina São Martinho, usineiros selectively mechanized the best cane fields, leaving the more challenging swampy, windy cane fields for manual cutters.[30]

Performing such arduous work, laborers often suffered work-related injuries. Deep lacerations on the arms and legs from the machetes were common, as were mangled limbs. Some workers died from heat exhaustion.[31] Other common ailments included breathing difficulty, cramps, dehydration, respiratory infections, poisoning, and animal bites. Usineiros hired their own medical staff, who were paid to downplay extensive work injuries, and their medical clinics often offered assistance to only the gravest cases.[32]. Without access to proper healthcare, workers had treatable ailments turn life-threatening and had to work through these conditions to make enough money to pay their own medical bills.

In addition to these accidents, workers endured poor air quality that put a constant strain on their respiratory systems. It was common practice to burn the cane at the beginning of the harvest to remove the tough straw exterior of the cane and facilitate faster and easier cane collection. Daily exposure to smoke-filled air and the soot that covered the fields, nearby streets, and houses affected workers and residents alike. City residents complained regularly. One claimed, "We spend the entire time swallowing that cane ash. We feel a bad fatigue and always have the flu."[33] Temporary workers were less vocal about the problem. As the wife of one temporary laborer noted, "The soot (of burned cane) is a sign that husbands have jobs."[34]

Transport to and from the cane fields also put workers' health at risk. Contractors often provided transportation to the fields in *pau-de-araras*, or open trucks with insecure benches, meant for forty-five passengers but often packed with sixty.[35] Sharp work tools, tightly packed trucks, and long, bumpy rides to and from the fields caused regular injuries from contact with equipment. Deadly injuries in highway accidents were also normal occurrences. These tragedies did little to bring additional safety measures, recompense, or improvements.[36]

Workers' housing did little to help their health conditions. Recruited seasonal workers lived in temporary housing provided by usineiros and contractors at or near usinas. These temporary units housed hundreds per barracks, ranging from 500 to 800 workers at times.[37] A 1984 exposé of a housing barracks on the Fazenda São Vicente that provided sugarcane for the Usina Santa Elisa noted:

> In each stall, in precarious bunks, around twenty workers sleep, on hay mattresses . . . They have no bathrooms or showers. They have to carry water from a dam near the barracks to bathe themselves. But cane debris and pigs have also contaminated the dam water. Bad smell, mosquitoes, this is the ambiance.[38]

These dams were likely linked to the decantation lakes that held excess vinasse and cane debris and all the contamination that specialists deemed "unfit to bathe in."[39] The São Paulo Federation of Agricultural Workers (Federação dos Trabalhadores na Agricultura do Estado de São Paulo) called the barracks "modern slave quarters (*senzalas*)," where breakouts of measles, rubella, conjunctivitis, and other such diseases were common.[40] Pedro Ulisses de Lima, a 55-year-old cane cutter for the Usina São Martinho in Guariba, told *Veja* reporters, "We live worse here than in the Northeast," a region known for its drought-riddled impoverishment.[41]

Permanent wage laborers displaced from the colonato system often lived in emerging "sleeper towns" on the periphery of the cities. These workers, upon being removed from the owners' land, mixed construction materials from the homes they formerly occupied on coffee plantations with adobe and other materials to build their homes. Known as sleeper towns because workers only occupied them at night after returning from the fields, their construction accelerated as sugar demand increased in the 1980s.[42]

Racial-ethnic lines and regional origins segregated these communities from the urban center.

Within these stratified towns, access to water and public services was particularly contentious.[43] The sole public service provided in the towns was piped water through the state-owned São Paulo State Basic Sanitation Company (Sabesp). Of the 280 municipalities serviced by Sabesp in the state, Guariba's water prices were among the highest in the region. Neighboring cities such as Araçatuba and Piracicaba paid Cr$1,220 and Cr$1,372 respectively for the minimum monthly service, while the local Sabesp manager Carlos Alberto Júlio da Rocha claimed that the majority of Guariba workers paid the minimum C$1,460 and Cr$1,560.[44] Despite these official rates, the popular magazine *Veja* reported that only 8 of the 3,950 households in Guariba paid the minimum price while the rest paid around Cr$11,000 per month, more than the typical wage for a day's work.[45] Sabesp continued to drive up tax rates and fees despite the limited financial means of the residents.[46]

On such tight budgets, laborers also had to pay for the costs of their own work tools. A machete cost Cr$4,000 to Cr$6,000 and a file Cr$1,500, which workers had to replace on average every five and three days, respectively, according to the temporary worker Paulo Soares Lima. To make ends meet, workers had to cut corners. Paulo Soares Lima told a reporter, "I have not bought clothes for a long time."[47] Dona Guiomar, one of the many women who worked in the cane fields of Guariba, labored alongside her two sons. From her expected monthly income of Cr$150,000, she paid Cr$30,000 per month to rent a room in a housing unit that she and her sons shared with two other female cane cutters.[48] Add to this the additional cost of tools for a month (Cr$32,000, a conservative estimate), and how little money is left over for emergencies in workers' monthly budgets becomes clear.[49]

In addition to the tight budgets imposed by work tools, housing, and poor pay, supermarket owners allied with contractors to exploit workers. In 1984, the 16-year-old bóia-fria João Lopes Fernandes remarked that supermarket owners kept increasing food prices to gouge temporary workers. The former sugarcane worker Élio Neves similarly pointed to food prices as a major hardship imposed on workers. He recalled:

> The supermarket had an alliance with the *gatos* [contractors], so that it was a connected purchase, that is to say, the worker picked up food from the

market and ended up owing the gato. And the market obviously charged how much it wanted, and the gato earned, the gato earned on the purchases that the workers were making . . . It was an employer scheme that exploited labor and exploited consumption."[50]

Such conditions pushed workers to the limit.

Workers finally cracked under the financial and physical strain of these conditions when usineiros in the region moved to a seven-row policy from the traditional five-row one at the start of the 1984 harvest.[51] Meeting the growing Proálcool demand for ethanol-fueled cars placed additional pressure on distillers to produce more sugarcane for ethanol per harvest. The seven-row system tried to extract an additional 2–3 hours of work out of each rural worker per day at minimum to meet new cutting and loading requirements. Producers manipulated the length and width of the rows, so workers were responsible for a far greater area. The new policy also required workers to carry the cane in their arms for another 3 meters to load it at a more distant main loading zone.[52] Thus, workers would spend more time transporting cut cane to loading areas, less time cutting, and were still expected to cut more cane per day. The extra loading time reduced their ability to maintain previous cutting production rates. Workers claimed they had to generally work more to earn the same wages in the seven-row system that they had made under the five-row system. Benedito Magalhães, the President of the Guariba Rural Workers Union (Trabalhadores Rurais de Guariba), asserted that the time the worker had to give to loading the cane cut their daily production by 60 percent, and he claimed that these changes ultimately drove average incomes down from Cr$150,000 per month in a five-row system to an average of Cr$90,000 in the seven-row system.[53] Not achieving the target set by the new row policy could lead directly to dismissal at the end of the month, suspension, or other coercive practices. At the same time, usineiros would need fewer workers per square hectare if workers covered the two additional rows demanded, which enabled them to further exploit the instability of the labor market.[54]

Multiple factors drove workers to the physical and financial brink. Their living conditions were extreme, their pay poor. Then the new harvest seemingly brought more exploitation. The widespread implementation of the seven-row policy threatened livelihoods. In addition, according to a *Veja* report, workers received notifications that Sabesp prices were going to increase by up to 900 percent in early May.[55] Temporary workers needed to act against a labor system structured against them.

Conflict Takes Shape: The CPT, Padre Bragheto, and Articulating a Common Goal

To assert their needs, workers had to make usineiros see them in a system that increasingly made them invisible. Conditions were ripe for mobilization, and Ribeirão Preto already had a robust history of rural labor mobilization, but divisions between workers based on their status as permanent or temporary obscured their common experience. In Guariba, organizers from the Catholic Church, such as Padre José Domingos Bragheto and the local Pastoral Land Commission (Comissão Pastoral da Terra [CPT]), played an important role in helping workers unify around the common interests that drove the strike. As the labor organizer and former cane worker Élio Neves asserts, Bragheto and the CPT "deepened a revolt that had been growing."[56]

Elements of the Brazilian Catholic Church arose as major grassroots organizers and anti-military leaders during the dictatorship. Although the Church as an institution had supported the coup in 1964, many moderate members began identifying the Church with "marginalized sectors of society and their hopes for justice."[57] Activist clergy and lay members repeated clashes with the military's repressive crackdown on internal threats to its authority drew the National Conference of Bishops of Brazil (Conferência Nacional dos Bispos do Brasil [CNBB]) into a more assertive position against the dictatorship's "torture, repression, and social and economic oppression."[58] As outspoken priests advocated for human rights in São Paulo, the Northeast, and the Amazon, some lay members identified more closely with urban periphery and rural workers than with elite government interests.[59]

After the 1968 Latin American Bishops' Conference in Medellín, Colombia, further asserted support for community-based engagement, Catholic priests, nuns, and lay members established Ecclesiastical Base Communities (Comunidades Eclesiais de Base- CEBs) across Brazil.[60] These CEBs became important bastions of rural mobilization in areas where rural workers had little or no access to organized labor groups. This was particularly true in the North and Northeast, where Brazilian bishops such as Dom Hélder spoke out against the injustices of the economic system and the failures of Brazilian agrarian reform. In response, priests in Goiânia, Goiás, founded the Pastoral Land Commission (CPT) in 1975 to support displaced workers and the struggle for land reform.[61] A product of these CEBs, the CPT became an important part of rural labor mobilization in the North and the South.

Padre José Domingos Bragheto, a young priest from the Jaboticabal diocese, and a few other members of the Archdiocese of Ribeirão Preto founded the first chapter of the CPT in the state of São Paulo in 1979. Jaboticabal, a satellite town within the greater Ribeirão Preto region, had a strong agricultural presence and a larger population than Guariba. Bragheto's work initially focused on traveling throughout the state of São Paulo, trying to create small CPT bases in different municipalities.[62] Having worked in two small parishes in the cities of Dobrado and Santo Ernestino, both in heavy sugar-producing areas, Bragheto was aware of the conditions in which seasonal workers lived. This exposure made him start "to think more on the agrarian question in the interior of the state" and become more vocal about the "injustices" that rural workers experienced.[63]

Bragheto and the CPT helped empower workers to assert their labor rights. They focused on "organizing workers through unions and fostering consciousness" or, as he stated in another interview, "In the time that we were out there, all the work [was] in this line of workers' rights, to organize workers who were completely disorganized and to organize through unions and . . . to foster consciousness."[64] They did this through informal meetings, assemblies, worker celebrations, and the creation of new unions to slowly build workers' own understanding of their situation. As he recalls:

> We started the work just, very simply, visiting those [workers] who lived in the city as much as those who lived . . . in the countryside, and we got up in the morning, and we approached the workers who caught the trucks in the cities, in the periphery."[65]

The CPT helped break down the worker divisions established by usineiros and legal worker status. As Bragheto explained, they gathered groups of salaried workers to "reflect in the light of faith in the situation in which they lived, the exploitation, the lack of adequate equipment," and groups "were made in the trucks while traveling together [to work]."[66] Through their teachings and gatherings, the CPT provided space and means for workers to articulate the injustice of the conditions in which they worked and lived and to contextualize their exploitation in broader terms. As Bragheto stated, "Then it was all a very difficult task, because the people were not very aware of the situation and this consciousness was awakening slowly."[67] Salaried workers, whether permanent or seasonal, increasingly saw themselves as a group of workers with the same struggles, which allowed them to assert themselves in the Guariba strikes.

The former sugarcane worker and union leader Élio Neves similarly recalls the importance of the CPT's work in the region. Neves began working in the cane fields at age 13 at the Usina Tamoio in nearby Araraquara, assumed the position of secretary of the Labor Union of Araraquara in 1980, and continued working in the fields until 1983. He remembers workers started doing what he calls "*grevinhas*" (small strikes) to demand better pay in 1983. Although these early strikes had little effect, they directly opposed the seven-rows policy from its first implementation in May 1983.[68] Unionizing was "absent" for cane cutters, as unions were focused more on "government ideology" and were "distant from bóias-frias." He notes that "In this absence of syndicalism, Padre Bragheto was very important in the process," because, through the CPT, he educated people and made them "aware" of their conditions. Through their teachings on Christianity, Bragheto and his team "ended up bringing knowledge to the workers . . . [and] this knowledge obviously contradicted with the reality [the workers] were living."[69]

Bragheto and the CPT also exposed how *pelego* leaders, or government union members who controlled the state-sanctioned unions, allied with usineiros and exploited workers for their own gains with business owners.[70] These unions "at most gave [the workers] a haircut, some health plan, but they did not defend the workers' rights."[71] The CPT gave workers an alternative space to mobilize, where, Bragheto felt, their rights were of foremost importance.

The rural labor union that the CPT helped organize in Jaboticabal met days before the strike began. Although workers and the CPT leadership, including Bragheto, agreed that conditions were not right for a strike during earlier meetings, workers began the strike a few days after the proposed Sabesp price hikes.[72] They seized an important moment, with the beginning of the new harvest, at a time when CPT leaders were unwilling to upset the status quo. Workers themselves were very much in control of the mobilization, despite newspaper reports that explicitly identified Bragheto as the leader of the strike.[73] Instead, in the days leading up to the strike, workers mobilized through smaller, informal methods such as "conversations in the bar, in the truck, during work breaks" and even, according to the cane cutter Zilda Bezerra of the Usina São Martinho, by approaching workers as they boarded transport for the fields the morning before the strike.[74]

Neves placed the start of the strike in an even broader context. He had "attended since the beginning of 1980, as a worker, some CPT meetings, meetings of workers, [and] small meetings" and recalled that they showed workers that the violence, extreme poverty, and exploitation associated with their lives as temporary workers was "not normal." Neves placed workers' actions in the context of the São Paulo metalworkers' strikes of 1979/1980 and particularly the sugarcane workers strikes in the Northeast, in which some migrant sugar workers in São Paulo had participated. All these factors allowed workers to understand their situation in a larger context.[75]

The CPT's presence in the region was important in shaping workers' mobilization in 1984. A central organization in spreading strikes in the North and Northeast, the CPT was new to the central-southern region, where landed elites had efficiently suppressed worker unrest for so long. Bragheto's work in raising workers' consciousness about labor exploitation and workers' rights enabled these same sugarcane laborers to assert these ideas of basic workers' rights in their Guariba strike demands.

Workers and the Strike

Following days of rumors and informal calls to protest, the "black day" arrived on Tuesday, May 15. When trucks arrived to transport over 10,000 daily workers to the local cane fields, protesters armed with their machetes for cane-cutting blocked the main exits of the city with tree branches and formed picket lines. Some workers got off the trucks and joined the protesters. By 7:30 a.m., over 1,000 protesters, men, women, and children, marched to the city center. Sabesp price increases, exploitative pricing at the local supermarket, and, above all else, low salary linked to the seven-row policy constituted the workers' key complaints.[76] However, their demands quickly expanded to broader labor rights as the strike spread. Ultimately, workers made nineteen demands, which included the immediate removal of the seven-row policy and a return to the five-row policy, pay based on set meters of cane cut rather than per ton, a written daily receipt of the amount of cane each worker cut and the price to be paid for it, a labor contract for the year, better transportation conditions, injury pay, free transport, and free equipment provided by employers.[77] After three days of strikes, workers and usineiros successfully came to a new labor agreement which ultimately shaped the industry's approach to labor during the Proálcool era and beyond. While the media credited union leaders, Padre Bragheto, and labor lawyers, workers in fact appointed their own leaders during the strike.

On the first day, workers marched through the city from the supermarket to the Sabesp, sacking businesses along the way, until the military police intervened, quelling the strikers' protests by noon. In the process, the police shot and killed one man, a bystander, Amaral Vaz Melone, and wounded twenty-nine others.[78] The military police remained in the city to prevent further unrest even after workers who had made it to the fields returned after 5 p.m. Protest quickly spread to neighboring cities in subsequent days, and the conflict escalated as more workers joined the strike. The Guariba Rural Labor Union president, Benedito Magalhães, claimed the event exploded "spontaneously," "with no outside influence."[79] Of course, that is not entirely true. Workers had been organizing small strikes without gaining media attention since 1983. Between those grevinhas and the CPT meetings, workers found spaces to organize their demands and articulate their struggles. However, media reports tried to blame outside influences such as the communist party, misnamed leaders, and presented workers' actions as leaderless and disorganized.[80]

Fig 5.1 The Guariba Strike. Pictured in the center, with the open shirt, Aderval Alcides, leader of the bóias-frias from the Usina Santa Adélia.
Source: Carlos Fenerich, Abril Comunicações S.A.

As strikes expanded on May 16 and 17, protesters escalated matters by burning cane fields at the peak of the harvest. The first night, protesters burned part of the Usina São Carlos harvest and threatened usineiros that they would burn more if their demands were not met.[81] The intentional burning put pressure on producers to concede to the workers' demands because the cane would only remain viable for cutting and processing twenty-four to forty-eight hours after burning. This strategic move allowed workers to quickly capture the attention of usineiros, government officials, and the national public and required an immediate response from producers. Workers believed that only fears of losing their entire harvest would get producers to pay attention to their demands for better working conditions and pay. Indeed, one usineiro estimated that each day cane-cutting stopped cost Cr$73 million (US$39,566) in profits.[82] The three-day conflict brought over twenty-five usinas, including the Usina Santa Elisa, to a halt after the strikes expanded to over five municipalities in the region.[83]

Some union leaders took the opportunity to criticize both usineiros and state officials. Francisco Benedito Rocha, the general secretary of the São Paulo State Agricultural Workers Federation (Federação dos Trabalhadores na Agricultura do Estado de São Paulo [FETAESP]), stated,

Fig 5.2 Caneworker Burning the Cane Fields
Source: Carlos Fenerich, Abril Comunicações S.A.

"What provoked all of this was the revolt of workers against the little income that they earned for cutting cane, the changes made by usinas to the cutting system, changing from five rows to seven, and the excessive increase in water prices that Sabesp charged." The Guariba Rural Workers Union president Benedito Magalhães affirmed this, stating, the "bóias-frias situation has been dramatic since last year, when the Usinas São Martinho (Pradópolis), Bonfim (Guariba), Santa Adélia, and São Carlos (Jaboticabal) changed the cane cutting system."[84]

Other officials looked at broader economic conditions as the cause. Sabesp was the subject of particular ire for bóias-frias, but the Sabesp manager Carlos Alberto Júlio da Rocha dismissed their grounds, saying the strike "is due to the fact that all of these people are living in an extreme situation of misery and hunger. The water bills are only a pretext."[85] Similarly, the Governor of São Paulo André Franco Montoro responded by placing workers' desperation in the context of national economic crises. The day after the strike, he noted that, with "inflation at over 200 percent and the federal government so focused on the external debt, the nation is approaching the tolerable limit," and Brazilians were bound to respond; the Guariba strikes were just one example. The São Paulo State Secretary of Labor Roberto Gusmão connected the national economy to usineiros own greed. In relation to inflation, he stated, "Bóias-frias are currently making less this year than last, and on top of that usineiros try to impose on them the increase in cane collection quotas."[86] More simply, according to Rogério Orsi, the President of the Sugarcane Commission of the São Paulo Agriculture Federation (Federação da Agricultura do Estado de São Paulo), when usineiros requested federal support from the notoriously violent Second Army of São Paulo to end the disturbance, the commander "responded that they ought to use good sense and treat their employees better."[87] These state officials used the strikes to criticize usineiros' actions and distance themselves from the conditions that drove workers to strike.

According to the union leader Élio Neves, the strike had even broader implications for workers: "There were lives lost, not only during the strike, but in the cane fields, workers who died during transportation accidents." Remembering them, he asserts, the strike "was a fight for the workers being transported by bus, a fight that I would say was almost like . . . for the end of slavery."[88] Working the cane, he concludes, "was inhuman business," and the strike was nothing short of reclaiming their humanity for those who had been exploited.

Faced with threats of more widespread cane burning at the beginning of the harvest, usineiros gave in to most of the rural laborers' demands. On the first night of the strike, usineiros informally agreed to revert to the five-row system at a meeting at the Jaboticabal Rural Union headquarters.[89] The next morning, over 2,000 cane cutters met in the Guariba municipal stadium to decide whether they would continue the strike. They elected strike leaders from the various groups of workers to meet with directors and lawyers from the unions and FETAESP that afternoon to negotiate their broader demands.[90] Neves was among those elected as a worker representative. These representatives were important for temporary workers whose interests were not represented within the formal union structure.[91]

On Wednesday, May 17, two days after the strike first started, a coalition of union, usineiros, and worker representatives met from 10 a.m. to 4 p.m. to negotiate a collective labor agreement. Participants included the São Paulo State Secretary of Labor Almir Pazzianotto Pinto, the FAESP Sugarcane Commission president Rogério Orsi, the Copersucar lawyer Márcio Maturano, and the presidents of rural unions from Jaboticabal, Guariba, Cravinhos, and Barrinha, and a commission of six bóias-frias from the strike.[92] Given such high stakes for workers and employers, the tone of the meeting was tense; Neves described it as an "ambiance of war."[93] Representatives, including Neves, took the proposal to a general assembly of bóias-frias at the municipal stadium, where they approved the agreement,[94] commonly known as the Guariba Accord. Workers won a return to the five-row system; an increased the set price of cane to Cr$2,100 per ton; employer-provided work tools and protective gear such as gloves and leather leg guards; free transportation to work; guaranteed worker registration; and payment on inclement weather days, holidays, and sick days. In fact, workers won all but one of their demands: a year-long contract that would ensure pay between harvests, which would have been a far more expensive commitment for employers.[95]

The Guariba strikes established that workers could win basic labor rights through such mobilization despite their limited political presence. As the president of the Jaboticabal Rural Labor Union and one of the workers' leaders in the negotiations noted at the time, "Just the fact of us sitting at a table to discuss with employers already is a great victory, an unprecedented milestone in rural labor history. With this many families will be able to survive."[96] Even today, Neves remembers the strike as a "conquest of the obvious" in which "anonymous" workers who had had "informal jobs, of slavery, a lack

Fig 5.3 Bóias-frias voting to end the strike, May 17, 1984
Source: Carlos Fenerich, Abril Comunicações S.A.

of respect" gained basic rights, particularly through registration that recognized employment. Similarly, Padre Bragheto recalls:

> Various laws arose afterward, in relation to salary, in relation to security on the job. Thus, from there, many things changed, so we like to say that [the Guariba strike] was a watershed moment. . . . Before Guariba it was one situation and after Guariba it was a different situation.[97]

The strike yielded the first collective bargaining agreement between usineiros and salaried workers in the region, while workers' actions brought the struggles and social costs of the ethanol program to national attention.

The Immediate Aftermath of Guariba in the São Paulo Countryside

Despite the concessions workers won in the Guariba Accord, producers quickly attempted to roll back their gains. A National Agrarian Reform newsletter reported:

> The Guariba agreement . . . has been bungled almost systematically by contractors who provide services for cane suppliers . . . One of the principal problems for workers is that they do not have anyone to rely on and it is made worse by the uselessness of the Ministry of Labor's supervision system and employers' continuing abuse of power.[98]

As a result, usineiros often broke the agreement, which led to workers striking intermittently throughout the 1984, 1985, and 1986 harvests. However, the enduring success of the Guariba strikes lay partially in the attention that continuing poor working and living conditions received after the event. As Padre Bragheto stated in an interview with *Folha de São Paulo* the day after the first momentous strike, "Only the government and usineiros don't want to see the problem [with work conditions]."[99] As strikes continued, negative media attention held employers accountable, not the government.

In these ongoing conflicts, usineiros and contractors used increasing violence to intimidate protesters and organizers. By late August 1984, workers in Araraquara, Ribeirão Preto, São Manuel, Sertãozinho, Arapoema, and Andradina had used strikes to combat employers' failure to comply with the accord or additional worker demands.[100] In the nearby city of Arapoema, São Paulo, a private owners' henchman (*jagunços do grileiro*), Gilson Santana, and the police ambushed and killed the secretary of the Rural Workers' Union Hugo Ferreira de Souza in August 1984.[101] Padre Bragheto said usineiros blamed him for the strikes and placed a target on his back for his continued work as a negotiator and representative of workers in disputes with usineiros. He regularly received death threats, was beaten by the police, and was imprisoned, among other forms of intimidation, before finally being driven out of the region in 1986.[102] He moved to the city of São Paulo, where he continued to mobilize workers as a member of the FETAESP leadership.

Despite the Guariba Accord's attempt to improve relations between workers and usineiros, later workers' strikes had less impact, gained less national attention, and were more violently suppressed. In the first Guariba strike, regional police used tear gas, invaded homes, and beat workers to suppress the protest; one bystander was shot.[103] In the conflicts following the accord, the government escalated the violence. When a major strike broke out in Guariba in January 1985, the beginning of the second harvest season, to demand better labor conditions, the state government sent in the São Paulo-based special task force, the Batalhão do Choque, to suppress the conflict.

Hundreds of soldiers confronted workers armed with sticks, stones, and fire. Witnesses reported that police used home invasions, brutal beatings, tear gas, electric batons, firearms, and clubs against men, women, and children, including journalists, union officials, and religious leaders, to suppress the strikes.[104]

Television news coverage brought important attention to the everyday violence in the region. However, the popular media, particularly larger outlets such as the *Estado de São Paulo*, often sided with the usineiros and reported in their favor. The first reports on the Guariba strike focused on the fear and violence of the confrontation rather than the reasons for the workers struggles. The reporter Galeno Amorim recalls that the conservative newspapers "tried to make the strike a political scandal the whole time."[105] Yet, after the strike, according to Neves, the facts were "undeniable," and the media was "forced" to print the truth.[106] A new tool, the television exposé helped bring workers' mobilization to the public eye. Shows such as *Jornal Da Terra* and *Globo Rural* continued to regularly run exposés on rural labor conditions that detailed the arduous lives exploited workers led.[107] As a FETAESP report stated, "After radio and the press, lately it is television that is becoming a medium through which the worker can speak of his problems, present his demands." According to Galeno Amorim, television was much more effective than print media because the latter focused on middle-class and elite audiences, while the masses had access to the former.[108] From the media's point of view, the Guariba strikes seemingly made for good television.[109]

Employers might not have cared about appeasing workers, but they did care about public perception, and they were eager to counteract negative public images of themselves. For example, on August 4, a local team of Globo TV reporters went to a workers' barracks with members from the offices of Labor and Health in Ribeirão Preto, Araraquara and Bebedouro unions, and FETAESP to expose the poor conditions on the São Vicente *fazenda* (plantation), owned by the Marchesi Group, which grew cane for the Usina Santa Elisa. A month later, the regional newspaper, the *Jornal do Interior*, reported that the Usina Santa Elisa bought thirty-five buses to transport bóias-frias to and from the fields a few months after the Guariba strikes. The buses held fifty to sixty-five passengers each and "were equipped with boxes for cane-cutting tools and reserves for up to 500 liters of potable water." Cláudio Borges, the transportation manager of the Biagi-owned Companhia Agricola Sertãozinho (CASE), of which Santa Elisa is a part, stated that the buses were part of an effort to "ensure more comfort for our rural workers."[110] The usina directed this publicized overture at regional businessmen and the urban elite in an effort to improve public perception of the usina.

The Usina Santa Elisa again presented its improved worker conditions in an exposé on a *Globo Rural* report. While most cane workers cooked their lunches and brought them in tin cans, the reporters also noted that some usineiros offered trailers that provided hot food. Workers paid Cr$1,460 per month for the company lunches. Paulo Magalhães, an Usina Santa Elisa representative, noted that the hot food gave "personal satisfaction" to cane workers.[111] Purchasing the hot food every month on top of the cost of workers' basic necessities surely meant that few could afford it. Nevertheless, the Usina Santa Elisa saw this story as a way to distance itself from the negative image of the Guariba strikes and prove to the public that it had made changes to improve workers' experience in the cane fields. In this respect, subsequent media attention after the strikes substantially strengthened workers' visibility, and stories about their conditions became a medium for holding usineiros and contractors somewhat accountable and promoting some labor improvements.

Guariba and Critiquing Proálcool

Beyond the strikes' immediate impact on rural labor rights, they also had a lasting influence on public debate about Proálcool. During their administrations, President Geisel and then President Figueiredo constructed and promoted Proálcool as a domestic solution to an international problem that would increase job opportunities for rural laborers throughout the country. Proálcool propaganda celebrated the rural jobs it supposedly created. The São Paulo sugar cooperative, Copersucar, regularly ran advertisements that praised the benefits of Proálcool beyond economic savings: "It creates higher-salary jobs, provides work in the countryside, alleviating urban problems, [and] increases the income of a considerable part of the population up to now marginalized economically."[112] Major producers such as Maurilio Biagi Filho continued to make this argument, even as the conditions of this labor expansion grew increasingly exploitative.[113] Events like Guariba brought the silent legal dismantling of social responsibility for workers through the Rural Worker Statute, the Land Statute, and other legislation under the dictatorship over the past forty years into sharper view. Efforts to redirect attention to the program's successful creation of jobs to win support for the program became increasingly difficult.

As the economy faltered, officials increasingly questioned the economic costs of the ethanol program. In 1982, the powerful Minister of Planning, Delfim Neto, called attention to the possible inflationary influence of the program and froze its national financing. He posited that Proálcool was becoming too expensive in the current economic climate.[114] Although his challenge only yielded a brief freeze on program financing and ethanol-fueled car sales quickly rebounded, the seeds of doubt quickly spread.

Some of the interest groups that had benefited most from the program wondered about its long-term durability. For example, in the midst of the program's economic struggles in June 1983, the new Anfavea (National Car Producers' Association) president Newton Chiaparini suggested that the government "limit the incentives for the ethanol car and questioned the production of a sufficient amount of ethanol fuel to supply the fleet at the current growth rate [of car sales]."[115] Doubters' voices grew louder as the program's dependence on national financing drew increasingly negative attention.

Critics of the program's social and environmental implications were also more vocal during the early 1980s. Beyond the water pollution issues linked to vinasse dumping that had drawn local attention for decades, national critics increasingly censured the program for causing extensive deforestation and the reduced variety of crops in favor of a single-crop economy. Professor Fernando Homem de Melo spoke out often against Proálcool. He argued that the program was really the product of sugarcane lobbyists who "pressur[ed] a political and economically authoritarian government" which supported a "coalition of planters, mill owners, equipment producers, the automobile industry, and middle- and high-income classes."[116] In an astute review of the program, he also highlighted the low production efficiency of the Brazilian sugar industry compared with that of Hawaii, Florida, and Australia. Instead, he pointed to more efficient fuel sources such as coal, shale oil, and hydroelectricity as better energy options.[117]

While program propaganda had praised Proálcool's positive impact on labor for years, the Guariba strikes briefly called national attention to the realities of the "modernized" agricultural industry and Proálcool's place in this process. As the National Agrarian Reform newsletter issued following the strikes in July 1984 stated, "The recent events in the countryside, the fights, the conflicts, and the violence in general against rural workers and their families have at their core the same cause: the model of economic development applied to the agricultural sector."[118] For many, it was increasingly clear that the Brazilian government employed Proálcool to fulfill its own economic and political needs, to the detriment of rural laborers. As José Gomes da Silva, the founder of the Brazilian Agrarian Reform Association and former Secretary of Agriculture under São Paulo State Governor André Franco Montoro stated, "The real victims of Proálcool . . . were the temporary workers [*volantes*] abandoned by the [federal] government."[119] Such opinions became increasingly common not only among rural workers but also among political appointees surrounding the Guariba strikes. Rural workers' actions successfully drew social and political leaders into a conversation about the broader social impact of Proálcool and the long-term effects of the military government's development agenda.

The Guariba strikes' spotlight on Brazilian sugarcane workers in Ribeirão Preto opened up another avenue of criticism against the ethanol program. Only five days after the strikes began a major newspaper, the *Estado de São Paulo*, published a news series, "O programa em debate," on Proálcool, in which specialists and businessmen interrogated the program's durability. Over nine days, eight specialists, from usineiros to program officials to policymakers, contributed to the debate. Of course, rural workers still remained outside the scope of many commentators' analyses. The engineer and automobile specialist João Augusto do Amaral Gurgel reasserted earlier claims of the program's inflationary effect on the economy, due to increased financing for production without increased income for the government.[120] The Minister of Industry and Commerce Camilo Penna quickly dismissed Gurgel's assessment and general doubts about the program expressed by the interviewer, Rodrigues dos Santos. He argued that Proálcool, fortified by World Bank financing, "adds up to internal investment to create jobs, open new economic frontiers, develop specific technology, reduce air pollution, secure contracts for the capital goods industries, balance sugar production, and favor the creation of new businesses."[121] Job creation remained a critical counterpoint for government analysis of the program.

And yet Guariba's influence did feature in some commentators' analyses. For example, Lamartine Navarro Jr., a paulista engineer, early architect of the ethanol program, and one of the first owners of an autonomous ethanol distillery, noted efforts to address Proálcool's social shortcomings.[122] Navarro drew attention to São Paulo State's proposal to make new selections for the program contingent upon the "fulfillment of labor legislation and collective bargaining in consultation with the Ministry of Labor, Rural Workers' Union, and the Federation of Agricultural Workers," which would ensure that the collective bargaining agreement achieved in Guariba would factor into future project approval protocol.[123]

The Guariba strikes certainly colored reporter Rubens Rodrigues dos Santos' views in his interview with Luiz Lacerda Biagi, the departing president of the Biagis' Zanini S.A. Referencing the recent Guariba strikes, Rodrigues dos Santos questioned Lacerda Biagi about whether the subsequent increase in labor costs due to the Guariba Accord would make the program unsustainable for producers. Lacerda Biagi gave an evasive answer. He noted that the IAA, which set sugar and ethanol prices, would have to consider salary increases in the next revision of national prices. Additionally, he blamed the exorbitant water and electricity price increases ("up to 1,000%") workers faced for the strikes. By focusing on the role of the IAA and the state utility prices, he put the blame on the government and not usineiros.[124] In the interview, Rodrigues dos Santos went further, asserting that rising ethanol prices would force the increase in labor costs on producers rather than the state. In response, Lacerda Biagi boasted of the profits the program generated, citing the statistic that "Anhydrous ethanol alone generates 700 million dollars per year for the public coffers." However, he particularly noted the jobs created by the program, stating that the industry "employs a contingent of around two million workers directly and indirectly."[125] Lacerda Biagi highlighted the program's wealth to assure the public of its viability but returned to Proálcool's contribution to increased employment to address the social issue.

After the news series on the program, Biagi's brother, Maurilio Biagi Filho, would reiterate the positive effect of job creation linked to Proálcool a year later as criticism continued. By late 1985, the program was in trouble as World Bank financing dried up and the Brazilian government was unable to support it. Strikes continued in the Ribeirão Preto region. Nationally, the transition to a democratic government began in earnest. Biagi Filho remained an enthusiastic supporter of ethanol and the government bureaucracy built to support it. In his praise of Proálcool's tenth year, he noted the important impact the program had had on job creation. However, he went out of his way to mention improved rural working conditions, noting that "Between August of 1984 and 1985, the average salary of rural workers for agricultural businesses connected to sugar usinas in the region of Ribeirão Preto increased by 300 percent, providing an excellent salary adjustment and certainly provoking replication in related areas of production."[126] Countering the social costs of the program since the previous year's Guariba strikes made this comment even more important for national promotion of the program.

Despite the wealth created through Proálcool in Ribeirão Preto, the Guariba strikes contributed to public disquiet about the long-term influence of the national program. While previously proponents of the program had solely focused on the alternative fuel's ability to save on petroleum imports and the program's contributions to job creation, increasingly they had to discuss social factors in their broader analysis of the program.

***

Proálcool pushed rural laborers to their physical limits as sugar production expanded to meet growing fuel demands. The historian Richard White noted, "For much of human history, work and energy have linked . . . humans and nature."[127] The Guariba strikes reasserted the fundamental connection between human labor and energy production. Rural workers' legal and social displacement facilitated the growth of the sugar sector in the 1960s and eventually the National Ethanol Program in the 1970s and early 1980s. In turn, ethanol demand incentivized producers to expand sugar production at rates that violently exploited workers. However, once rural workers understood their daily plight as one that united them across the region, ethanol demand also provided workers with additional collective leveraging power against producers on tight production schedules. Conflict over labor to produce energy revealed a new limit to ethanol's expansion. Exploited workers asserted their grievances in a way that gained national attention and revised relations between workers and producers with the first rural labor collective bargaining agreement. Consequently, the alternative fuel's development was an important part of changing rural labor's social fabric.

Rural workers' efforts to contest this exploitative labor system through the Guariba strikes shook traditional promotion of Proálcool as a job creator just as the program's broader economic foundations began to collapse. Environmental and social questions seeped into growing national debate about the program's long-term viability. Producers faced a more hostile national discourse about Proálcool's value amidst a shifting understanding of the program's costs.

6
Proálcool Reimagined, 1985–2003

> "The sugarcane usineiros, who ten years ago were seen as agribusiness bandits, are turning into national and world heroes, because all the world is looking at ethanol."
>
> President Luiz Inácio Lula da Silva (2007)

When President Luiz Inácio Lula da Silva remarked on the major transformations of the ethanol industry between 1985 and 2003,[1] he was implicitly congratulating the Brazilian nation on its foresight in continuing to promote an alternate energy source despite setbacks. Government officials declared Proálcool and its ethanol-fueled car a triumphant success by the mid-1980s despite the labor issues and environmental degradation they caused. According to the President of the National Car Producers' Association (Anfavea) in 1986, "The program saved the country and the auto industry from a big crisis."[2] Yet, only three years later, the celebrated program was in free fall due to ethanol shortages and its producers seen as "irresponsible" and "selfish."[3] Although there were repeated public demands to end the program, the government continued to support a reformed program focused on promoting ethanol's environmental, green benefits in the 1990s rather than the foreign exchange benefits it had brought during the 1970s and 1980s. This new emphasis paved the way for the revival of the ethanol market and producers' redemption as "world heroes" when the flex-fuel car was launched in 2003.

This chapter follows Proálcool's transformation from the height of nationalist development in the mid-1980s through the sugar alcohol industry's reputational descent into "agribusiness banditry" in the 1990s and its resurgence in the 2000s with the flex-fuel car. Buoyed by government support, ethanol car sales climbed in the mid-1980s before multiple factors caused massive ethanol shortages in 1989 and 1990. Thereafter, public support for the ethanol car and Proálcool more broadly collapsed. However, from the late

Sweet Fuel. Jennifer Eaglin, Oxford University Press. © Oxford University Press 2022.
DOI: 10.1093/oso/9780197510681.003.0007

1980s, private producers and government officials intentionally refocused Proálcool promotion on technological advances and ethanol's lower carbon emissions compared with those of gasoline in order to sell it as an efficient and environmentally beneficial energy solution. Despite the ongoing pollution caused by the industry, this new focus won federal support from Brazil's neoliberal governments, which remained committed to removing government subsidies from the ethanol market throughout the decade. Even after Proálcool supports formally ended in 1999, the government built on its green energy image by offering incentives for ethanol cars during the 2000s. Incentives introduced in 2003 shifted support to the newly launched flex-fuel cars, which ran on any combination of ethanol and/or gasoline, thus re-establishing ethanol's place in the Brazilian fuel market.

Even after multiple political, economic, and environmental crises compromised Proálcool in the 1980s, a combination of factors, mostly linked to car buyers, sustained the government's commitment to the program in the 1990s and solidified ethanol's place in the Brazilian energy market in the 2000s.[4] The automobile's special place in Brazilians' national imaginary has been well established, but its connection to the ethanol car less so. Popular discontent with ethanol should have ushered in liberalized management of the ethanol industry in the 1990s as neoliberal reforms spread in the country, but the Brazilian government never completely gave up on centralized management in favor of the neoliberal ideology it espoused.[5] This was particularly true of the auto industry and the sugar sector.[6] Ethanol, through Proálcool and the ethanol car, merged the two. Branding ethanol a "green fuel" became the key tool for appealing to cost-averse car consumers, extending government support, and launching Brazil as a global alternative energy leader in the 1990s. By examining the political, private, and international actors and influences that enabled persistent and often controversial government support for ethanol-fueled cars and the eventual launch of the flex-fuel car, this chapter reveals how ethanol became a standard part of Brazil's national energy matrix in the twenty-first century.

Ethanol Shortages and the Beginning of Proálcool's Demise, 1985–1990

After ethanol went from a supplement to a fuel replacement in 1979 with the launch of the ethanol car, its national production exponentially expanded to accommodate the growing demand. Nonetheless, environmental, political, and economic mismanagement ensured that the fuel's demand exceeded market supply by the late 1980s. The resulting shortages damaged public opinion of ethanol cars and brought a rapid end to Proálcool as a full fuel replacement program by 1990.

A severe drought in the southern region in 1985 and subsequent droughts across the country significantly compromised the national ethanol supply. A major drought hit São Paulo in May 1985 and continued through November, described as "the harshest drought of the last fifty years."[7] While Ribeirão Preto's annual average rainfall is around thirty-six inches, a local distillery noted that only a little over seven inches fell during those months.[8] The weather pattern seriously harmed the earlier 1984 planting and the entire 1985 harvest and delayed the new planting in the process.

The significant upfront sugarcane losses due to the drought had a major impact on the long-term trajectory of Proálcool. The drought caused a drop of over 8 million tons in sugarcane production during the 1986/1987 harvest. São Paulo had seen a gain of over 70 million tons in cane production over the previous three harvests, which had largely gone directly to additional ethanol production, doubling the country's ethanol production between 1982 and 1985. However, the drought substantially affected the amount of cane used for ethanol production in the 1986/1987 harvest. The drop of 8 million tons in sugarcane production meant a loss of nearly 64 million liters of ethanol.

At the same time, international market demands shifted private sugar and ethanol producers' interests toward the world sugar market. World sugar prices rose from US$54 per ton in June 1985 to over US$160 in April 1986. Most producers had ethanol distilleries attached to their sugar mills that allowed them either to produce ethanol or to process sugar from sugarcane at almost no cost differential. By November 1986, ethanol production in São Paulo fell by 15–20 percent as producers were incentivized to prioritize sugar production over subsidized ethanol production.[9]

Just as the drought drove ethanol production prices up, international oil prices collapsed. From November 1985 to July 1986, oil prices dropped from US$30 to below US$12 per barrel and remained below US$20 through the rest of the decade.[10] Since ethanol production cost about US$45–50 per barrel, it could not compete without heavy government subsidies on the price per barrel.[11] Between the shortages in cane caused by drought, the shortages of ethanol due to high sugar export prices, and the drop in gasoline costs, ethanol was in trouble by 1986.

Table 6.1 Sugarcane, Sugar, and Ethanol Production in São Paulo, 1985–1990

Year	Sugarcane (1,000 tons)	Sugar (1,000 tons)	Ethanol (billions of liters)	National Ethanol Production (billions of liters)
1982/1983	49,094	4,300	3.815	5.823
1983/1984	50,446	4,342	5.391	7.864
1984/1985	11,887	4,106	6.023	9.192
1985/1986	122,584	3,607	7.624	11.829
1986/1987	114,573	3,617	6.190	10.505
1987/1988	125,457	3,838	7.329	11.458
1988/1989	124,556	4,001	7.724	11.645
1989/1990	122,675	3,032	7.775	11.920

Source: Unica, http://www.unicadata.com.br/

The drop in ethanol production affected the drivers of the nearly three million ethanol-fueled cars on the road in 1986.[12] It was government policy for Petrobras to store one month's reserve of ethanol for any unforeseen shortages, and the government accordingly had stored 2.1 billion liters of excess ethanol from the previous year. However, the drought reduced available reserves for the following year. Sugar producers and government officials assured the public and the car industry that they could continue to meet fuel demands. Then, drought in the Northeast further reduced supplies in 1987. Thereafter, worries about the ethanol supply in the months between harvests became increasingly regular.

Criticism of Proálcool increased as these multiple factors changed the market reality for ethanol. The most outspoken critics often came from Petrobras, the official government distributor of ethanol fuel and a long-time opponent of the program's growth. Company officials had long bemoaned the "ethanol bill," which the company accumulated from purchasing ethanol from producers, storing the alternative fuel, and distributing it at subsidized rates to consumers. In 1983, officials, including the National Petroleum Council president Colonel Hilton Vasconcellos complained of the cost of storage as overproduction of ethanol threatened the market.[13] By the late 1980s, they complained that the reduced reserves of the overpriced, subsidized fuel threatened the market and company's finances. Reports claimed that the "famous ethanol bill" had already cost

Petrobras Cz$29 billion in subsidies by mid-1988. Petrobras fueled consumer doubts about the program's long-term ability to meet ethanol fuel demands across the country at competitive prices as world oil prices fell. As Gil Siuffo, the president of the National Federation of Gas Stations, asked, "Why would a country prefer to impose on its people a product that costs US$45 a barrel and discourage another that, with the same properties, is costing only US$14 per barrel?"[14]

Frustration with ethanol grew as the government's ability to support the program collapsed. A set and subsidized price ratio that kept ethanol prices below those of gasoline had long been one of the most important incentives for promoting ethanol cars, but during the economic crisis of the 1980s this price ratio was gradually decreased. While policymakers initially priced ethanol at 59 percent of gasoline, by July 1988 they had increased ethanol's ratio to 69 percent of gasoline.[15] As prices rose, ethanol car owners grew wary. After a price increase in May 1988, Daniel Alberto Wilhems, a 40-year-old commercial manager, stated:

> This is absurd. We work all day, earn little, and still have to put up with this abuse. I use three tanks of ethanol per week, which is more than Cz$9000, but still I manage to cover these increases. But the salaried [workers], poor guys, what do they do? The worst is that ethanol can go up more, which is not fair. In the end, the government always incentivized the purchase of the ethanol-fueled car, and now it betrays the consumer.[16]

Another car owner, the chemistry professor Lupéricio Augusto Santos, stated, "The ethanol car is good, but it is difficult to live with it without the government incentive." Indeed, Santos was considering becoming one of the many who converted their ethanol engines to gasoline motors.[17]

Ethanol shortages finally arrived during the 1988/1989 harvest year. In mid-July, they began in the Northeast. By September, reports emerged of gas station owners in Pernambuco and Paraiba lacking pre-ordered ethanol to fill their pumps.[18] By May 1989, ethanol shortages endangered fuel supplies throughout São Paulo and Rio de Janeiro in the southern region. Across the state of São Paulo, multiple distributors shut down their pumps. Motorists parked at gas stations to wait for distribution trucks.[19] As one report noted, "the ethanol shortage this month shatters the image of Proálcool."[20] When reports confirmed that ethanol supplies would not recover until July, panic set in.

The ethanol shortage drew government officials to increasingly question, if not altogether withdraw, public support for the program. The Minister of Mines and Energy, Vicente Fialho, announced that ethanol car production would be limited to 350,000 cars that year, about 50 percent of the total expected output, in response to the shortages. One minister stated that "The current problems are helping to revise the program in order to maintain it on 'consistent bases' so as not to repeat the fuel shortage in the future."[21] The strongest attacks on Petrobras still came from within, as the company had won control of ethanol distribution back in 1979. After years of calling for the government to readjust the price of ethanol and reduce its production, in 1989, the Petrobras president Carlos Sant'Anna called for a freeze on the program until 1995 because of ethanol's unjustifiably high production cost in relation to that of gasoline. He compared the program to the Titanic, with the collapse of oil prices its iceberg.[22]

However, Sant'Anna's focus on low global oil prices undercut the multiple factors that undermined the program's long-term viability. Sales of ethanol cars, whose fuel and price remained subsidized by the government, continued to increase even after oil prices fell. In total, 698,563 ethanol cars were sold in 1986 (92.1% of the market) and 459,222 (94.4%) in 1987. Even in 1988, ethanol car sales (566,610) exceeded those of the previous year, although the percentage of the market fell slightly (88.4%).[23] However, between 1985 and 1989, ethanol consumption grew by 60 percent, while production only grew by 21 percent.[24] Yet supply shortages and recurring droughts in São Paulo were finally breaking ethanol car owners' confidence in the ethanol market.

By the end of May 1989, the once effective promotion of Proálcool as a fuel alternative program had completely changed. Reporters increasingly described the program as "expensive and ambitious" and a "dramatic farce that makes up the Brazilian consumer's everyday."[25] Ethanol shortages peaked in early 1990. Government officials rolled out plans for rationing and accused usineiros of "blackmail" of the public.[26] Given the initial implementation of Proálcool as a way to avoid oil shortages, it was ironic that ethanol shortages and lines at ethanol pumps plagued the program. Eventually, Petrobras mixed wood-based methanol and ethanol imports into the ethanol fuel supply to service the millions of ethanol cars on the road.[27] Sugar producers blamed government planning for the shortages, while the public blamed sugar producers. Proálcool entered full crisis in 1990.

Proálcool Reimagined

As Proálcool faltered, producers and government officials turned to new research and development to proactively redirect promotion of the ethanol industry toward green or renewable energy over the first half of the 1990s. This new focus informed ethanol car promotion, the reorganization of sugar and ethanol's administration, and the program's national goals over the first half of the 1990s even as ethanol car sales collapsed.

Researchers at the University of São Paulo (USP) began studying the impact of ethanol on air quality soon after the ethanol car's launch in 1979. Founded in 1979 by the professor of Pathology, György Miklós Böhm, the Laboratory of Experimental Atmospheric Pollution at USP's Medical College ran experiments on air pollution and pulmonary pathology. The laboratory led a series of studies comparing the effects of acute exposure to ethanol exhaust and to gasoline exhaust. The researchers' early findings showed that, on average, ethanol cars released 65 percent less carbon monoxide, 13 percent less nitrogen oxide, and 69 percent less hydrocarbons but 441 percent more aldehydes, namely acetaldehyde and formaldehyde.[28] Later studies proved that aldehydes react to sunlight to create additional air pollution, such as smog, but their immediate impact on air quality was far less clear than the benefits of reduced carbon emissions from gasoline fumes.[29] When the group began presenting and publishing its findings in 1983, they quickly caught the attention of government officials and sugar producers, among others. Despite data illustrating the pulmonary stress caused by increased aldehyde emissions, their research definitively proved that ethanol cars significantly reduced toxic carbon emissions caused by gasoline automobiles.

Ethanol's environmental benefits gained further support from an important nuclear physicist and later policymaker, José Goldemberg, who began publishing on the energy benefits of sugar-based ethanol in the late 1970s. His research proved not only that ethanol released lower carbon emissions than petroleum but also that sugarcane was the most efficient renewable input for producing ethanol.[30] Goldemberg argued that ethanol exemplified how developing countries uniquely contributed to lowering greenhouse gas emissions on a larger scale than developed countries like the United States, which relied so heavily on high-emission petroleum.[31]

The data on air pollution in the São Paulo metropolitan area supported the promotion of ethanol fuel as an environmental boon. In addition to launching cars running exclusively on ethanol, Brazil replaced lead in regular gasoline with ethanol in the 1980s. Thereafter, the metropolitan area, in which thermal inversion produces dangerously concentrated levels of air pollution during the winter months, experienced a 92 percent decline in lead concentrations, dropping from 1.4 mg per cubic meter in 1978 to less than 0.1 mg in 1991.[32] Exhaust emissions fell from 100 mg per cubic meter in 1978 to 60 mg in 1989. Even more noticeably, carbon dioxide emissions fell from 130 mg per cubic meter in 1977 to 60 mg per cubic meter in 1989.[33] As the largest, most concentrated car-driving city in the largest car-driving state in Brazil, these atmospheric changes were pronounced across São Paulo state. One study indicates that in São Paulo state alone "use of ethanol as a fuel avoided the emission of 82 million tons of carbon dioxide equivalent from 1980 to 2003."[34]

In addition to ethanol's positive influence on urban air pollution, the creation of another sugar byproduct became a major part of the ethanol industry's reinvention. Like vinasse, bagasse, the dried husk of sugarcane, had long been a problematic byproduct of ethanol production. Some sugar producers had used bagasse as a firewood alternative in times of wood shortages. However, when usinas moved to fossil fuels to power sugar and ethanol processing, alternative bagasse use decreased and producers often threw the byproduct in the water or burned it to use as a fertilizer along with vinasse.[35] As sugar cultivation increased under Proálcool so too did wasted bagasse. In 1980, specialists estimated that each ton of cane produced 270 kilos of bagasse, in addition to 70 liters of ethanol and 910 liters of vinasse. In the 1980/1981 harvest, bagasse production reached over 37 million tons nationwide, 24 million tons of which came from São Paulo alone. Like vinasse, bagasse storage created numerous environmental issues, including air pollution from open burning. In the early 1980s, large usinas in the Ribeirão Preto region, like Usina Santa Lydia, promoted burning the product for energy, not in the open air, as was traditionally done, but in processing centers that would redirect that thermal energy back into an electrical energy source for the usina itself. Producers highlighted how this process of electricity production, known as cogeneration, provided the possibility of self-sufficiency for high energy-consuming usinas that invested in such a processing plant on their own premises.[36] Some had promoted the practice earlier, including the researcher José Goldemberg and Maurilio Biagi of the Usina Santa Elisa. However, as cogeneration produced more energy than was required to run the usinas, producers looked to contribute the excess electrical energy to the Brazilian energy market.[37]

Fig 6.1 Accumulated bagasse waste

Source: José Coronado, "Bagaço aquece a indústria," *Química e derivados* 16, no. 190 (1982): 44. APHRP Caixa 192.

Cogeneration provided a possible solution to the climatic shocks that endangered the country's electricity supply in the late 1980s and early 1990s. By 1989, the greater São Paulo and interior regions like Ribeirão Preto were experiencing intense cyclical droughts.[38] After the disastrous 1985 drought, the region experienced drought conditions again in 1987, 1989, 1992, and 1995 that endangered hydroelectricity production in the entire southern region of Brazil and led politicians to look for solutions to the pending energy crisis. Sugar producers presented cogeneration as a potential solution, since sugar harvests, and thus cogeneration, came in during dry seasons when hydroelectric water supplies would be at their lowest.[39]

These newly recognized environmental benefits of the ethanol car and cogeneration, however, did not change many of the ongoing environmental costs linked to ethanol production, especially the water pollution from vinasse. For example, a 1992 CETESB report on the two major rivers in the Ribeirão Preto region listed sugar and ethanol distillers as the top two polluters in the Mogi-Guaçu and two of the top three polluters in the Pardo basin.[40] At the same time, the industry's contributions to air pollution in São Paulo's sugar-producing countryside gained more attention. To breakdown sugarcane quickly and facilitate manual cutting, producers used controlled burning, known as *queimadas*, during the harvest. One 1982 report described the countryside as a "bonfire," as regions covered in cane were intentionally set on fire every harvest.

Burning cane initially remained a legally supported part of cane production, defended by rural cane workers and producers alike. For rural workers, cutting cane without burning the husk around it first, that is, cutting "green cane," caused more injuries and slowed worker productivity.[41] For producers, manual laborers remained cheaper than machines when cutting burned cane, but cutting green cane incentivized mechanization to cut at faster rates than manual laborers over several harvests.[42]

However, public pressure on producers about the poor air quality caused by burning highlighted the connection between city and countryside in the 1980s. Residents of the urban centers like Ribeirão Preto, Sertãozinho, Piracicaba, and Araraquara increasingly complained of the "black soot (*fuligem*)" that hung overhead during the harvest periods.[43] In 1982, Araraquara and other sugar-producing cities, including Sertãozinho, sent a proposal to the state government to prohibit cane burning in a 10 km radius of the urban perimeter.[44] That proposal failed, but the Council of Environmental Defense of the city of Araraquara proposed prohibiting burning in a radius of 5 km from the urban areas in 1985. Three years later, on August 30, 1988, the São Paulo State governor Orestes Quércia finally passed Decree no. 28.848, which officially prohibited "any form of fire use to clean and prepare soil in the State of São Paulo, including for the preparation of planting and for the collection of sugarcane."[45] As the first formal outlawing of queimadas in the rural zone, the decree cleared the path for CETESB to impose fines on fazendas (plantations) and usinas that continued the practice.[46]

Usineiros and agricultural groups led by the state's sugar cooperative, Copersucar, formally complained to the governor after the decree, claiming that the measure "paralyzes activities in the countryside." They argued that "Collecting cane without burning would make the commercial exploitation of cane impossible on a large scale" and would require tripling manual workers "at minimum" to meet the additional labor demanded.[47] Governor Quércia relented and amended the full prohibition less than a month later. The new decree added stipulations that burning for cane collection was acceptable under certain conditions if neighbors were adequately warned at least forty-eight hours in advance, and if it occurred at least one kilometer from the "urban perimeter of the cities."[48]

Producers continued the practice, but negative publicity about burnings escalated over the next several years. Some news reports focused on the subsequent soil erosion that accompanied burnings, the organic material destroyed, the water used, the dirt produced, and other problems linked to smoke and soot distribution. Reporters repeatedly cited the complaints of the housewives who had to deal with the nuisance in the region. Others drew attention to the increased toxic gases and greenhouse emissions produced by burnings and their impact on public health that had previously gone unaddressed. Just as attention to the ethanol car's contributions to reducing greenhouse gases gained momentum, critics questioned the long-term health implications of exposure to the concentration of the ozone in the lower atmosphere that such burnings, which had been central to producing ethanol at cheaper prices, generated.[49]

Although cane burning remained common, producers embraced mechanization as the future of the industry in the 1990s. Researchers began developing cane varieties best suited for mechanical cutting, which would enable the industry to move to cutting more crude cane with fewer manual laborers.[50] Producers followed trends already established in Australian and Cuban sugar harvesting. Cane-cutting machines slowly replaced large swaths of the labor market. Each machine cuts 600 tons per day, or the equivalent of at least ten workers. In 1993, 40 percent fewer cutters worked the cane fields during the harvest than in 1973, despite increased production of cane.[51] While specialists celebrated the reduced air pollution, rural workers lost jobs.

The industry's negative environmental impact won less and less attention as producers tried to change Proálcool's image to that of an environmental savior. Very few critics of the program directly pointed to the industry's poor environmental record by the mid-1990s. In one rare editorial, a paulista citizen noted that the claim that ethanol does not pollute was:

> false, its production is highly polluting. Burning millions of hectares of cane adds to the greenhouse effect. And more, the *restilo* [vinasse], which in part is dumped in rivers, is as polluting as the waste of a city with a million inhabitants! I remind you that the modern cars, [which run] on gasoline, are adapted to catalyze to reduce pollution. Ethanol is an energy fallacy. It wastes more energy in manual production of cane, in transport to usinas, in the "trip" from usinas to distributors, to the gas station, etc.[52]

However, these outspoken views were ever more infrequent at a time when the overwhelming perspective was that the industry did more good for the environment than bad. Growing international and domestic attention to the environment as an important policy factor became political fodder for the ethanol industry. Even as vinasse and queimadas regularly exposed the countryside to water and air pollution, ethanol supporters built a campaign focused on ethanol's environmental benefits that targeted urban car owners and international politics and policy in order to win continued federal support for the program in the early 1990s.

Rejuvenating Proálcool

Ethanol's economic advantage over gasoline on the fuel market had collapsed by 1990. However, with the program's new focus on the ethanol car's improvement of urban air quality and the possibilities of cogeneration as an energy-saving measure, the sugar ethanol industry began to relaunch Proálcool as an environmentally beneficial and efficient program, overlooking its reduced direct economic benefits. Promoting these advantages to the public became the mission of producers.

Well aware of the deteriorating public opinion of them and Proálcool amid the ethanol shortages of 1989, sugar producers from the Northeast and the Center-south, especially São Paulo, launched a new campaign to "neutralize" the negative attention the industry was receiving by focusing on the alternative fuel's connection to improved air quality in major cities. The University of São Paulo pathologist, György Miklós Böhm, and his team's findings became an important part of this strategy. São Paulo producers spearheaded the idea as the "cold war" with Petrobras heated up in late 1989, when ethanol shortages put Petrobras and producers at odds over the use of the limited supplies for the national fuel mixture or ethanol cars.[53] In December, all the major sector leaders, from Copersucar to sugar, ethanol, and cane unions and state associations, approved the industry-wide plan to rebuff growing national anti-ethanol sentiments as Petrobras unofficially began incentivizing car owners to convert their ethanol engines back to gasoline motors.[54] In the short-term first phase of the plan, producers would focus national and regional media attention on "the sector's version that the blame for the eventual crisis ought to be credited exclusively to the government" while mobilizing "public opinion with their arguments in favor of the environment and energy independence." In phase two, three to four months later, usineiros planned to launch a "new institutional campaign" to stimulate ethanol car sales and rebuild consumer trust "that the product would never run out." This "counterattack in the fuels war" against pro-petroleum interests, particularly Petrobras, explicitly included lobbying the newly elected president, Fernando Collor de Mello, and his administration.[55] Thus, convincing the new democratic government to continue support for Proálcool and ethanol followed similar channels used to entice Military President Ernesto Geisel to support the creation of the program back in 1975.

Changing the economic pitch used two decades earlier, the industry tried to sell the public on ethanol's environmental benefits. A two-page promotion advertisement announced that "With the ethanol car you help depollute the air of your city." The advertisement shows the São Paulo skyline filled with smog, with a skull, the traditional sign for poison and other biohazards, peeking through. The text of the advertisement details seven different pollutants most reduced by ethanol cars: lead, carbon monoxide, hydrocarbon carcinogens, sulfur, black smoke, aldehydes (which it calls "tiny" and "below the limit established by international norms"), and the greenhouse effect. It prominently includes a detailed quotation from Professor Böhm: "The toxic effects of gases emitted by gasoline motors are brutally more serious than those of ethanol motors." The message seeped into other media. A journalist reporting on pending anhydrous alcohol shortages in late 1989 claimed that the product was primarily mixed in the Brazilian fuel supply to "reduce carbon monoxide emissions in the atmosphere of the Brazilian capitals."[56] As ethanol shortages also threatened a return to the use of lead and/or other toxic mixtures in the national fuel supply in order to increase fuel efficiency, specialists repeatedly highlighted ethanol's unique contributions to air quality improvements.[57] Such assertions affirm the growing perception that anhydrous ethanol was used for environmental reasons even though the government had reduced the mixture rate to 12 percent from the 20 percent used in 1980s. Furthermore, the advertisement implied the approach was new, despite the fact that some level of mixture had been mandated since the 1930s.

While media and marketing provided the foundations for the first phase of the sugar industry's campaign to renew support for Proálcool, convincing the new president was a more difficult task. Once the centerpiece of a petroleum substitution initiative, the program was imperiled by the country's economic crisis, heavy government financing, and declining international petroleum prices. In one of his first actions as the first democratically elected

Fig 6.2 Ethanol car advertisement (after 1989): "With the ethanol car, you help depollute the air in your city."
Source: APHRP Caixa 192.

president in over thirty years, in March 1990 President Collor dismantled the IAA, which had been the sugar and ethanol policy body for over a half-century. He threatened to dismantle Proálcool next.[58]

The future of Proálcool remained in limbo for months.[59] The state-owned oil distribution company Petrobras had long bemoaned the program's inefficient production costs. By late 1989, the Petrobras president Carlos Sant'Anna openly advocated freezing the costly ethanol program. Major car manufacturers such as GM and Volkswagen also grew skittish amid the uncertainty about the future of the program and practically halted all ethanol car production by July 1990.[60] Others in the auto sector were more outspoken. João Augusto Conrado do Amaral Gurgel, the São Paulo businessman whose domestic car company built the first national car in the 1970s, remained an outspoken critic of the subsidies used to support the ethanol industry, which, he complained, consumed huge amounts of diesel fuel to power its usinas and distilleries and kept Brazilian fuel prices high unnecessarily. He claimed it was time to end "problems like Proálcool" and lower the cost of gasoline in the country to accelerate the decline of the ethanol fleet.[61] Gurgel's critique of the ethanol program reflects how important government incentives for both the car and the fuel were to the ethanol car's success. However, ultimately, Proálcool's fate lay in President Collor's hands.

During this period, the renowned physicist and ethanol supporter José Goldemberg joined Collor's administration as Federal Secretary of Science and Technology in March 1990.[62] Goldemberg became pivotal to reshaping Collor's broader environmental policy and Proálcool's place within it. Although Brazil had a long history of domestic environmental activism, Brazilian officials had maintained a "defensive position" against international pressure to reduce carbon emissions. The previous president José Sarney famously promised to "let pollution come, as long as the factories come with it."[63] By the late 1980s, the United Nations was calling for countries to reduce greenhouse gas emissions linked to fossil fuel consumption in an effort to establish a more "sustainable" world for future generations.[64] Growing international attention to environmental concerns, particularly deforestation in the Amazon, made Brazil's position increasingly contentious in international circles in the 1980s. As the country distanced itself from its twenty-year dictatorship and renewed democratic connections abroad, Collor sought to improve its position on the world stage. The professionalization of environmental activism in the 1990s led to environmental reforms becoming an important political platform domestically and internationally.[65] As a country that had already established a large diversified energy infrastructure, refocusing attention from the Amazon onto ethanol's lower carbon emissions in the transportation sector became politically advantageous. Thus, political interest in solidifying the ethanol industry's image as green aligned with producers' interest in shifting attention to ethanol's environmental benefits regardless of its actual history of water pollution.

The new Science and Technology Secretary José Goldemberg, along with the renowned Brazilian environmentalist and new Secretary of the Environment José Lutzenberg, became the face of Collor's strategy to lead the Third World in international efforts to lower emissions.[66] In a detailed account of the new strategy, Goldemberg explained Collor's two-pronged approach: first, drastically reduce Amazonian deforestation by eliminating subsidies and agricultural projects in the region and increasing national oversight of environmental laws, and second, create a national energy rationalization program to reduce the growth of electricity and petroleum consumption. Collor's administration promoted "the country's new mature and adult position" on the environment with explicit hopes that it would "help repair our image abroad, and possibly, influence even the renegotiation of the foreign debt that is now underway."[67] Goldemberg was a critical part of this outreach as he regularly presented internationally on global alternative energies using Brazil as a case study.

All the while, sugar and ethanol producers aggressively lobbied behind the scenes for the president to continue Proálcool. The alliance between northeast and paulista sugar producers worked to their advantage. Collor was a native of the northeastern state of Alagoas, the second largest sugar- and ethanol-producing state in the country, so the region's influential usineiros directly pressed him to continue support for ethanol. The Alagoas state senator Teotônio Vilela Filho, who was the president of the Senate Infrastructure Commission, finally convinced Collor to revitalize Proálcool by telling him that he could avoid the impending energy crisis without spending money or financing a deficit program. Senator Vilela Filho said Collor's "eyes bulged and he asked who in the government knew of this. The next day, he set up a meeting with Goldemberg and resolved to invest in the idea."[68] Evidently, Goldemberg closed the deal.

In August 1990, just months after he promised to abolish the program, Collor called Proálcool a "national treasure," just like Petrobras, and guaranteed sugar producers continued government support and investment in research.[69] He auspiciously and strategically announced his decision at a sugar producers' meeting in his home state of Alagoas. Collor restructured the National Ethanol Program, noting the limits of ethanol as a petroleum replacement, but very distinctly continuing support for the program as a fuel supplement initiative.[70]

To justify his decision, Collor emphasized the established importance of the industry for fuel security in a time of energy uncertainty. The program had been part of the military government's larger agenda to reduce the country's dependence on foreign oil, particularly from the Middle East.[71] By the end of the 1980s, oil represented a smaller, but still significant percentage of Brazil's overall imports. Thus, when Saddam Hussein's Iraqi troops invaded Kuwait in August 1990, Collor specifically identified the threat of renewed oil shortages as a factor in his decision-making.[72] The new crisis certainly affected consumer behavior, as ethanol car sales jumped in August 1990, which car retailers directly attributed to consumer fears of the international conflict.[73] However, sugar lobbying clearly influenced Collor's commitment too, as he praised cogeneration's ability to "provoke[e] a real revolution in the sector" at the same event at which he announced renewed support for ethanol.[74]

Proálcool II, the new ethanol program, promised sugar producers immediate subsidies and financial support to incentivize a return to ethanol production, but it also focused on slowly transitioning the industry toward privatization and self-sufficiency in line with neoliberal expectations. Again, sugar producers were offered preferential financing with government-supported 12 percent interest rates. The government also finally gave in to usineiros' demands for price increases. The government continued the differential between gasoline and ethanol fuel, although officials had already increased ethanol's price from the controversial 65 percent of the price of gasoline to the less favorable 75 percent.[75] However, Collor specifically called for innovation in order to make the industry more efficient and self-sustaining in the near future. He stated, "Without subsidies or the protection of the government, which requires public spending . . . businessmen will have to use greater creativity to reduce their spending and make the alternative fuel economically viable."[76] This triggered an expansion of cogeneration, which simultaneously met Collor's various political and economic goals.

National promotion of ethanol's environmental benefits continued after Proálcool's rejuvenation. President Collor and Goldemberg, who was newly appointed Minister of Education and interim Secretary of the Environment, pivoted their propaganda toward the United Nations Conference on the Environment and Development held in Rio de Janeiro in June 1992. The international conference, for which Brazil won the hosting rights in the late 1980s, became the central platform for promoting the country's new environmental image. With panels on agriculture and the environment, sustainable development, models of energy use, environmental law, deforestation, and the Amazon, the conference agenda focused on drawing positive international attention to the country's leadership on environmental topics despite its historically large share of air pollution from land change linked to burning the Amazon rainforest.

Brazilian leadership showcased the seventeen-year-old ethanol program as a solution to environmental challenges. The day after a session on Brazilian air pollution, one reporter noted, government officials and industry specialists presented Proálcool "as a helpful model for preserving the environment" and a "unique program that worked" to the businessmen, ecologists, and heads of government in attendance.[77] This redirection included glowing reviews of the advances in the industry's reuse of its byproducts, particularly vinasse and bagasse, which one reporter claimed "used to pollute the environment and were reasons for harsh criticisms from ecologists" in the past.[78] Instead, Clésio Balbo of the Usina Santo Antonio in the Ribeirão Preto region claimed that the industry was now "a self-sustaining activity in which nothing is lost."[79]

Usineiros used international attention on the conference to expand their international image and promote export opportunities. Usineiros such as Maurilio Biagi Filho promoted the "clean and renewable" fuel's impact on air pollution in big cities and Brazil's sugar ethanol as a potential global replacement for tetraethyl lead, which was commonly mixed in fuels around the world at the time. Biagi affirmed that "Brazil is the world leader in the replacement of lead in gasoline, produces the world's cheapest ethanol, and can perfectly meet the demand of the first world."[80] US officials visited Ribeirão Preto to learn more about the ethanol program, and particularly bagasse energy production, during the Rio conference. After going to Biagi's Usina Santa Elisa and Zanini during the conference week, the US Undersecretary of Energy John Michael Davis declared that "The Brazilian program of liquid alternative fuels is the largest, best, most successful, and most competitive in the world."[81]

Wih government and international support, Proálcool II completely reversed the direction of the struggling program. With Proálcool II incentives, production continued at a maximum capacity of 12.5 billion liters in 1991, and Collor set a new goal of 15 billion liters annually and, later, 18 billion per year.[82]

The Collapse of Proálcool and the Ethanol-Fueled Car

Despite Proálcool's renewed purpose under a "green fuel" banner and the additional financial support it provided, not all were convinced that the program needed reinvigoration, as demand for ethanol cars was actually falling in the early 1990s.[83] In fact, the remarketing and revival of Proálcool did little to change consumers' opinion of ethanol and its producers over the course of the decade. As government support for Proálcool rose, public support waned.

All the Proálcool fanfare on an international stage did not change the domestic ethanol market's struggles in the 1990s. Despite maintaining the ethanol mixture in the national fuel supply at 20 percent, ethanol cars sales dropped after the loss of consumer confidence caused by the 1989 and 1990 fuel shortages and as a result of low oil prices, which enticed some to convert back or upgrade to gasoline cars.[84] In 1990, car producers only manufactured 83,259 new ethanol cars, compared with nearly 400,000 the previous year. While ethanol car sales had accounted for over 90 percent of car sales as late as 1987, they represented only 13.2 percent in 1990. Advertisements promoting the ethanol car's environmental benefits in the 1990s tried to stave off the collapse. In one advertisement, Böhm specifically warned that "The return of the gasoline car would tragically overload the city of São Paulo. It is makes no sense: at the same time people are prepared for emergency scenarios—on the other hand, the return of the gasoline car is incentivized." Such efforts were unconvincing to new buyers focused on cost.

The arrival of new "popular cars" broadened Brazilian car ownership dramatically in the 1990s. Historically, only a small percentage of the population could afford to buy a car. In 1960, 0.57 percent of Brazilians owned a car; by 1980 that number had only risen to 5 percent.[85] Even with the incentives provided for ethanol cars in the 1980s, few could afford this luxury, and critics highlighted how few everyday Brazilians benefited from the program.[86] Still, ethanol cars were many middle-class Brazilians' first cars in the 1980s, in part thanks to the incentives provided. However, Brazilian carmakers, including João Gurgel who had been manufacturing small cars since the 1970s, argued that a simple, basic, cheap "popular car" would expand access to car ownership and yield greater profits for the domestic industry and the national government, just as the Ford Model T had in the United States, the Volkswagen Beetle in Germany, and the Fiat 500 in Italy decades before.[87] In 1990, Fiat successfully lobbied the Collor administration for approval of a tax reduction on compact cars with a 1.0-liter engine. Conveniently, only Fiat's Uno Mille model qualified at the time. Between September 1990 and November 1992, Uno Mille sales pushed Fiat's market share up from 14 percent to 22 percent of the Brazilian market. Thereafter, other automakers pushed for similar tax breaks for their own specific individual popular models. In April 1993 Collor's successor, Itamar Franco, formally supported the creation of popular cars targeting average Brazilian workers, with tax rates below the market rate and priced below US$7,000 to expand access to car ownership. Approved popular cars transformed the car sector as new buyers flooded the market.[88] Many manufacturers offered models in both gasoline and ethanol versions but new buyers increasingly purchased gasoline cars.

Ethanol cars in the 1980s and, even more, popular cars in the 1990s broke the exclusive relationship between middle-class status and car ownership.[89] New buyers, including middle-class women in search of second family cars, had entered the market in the 1980s. During the next decade working-class men and women entered the market. More so than the United States, Argentina, and Venezuela, Brazilians, regardless of class, consistently proved sensitive to price, preferring cost-efficient models and often using public transport to commute to work even if they owned a car.[90] During this demographic shift, ethanol fuel car sales rebounded between 1991 and 1994, but the ethanol car never went above a third of the market share again. Between conversion and cheap, new gasoline car sales, ethanol cars represented only 5 percent of the expanded market by 1995.[91]

Ethanol car sales fell as a national crisis further compromised sugar producers' position in the economy. The military government's massive infrastructure investments in the 1970s and early 1980s, including Proálcool, as well as the construction of the world's largest hydroelectric dam, Itaipu, drove up inflation by the mid-1980s. The failed economic stabilization programs of the late 1980s pushed inflation into quadruple digits by the early 1990s.[92] Proálcool II buoyed sugar producers in the midst of this economic crisis by providing price readjustments for sugar and ethanol subsidies. In February 1993, the Itamar government approved a US$1.17 billion financial

Table 6.2 Ethanol Car Sales

Year	Cars Sold	Percentage of the market
1986	698,563	92.1%
1987	459,222	94.4%
1988	566,610	88.4%
1989	399,578	61.0%
1990	82,001	13.2%
1991	150,985	22.1%
1992	195,510	28.5%
1993	264,235	26.7%
1994	141,835	12.2%
1995	40,707	3.0%
1996	7,647	.5%
1997	1,120	.1%
1998	1,224	.1%

Source: Cleide Silva, "Aumenta a procura para carros a álcool," *ESP* (April 26, 1999), B4; Anfavea, *Anuário da Indústria Automobilística Brasileira*, 59.

support package for the sugar ethanol sector, which included US$500 million for ethanol production, US$500 million to support the cost of the harvest, and US$170 million to finance strategic stock storage.[93] In response, news reports bemoaned the cost of government subsidies to finance the "inept, deficit sector" and the heavily indebted usineiros who exploited the Bank of Brazil's financial obligations to Proálcool.[94]

Ethanol required heavy subsidies because production remained more expensive than that of petroleum. Throughout the 1990s, petroleum remained between US$14 and US$22 on the world market, well below the prices during the oil crisis era of the 1970s and early 1980s. Although fears of an increase were triggered by the Persian Gulf Crisis in 1990, prices never surpassed US$30, which was still far lower than ethanol production costs of US$45 per barrel. Indexing ethanol prices to petroleum prices remained standard Brazilian policy to keep the alternative fuel competitive with petroleum at the pumps. Thus, low international petroleum prices forced ethanol prices below production costs, which then required ongoing subsidies to compensate sugar and ethanol producers.

Although critics bemoaned ongoing ethanol subsidies, the sugar sector played an important role in the new government's economic recovery strategy in the mid-1990s. Franco's administration finally contained inflation with the Real Plan, designed and implemented by his Minister of Finance, the sociologist and development theorist Fernando Henrique Cardoso, in 1993. The plan, centered around a new currency—the real— successfully reduced inflation from a dizzyingly high 1,094 percent to the far more reasonable 15 percent between 1994 and 1995.[95] The feat won Cardoso the presidency in 1994, after which his administration advanced the neoliberal agenda first initiated by Collor to stabilize the economy and balance the exorbitant federal budget by aggressively privatizing state enterprises, promoting exports, and cutting state programs.[96] For politicians, officials, and the public, ethanol had become synonymous with costly subsidies.[97] Yet sugar exports supported the economic stability established by the Real Plan. While the industrial and financial sectors shrank in 1995 and 1996 due to the high interest rates imposed to keep inflation down, the agricultural sector, led by agro-industries such as the sugar sector, grew by 4.1 percent. In 1996, the sugar sector produced a surplus of US$1.43 billion, which contributed to the reduction of the US$5 billion Brazilian balance of trade.[98] In an interview with the news magazine *Imprensa*, Maurilio Biagi Filho asserted that agro-industry, particularly the growing soy industry and the sugar sector, was the "green anchor" of the real that steadied the Brazilian economy.[99]

Renewed debate over continuing Proálcool ensued as the program approached its twentieth birthday. Politically powerful sugar and ethanol producers called for increased government support to counteract the catastrophic collapse of the ethanol car market and to save the program. In February 1995, Cicero Junqueira Franco, the owner of the Usina Vale do Rosario of Morro Agudo in the greater Ribeirão Preto region, noted that, "If nothing is done, the ethanol car will simply stop being produced in less than two months and this will signal the death of Proálcool, provoking social and economic chaos of great proportion for the entire country."[100] Government officials proposed reducing the IPI tax on ethanol cars by 5 percent to ensure they remained cheaper than competing gasoline cars, but producers wanted more aggressive supports, including a fixed 20 percent of the market for ethanol cars.[101]

In their defense, Proálcool supporters almost completely focused on the program's environmental benefits. Industry boosters argued for the need to continue Proálcool on the grounds of the "preservation of technological conquest," "the environmental question," and job creation.[102] Many supporters also pointed to worsening traffic in major cities, particularly São Paulo, to justify continued government support for the alternative fuel. As ownership of predominantly gasoline popular cars expanded, they brought additional urban traffic.[103] In mid-1994, daily traffic congestion on roads extended for an average of 50 to 80 km across the city; by the end of 1995 that average reached over 95 km at peak times. More generally, a 1995 report noted that average traffic speed for cars was only 20 km per hour and over 3.2 million cars circulated around the city each day.[104] Traffic became so bad that the city government implemented an experimental traffic program, the *rodízio*, which attempted to limit drivers on the roads to certain days on the basis of their license plate numbers. Officials from the São Paulo Technological Center for Basic Sanitation (CETESB) supported the proposal of producers for the government to exclude ethanol-fueled cars from the voluntary program's restrictions as a way of incentivizing ethanol. Cicero Junqueira Franco claimed that, with the ethanol car's exclusion, "The population would remain more aware of the efficacy of its use in large cities as a pollution reducer."[105] Similarly, the President of the National Federation of Gas Stations Gil Siuffo, who notably spoke out against ethanol in the late 1980s, stated that, given the way traffic had worsened, "Ethanol ought to be promoted as being less polluting." While the initial *rodízio* failed, it provided another platform to promote ethanol's environmental benefits despite its cost.[106]

Ethanol's opponents continued to attack the fuel as a burden on the state. One report noted the country's growing public debt in 1995 and the ongoing burden of continued subsidies for ethanol. Countering the main argument of ethanol supporters, it claimed that, if incentivizing the program relied solely on ethanol's environmental benefits, it was "better to invest in railroads, trains, and metro transport, which pollutes little, if at all."[107] Opponents also criticized the exploitation of the program by sugar producers. For example, the Bank of Brazil was reluctant to continue financing the program because of its "low return, high defaults, waste, and siphoning of resources by owners."[108]

While public debate over Proálcool's future continued, internal division in the federal government finally and unexpectedly brought Proálcool price supports to an end. In late October 1995, the federal government called together an interministerial commission, including the Ministers of Finance, Industry and Commerce and Tourism, and Mines and Energy to again redefine the program.[109] However, the team could not agree on price supports.[110] Lower ethanol fuel prices had proven the bedrock of Proálcool, but the Finance Minister Pedro Malan argued subsidizing the price differential between cheaper gasoline and ethanol was no longer financially sustainable. Even as the Ministry of Industry, Commerce, and Tourism, long the protector of sugar and ethanol policy, proposed viable ways to continue financing the program, Malan bypassed Proálcool negotiations and liberated price restrictions on sugarcane products. Citing the benefits floating prices would have on sugar exports, Malan's Directive no. 64, passed in early 1996, set the date to activate full free market pricing of the sugar and ethanol market for January 1, 1997.[111] Slowdowns and setbacks delayed the price liberalization by two years, but in the interim, producers began negotiating prices for sugar directly with sugar suppliers and for ethanol with distributors, which signaled producers' gradual acceptance of the end of Proálcool's ethanol price controls.[112]

Government control of ethanol pricing finally ended on January 1, 1999 and, with it, the nearly twenty-five-year-old ethanol program. Ethanol production still continued at free and floating prices dictated by market demand, but the subsidized ethanol prices set below gasoline prices that had defined the program disappeared. Even so, producers pushed for continued government support for ethanol cars on the federal and state level. No matter how many parts of the program were stripped away, ethanol cars tied government officials to sustaining some sort of ethanol supports.

The Death of the Ethanol Car

By 1999, over 4.5 million ethanol cars remained on the road, but 83 percent were more than ten years old, relics of peak sales in the late 1980s.[113] Gasoline-powered popular cars dominated sales and roads. Sugar producers and other interest groups' attempts to gain government support to attract consumers back to ethanol cars met fleeting success. By the end of the 1990s, the ethanol car market was all but dead. Repeated government intervention, however, reveals how much influence these interest groups still had in Proálcool's wake.

By 1999, ethanol prices were free and floating. The government continued mixing anhydrous ethanol, the more expensive of the two ethanol varieties, into the national fuel supply at a 22 percent rate and above. However, the floating price change initially created a rather disastrous disparity between demand for hydrous ethanol, which decreased without ethanol car sales, and supply. Contrary to the laws of supply and demand, ethanol prices did not decrease as supply increased. Instead, the formerly subsidized prices continued to rise as ethanol supply oscillated between harvests. Oil prices bottomed out at US$11 per barrel in early 1999, while ethanol prices rose to US$28.60 per barrel. While the state had maintained 65 percent parity in the past to keep ethanol economically competitive with gasoline, ethanol burns faster than gasoline and thus at least 85 percent price parity is necessary for the fuel to reach similar usage efficiency as gasoline. At nearly triple the price of gasoline, ethanol became both cost- and fuel-inefficient. By late April 1999, usineiros and distillery workers clamored for the reactivation of Proálcool price supports.[114]

Brief spikes in ethanol car sales gave some hope for renewed demand. A bump in domestic gasoline prices that followed a slow increase in international oil prices boosted ethanol car sales for the first time in years in early 1999. In the first four months of that year, oil prices increased by nearly 30 percent on the international market from US$12.50 to US$17.30, and they continued rising.[115] In the same time period, more ethanol cars were sold between January and April 1999 (1,278) than had been sold the entire year before (1,224).[116]

Multiple actors responded positively to the unanticipated bump in sales. During the brief bump in gasoline prices, the federal government ordered a new "Green Fleet," which called for completely renovated federal government cars and taxis to run on ethanol. The auto industry remained skeptical, and only Volkswagen and Fiat invested in new ethanol models. Increased demand delayed the delivery of new cars to major ethanol consumer markets like Ribeirão Preto and São Paulo. Clients waited for months for the new cars, up to three months in some cases, thus missing the brief decline in ethanol prices.[117] Thereafter, the sugar interests pushed for broader federal ethanol price supports to no avail. Notably, Aproverde, a pro-ethanol organization composed of usineiros and workers in the sector and led by Maurilio Biagi Filho, even organized a protest in the nation's capital, Brasilia, in late May to pressure the government to adopt measures to protect the sugar ethanol sector, including renewed incentives for ethanol cars.[118]

In response to ethanol producers' demands and rising oil prices, the state of São Paulo sought to reinvigorate the ethanol market with an incentive program in August 1999. Even though ethanol car sales remained uncertain, the São Paulo state government, with its close ties to powerful sugar and ethanol producers, launched an ethanol car incentive program in 1999, following its 1992 initiative. The 1999 project, "São Paulo on the Front for the Ethanol Car (São Paulo na Frente pelo Carro a Álcool)," aligned the state government with São Paulo producers, Petrobras, and Volkswagen and Fiat retailers to offer a series of discounts and bonuses to make the ethanol car more attractive to consumers, and by extension Proálcool, which it described as "a generator of jobs and technological development." Launched through December 31, 1999, the government offered free car ownership tax (*imposto na propriedade de veículos automóveis*) in 1999/2000. Petrobras offered 1,000 liters of free ethanol fuel through fuel coupons at gas stations in São Paulo. Car retailers provided 3–5 percent discounts on overall ethanol car prices compared with those of similar gasoline models. Advertisements celebrated Proálcool's contribution to domestic jobs and clean air. The campaign compared the progressive nature of ethanol in reducing greenhouse gas emissions and the inferior status of competing developed countries, like the United States. Indeed, the campaign slogan referenced the popular car-centered film, *Back to the Future* (1985), with the slogan, "You [go] back to the future," attempting to assert that the ethanol car was both the car of the 1980s and the future.[119]

Despite early success, the rise in ethanol prices undercut the initiative. With the program's incentives, sales briefly climbed, but between May and November 1999, free market ethanol prices doubled as demand increased.[120] Ethanol production exceeded demand and, without the price subsidies, consumers had no incentive to buy ethanol cars. The federal government was reduced to public auction sales of ethanol reserves to ensure fuel distributors could maintain their stocks at stable prices, beginning in November 1999.[121] However, the damage was done. As ethanol prices increased, sales suffered. Ethanol cars sat in lots, unsold, for months. As one car salesman noted in January 2000, "The search for a car that runs on [ethanol] is almost zero." A Volkswagen manager indicated that ethanol car sales were so poor that he preferred to literally "*burn* the last units they have in stock."[122] Car salesmen and consumers had no interest in reviving ethanol cars after the failed São Paulo incentive program.

By early 2000, ethanol as an independent fuel and its cars was at death's door. While its former success affirmed that consumers would buy ethanol cars if the fuel were available at competitive prices, the previous year had again shown that ethanol cars could not compete with the cheaper gasoline cars in the current market.

The Rise of the Flex-Fuel Car

Ethanol's place in the Brazilian fuel market, and more broadly in the national energy matrix, remained uncertain at the turn of the century. Even with anhydrous ethanol mixed into the national fuel supply, ethanol stocks grew at less favorable prices as production exceeded demand. Ethanol producers remained unpopular in the public eye, but supporting ethanol, and thus sugar interests, was still good business because of the sugar sector's continued political clout. A confluence of factors, including global market changes, private industry investment, and fresh support for ethanol incentives from Lula and his political party, the Worker's Party (Partido dos Trabalhadores [PT]), ushered in a new celebratory era of ethanol fuel and its producers with the launch of the flex-fuel car in 2003.

The development of the flex-fuel engine was central to the rebirth of the Brazilian ethanol market in the 2000s. The motor, which could run on any combination of ethanol and gasoline, was originally developed in the late 1980s in response to new US legislation requiring adaptation of part of the American fleet to alternative fuels as part of evolving emissions requirements. As Silvio de Andrade Figueiredo, the chief of the Engine Group in the Mechanical Division at the Institute for Technological Research (Instituto de Pesquisas Tecnológicas [IPT]), noted, the car never picked up in the United States because "legislation required [the American market] to have the vehicles but not to use the fuel."[123] As the US market shifted back to bigger, fuel-guzzling vehicles in the 1990s, developers turned their attention to other potential markets. Given Fiat's growing share of the Brazilian market in the 1990s and its earlier success with the first ethanol car in the 1980s, Italian automakers and developers would have been particularly attuned to a dual fuel system's potential in the country. In the mid-1990s, a former Volkswagen employee, Fernando Damasceno, drove development of the adapted technology as a program manager at Magneti Marelli, an Italian auto parts company. The new flex-fuel engine included a chip that identified how much ethanol and how much gasoline were in the engine and adjusted accordingly. In 2002, Marelli sold the technology to Volkswagen, which incorporated it into its original flex-fuel model. Thereafter, Marelli sold the technology to other Brazilian manufacturers, including Ford, which had first sold flex-fuel cars in the United States in 1991.[124]

At the same time, global petroleum prices finally swung upward, as ethanol supporters had warned would happen. For the first time since 1990, growing international demand drove oil prices above US$30 per barrel in June 2000, and they remained at that level for the remainder of the year.[125] While prices decreased in 2001 and 2002, the sustained fluctuation in oil prices renewed interest in alternative options in the Brazilian market.

Meanwhile, savvy Brazilian politicians such as Lula looked to benefit from the sugar ethanol sector's continued ties to government even after ethanol prices became free and floating in 2000. Although Lula had been an adamant opponent of the sugar sector for decades, the three-time presidential candidate and honorary president of the Workers' Party began trying to build support among groups that had strongly opposed his candidacy in the past, including the sugar sector. He claimed he did not want the party to "fall into the common pit of the Brazilian political experience" and instead wanted to prove that "it is possible to govern in a different way."[126] This outreach began with Lula's own nongovernmental organization, the Instituto Cidadania, hosting a seminar entitled "Ethanol: Fuel of the New Millenium?" in March 2000 for governors, usineiros, and the Minister of Agriculture. After the PT won the 2000 general elections, Lula solidified his allegiance at a meeting of a group of usineiros in São Paulo in 2002, during his first successful presidential campaign, by promising, if elected, to incentivize ethanol car production and renew the country's car fleet. His PT campaign team member, Antônio Palocci, the mayor of Ribeirão Preto, positioned Lula and the PT well to win the sugar lobby's support. After the meeting, Palocci stated, "We have a commitment to Proálcool, and our idea is to give incentives in order that the consumer trade in the old car for a new one, run on ethanol, at popular prices."[127] These campaign promises had all been heard before, but not from Lula or the PT. Lula's success highlights the continued importance government officials placed on appeasing the sugar ethanol sector with ethanol incentives.

Even after ethanol car sales had all but died in 1999 and more domestic incentives seemed useless, burgeoning international pollution agreements resuscitated domestic production and the promotion of ethanol cars. The Kyoto Protocol produced at the 1992 UN Environmental Conference in Rio and adopted in December 1997, set "internationally binding emission reduction targets" for committed parties to come into effect in February 2005.[128] The protocol placed more responsibility on developed countries to reduce greenhouse gas emissions because of their disproportionate influence on climate change. While it called for countries to reduce domestic emissions, it also provided international emissions trading, a clean development mechanism, and joint implementation as market-based means for wealthy countries to fund emission reduction efforts in developing countries in order to reach lower emission goals. On the premise of ethanol car's lower carbon emissions, the Brazilian Foreign Minister, the economist Celso Lafer, constructed a deal in 2002 with the German government to count investment in Brazilian ethanol car sales toward credits for the European country's required carbon emissions abatement. In August 2002, President Fernando Henrique Cardoso and the German chancellor Gerhard Schröder, known as the "Car Chancellor" in Germany because of his previous ties to Volkswagen and consistent support of auto interests, signed the agreement, which committed Germany to invest R$100 million (US$34.2 million) in the production of 100,000 ethanol cars. According to the agreement, the Brazilian government would redirect those funds to produce a subsidy of R$1,000 on ethanol cars for taxis and government vehicles to ensure the car remained cheaper than gasoline cars and thus incentivize an expansion of ethanol fuel consumption. Germany would then get credit for the reduction of 100,000 vehicles' emissions.[129]

Volkswagen, Brazil, and Germany all benefited from this deal. For one thing, Germany further enhanced its reputation as an environmental policy leader among Western industrial countries. But beyond the political interests served by committing to the "pilot experiment," the deal bolstered Volkswagen's struggling Brazilian subsidiary. Volkswagen do Brasil and Fiat were the only two companies to continue production of ethanol cars throughout the 1990s. Although Volkswagen do Brasil had led the market since the 1960s, Fiat won market dominance in 2001 largely due to its successful popular cars like the Mille Electronic. Volkswagen sought to launch a new popular car, which represented 69.8 percent of registered new cars in 2001, and subsequently the flex-fuel car as a way to regain the market lead. Additional incentives to buy ethanol cars further benefited one of Volkswagen's most profitable subsidiaries' bottom-line as well. As the new Volkswagen do Brasil president Paul Fleming noted, "For each R$1,000 that is reduced on the price of the car, the market grows by 50,000 units. If we had conditions to make an automobile for R$12,000, we would aggregate, per year, 250,000 new consumers to the market."[130] Given the simple math of expanding access to cars in Brazil, Germany's commitment served its own domestic company's economic interests by potentially advancing Brazil's ongoing push to expand car ownership.

However, Volkswagen's launch of the flex-fuel car quickly overshadowed its commitment to the ethanol car. Volkswagen do Brasil began promotion of the flex-fuel car only a month after Brazil and Germany signed the mutual agreement. Volkswagen and Marelli adapted the technology to the Gol, the Brazilian adaptation of the Golf, the global leader and the Brazilian market's top model of the previous sixteen years.[131] Even before its arrival, the National Car Producers' Association (Anfavea), which had been central to facilitating the arrival of the first ethanol car on the market in 1979, won similar tax incentives for the flex-fuel car. Incentives were tiered: ethanol cars still enjoyed the highest tax breaks, particularly on the IPI, but at 13 percent, the flex-fuel car's IPI was lower than gasoline cars' standard 15 percent. The necessary add-ons for ethanol cars, like larger batteries and cold start ignition starters to address standard market issues, made the flex-fuel car immediately competitive against both gasoline and ethanol models upon its launch in 2003. Finally, the 1.6 flex-fuel engine was larger than the popular 1.0 (1,000 cc), but with the promise of being able to use the cheapest fuel and government incentives, it was also able to compete with the popular cars.[132]

Volkswagen launched the Gol Total Flex in March 2003 during the company's fiftieth anniversary in the country. It initially offered purchase exclusively on the internet. The car was an immediate success. The President of Volkswagen Global Bernd Pichetsrieder presented the car as a gift to the recently inaugurated new President Lula, who had already proven himself an opportune salesman. Lula repeatedly noted his administration's focus on

Fig 6.3 President Lula and Volkswagen do Brasil President Paul Fleming at the Fiftieth Brazilian Anniversary of Volkswagen do Brasil with the new flex-fuel car, March 24, 2003.
Source: Marcello Casal Jr, Agência Brasil

hunger and producing jobs. Volkswagen executives responded by donating a flex-fuel car to his Zero Hunger (Fome Zero) campaign and committing to give 600 young people internships at each of its plants. Additionally, the company and the media made sure to capture the moment, photographing the president filling up the car. Given Lula's pop star status, this was the best free promotion for the new product that the company could get.[133]

While Volkswagen was the first to launch the flex-fuel car, the other major car companies in Brazil were quick to follow. GM launched the Corsa Flexpower, its first flex-fuel model, in June 2003. Fiat launched the Palio 1.3 Flex in October 2003, and Ford launched the Fiesta 1.6 Flex in September 2004.[134] In 2005, Volkswagen and Fiat launched 1.0 popular models, which had been so important in reclaiming gasoline's dominance in the 1990s, with a flex-fuel engine. So popular was the new flex-fuel engine that some manufacturers stopped producing their non-flex-fuel gasoline options for the Brazilian market. After the Brazil-Germany agreement signing in August 2002 between Volkswagen and Fiat, only 109,734 more ethanol cars were manufactured in the entire country between 2003 and 2006 before producers completely switched to flex-fuel cars. In 2006, 85 percent of all new cars sold in Brazil had flex-fuel motors, equaling the success of the ethanol car two decades earlier.[135]

***

The transformation of ethanol and its producers from bandits to world heroes was complete by the mid-2000s. As oil prices rose around the world, Brazilian producers such as Biagi Filho enjoyed the fruits of another ethanol boom. New jobs brought workers to the Ribeirão Preto region, and unemployment in Sertãozinho, home to Biagi's long-time holding, the Usina Santa Elisa, hit zero. As one report stated, all Brazilians could do was "laugh" as the world looked for ways to diversify their energy sources.[136] By 2006, the Brazilian government anticipated ethanol exports would double from US$600 million in 2005 to US$1.3 billion in 2010.[137] Brazilian sugar and ethanol producers' renewed position in the economy and the country emerged from the death of the ethanol car and Proálcool as an economic program with the birth of the flex-fuel car and Proálcool as an environmental savior over the course of the late 1980s and the 1990s. Government support for ethanol-fueled cars was questioned but persisted, despite rhetoric to the contrary. Even after government officials ended ethanol subsidies and price protections in 1999, the ethanol car market won preferential treatment on the basis of this environmental focus.

Celebration of ethanol as a green alternative energy source, both for fuel and electricity in the form of cogeneration, gave the ethanol sector an environmentally positive image. Germany's investment in the ethanol car for the Kyoto Protocol objectives further illustrated how the environmental benefits of ethanol fuel as a lower carbon gas-emitting product overshadowed the sugar and ethanol sector's water and air pollution in the countryside. Instead, ethanol was finally transformed from a domestic solution to the international oil crisis during the 1970s into a global solution to a global climate crisis in the twenty-first century.

However, such shortsighted praise of ethanol illustrates the environmental and social costs that car-driving societies are willing to incur to sustain the current energy consumption status quo with alternative fuels. City dwellers disproportionately benefit from the improved air quality these fuel alternatives bring to major cities without reducing still unsustainable energy consumption practices. In exchange, they sacrifice water and air quality in the countryside, where rural laborers and residents disproportionately suffer the costs, with poor working conditions, regular exposure to agro-industrial pollution in their water, and reduced air quality during the harvest seasons. In turn, ethanol's history warns of a future where green economies, not unlike the fossil fuel economies of the past, may turn whole regions, mostly rural, into sacrificial zones like the vinasse-laden lakes of sacrifice dotting sugar and ethanol regions, in order to accommodate urban, car-driving citizens.

Epilogue

In 2009, in the middle of his second term, President Lula proclaimed that, thanks to ethanol, Brazil would become the world's largest fuel supplier by 2030. Implied in this statement, as one journalist wrote, was the promise that, with ethanol, no one has to consume less because when "powered by the sun," one can "step on the gas with a clear conscience."[1] Such gleaming optimism is nothing new; Brazilians embraced similar rhetorical flourishes in the 1930s and 1970s despite the highs and lows the ethanol industry experienced and the environmental and labor outcomes that came along with them. However, consistent with ethanol's development in the course of the twentieth century, shifts in sugar and ethanol demand, petroleum pricing and availability, international crises, rural labor exploitation, drought, pollution problems, and global marketing have continued to affect ethanol's value as a fuel alternative in the twenty-first century.

This epilogue traces the fifteen years after Brazilian ethanol's ascendance as a global fuel source in 2003. Rather than live up to Lula's optimistic vision of global ethanol demand, the alternative fuel endured another bust cycle that mirrored that of the late 1980s. Examining the industry's evolution between 2003 and 2019 reveals how ethanol's fluctuations parallel not only earlier periods in its brief history but also those of other energy commodities, particularly petroleum. Such similarities have direct implications for what a transition to a green energy economy might look like in the near future.

Brazilian Ethanol's Highs and Lows in the Twenty-First Century

By the mid-2000s, rising oil prices seemed to promise ethanol's prosperity in the twenty-first century, but the next fifteen years turned out to be rocky for the Brazilian fuel and its producers. After the launch of the flex-fuel vehicle in 2003, President Lula promoted ethanol production and consumption around the world, selling Brazil's expertise and exports.[2] Rising oil

Sweet Fuel. Jennifer Eaglin, Oxford University Press. © Oxford University Press 2022.
DOI: 10.1093/oso/9780197510681.003.0008

prices— driven by increased global demand, speculation, and fears of petroleum shortages linked to climate change— produced what some have called a third oil crisis from 2003 to 2009.[3] In response, ethanol production boomed, just as it had in the early 1980s. After ethanol sales surpassed those of gasoline in 2004, the scholar and policy specialist Dr. Marcos Jank called gasoline Brazil's "alternative energy," because ethanol dominated.[4] By the beginning of 2010, there were over 10 million flex-fuel cars on Brazil's roads.[5] As flex-fuel cars took over Brazilian roads, export opportunities for ethanol expanded. However, despite ethanol's renewed popularity, many of the same issues the industry had faced in the mid-1980s have continued to threaten long-term evaluations of the industry.

In comparison with competitors, such as the United States' corn-based ethanol, rhetoric about sugar-based ethanol as a clean energy of the future grew. Global critics noted the corn-based ethanol industry's connections to rising food prices, less competitive energy production, and questionable environmental impacts. In the production process, fuel from sugarcane produces 8.2 joules of energy per joule of fossil fuel used, while corn ethanol only produces 1.5 joules per unit. In contrast, gas and diesel production produces less than1 joule of energy per unit of fossil fuel consumed. Due to additional input costs, including gasoline to avoid an American alcoholic beverage tax, corn-based ethanol production is at least 30% more expensive than sugar-based ethanol.[6] Brazilian ethanol specialists such as the former Environment Minister José Goldemberg regularly critiqued the American corn option on the international stage for its more visible environmental shortcomings, particularly the use of petroleum in its production process, and celebrated Brazilian ethanol's cogeneration as superior to other competitors.

Critics of ethanol revived long-held complaints about the biofuel's environmental and social costs. Increased corn-based ethanol production reignited food versus fuel debates from the 1970s and 1980s.[7] Latin American leaders, such as Fidel Castro in Cuba and Hugo Chavez in Venezuela, spoke out against the US and Brazil's unfettered promotion of ethanol and other biofuels as US-Brazil joint efforts particularly targeted expanding ethanol production in the Caribbean.[8] Critics also noted sugar ethanol's continued connection to labor exploitation. As ethanol sales rose, Father Tiago, a Catholic monk who worked with the Pastor Land Commission (Commissão Pastoral da Terra [CPT]), the same organization that had helped organize bóias-frias in the Ribeirão Preto region in the 1980s, asserted that "The promise of biofuel is a lie. Anyone who buys ethanol is pumping blood into his tank. Ethanol is produced by slaves."[9]

Supporters drowned out critics by diverting attention to the energy possibilities that a non-fossil fuel provided for the future. Lula promoted joint efforts of the United States and Brazil to expand ethanol production around the globe.[10] Sugar ethanol supporters deflected questions about the global ethanol industry's connection to rising food prices by insisting that sugarcane, unlike corn, was not a primary food source. When critics linked the expansion of sugar ethanol production to Brazil's rapid razing of the Amazon rainforest, Lula denounced the association as "absurd."[11] Instead, Lula focused on the alternative energy's possibilities for non-oil-producing countries. He reasserted at the UN's Food and Agricultural Organization in April 2008 that "Biofuels aren't the villain that threatens food security . . . On the contrary . . . they can pull countries out of energy dependency without affecting foods."[12]

Lula's idyllic vision for ethanol did come to fruition, but instead, just as in the 1980s, a confluence of global and economic factors combined to derail ethanol's ascendancy once again in the late 2000s and early 2010s. Brazil discovered the largest deepwater oil reserves in history off the coast of Espirito Santo and Rio de Janeiro in 2007, and by the end of the decade, Brazil's oil-producing possibilities replaced ethanol as its premier political and economic tool in global affairs.[13] At the same time, ethanol's popularity in the early twenty-first century transformed the industry into a hotbed of multinational investment. Many domestic ethanol producers sold out to foreign investors, including the patriarch of the Usina Santa Elisa, Maurilio Biagi Filho.[14] However, international exposure more explicitly connected the ethanol industry to global market shifts. The foreign investment that poured into Santa Elisa and other formerly domestic owned sugar companies in the peak years of 2006 and 2007 became liabilities in 2009 and 2010 as global financial markets collapsed. Recognizing the impact of this important shift, in 2011 Biagi Filho observed, "Our sugarcane agro-industry has entered the era of large international capitalist groups, represented by agri-food transnationals, oil companies and national capital contractors, which already control at least one-third of our sugar and ethanol production."[15] The deeper incorporation of foreign interests decentered nationalist rhetoric of the earlier ethanol booms just as new crises engulfed the industry.

Just as they had in the mid-1970s and mid-1980s, severe droughts and global price changes led some producers in financial crisis to look for government support again by the end of the 2010s. Floods and droughts affected the harvests in both the major sugarcane-producing markets of India and Brazil and drove global sugar prices up, which in turn drove up the price of ethanol production.[16] Severe droughts in São Paulo led to another ethanol production collapse in 2011.[17] Export opportunities eroded as advances in fracking technology allowed greater exploitation of oil reserves around the world, and major potential consumers such as the United States became more energy-independent due to their shale reserves. Then oil prices collapsed in 2016. Petrobras, Brazil's oil and ethanol distributor, imploded as investigators unearthed the largest corruption scandal in modern global history linked to the deepwater oil reserves.[18] Despite these economic woes, the ethanol industry's connections in the government unsurprisingly led to renewed discussion of government support. In response to the industry's troubles, in 2017 the Chambers of Foreign Trade even proposed reinstituting a 20 percent tariff on ethanol imports that had been removed nearly a decade earlier during the industry's boom years.[19] Thus, the nearly century-long dance between private producers and government support that defined ethanol's development continued.

Ethanol's ongoing vinasse issue also has colored assessments of the industry in the twenty-first century. By the 2010s, some producers used processed vinasse to generate algae for use in biodiesel production or as biogas from anaerobic fermentation for heat and electricity to maximize the byproduct and diminish waste.[20] However, the vinasse problem has not disappeared. One specialist noted that second-generation ethanol produced from cellulosic materials will produce more vinasse, around 20 liters per gallon of ethanol, compared with the average 13 liters for traditional sugarcane ethanol.[21] Greater quantities of vinasse will only put more pressure on producers, government officials, and local citizens to enforce redirection of this voluminous waste away from cheaper, harmful dumping. As one specialist noted, when it comes to vinasse, "environmental monitoring will always be necessary."[22]

The industry has continued to use surface-level tanks, the cheapest vinasse storage option, despite the environmental damage they cause. Subject to leaks and flooding, they have remained smelly pits that attract many of the same issues identified in the 1950s in Piracicaba, particularly large numbers of mosquitoes.[23] Anti-dumping legislation has expanded, but transportation and application costs remain higher for vinasse than for traditional mineral fertilizers. Researchers have continued working to encourage more producers to use vinasse as a fertilizer to improve soil fertilization. However, studies of vinasse's environmental impact on groundwater have proven that concentrated and untreated vinasse causes increased leaching of chloride, nitrate, and calcium ions into the soil in a short period of time. Research continues on vinasse applications' impact on greenhouse gas emissions.[24]

The industry continued to impact rural labor relations as well. Booming ethanol investment in the 2000s incentivized producers to accelerate mechanization as never before. The temporary labor force peaked in 2008–2009 at 1.2 million workers. Peak ethanol production during the new ethanol boom (26.6 billion liters of ethanol in 2008) drew increased attention to labor violations in the sector. As labor organizations pressured government oversight to address egregious human rights abuses in the industry, heavy foreign investment in the industry allowed producers to accelerate mechanization as a solution.[25] By 2019, the industry only employed 850,000 manual cane workers.[26] However, in the midst of the industry's economic downturn, some manual workers have returned to the fields as the ethanol crisis has incentivized producers to use cheap manual labor rather than incur the costs of mechanization again. Producers again spun the move as environmentally friendly, claiming manual laborers were more efficient because they did not "compact the earth" or "waste raw material."[27] The truth is that workers again became cheaper than machinery in a depressed market. Competition for such limited jobs creates the same exploitative conditions that allowed usineiros and their labor contractors to push rural workers to their physical limits with minimal oversight in 1984. The instability and precariousness of the rural labor sector has remained a defining aspect of Brazilian ethanol's legacy.

Lessons on Energy Transitions

Many recent energy histories have sought to address what energy transitions might look like in the near future. Most have been Eurocentric histories, using earlier transitions to or between fossil fuels, particularly petroleum-based derivatives, to inform their analyses.[28] In contrast, Brazilian ethanol's history, which involved a more sustained effort to diversify away from fossil fuel energy, reveals important lessons about what potential transitions to green energies might look like in the twenty-first century.

Energy transitions require serious government intervention. The history of Brazilian ethanol demonstrates that Brazilians have been trying to make ethanol "work" forever. Government intervention, first through ethanol incentives, then agro-industrialization efforts, and then both, was critical to the industry's creation and expansion. This commitment was not limited to the industry's initial years but rather recurred at varied times when oscillations in the sugar market, climatic events, and the energy market required it. As the world embarks on an effort to transition away from a fossil fuel-centered energy system, Brazil's experience with ethanol illuminates just how much "public will," in the form of repeated government support, incentives, and marketing is necessary to make a long-term transition work.

Energy transitions are fragile. Brazilian ethanol's history adds the single example of a brief but significant successful transition to a non-carbon-based car fuel. In 1985, ethanol cars ruled the roads, and yet only a few years later they were outdated and unreliable products of government mismanagement and waste. The present-day Brazilian ethanol industry required producers, government officials, local politicians, scientists, and others to embrace, challenge, exploit, celebrate, market, and remarket ethanol as a viable fuel source. While the full fuel transition was brief and incomplete—gasoline cars remained on the roads—it paved the way for large-scale adaptation of other fueling innovations such as the flex-fuel car. Ethanol cars may have ruled the road for a brief period but flex-fuel cars have sustained longer, fuller adaptation. By 2018, fifteen years after their introduction onto the market, over 70% of Brazilian cars were flex-fuel cars.[29] Brazil's large-scale adoption of a non-petroleum transportation fuel reminds us how tenuous a full shift can be and how long an energy transition can take. Success may be determined less by immediate markers and more by long-term shifts. Any large-scale transition to a non-carbon energy source will require long-term assessments beyond short-term economic markers to ever truly work.

Energy transitions have uneven outcomes in which some parties unequivocally win. Sugar has defined Brazil's political, social, and economic reality since its inception.[30] Government provided such large-scale intervention and unflinching commitment to ethanol to buoy a politically powerful sugar sector linked to a traditional commodity of national importance in Brazil. Private producers in São Paulo such as the Biagis were able to guide government intervention and benefit from unyielding government support for sugar interests. They took risks to build an ethanol empire but with the confidence that Brazilian sugar would always have the support of government officials. Increasing government support further empowered influential private sugar producers to dictate the terms of the sugar market and government support itself throughout much of the twentieth century. When the sugar sector hit hard times, these small groups of wealthy owners continued to get cheaper financing, tax breaks, and other incentives even when their public image was in disrepute.

Similarly, energy transitions burden some parties more than others. Rural workers fought to assert their voices and influence Proálcool's trajectory but over the course of the industry's growth they were persistent losers in the expansion of the sugar sector. Rural residents also lost as government policies and relaxed enforcement favored industry time and again. Despite their efforts, more often than not both rural workers and residents were unable to bring about the change they needed. This should remind us that large-scale industries producing future energy options will, if given the unlimited government support necessary for successful transitions, exploit land and people as they expand. Thus, bottom-up public resistance will be important in demanding government oversight and regulation. While international energy agencies have deemed the Brazilian biofuel a key part of the path forward for a "decarbonized" and "sustainable" future, this history reveals the industry's deep ties to extensive water pollution and labor exploitation.[31] A successful large-scale energy transition will also require that society prepare for and mitigate negative outcomes connected with heavier dependence on a single or multiple fuel sources.

Ethanol and Fossil Fuel Histories

The Brazilian example exposes the ongoing challenges to an energy transition for a society singularly focused on production-side solutions rather than consumption issues. The transportation sector remains the world's largest consumer of fuel and the largest greenhouse gases emitter.[32] Policymakers in Western industrial, historically large fuel-consuming countries have turned their attention to alternative fuel options, assuming that non-fossil fuel energy must be better for the environment, but a historical assessment of this non-fossil fuel's social and environmental impact defies that assumption. As investments in energy alternatives expand to accommodate voracious human energy consumption,[33] comparing ethanol and petroleum's similar historical trajectories warns of the potential costs of expanded green fuel economies in such a fuel transition.

Ethanol's history at times mirrors that of its fossil fuel competitor. Petroleum was first a byproduct of oil used for lighting lamps, just as ethanol was once simply a byproduct of sugarcane with no market value. Petroleum only became a major fuel source as gasoline-powered cars became more popular. The petroleum market, like that of ethanol, also required continued government intervention over the course of the twentieth century. The United States bailed out oil companies in the 1930s due to overproduction.[34] Prices have regularly plummeted with unstable supply and shifting demand. Geopolitics drove the oil crises of the 1970s and 1980s as OPEC used intentional withholding of supply and production to contest American political and military decisions. Today, OPEC+ countries continue to collectively set production levels to ensure price stabilization. Fuel prices are heavily subsidized in the United States, and government support has never been far from the energy sector's side in the twentieth and twenty-first centuries.

Ethanol and petroleum's similarities extend beyond price manipulation. Ethanol's history of extensive environmental pollution and labor exploitation, even if the industry claimed they had been solved, parallels that of petroleum. The systematic dumping of vinasse and the exploitation of rural sugar workers enabled the expansion of the "lean, modern, technological" sugar-ethanol sector that made possible the Usina Santa Elisa's growth.[35] The early petroleum industry's development in Mexico, for example, paints a similarly chilling picture of the lives lost, lands sacrificed, and people displaced in the rise of the oil industry at the beginning of the twentieth century. The rush to exploit the region's oil reserves politicized land and laborers as foreign-owned oil production contaminated the water and air while exploiting a largely migrant Mexican labor force in the early twentieth century.[36] Such devastation in the name of energy production echoes the exploitative realities of Brazil's sugar-ethanol production by the 1980s. Only ethanol's remarketing as a non-carbon-producing fuel allowed an industry once seen as an uncaring polluter to shake its dirty image and transform into a green industry.

However, vinasse waste reveals a more upsetting story of sacrifice linked to alternative energy industries. The fossil fuel and automobile industries were notorious for polluting nearby waterways by the 1940s.[37] Sacrifice zones are typically connected to fossil fuel industries, whether mining, oil extraction, or plastic debris in the ocean, that cover the globe in societies dominated by capitalist accumulation. As the theorist Naomi Klein has asserted, "Fossil fuels require sacrifice zones: they always have."[38] However, from ethanol's lakes of sacrifice to wind turbine areas to solar farms, alternative fuel industries too require sacrificial zones.[39] Ethanol's history of vinasse disposal is another reminder that alternative fuels are not free of environmental costs just because they provide alternatives to fossil fuels.

The whitewashing of ethanol's complicated environmental and social history has enabled Brazilian policymakers to tout their ethanol as a "green energy" in the relatively recent marketing of non-fossil fuel options as environmentally friendly.[40] The industry's historical environmental and social record offers a cautionary tale about what may be left out of the public image of other green industries. If anything, this history debunks the idea that green industries exist. As this book has shown, Brazilian ethanol's green status was deeply political. Ethanol production expanded to service a growing Brazilian car fleet, with little regard for its environmental and social costs. Politicians and businessmen alike promoted the program as environmentally beneficial to an urban population of drivers who would not experience the daily air and water pollution issues the industry inflicted on the countryside. Instead, the focus on air quality improvements in densely populated cities transformed ethanol into the beacon of Brazilian environmental ingenuity of the twenty-first century.[41]

Recounting Brazilian ethanol's history of water pollution reveals the hidden costs associated with green industries today, but its amelioration also provides a story of hope.[42] The industry's history can also be viewed as a story of continued human innovation as two byproducts of destruction were repurposed: vinasse, from liquid waste, was turned into a viable fertilizer and bagasse, from solid waste, was transformed into another electrical energy source through cogeneration.

However, the industry's history of destruction is just as important as its history of improvement. The Brazilian ethanol industry's image as an "advanced fuel with lower carbon emissions" today does not negate the damage done historically to earn that status.[43] Instead, it underscores the pressures necessary to clean up a dirty industry and the possible fruits that such continued pressure can yield. Local actors forced government action to address environmental degradation, and rural labor strikes provided moments of resistance to the labor exploitation at the center of the industry's production nexus. The Brazilian experience illuminates how green policies focused on lower-carbon industries have ignored their impact on lower-income, rural, and minority populations. It also shows how building a consensus around environmental and social issues can be an effective way to demand market changes in the long term.

Was the sugar ethanol industry's development worth it in the end, given its many ups and downs and the considerable costs that accompanied the creation of the industry? In a word, yes. From a purely economic position, the ethanol industry has required some form of government support, whether through incentives and/or marketing, throughout its entire existence. But Brazil managed to do something that no other country has done on a large scale: diversify away from gasoline for a car-dominant society. Active investments by public and private actors alike yielded the most integrated and advanced alternative to gasoline for car fuel in the world. Such rare examples are important for a society at a crossroads in the escalating climate crisis even if such an energy alternative increased car use in the past.

The truth is that whether the industry's creation was worth it is the wrong question; rather, what does Brazil's ethanol history tell us about energy solutions going forward? In the search for answers to the global climate crisis, policymakers have sought and celebrated alternative fuels that allow us to sustain the same levels of energy consumption without using carbon-based fuels as intensely. However, ethanol's history illustrates that large-scale production of non-fossil fuels brings its own environmental and social issues. Consequently, it stresses that alternative fuel production cannot solve the climate and toxic pollution crises alone. Instead, changing consumption practices must be part of, if not central to, a real, long-term energy solution. Otherwise, we will continue to celebrate the industries such as Brazilian ethanol that let us continue down this destructive path of human consumption as we continue to lay waste to our planet.

Still, as the world continues to devour natural resources at unmitigated levels and the need for immediate and drastic reductions in global carbon emissions rises,[44] the road to a non-carbon-based world will likely be paved at least in part with sugar-based ethanol. The infrastructure is already in place, and the fuel's lower carbon emissions easily imprint onto our current carbon-based transportation system. How distant a world without individual car transportation is and what new fuel options may enable full decarbonization will determine how extensive ethanol's role will be in the future. As Lula said in 2009, the "world must become cleaner,"[45] and one thing seems certain: Brazilians will get there driving on ethanol.

Appendix

Table A.1 National Ethanol Production, Ethanol Consumption as a Fuel, and Its Impact on National Petroleum Metrics, 1932–1990

YEAR	Total Ethanol Produced (in millions of liters)	Anhydrous (millions of liters)	Hydrous (millions of liters)	Ethanol delivered for fuel use	Value equivalent to gasoline substituted by alcohol (Cr$)
1930	48.9	—	48.9		
1931	43.8	—	43.8		
1932	63.3	—	63.3		3,328,540
1933	55.1	0.1	55.0		3,030,379
1934	53.3	0.9	52.4	1.0	3,373,715
1935	51.3	5.4	45.9	3.5	5,876,423
1936	65.8	18.5	47.3	15.4	8,519,138
1937	59.1	16.4	42.7	14.6	6,991,279
1938	81.0	31.9	49.1	24.4	11,408,768
1939	96.7	38.2	58.5	33.1	21,539,698
1940	116.5	53.5	63.0	36.3	17,664,608
1941	133.2	76.6	56.6	74.5	45,741,333
1942	147.6	82.2	65.4	62.3	46,588,000
1943	121.5	50.2	71.3	30.8	55,838,519
1944	122.5	41.0	81.5	25.9	40,587,495
1945	108.5	22.8	85.7	12.3	15,284,575
1946	116.6	30.2	86.4	16.7	13,264,193
1947	126.5	50.5	76.0	49.5	39,783,096
1948	154.8	65.4	89.4	62.5	48,588,448
1949	153.7	56.9	98.8	52.6	40,525,302
1950	135.2	18.6	116.6	76.1	6,392,087
1951	168.0	38.0	130.0	23.1	8,568,487
1952	204.0	71.6	132.4	60.7	33,485,470
1953	269.0	137.2	131.8	117.4	71,827,868
AFTER THE CREATION OF PETROBRAS IN 1953					National dependence on foreign oil imports (%)
1954	304.1	163.4	140.7	129.2	65.8
1955	290.3	177.8	112.5	170.0	92.8
1956	241.3	97.4	143.9	86.7	92.3
1957	367.4	214.0	153.4	154.9	79.3
1958	435.3	280.5	154.8	252.0	81.1
1959	480.9	341.5	139.4	295.2	76.6

Table A.1 *Continued*

YEAR	Total Ethanol Produced (in millions of liters)	Anhydrous (millions of liters)	Hydrous (millions of liters)	Ethanol delivered for fuel use	Value equivalent to gasoline substituted by alcohol (Cr$)
1960	476.3	188.6	287.7	228.2	64.0
1961	419.5	181.5	238.0	128.2	58.6
1962	382.6	132.4	250.2	124.0	71.0
1963	387.5	111.2	276.3	56.5	68.4
1964	375.6	62.2	313.4	69.3	69.7
1965	559.1	305.9	253.2	184.7	69.1
1966	674.8	362.0	312.8	365.9	65.1
1967	765.7	432.6	333.1	437.2	58.7
1968	499.2	171.1	328.1	191.3	60.3
1969	459.7	98.4	361.3	31.8	62.9
1970	625.3	233.0	392.3	183.6	67.7
1971	624.7	394.5	230.2	253.8	71.2
1972	684.0	399.3	284.7	391.1	76.5
1973	652.8	319.7	333.1	308.8	80.1
1974	614.9	215.1	399.8	190.2	79.4
1975	580.1	220.3	359.8	162.2	82.5
1976	642.1	272.3	369.8	171.6	77.2
1977	1387.6	1087.9	299.7	639.0	82.9
1978	2359.1	1959.9	399.2	1505.7	84.6
1979	3448.3	2830.0	618.2	2219.1	85.5
1980	3676.1	2171.5	1504.7	2253.1	83.4
1981	4206.7	1347.6	2859.1	1146.1	81.7
1982	5618.2	3527.4	2090.7	2020.0	77.7
1983	*	*	*	*	68.6
1984	*	*	*	*	58.6
1985	*	*	*	*	49.3
1986	*	*	*	*	49.5
1987	*	*	*	*	51.4
1988	*	*	*	*	52.8
1989	*	*	*	*	49.6
1990	*	*	*	*	**45.3**

Sources: Santos, *Política e políticas de uma energia alternativa*, 302, 322; "Uma revolução agrícola e industrial," *Álcool e alcoolquímica* 1, no. 1 (1984): 6; Serviço de Estatística e Cadastro do IAA, *Álcool e Álcool Motor: Produção e Consumo, Safras de 1951/52 e 1952/53* (IAA: Rio de Janeiro, 1954): 13; Biblioteca do Ministerio da Fazenda: Rio de Janeiro; Randall, *The Political Economy of Brazilian Oil*, 13.

* data not available in the same units.

Table A.2 Ethanol Production in Brazil, 1980–2004

Harvest Year	National Total Anhydrous Ethanol Produced	National Total Hydrous Ethanol Produced	National Total Ethanol Produced
1980/1981	2.105	1.601	3.706
1981/1982	1.453	2.787	4.240
1982/1983	3.549	2.274	5.823
1983/1984	2.469	5.395	7.864
1984/1985	2.103	7.089	9.192
1985/1986	3.196	8.633	11.829
1986/1987	2.163	8.342	10.505
1987/1988	1.982	9.476	11.458
1988/1989	1.716	9.928	11.645
1989/1990	1.453	10.468	11.920
1990/1991	1.287	10.229	11.515
1991/1992	1.987	10.735	12.722
1992/1993	2.216	9.513	11.729
1993/1994	2.253	8.770	11.292
1994/1995	2.876	9.876	12.752
1995/1996	3.009	9.602	12.611
1996/1997	4.616	9.779	14.395
1997/1998	5.683	9.732	15.415
1998/1999	5.667	8.209	13.876
1999/2000	6.112	6.871	12.983
2000/2001	5.621	4.971	10.592
2001/2002	6.465	5.071	11.536
2002/2003	7.015	5.608	12.623
2003/2004	8.876	5.861	14.736

Note: Unit: billions (published as 1,000 cubic meters, i.e., 2,105,000,000).

Source: Unicadata, "Histórico de produção e moagem," https://observatoriodacana.com.br/sub.php?menu=producao, accessed October 6, 2021.

Table A.3 The Usina Santa Elisa's Total Ethanol Production Compared with State and National Production, 1976–1985

Harvest	Santa Elisa Ethanol (liters)	Santa Elisa's Share of São Paulo State's Ethanol Production (%)	São Paulo State's Share of National Ethanol Production (%)
1976/1977	8,712,000	1.8	69.8
1977/1978	50,007,713	4.5	74.5
1978/1979	64,181,000	3.5	72.7
1979/1980	71,001,000	2.8	72.7
1980/1981	60,737,000	2.3	70.3
1981/1982	57,263,000	2.0	66.8
1982/1983	84,151,000	2.2	65.5
1983/1984	135,000,000	2.5	68.6
1984/1985	158,004,000	2.6	65.1

Sources: MIC/IAA/DCP, *Brasil: Produção de Álcool, Safra de 1984*/85, Safra de 1983/84, Safra de 1982/83, Safra de 1981/82, Safras 1959–1978, (Divisão de Estatísticas, 1985), BR RJANRIO IY F4.05 Caixa 2668.

Notes

Introduction

1. Robin McKie and Ned Temko, "Could Sugar Cane Save the Planet?" *The Guardian* (September 17, 2006), https://www.theguardian.com/environment/2006/sep/17/energy.transportintheuk, accessed September 27, 2021.
2. Brazilian sugar ethanol produces at least five times more energy per hectare than American corn-based ethanol and palm oil biofuel, which led the US Environmental Protection Agency to name Brazilian sugarcane ethanol an "advanced biofuel." For a comparison of ethanol productivity levels, see Eduardo L. Leão de Sousa and Isaias de Carvalho Macedo, eds., *Ethanol and Bioelectricity: Sugarcane in the Future of the Energy Matrix*, trans. Brian Nicholson (São Paulo: Unica, 2011), 194–220.
3. Ana Ionova and Marcelo Teixeira, "Betting on Ethanol, Brazilian Mills Turn Sour on Sugar," *Reuters.com* (December 3, 2018), https://www.reuters.com/article/us-brazil-ethanol-insight-idUSKBN1O20L7, accessed September 27, 2021. In the US, George Bush originally initiated ethanol mandates in 2007, which subsequent presidents Barack Obama and, reluctantly, Donald Trump have upheld. See Ellen R. Wald, "Trump's New Ethanol Rule Explained (And What It Means for Gasoline)," *Forbes Magazine* (October 9, 2018), https://www.forbes.com/sites/ellenrwald/2018/10/09/trumps-new-ethanol-rule-wont-change-your-gasoline/?sh=286e997d7d96, accessed September 27, 2021.
4. Anfavea, *Anuário da Indústria Automobilística Brasileira* (São Paulo: Anfavea, 2015), 59.
5. Jennifer Eaglin, "The Demise of the Brazilian Ethanol Program: Environmental and Economic Shocks, 1985–1990," *Environmental History* 24 (2019): 104–129.
6. Ionova and Teixeira, "Betting on Ethanol, Brazilian Mills Turn Sour on Sugar."
7. Northeastern ethanol development differed greatly from the experience in São Paulo. On the Northeast's diverging sugar and ethanol industry, see Pedro Ramos, *Agroindústria canavieira e propriedade fundiária no Brasil* (São Paulo: Editora Hucitec, 1999); Tamás Szmrecsányi, *O planejamento da agroindústria canavieira do Brasil 1930/1975* (São Paulo: Editora Hucitec, 1979); Barbara Nunberg, "State Intervention in the Sugar Sector in Brazil: A Study of the Institute of Sugar and Alcohol," (Ph.D. diss., Stanford University, 1979); Amanda Hartzmark, "Businesses, Associations, and Regions in the Brazilian Sugar Industry, 1920–1990," (Ph.D. diss., University of Chicago, 2014).
8. Jorge Licurci, "Os náufragos do 'mar de cana,'" *Revista Globo Rural* 1, no. 9 (1986): 68–69. President Luiz Inácio Lula da Silva would later echo this terminology. See Clemens Höges, "The High Price of Clean, Cheap Ethanol," *Der Spiegel* (January 22, 2009).

9. This builds on some existing histories of ethanol and the Biagi family. Margarida Cintra Gordinho, *Do álcool ao etanol: Trajetória única* (São Paulo: Terceiro Nome, 2010); Geraldo Hasse, *Maurilio Biagi: O semeador do sertão* (Ribeirão Preto, SP: Editora Ceu e Terra, 2003); Geraldo Hasse, *Filhos do fogo: Memória industrial de Sertãozinho, 1896–1996* (Ribeirão Preto, SP: Editora Ceu e Terra, 1996).
10. Daniel Gallas, "Brazil's Biofuel Industry Finds New Sweetspot," *BBC News* (June 23, 2015), https://www.bbc.co.uk/news/business-33114119, accessed September 28, 2021.
11. Stuart Schwartz, *Sugar Plantations in the Formation of Brazilian Society: Reconcavo, Bahia, 1550–1835* (Cambridge: Cambridge University Press, 1985), 106.
12. Szmrecsányi, *O planejamento*, 41–53.
13. Hal Bernton, William Kovarik, and Scott Sklar, *The Forbidden Fuel: A History of Power Alcohol* (Lincoln, NE: University of Nebraska Press, 2010), 3–4.
14. Gilberto Freyre, *Nordeste: Aspectos da influencia da cana sobre a vida e a paisagem do nordeste do Brasil* (Rio de Janeiro: J. Olympio Editora, 1937).
15. Schwartz, *Sugar Plantations in the Formation of Brazilian Society.*
16. Peter L. Eisenberg, *The Sugar Industry in Pernambuco: Modernization without Change, 1840–1910* (Berkeley, CA: University of California Press, 1974), 48.
17. Warren Dean, *With Broadax and Firebrand: The Destruction of the Brazilian Atlantic Forest* (Los Angeles, CA: University of California Press, 1995); Hasse, *Filhos do fogo*, 25. The red soil is found in only three places in the country: northeast São Paulo, northeast Paraná, and northern Tocatins.
18. Governo do Estado de São Paulo, *Estudo do macrozoneamento das bacias do rios Mogi Guaçu, Pardo, e Médio-Grande* (São Paulo: SMA/SAA/SEP, 1995), 17; João Garcia, "Aventuras de um rio teimoso," *Globo Rural* (October 1987), 33.
19. Steven Topik, *The Political Economy of the Brazilian State, 1889–1930* (Austin, TX: University of Texas Press, 1987), 89–92.
20. Eve Buckley, *Technocrats and the Politics of Drought and Development in Twentieth-Century Brazil* (Chapel Hill, NC: University of North Carolina Press 2017); Barbara Weinstein, *The Color of Modernity: São Paulo and the Making of Race and Nation in Brazil* (Durham, NC: Duke University Press, 2015).
21. Joseph L. Love, *São Paulo in the Brazilian Federation, 1889–1937* (Stanford, CA: Stanford University Press, 1980), ch. 8.
22. Eisenberg, *The Sugar Industry in Pernambuco*, 26–29.
23. Murilo Pinheiro, ed., *Ribeirão Preto* (Ribeirão Preto: MIC Editorial Ltda, 1995), 20; Ida Pizzoli Marchesi, *João Marchesi: História de um imigrante* (Ribeirão Preto: Editora Colégio, 1987), 59–60; Hasse, *Filhos do fogo*, 33–37. See also Hartzmark, "Businesses, Associations, and Regions," 231–232; Ramos, *Agroindústria canavieira*, 100.
24. Moacyr Castro, "Pedro Biagi," in *Os desbravadores*, ed. Galeno Amorim (Ribeirão Preto: Palavra Mágica, 2001), 128–129.
25. Castro, "Pedro Biagi," 128–129.
26. Historians of the Brazilian ethanol industry must also be historians of the Brazilian sugar industry because both agricultural and industrial aspects have shaped its trajectory. Yet studies often disaggregate the two. See Michael Barzelay, *The*

Politicized Market Economy: Alcohol in Brazil's Energy Strategy (Los Angeles, CA: University of California Press, 1986); F. Joseph Demetrius, *Brazil's National Alcohol Program: Technology and Development in an Authoritarian Regime* (New York: Praeger, 1990); Maria Helena de Castro Santos, *Política e políticas de uma energia alternativa: O caso do Proálcool* (Rio de Janeiro: Notrya, 1993); Márcia Azanha Ferraz Dias de Moraes and David Zilberman, *Production of Ethanol from Sugarcane in Brazil: From State Intervention to a Free Market* (New York: Springer, 2014).

27. Summarized by Antoine Acker, *Volkswagen in the Amazon: The Tragedy of Global Development in Modern Brazil* (Cambridge: Cambridge University Press, 2017), 5. See also Arturo Escobar, *Encountering Development: The Making and Unmaking of the Third World* (Princeton, NJ: Princeton University Press, 1995), 3–4.
28. For an overview, see Rafael Ioris, *Transforming Brazil: A History of National Development in Postwar Brazil* (New York: Routledge 2014); Joseph Love, *Crafting the Third World: Theorizing Underdevelopment in Rumania and Brazil* (Stanford, CA: Stanford University Press, 1996), ch. 10.
29. See, for example, Raúl Prebisch, *The Economic Development of Latin America and Its Principal Problems* (Lake Success, NY: United Nations Department of Economic Affairs, 1950).
30. Fernando Henrique Cardoso and Enzo Faletto, *Dependency and Development in Latin America* (Berkeley, CA: University of California Press, 1979); Peter Evans, *Dependent Development: The Alliance of Multinational, State, and Local Capital in Brazil* (Princeton, NJ: Princeton University Press, 1979).
31. Stephen Haber, ed., *How Latin America Fell Behind: Essays on the Economic Histories of Brazil and Mexico* (Stanford, CA: Stanford University Press, 1997).
32. On neo-institutionalism, see Gail Triner, *Mining and the State in Brazilian Development* (London: Pickering & Chatto, 2011).
33. Buckley, *Technocrats and the Politics of Drought*, 132.
34. Triner, *Mining and the State*, 80.
35. Evans, *Dependent Development*.
36. Hartzmark, "Businesses, Associations, and Regions."
37. Government officials did this without transforming the industry into a state owned enterprise, which contravened other state-led development efforts of the era. On comparative state owned enterprises, see Triner, *Mining and the State*, 5.
38. Peter Evans famously argued that foreign capital through multinational companies combined with private enterprises and government intervention to form a particular model of Brazilian development called the "tri-pé," or Triple Alliance. More recently, Marshall Eakin expanded that formation to a quadruple alliance, specifically adding an *absence* of technological innovation to Brazilian development efforts. See Evans, *Dependent Development*; Marshall Eakin, *Tropical Capitalism: The Industrialization of Belo Horizonte, Brazil* (New York: Palgrave, 2001), 3.
39. F. Joseph Demetrius similarly argues that the selection of certain technologies drove the program and that domestic innovation was an important factor in these decisions but exclusively focuses on car technology developed during the program. See Demetrius, *Brazil's National Alcohol Program*, 2–4.

40. João Batista Olivi, "CTA ditará padrões para motor a álcool," *ESP* (April 27, 1979), 30. Bernton, Kovarik, and Sklar, *The Forbidden Fuel*, 145–154. Antoine Acker highlighted how Volkswagen successfully linked its achievements to Brazilian national rhetoric thus the ethanol car could be seen as even more Brazilian because of Volkswagen's own "Brazilianization" during the dictatorship. See Acker, *Volkswagen in the Amazon*, 46–49.
41. See Jennifer Eaglin, "'More Brazilian than Cachaça': The Development of the Brazilian Sugar-Based Ethanol Industry," *Latin American Research Review* 54, no. 4 (2019): 927–943. On the automobile's importance in Brazilian development and ideas of modernity, see Shawn William Miller, *The Street Is Ours: Community, the Car and the Nature of Public Space in Rio de Janeiro*. (New York: Cambridge University Press, 2018); Joel Wolfe, *Autos and Progress: The Brazilian Search for Modernity* (Oxford: Oxford University Press, 2010); Brian Owensby, *Intimate Ironies: Modernity and the Making of Middle-Class Lives in Brazil* (Stanford, CA: Stanford University Press, 2002).
42. In Latin American studies, limited examples include Fernando Coronil, *The Magical State: Nature, Money, and Modernity in Venezuela* (Chicago, IL: University of Chicago Press, 1997); Myrna Santiago, *Ecology of Oil: Environment, Labor, and the Mexican Revolution, 1900–1938* (Cambridge: Cambridge University Press, 2010). Eurocentric recent energy humanities studies include Timothy Mitchell, *Carbon Democracy: Political Power in the Age of Oil* (London: Verso, 2011); Christopher Jones, *Routes of Power: Energy and Modern America* (Cambridge, MA: Harvard University Press, 2014); Andreas Malm, *Fossil Capital: The Rise of Steam Power and the Roots of Global Warming* (London: Verso, 2016).
43. For example, Dean, *With Broadax and Firebrand*; Reinaldo Funes Monzote, *From Rainforest to Canefield: An Environmental History Since 1492* (Raleigh, NC: University of North Carolina Press, 2008).
44. There is a growing literature historicizing green industries. See, for example, Alexis Madrigal, *Powering the Dream: The History and Promise of Green Technology* (Cambridge, MA: Da Capo, 2011). See also Jennifer Eaglin, "Fuel in the Age of the Great Acceleration," in *A Cultural History of the Environmental*, ed. Jessica van Horssen (London: Bloomsbury, forthcoming).
45. Ricardo Bueno, *Pró-Álcool: Rumo ao desastre* (Petrópolis, RJ: Editora Vozes Ltda, 1980).
46. Freyre, *Nordeste*; See also Regina Horta Duarte, "Nature and Historiography in Brazil, 1937–1945," *Iberoamericana* 3, no. 10 (2003): 23–36.
47. José Augusto Pádua, "Natureza e projeto nacional: As origens da ecologia política no Brasil," in *Ecologia e política no Brasil*, ed. José Augusto Pádua (Rio de Janeiro: Espaço e Tempo, 1987), 11–59; Dean, *With Broadax and Firebrand*; Shawn William Miller, *Fruitless Trees: Portuguese Conservation and Brazil's Colonial Timber* (Palo Alto, CA: Stanford University Press, 2000).
48. Kathryn Hochstetler and Margaret Keck, *Greening Brazil: Environmental Activism in State and Society* (Durham, NC: Duke University Press, 2007).
49. James Scott, *Seeing like a State: How Certain Schemes to Improve the Human Condition Have Failed* (New Haven, CT: Yale University Press, 1998).

50. History of technology scholars have long debated whether technology influences society or society influences technology. On the broader history of technology debates on energy, see Jones, *Routes of Power*, 8; Gabrielle Hecht, *The Radiance of France: Nuclear Power and National Identity after World War II* (Cambridge, MA: MIT Press, 2000 [2009]), 8–9.
51. IAA, *Anuário Açucareiro: Safras de 1960/61–1965/66* (Rio de Janeiro: IAA, 1967), 4; Câmara dos Deputados, "Relatório da subcomissão especial para exame da situação do setor sucroalcooleiro brasileiro" Brasília, DF (June 1991), 46. Arquivo Público e Histórico de Ribeirão Preto (APHRP) Caixa 193.
52. On ethanol and the economic crisis, see Eaglin, "The Demise of the Brazilian Ethanol Program."
53. "Collor manda estudar extinção do Proálcool" *ESP* (March 8, 1990), 55.
54. For example, György Miklós Böhm, "O álcool combustível e a saúde da população," Edição Associação das Indústrias de Açúcar e de Álcool do Estado de São Paulo (AIAA), no. 3 (August 1991). See also Ogenis Magno Brilhante, "Brazil's Alcohol Program: From an Attempt to Reduce Oil Dependence in the Seventies to the Green Arguments of the Nineties," *Journal of Environmental Planning & Management* 40, no. 4 (1997): 435–449.
55. Lester R. Brown, Christopher Flavin, and Colin Norman, *The Future of the Automobile in an Oil-Short World*, Worldwatch Paper 32 (Washington DC: Worldwatch Institute, 1979); and Lester Brown, *Food or Fuel: New Competition for the World's Cropland*, Worldwatch Paper 35 (Washington DC: Worldwatch Institute, 1980).
56. Anthony W. Pereira, *The End of the Peasantry: The Rural Labor Movement in Northeast Brazil, 1961–1988* (Pittsburgh, PA: University of Pittsburgh Press, 1997); Clifford Andrew Welch, *A semente foi plantada: As raízes paulistas do movimento sindical camponês no Brasil, 1924–1964* (São Paulo: Editora Expressão Popular, 2010); Thomas Rogers, *The Deepest Wounds: A Labor and Environmental History of Sugar in Northeast Brazil* (Chapel Hill, NC: University of North Carolina Press, 2010); Adriano Pereira Santos, *A usinagem do capital e o desmonte do trabalho: Reestruturação produtiva nos anos de 1990, o caso da Zanini S/A de Sertãozinho-SP* (São Paulo: Editora Expressão Popular, 2010).
57. See, for example, Barzelay, *The Politicized Market Economy*; Demetrius, *Brazil's National Alcohol Program*.
58. Maria Conceição D'Incao e Mello, *O bóia-fria: acumulação e miséria* (Petrópolis, RJ: Editora Vozes, 1975); Maria Aparecida de Moraes Silva, *Errantes do fim do século* (São Paulo: Fundação Editora da UNESP, 1999); Welch, *A semente foi plantada*.
59. Angus Wright and Wendy Wolford, *To Inherit the Earth: The Landless Movement and the Struggle for a New Brazil* (Oakland, CA: Food First Books, 2003).
60. Classic studies include John French, *The Brazilian Workers' ABC: Class Conflict and Alliances in Modern São Paulo* (Chapel Hill, NC: University of North Carolina Press, 1992); Joel Wolfe, *Working Women, Working Men: São Paulo and the Rise of Brazil's Industrial Working Class, 1900–1955* (Durham, NC: Duke University, 1993); Barbara Weinstein, *For Social Peace in Brazil: Industrialists and the Remaking of the Working Class in São Paulo, 1920–1964* (Chapel Hill, NC: University of North Carolina Press,

1996). More recent studies on citizenship still focus on urban dwellers. See Brodwyn Fischer, *A Poverty of Rights: Citizenship and Inequality in Twentieth-Century Rio de Janeiro* (Stanford, CA: Stanford University Press, 2008); James Holston, *Insurgent Citizenship: Disjunctions of Democracy and Modernity in Brazil* (Princeton, NJ: Princeton University Press, 2009).

61. Kathryn Sikkink and Margaret E. Keck, *Activists beyond Borders: Advocacy Networks in International Politics* (Ithaca, NY: Cornell University Press, 1998); Hochstetler and Keck, *Greening Brazil*; Seth Garfield, *A luta indígena no curação do Brasil: Politica indigenista, a marcha para o oeste e os índios xavante (1937–1988)* (São Paulo: UNESP, 2011).
62. On local influence on non-Western state-led development programs, see Scott, *Seeing like a State*. By linking the ethanol industry to broader social and environmental concerns, this book joins a limited few scholars addressing the costs and benefits of Brazilian sugar-ethanol development. See, for example, Renata Marson Teixeira de Andrade and Andrew Miccolis, "The Expansion of Sugarcane Ethanol in Brazil and Controversies Surrounding Human Rights," in *Controversies in Science and Technology: From Evolution to Energy Vol. 3*, ed. Daniel Lee Kleinman, Jason A. Delborne, Karen A. Cloud-Hansen, and Jo Handelsman (New Rochelle, NY: Mary Ann Liebert Inc., 2010), 214–228; Kate B. Showers, "Biofuels' Unbalanced Equations: Misleading Statistics, Networked Knowledge and Measured Parameters," *International Review of Environmental History* 5, no. 1 (2019): 61–83.

Chapter 1

1. Hasse, *Maurilio Biagi*, 189.
2. Triner, *Mining and the State*, 80.
3. Topik, *The Political Economy of the Brazilian State*, 70–81. The state and federal government would continue the program on and off through the 1910s and 1920s.
4. Topik, *The Political Economy of the Brazilian State*, 71.
5. Triner, *Mining and the State*, 80. Triner's examination of state economic planning in the mining industry during the Vargas era reveals notable similarities.
6. Joel Wolfe, "Change with Continuity: Brazil from 1930–1945," *The Great Depression in Latin America*, ed. Paulo Drinot and Alan Knight (Durham, NC: Duke University Press, 2014), 81.
7. Szmercsányi, *O planejamento*, 172.
8. Szmrecsányi, *O planejamento*, 172.
9. Szmrecsányi, *O planejamento*, 174, n. 22.
10. "O Banco do Brasil e seu novo presidente," *Brasil Açucareiro* 3, no. 5 (1934): 300.
11. Steven Topik, "State Enterprise in a Liberal Regime: The Bank of Brazil, 1905–1930," *Journal of Interamerican Studies and World Affairs* 22, no. 4, Special Issue: Public Enterprise in Latin America (1980): 408–413. More recent studies have unveiled a far more interventionist role taken by the state and the Bank of Brazil during the

First Republic beyond just coffee support. See Gail D. Triner, *Banking and Economic Development: Brazil, 1889–1930* (New York: Palgrave, 2000), 8–9.

12. Peter Houtzager argues that the Bank of Brazil "as the principal conduit for credit became the state's arm for capital accumulation in rural areas." See Peter Houtzager, "State and Unions in the Transformation of the Brazilian Countryside, 1964–1975," *Latin American Research Review* 33, no. 2 (1998): 115.
13. Cf. "Nosso Programa", Economia e Agricultura 1, no. 1 (1932): 1–2 , cited in Szmrecsányi, *O planejamento*, 174, nn. 22–23. Also note that the magazine *Economia e Agricultura* became *Brasil Açucareiro* in 1934.
14. Thomas Walker, "From Coronelismo to Populism: The Evolution of Politics in a Brazilian Municipality, Ribeirão Preto, São Paulo, 1910–1960" (Ph.D. diss., University of New Mexico, 1974), 28–30; Love, *São Paulo in the Brazilian Federation*, 119. In an effort to centralize his own power, Vargas handpicked caretaker governors (interventors) rather than electing governors to govern state politics. That a northeasterner would hold such a position in São Paulo would exacerbate already established racial and social divisions between formalizing ideas of paulista identity in contrast to northeastern identity. See also Weinstein, *The Color of Modernity*.
15. Thomas Skidmore, *Politics in Brazil, 1930–1964: An Experiment in Democracy* (New York: Oxford University Press, 1967), 12–21; Wolfe, "Change with Continuity," 86.
16. Comissão de Defesa da Produção do Açúcar 1932 Report, sent December 8, 1932 to the Labor, Industry, and Commerce Minister. BR RJANRIO IY Caixa 458.
17. The question of oil rather than alcohol for combustion engines was more political than technical. Bill Kovarik argues that petroleum interests were able to edge out the ethanol market in favor of oil using biased scientific reports. See Bill Kovarik, "Henry Ford, Charles Kettering and the Fuel of the Future," *Automotive History Review* 32 (1998): 7–27; Maria Helena de Castro Santos, "Alcohol as Fuel in Brazil: An Energy Policy Analysis," (Ph.D. diss., Massachusetts Institute of Technology, 1984), 18–21.
18. Regina Machado Leão, *Álcool: Energia verde* (São Paulo: IQUAL, 2002), 89–90. Sabino de Oliveira later published this work in 1930. See Eduardo Sabino de Oliveira, *Álcool motor e motores a explosão* (Rio de Janeiro: Ministério do trabalho, indústria, e comercio, Instituto de tecnologia, 1937).
19. Santos, "Alcohol as Fuel in Brazil," 33.
20. Joaquim de Melo, *A política do álcool-motor no Brasil* (Rio de Janeiro: Instituto de Açúcar e do Álcool, 1942), 25–26.
21. On automobile ownership, see Wolfe, *Autos and Progress*, 14.
22. Presidential message of 1922 to Congress, President Epitácio Pessoa in Almir de Andrade, *Contribuição à História Administrativa do Brasil* vol. I (Rio de Janeiro: Livraria José Olympio Ed., 1952), 94.
23. "Fontes de energia," *ESP* (January 21, 1927), 3; Nelson Coutinho, "Economia e Indústria Álcooleiras (III)," *Brasil Açucareiro* 26, no. 3 (1958): 182 , quoted in Santos, "Alcohol as Fuel in Brazil," 39; Szmrecsányi, *O planejamento*, 178.
24. Coffee prices fell to a third of their average price from 1925 to 1929; foreign capital investment also dried up by 1932. By 1931, the country had an external debt of over

US$1.3 billion. See Werner Baer, *The Brazilian Economy: Growth and Development* 7th edn (Boulder, CO: Lynne Rienner, 2008), 37; Marcelo de Paiva Abreu, ed., *A ordem do progresso: Cem anos de política econômica republicana, 1899–1989* (Rio de Janeiro: Campus, 1989), 399.

25. Moacyr Soares Pereira, *O problema do álcool-motor* (Rio de Janeiro: Livraria José Olympio Editora, 1942), 6.
26. De Melo, *A política do álcool-motor no Brasil*, 22. Probably the most popular early commercial alcohol mixtures were the USGA and Azulina brands, produced in Alagoas and Pernambuco, respectively, from 1928. In São Paulo, the most popular brand was Cruzeiro do Sul.
27. Santos, "Alcohol as Fuel in Brazil," 56–58.
28. Pereira, *O problema do álcool-motor*, 8–9.
29. Santos, "Alcohol as Fuel in Brazil," 57, n. 22, citing Pereira, *O problema do álcool-motor*, 11–12.
30. De Melo, *A política do álcool-motor no Brasil*, 21; Santos, "Alcohol as Fuel in Brazil," 58–59.
31. Szmrecsányi, *O planejamento*, 172.
32. Santos, "Alcohol as Fuel in Brazil," 64.
33. Pereira, *O problema do álcool-motor*, 21.
34. These autarkies, including those for coffee and cotton, reflect Vargas's protectionist policies, which were part of his broader policy of *dirigismo econômico*, which dominated Brazilian industrialization policies in the 1940s and 1950s. See Nunberg, "State Intervention," 13–18; Love, *Crafting the Third World*, 147. Amanda Hartzmark provides an interesting analysis of the power of the IAA compared to other autarkies in the period. See Hartzmark, "Businesses, Associations, and Regions," 59–61.
35. Szmrecsányi, *O planejamento*, 180–185.
36. Hartzmark, "Businesses, Associations, and Regions," 67.
37. Léo da Rocha Lima and Aluizio de Abreu Marcondes, *Álcool carburante: Uma estratégia brasileira* (Curitiba: Editora UFPR, 2002), 48–49. The IAA set the selling price of anhydrous alcohol delivered to gasoline distributors while the National Petroleum Council (CNP) adjusted alcohol mixture prices on the basis of the IAA's pricing as stipulated in Decree no. 22,799 of 1933. See Santos, "Alcohol as Fuel in Brazil," 129, 149–150.
38. Pereira. *O problema do álcool-motor*, 16; Márcia Azanha Ferraz Dias de Moraes, *A desregulamentação do setor sucroalcooleiro do Brasil* (Americana, SP: Caminho Editorial, 2000), 50–53.
39. Gercino de Pontes, " A indústria no Brasil, depois de 1928–1929," *Brasil Açucareiro* 6, no. 1 (1935): 21. Economically speaking, "dumping" meant selling underpriced products on the world market to manipulate global prices. The IAA approved dumping some sugar on the world market to reduce stocks for northeastern producers by selling under the regulated price in order to manipulate and stabilize prices on the domestic market.
40. Santos, "Alcohol as Fuel in Brazil," 67, citing Pereira, *O problema do álcool-motor*, 18.

41. De Melo, *A política do álcool-motor no Brasil*, 69.
42. According to de Melo, Pernambuco, Paraiba, Rio Grande do Norte, Alagoas, and Sergipe exceeded the mandate with 40% alcohol and 60% gasoline. Alcohol-motor still failed to reach mandated distribution and consumption in certain areas of the country, including the interior of São Paulo. See de Melo, *A política do álcool-motor no Brasil*, 69.
43. De Melo, *A política do álcool-motor no Brasil*, 73.
44. De Melo, *A política do álcool-motor no Brasil*, 42–45.
45. "Gazolina Rosada," *A Gazeta* (July 29, 1936), as republished in *Brasil Açucareiro* 7, no. 6 (1936): 402.
46. "Gazolina Rosada," *A Gazeta* (July 29, 1936), as republished in *Brasil Açucareiro* 7, no. 6 (1936): 402. Composed of 90% gasoline and 10% anhydrous alcohol, "gazolina rosada" was the commercialized name of the first official alcohol-motor mixture. See de Melo, *A política do álcool-motor no Brasil*, 46.
47. De Melo, *A política do álcool-motor no Brasil*, 30, citing Decree no. 22.789 of June 1, 1933.
48. De Melo, *A política do álcool-motor no Brasil*, 50–53; Santos, "Alcohol as Fuel in Brazil," 75, n. 36. The six initial distilleries that received 50% of the funding from the IAA for installation were the Distillaria dos Productores de Pernambuco (Azulina), the Distillaria dos Productores de Pernambuco (nova), Usina Catende, Central Barreiros, Distillaria de Alagoas, and the Cia Industrial Paulista S.A. The first four were located in Pernambuco. The last was a São Paulo distribution company, which worked in association with the IAA. A third IAA-owned and operated distillery, located in Alagoas, opened in 1960.
49. Leonardo Truda, "A victoria do alcool motor," *Brasil Açucareiro* 10, no. 2 (1937): 94–104; "Associação dos Usineiros de São Paulo," *Brasil Açucareiro* 10, no. 1: 73. See also, de Melo, *A política de álcool-motor no Brasil*.
50. Leonardo Truda, *A defesa da produção açucareira* (Rio de Janeiro: IAA, 1971), 50.
51. Truda, *A defesa da produção açucareira*, 77.
52. For example, Celso Furtado, *A operação nordeste* (Rio de Janeiro: Ministério da Educação e Cultura, Instituto Superior de Estudos Brasileiros, 1959); Caio Prado Junior, *História econômica do Brasil* (São Paulo: Brasiliense, 1967); Celso Furtado, *Formação econômica do Brasil* (São Paulo: Companhia das Letras, 2006). See, more recently, Weinstein, *The Color of Modernity*, 2–5; Buckley, *Technocrats and the Politics of Drought and Development in Twentieth-Century Brazil*.
53. Szmrecsányi, *O planejamento*, 172.
54. Dean, *With Broadax and Firebrand*, 173–176; Shawn William Miller, *An Environmental History of Latin America* (Cambridge: Cambridge University Press, 2000), 79–87. On cane varieties and conditions for growing, see Richard Tucker, *Insatiable Appetite: The United States and the Ecological Degradation of the Tropical World* (Berkeley, CA: University of California Press, 2000), 18–19.
55. A similar shift from coffee to sugar production occurred in the Caribbean in the nineteenth century because hurricanes threatened the long-term investment prospects for

coffee compared with those for sugarcane, whose roots could better survive storms and whose short time frame from planting to yield provided better economic stability. See Stuart Schwartz, *Sea of Storms: A History of Hurricanes in the Greater Caribbean from Columbus to Katrina* (Princeton, NJ: Princeton University Press, 2015), 73.

56. Gileno Dé Carli, "Geografia econômica e social da canna de açúcar no Brasil," *Brasil Açucareiro* 10, no. 5 (1938): 391.
57. The firm owned five usinas altogether, namely, the Villa Rafard, Porto Feliz, and Piracicaba usinas in São Paulo and the two in Rio de Janeiro. ."Notas e Comentarias," *Brasil Açucareiro* 3, no. 4 (1934): 239; de Melo, *A política do álcool-motor no Brasil*, annex.
58. Castro, "Pedro Biagi," 129. The Biagis' cousin, João Marchesi, founded the Santa Elisa engenho and named it after his deceased daughter. This is the mill that the Biagi brothers would then purchase in 1936 and transform into an usina.
59. Ramos, *Agroindústria canavieira*, 86–89, 100. Hartzmark, "Businesses, Associations, and Regions," 231–232.
60. De Melo, *A política do álcool-motor no Brasil*, 49–53.
61. C. Boucher, "Algumas deducções tiradas das estatisticas publicadas no 'annuario açucareiro,'" *Brasil Açucareiro* 6, no. 1(1935), 15–18.
62. Leonardo Truda, "A Victoria do Álcool," *Brasil Açucareiro* 10, no. 2 (1937): 93–105.
63. Hasse, *Filhos do fogo*, 90. The Usina Santa Elisa's first harvest produced 18,781 sacks of sugar.
64. "Á Nação," *Brasil Açucareiro* 10, no 3 (1937): 175.
65. Ramos, *Agroindústria canavieira*, 107.
66. Ramos, *Agroindústria canavieira*, 108–109. São Paulo production grew by 132% (11% per year) between 1932 and 1940, while it grew by an annual rate of 7.2% between 1940 and 1944.
67. Santos, "Alcohol as Fuel in Brazil," 112–123. See Table 1 in the Appendix for overall alcohol production from 1930 to 1982. See also Dias de Moraes, *A desregulamentação*, 49.
68. Wolfe, *Autos and Progress*, 107.
69. Santos, "Alcohol as Fuel in Brazil," 113.
70. Decree no 3.755 was issued on October 24, 1941. The IAA reported on the first meeting of the commission in the December 1941 issue of *Brasil Açucareiro*.
71. Skidmore, *Politics in Brazil, 1930–1964*, 48–54.
72. Skidmore, *Politics in Brazil, 1930–1964*, 69.
73. The IAA's monthly magazine republished numerous articles and excerpts from the *Correia de Manhã*, *Diário Carioca*, and other newspapers to rebut their claims in the January and February 1946 editions amongst others.
74. "Em defesa do Instituto do Açúcar e do Álcool," *Brasil Açucareiro* 27, no. 4 (1946): 336–40.
75. Szmrecsányi, *O planejamento*, 213, n. 84. For more on the heated battle to end the IAA, paulista producers' role in the battle, and the IAA's defense, see Santos, "Alcohol as Fuel in Brazil," 125–126.
76. Szmrecsányi, *O planejamento*, 214.

77. On the divergence of the southern and northeastern sugar industries, see Ramos, *Agroindústria canavieira*, 115–139; Hartzmark, "Businesses, Associations, and Regions," chs 3 and 5.
78. Dias de Moraes, *A desregulamentação*, 50–51; Ramos, 138.
79. IAA, *Anuário Açucareiro* 16 (Rio de Janeiro: IAA, 1950–1), 74. Over 90% of the 1950/1951 harvest's alcohol was hydrated rather than anhydrous.
80. "Editais do IAA", *Brasil Açucareiro* 27, no. 1 (1946): 36.
81. Szmrecsányi, *O planejamento*, 221.
82. Santos, "Alcohol as Fuel in Brazil," 130. Lower-grade alcohol from reprocessing had lower prices.
83. Hasse, *Filhos do Fogo*, 69–70, 102–105; Marchesi, *João Marchesi*, 22.
84. Hasse, *Maurilio Biagi*, 185–186, 190; Hasse, *Filhos do fogo*, 94–95; "Assim nasceu Santa Elisa," *A Revista Santa Elisa: Uma Historia de Trabalho e Desenvolvimento*, Isabel de Farias (directora) (Ribeirão Preto: MIC Editorial Ltda, 1996), 15; Santa Elisa Proálcool II Application, November 13, 1980. BR RJANRIO IY Caixa 1.978, código 211.2.
85. José Rubens da Silva, "Assim nasceu a Santa Elisa," 15.
86. Hasse, *Maurilio Biagi*, 183.
87. Hasse, *Maurilio Biagi*, 182–194. Eventually the youngest sibling, Oswaldo Biagi, became the president of Solorrico.
88. Adelino Deícola dos Santos, "Modernização da lavoura canavieira," *Brasil Açucareiro* 25, no. 6 (1945): 61; Jaime Rochas de Almeida, "Canas queimadas," *Brasil Açucareiro* 27, no. 1 (1946): 51. For more on cane burning and the harvest, see Rogers, *The Deepest Wounds*, 142–155.
89. Hasse, *Filhos do fogo*, 111–114.
90. Hasse, *Filhos do fogo*, 146.
91. Hasse, *Filhos do fogo*, 150–152. As the historian Geraldo Hasse described it, the Usina Santa Elisa and Zanini would have a somewhat symbiotic relationship, in which the two grew together. The usina served as a test site for Zanini products during the usina's development and the company's growth. Although majority ownership changed hands early in the first decade of Zanini's existence, Biagi would remain the guiding force behind the company's growth in the 1950s.
92. This strategy included using interpersonal and familial connections to consolidate holdings. This is consistent with other sugar producers in the region according to Amanda Hartzmark and occurred in textile and pharmaceutical industries as well according to Peter Evans. See Hartzmark, "Businesses, Associations, and Regions," 232; Evans, *Dependent Development*, 281.
93. Skidmore, *Politics in Brazil, 1930–1964*, 70.
94. Ioris, *Transforming Brazil*, 30–33; Triner, *Mining and the State*, 108–109; Love, *Crafting the Third World*, 120–121; Skidmore, *Politics in Brazil, 1930–1964*, 86–89.
95. Vargas supported the populist campaign, "O petróleo é nosso," on his return to power with his promise to nationalize domestic oil exploration and refining, which led to the founding of the Brazilian National Oil Company, Petrobras in 1953. See Maria Augusta Tibiriça Miranda, *O petróleo é nosso: A luta contra o "entreguismo" pelo*

monopólio estatal, 1947–1953 (Petrópolis: Vozes, 1983); John Wirth, *The Politics of Brazilian Development, 1930–1954* (Stanford, CA: Stanford University Press, 1970), chs 8 and 9.

96. Triner, *Mining and the State*, 115. Classic analysis has focused on Petrobras and petroleum as the key strategic industry developed under Vargas's economic nationalist agenda, but this work contributes to newer studies that have revealed the farther-reaching influence of Vargas's state-led intervention into not only agro-industrial planning, but also the creation of the iron ore and steel state-owned industries for example. For classic interpretations, see Skidmore, *Politics in Brazil*. For newer analyses of other state-led development projects, see Triner, *Mining and the State*, ch. 7.
97. Wolfe, *Autos and Progress*, 115.
98. Wolfe, *Autos and Progress*, 137.
99. Wolfe, *Autos and Progress*, 119–121 and 234, n. 63. Wolfe's own dismissal of the important role ethanol played in the Brazilian energy matrix prior to the 1950s highlights the detrimental effect the obsession with oil and industrialization in the 1950s had on ethanol's place in the national economy as an oil supplement and substitute. After citing the IAA's creation in the 1940s rather than the 1930s, he claims that the gasogene alternative had a far greater impact on the national energy economy while ethanol production only "slightly diminished fuel shortages" in the war era. He makes no other mention of the ethanol mixture before the oil crisis of 1973.
100. Brazil relied on foreign oil for 92.8% of its oil in 1955. This percentage fell to as low as 58% twice in the 1960s (1960 and 1967) before rising to 80% in 1973. See Laura Randall, *The Political Economy of Brazilian Oil* (Westport, CT: Praeger, 1993), 12–13.
101. Santos, "Alcohol as Fuel in Brazil," 107–108, 154. With the exception of 1958 and 1959, at which point the requirement increased to 7 and 7.5% respectively.
102. "Política Açucareira," *Brasil Açucareiro* 37, no. 3 (1951): 3–4, 10–19. The IAA's executive commission began issuing separate sugar crop plans and alcohol plans each year in 1939. The plans delineated the quotas for the year, which national production systematically exceeded from 1946. See Ramos, *Agroindústria canavieira*, 120.
103. Ramos, *Agroindústria canavieira*, 120. The IAA would again readjust quotas to account for sugar overproduction in 1952, 1957, and 1963.
104. IAA, *Anuário Açucareiro* 20 (IAA: Rio de Janeiro, 1960–6), 32.
105. Other stipulations of the resolution required the usina to process ethanol directly from sugar rather than from another byproduct such as molasses and allowed the ethanol to be sold for other industrial uses beyond just fuel.
106. IAA, *Anuário Açucareiro* 18 (IAA: Rio de Janeiro, 1953–6), 40.
107. IAA, *Anuário Açucareiro* 18, xiii.
108. Hasse, *Filhos do fogo*, 70.
109. "Parceiros e Colaboradores," *A Revista Santa Elisa: uma história de trabalho e desenvolvimento*, (Ribeirão Preto: MIC Editorial Ltda, 1996), 21; See volumes 16–20 of the IAA's *Anuário Açucareiro* for further data.
110. The other five usinas were located in different regions across the state. They were the Usinas Tamoio (in Araraquara), Porto Feliz (near Sorocaba), Itaiquara (in

Campinas), Santa Bárbara (Santa Bárbara do Oeste), and Monte Alegre (Piracicaba). Agro-engineers reported their findings in a series of articles published in the Agronomic Institute of Campinas's technical bulletin, *Bragantia*. See, for example, A. L. Segalla and R. Alvarez, "Variedades de cana-de-açúcar: II, Série de ensaios realizados no período de 1953–1956," *Bragantia* 17 (1958): 45–79.

111. Hartzmark, "Businesses, Associations, and Regions," 234.
112. On the formation and early work of Copereste and its counterpart, Copira, the Piracicaba cooperative, see Hartzmark, "Businesses, Associations, and Regions," ch. 6, esp. 233–245.

Chapter 2

1. Speech at the Palácio do Itamaraty, Brasilia, April 20, 1970, as published in Emílio Garrastazu Médici, *A verdadeira paz* (Brasilia: Departamento de Imprensa Nacional, 1971), 29.
2. "Basta um argumento para a Usina Santa Elisa comprar 15 caminhões Dodge este ano," *ESP* (June 13, 1971), 47.
3. Many European nations protected their markets to favor current and former sugar-producing colonies.
4. A C Hannah and Donald Spence, *The International Sugar Trade* (New York: John Wiley & Sons, Inc, 1997), 94–95; Richard Tucker, *Insatiable Appetite: The United States and the Ecological Degradation of the Tropical World* (Berkeley, CA: University of California Press, 2000), ch. 1.
5. Szmrecsányi, *O planejamento*, 245–250; IAA, *Anuário Açucareiro* 18 (Rio de Janeiro: IAA, 1953–1956), 53–56; 79th Ordinary Session of July 23, 1959; "Atas da Comissão Executiva do IAA," *Brasil Açucareiro* 56, no. 1, (1960): 26.
6. Tucker, *Insatiable Appetite*, 48–49.
7. Gail M. Hollander, *Raising Cane in the 'Glades'" The Global Sugar Trade and the Transformation of Florida* (Chicago, IL: University of Chicago Press, 2008), 287; Szmrecsányi, *O planejamento*, 260, n. 139; Nunberg, "State Intervention," 101–105.
8. M. Golodetz & Co., "Mercado Internacional do Açúcar," *Brasil Açucareiro* 56, no. 2 (1960): 105–106; IAA, *Anuário Açucareiro: Safras de 1960/61–1965/66* (Rio de Janeiro: IAA, 1967), 54–56; Szmerscányi, *O planejamento*, 254, n. 127.
9. Tucker, *Insatiable Appetite*, 56–61; Hasse, *Filhos do fogo*, 123–124. Other soda and beer producers opened factories in Ribeirão Preto, including the popular domestic company, Antarctica.
10. Szmrecsányi, *O planejamento*, 256.
11. "Notas e Comentários," *Brasil Açucareiro*, 59, nos. 1–2 (1962): 3–5.
12. Hartzmark, "Businesses, Associations, and Regions," 96–98.
13. Nunberg, "State Intervention," 108.
14. Hartzmark, "Businesses, Associations, and Regions," 310–314; Santos, "Alcohol as Fuel," 145, 174; Szmrecsányi, *O planejamento*, 268–269, n. 149.

15. Hartzmark, "Businesses, Associations, and Regions," 111; see also Santos, "Alcohol as Fuel," 161–162; Ramos, *Agroindústria canavieira.*
16. Szmerscanyi, *O planejamento*, 256–263. A year later Cuba set the goal of producing ten million tons of sugar in a single harvest by 1970, which failed primarily because they could not adequately increase agricultural yields. However, São Paulo producers successfully implemented new cane varieties, expanded irrigation, and increased fertilizer and insecticide use unavailable to the Cubans. See Manuel R. Moreno Fraginals and Teresita Pedraza Moreno, "The Ten Million Ton Sugar Harvest," https://snimsib.files.wordpress.com/2017/11/ten-million-ton-sugar-harvest.pdf, accessed September 30, 2021.
17. The president and the Executive Commission created the first with Decree no. 51.104 on August 1, 1961 and the second on November 17, 1961 under Decree no. 156. See Szmrecsányi, *O planejamento*, 265–267.
18. Szmrecsányi, *O planejamento*, 273, n. 154; Verena Stolcke, *Coffee Planters, Workers, and Wives: Class Conflict and Gender Relations on São Paulo Coffee Plantations, 1850–1980* (New York: St. Martin's Press, 1988), 97–100.
19. Ioris, *Transforming Brazil*, 3; Skidmore, *Politics in Brazil, 1930–1964*, 303–304. See also Eaglin, " 'More Brazilian than Cachaça,' " 932–934. For a more detailed account of the factors and events leading up to the coup, see Thomas Skidmore, *The Politics of Military Rule in Brazil, 1964-1985* (New York: Oxford University Press, 1990), 3–17; Alfred Stepan, *The Military in Politics: Changing Patterns in Brazil* (Princeton, NJ: Princeton University Press, 1971), 139–142.
20. Stepan, *The Military in Politics*, 178.
21. Skidmore, *The Politics of Military Rule*, 160–161; see also Stepan, *The Military in Politics*, 174.
22. Maria Helena Moreira Alves, *State and Opposition in Military Brazil* (Austin, TX: University of Texas Press), 1985, 14–23; Guillermo O'Donnell, *Modernization and Bureaucratic-Authoritarianism: Studies in South American Politics* (Berkeley, CA: University of California Press, 1973), 2–4; David Collier, "The Bureaucratic-Authoritarian Model," in *The New Authoritarianism in Latin America*, ed. David Collier (Princeton, NJ: Princeton University Press, 1979), 26–27.
23. Skidmore, *The Politics of Military Rule*, 66–71, 89–90; Baer, *The Brazilian Economy*, 462; Federative Republic of Brazil, *First National Development Plan 1972–1974* (Brasilia: Federative Republic of Brazil, 1971), xii and 17–18.
24. Alberico Leite, "A nova política," II *Encontro Nacional dos Produtores de Açúcar* (Campos, RJ: COPERFLU, 1974), 77.
25. Szmrecsányi, *O planejamento*, 273–274.
26. "Occorrencia do petroleo no estado de S. Catarina" *ESP* (October 15, 1955), 9; "A Petrobrás exportará e importará petroleo" *ESP* (January 6, 1959), 5; Szmrecsányi, *O planejamento*, 107–108; Santos, "Alcohol as Fuel," 171–178.
27. *Anuário Açucareiro: Safras de 1960/61–1965/66*, 40.
28. Santos, "Alcohol as Fuel," 177.
29. Barbara Nunberg, "Structural Change and State Policy: The Politics of Sugar in Brazil since 1964," *Latin American Research Review* 21, no. 2 (1986): 63–64.

30. Simon Schwartzman, *A Space for Science: The Development of the Scientific Community in Brazil* (University Park, PA: Pennsylvania State University Press, 1991), 142–144. See also Hartzmark, "Businesses, Cooperative, Associations," 233–245; Franz O. Brieger, *Noções básicas e métodos analíticos para a indústria açucareira* (Ribeirão Preto: Copereste, 1964), 29–30.
31. Jorge Wolney Atalla, *Reflexões e sugestões para o desenvolvimento brasileiro* (Brasilia: Confederação Nacional da Agricultura, 1979), 75; Nunberg, "State Intervention," 189; "Morre Jorge Wolney Atalla," (August 4, 2009) *Unica (União da indústria de cana-de-açúcar)* (São Paulo), accessed January 28, 2015, <https://unica.com.br/noticias/morre-jorge-wolney-atalla/>
32. Regina Machado Curi, "Os barões do açúcar," *Veja* 411 (July 21, 1976), 78.
33. See, for example, Jorge Wolney Atalla, "Álcool é pouco e irregular na gasolina," *ESP* (November 5, 1972), 57.
34. Santos, "Alcohol as Fuel," 145 and Curi, "Os barões do açucar," 78.
35. Hasse, *Filhos do fogo*, 37, 70, 156, 163.
36. José Rubens da Silva, "De pai para filho," *A Revista Santa Elisa: Uma história de trabalho e desenvolvimento* (Ribeirão Preto: MIC Editorial Ltda, 1996), 23–24; Hasse, *Filhos do fogo*, 193–194.
37. Zanini S.A. Equipamentos Pesados, "Perfil Técnico 1973" (Banco Safra de Investimentos S.A.), 18. APHRP Caixa 193. José Rossi Jr., an engineer who joined Zanini in 1961, assumed the presidency, but Lacerda Biagi would remain the spokesperson of Zanini operations from 1970 to 1985. Hasse, *Filhos do fogo*, 146–148, 162–163, 167–168.
38. Prices originally given in US dollars per lb. Conversions are my own. Coffee held the top export earning spot from the 1840s. See Nunberg, "State Intervention," 135.
39. According to Barbara Nunberg, the new IAA president had no previous experience in the sugar industry. See Nunberg, "State Intervention," 208.
40. Ramos, *Agroindústria canavieira*, 159.
41. Szmrecsányi, *O planejamento*, 298–304. On Planalsucar, see Roberto Manera, "Há 4 séculos o Brasil planta errado," *Revista Globo Rural*, 1, no. 9 (1986): 54–58. See also Gilberto Miller Azzi, "Planalsucar: Por que? O que? O como?" *Brasil Açucareiro* 85, no. 3 (1975): 46–50.
42. Azzi, "Planalsucar: Por que? O que? O como?"; Santa Elisa GEAT form of 23/08/1973. BR RJANRIO IY A6.06 Caixa 0393.
43. Evans, *Dependent Development*, 120–121.
44. This aligns with historian Marshall Eakin's assertion that foreign technology was the fourth prong in Brazilian industrial development. See Eakin, *Tropical Capitalism*, 3.
45. Zanini S.A. Equipamentos Pesados, "Perfil Técnico 1973," 7; Zanini history pamphlet, "Zanini S.A. Equipamentos Pesados," n/d, 36–40. APHRP Caixa 193; Hasse, *Filhos do fogo*, 155–156. Biagi first bought the Danish company's technology in the early 1960s and Zanini adapted it throughout the decade. Hasse states that Zanini paid US$50,000 in royalties for the Atlas turbine technology.

46. Santos, "Alcohol as Fuel," 380; Hasse, *Filhos do fogo*, 194. In its stead, producers founded the Society of Producers of Sugar and Ethanol (*A Sociedade de Produtores de Açúcar e do Álcool*) to contest Copersucar's dominance in 1975.
47. Houtzager, "State and Unions," 116, n. 30.
48. Senna notably signed off on all of the Usina Santa Elisa's first Proálcool applications a little over a year later. See Usina Santa Elisa Proálcool Application, CNAl n. SP06/76. BR RJANRIO IY A6.16 Caixa 0443. Historian Geraldo Hasse asserts that "the discovery of the government market" encouraged the Biagis to hire "a military man [Senna] to lobby at the federal level." Hasse, *Filhos do fogo*, 170.
49. Funproçúcar approval letter from General Tavares Carmo to the Usina Santa Elisa on April 4, 1974. GPCt 515/74, BR RJANRIO IY A6.16 Caixa 0443.
50. Internal economic report with the Santa Elisa Funproçúcar application by the economist Roberto de Oliveira and approved by the economic adviser Carlos Alfredo Hiss to the executive secretary of GEAT in Rio de Janeiro on October 23, 1973. BR RJANRIO IY A6.06 Caixa 0393.
51. President of the State BADESP President Alvaro Coutinho, "The Role of State Banks," Presentation to the ACI-RP on April 19, 1974. Arquivo da Associação de Comércio e Indústria Ribeirão Preto Caixa 187.
52. "Conjuntura açucareira é analisada pelo President do IAA no Senado Federal," *Brasil Açucareiro*, 83, no. 1 (1974): 18, as cited in Ramos, *Agroindústria canavieira*, 160–161.
53. Santa Elisa GEAT form of August 23, 1973. BR RJANRIO IY A6.06 Caixa 0393; See also the applications of the Usinas Santa Lydia and Nossa Senhora da Aparecida for more examples. GEAT form of August 23, 1973 of A6.06 Caixa 0395 and GEAT form of October 12, 1973 of A6.03 Caixa 0378, BR RJANRIO IY.
54. See also Santos, "Alcohol as Fuel," 255; Barzelay, *The Politicized Market Economy*, 183.
55. Funproçúcar approval letter from General Tavares Carmo to the Bank of Brazil President Dr. Ángelo Calmon de Sá on April 4, 1974. GPO 324/74, BR RJANRIO IY A6.16 Caixa 0443; Cédula de Credito Industrial contract between the Bank of Brazil and the Santa Elisa shareholders, Maurilio Biagi Sr. (director), Maurílio Biagi Filho (superintendent director), Edilah Lacerda Biagi, and Luiz Lacerda Biagi on May 6, 1974 and the annexed equipment budget of May 3, 1974.
56. Evans, *Dependent Development*, 120–121.
57. For a more detailed history of the Zanini company and its impact on the region, see Santos, *A usinagem do capital*, 33–47.
58. GECEP-544/74 of April 16, 1974. BR RJANRIO IY A6.16 Caixa 0443. The IAA tasked two groups with administering Funproçúcar: the Special Technical Assistance Group (Grupo Especial de Assistência Técnica- GEAT) and its administrative organ, the Special Group for Executive Control of Projects (Grupo Especial de Controle Executivo de Projetos- GECEP).
59. Médici, *A verdadeira paz*, 29.
60. GEAT-III-86/74, Report on the Usina Santo Antonio-SP, BR RJANRIO IY A6.07 Caixa 0397.
61. Baer, *The Brazilian Economy*, 87.

62. Randall, *The Political Economy of Brazilian Oil*, 15; Santos, "Alcohol as Fuel," 195–196.
63. "Pratini vê maior uso de álcool na gasolina," *Jornal do Brasil* (December 11, 1973), 20; see also "MIC estimula produção de álcool combustível," *Gazeta Mercantil* (December 11, 1973). In Santos's study of Proálcool, she identifies this as the moment that the National Ethanol Program truly began. See Santos, "Alcohol as Fuel," 232.
64. Szmrecsányi, *O planejamento*, 310. Although it was anonymous upon distribution in 1974, Copersucar usineiros were generally considered to be the authors. Maurílio Biagi Sr. was one collaborator to later claim authorship.
65. Interview with Maurilio Biagi Filho, May 20, 2013, Ribeirão Preto, São Paulo.
66. Szmrecsányi, *O planejamento*, 310–311. Approved autonomous distilleries had to have a minimum production capacity of 60,000 liters per day and predominantly produce anhydrous ethanol for the fuel supply. These distilleries could produce ethanol from sugar directly or from a residual source such as molasses.
67. Letter from Maurilio Biagi Filho to General Tavares Carmo, June 16, 1974, BR RJANRIO IY A6.16 Caixa 0443.
68. Funds request letter from Maurilio Biagi Filho to the IAA president General Alvaro Tavares Carmo on June 17, 1974. BR RJANRIO IY A6.16 Caixa 0443.
69. Ibid.
70. Ibid.
71. Ibid.
72. Hasse, *Filhos do fogo*, 127.
73. GEAT Processo III-22/73, Usina Santa Lydia Credit Supplement, signed by the chemical engineer Manoel M. de M. Correia on June 2, 1975. BR RJANRIO IY A6.06 Caixa 0395.
74. GPCt/GECEP-67/74, Letter to the Usina Santa Elisa on July 30, 1974. BR RJANRIO IY A6.16 Caixa 0443.
75. Santa Lydia GEAT Processo III-22/73, Letter from the economist Terezinha Florencio to the economic adviser Carlos Alfredo Hiss, May 27, 1975. BR RJANRIO IY A6.06 Caixa 0395. This is my assessment of the filed projects based on the Bank of Brazil branches used for the respective projects as issued by Pedro Cabral da Silva, director of the Department of Modernization of Sugar Agroindustry in the attachment to Of. DMA- 207/80, June 17, 1980. BR RJANRIO IY A6.23 Caixa 0480. More generally, of the 111 approved projects by January 1, 1975, 21 were in Pernambuco, 17 in Alagoas, 9 in Rio de Janeiro, 5 in Minas Gerais, and the rest were individually dispersed between 6 other states.
76. Usina Santa Elisa Proálcool Application, Maurilio Biagi Filho to the IAA president Tavares Carmo, February 13, 1976. National Ethanol Commission, Division of Assistance for Production N. SP06/76, February 12, 1976. BR RJANRIO IY A6.16 Caixa 443.
77. Ibid.
78. Albert Viton, *The International Sugar Agreements: Promise and Reality* (West Lafayette, IN: Purdue University Press, 2004), 183–192, 225. See also Tucker, *Insatiable Appetite*, 60.

79. "Na Mogiana, só a previsão preocupa," *ESP* (July 19, 1975), 9; "Na região Alta Ararquarense prejuízo foi total," *ESP* (July 19, 1975); Cláudio Perani, "A greve dos bóias-frias em São Paulo," *Cadernos do CEAS* 93 (September/October 1984): 17–23.
80. Letter to the IAA from Maurilio Biagi Filho, September 15, 1975. BR RJANRIO IY A6.16 Caixa 0443.
81. MIC/IAA, *Relatório 75* (Rio de Janeiro: IAA).
82. GECEP release approval, April 24, 1975. Opinion no. 307/75; GECEP letter to IAA November 6, 1975. The IAA president Tavares Carmo approved the proposal on November 7, 1975. BR RJANRIO IY A6.16 Caixa 0443.
83. Letter from President Tavares Carmo to the manager of the Bank of Brazil, Ribeirão Preto Branch, on November 7, 1975. GPCt-604 and GPCt-590, BR RJANRIO IY A6.16 Caixa 0443.
84. Minas Gerais, Paraná, and Rio de Janeiro also received interest suspensions accounting for a little over Cr$52,558,000 collectively. See MIC/IAA, *Relatório 75* (Rio de Janeiro: IAA).
85. See Barzelay, *The Politicized Market Economy*, ch. 5; Demetrius, *Brazil's National Alcohol Program*, 10–11; Santos, "Alcohol as Fuel," 321–322, n. 44.

Chapter 3

1. Maurilio Biagi Filho, "O álcool é nosso," *FSP* (May 9, 1983).
2. Conversely, Barzelay asserts that Proálcool was the quintessential example of Peter Evan's triple alliance development strategy. My interpretation aligns more with Barzelay's contemporary, Demetrius, and more recent work by Dias de Moraes. See Demetrius, *Brazil's National Alcohol Program*, 100; Barzelay, *The Politicized Market Economy*, 195. Dias de Moraes, *A desregulamentação*, 15–18.
3. Baer, *The Brazilian Economy*, 79.
4. Skidmore, *Politics in Brazil l, 1930–1964*, 160–161; President Ernesto Geisel statement at the Meeting of Ministers of September 10, 1974 in Federative Republic of Brazil, *Second National Development Plan-II PND (1975–1979)* (Brasilia, Federative Republic of Brazil, 1974), 3.
5. Geisel, *II PND*, 3–4; Baer, *The Brazilian Economy* 6th ed., 79.
6. Quote in Geisel, *II PND*, 44; see also Geisel, *II PND*, 17, 81–83.
7. Ozires Silva and Decio Fischetti, *Etanol: A revolução verde e amarela* (São Paulo: Bizz Communicação e Produções, 2008), 47–51.
8. "CTA revela a Geisel pesquisa sobre álcool," *ESP* (June 28, 1975), 14.
9. "CTA revela a Geisel pesquisa sobre álcool," 14; Silva and Fischetti, *Etanol*, 75.
10. Allen L. Hammond, "Alcohol: A Brazilian Answer to the Energy Crisis," *Science* 195 (1977): 564–566.
11. "CTA revela a Geisel pesquisa sobre álcool," 14.
12. Szmerscányi, *O planejamento*, 277; Skidmore, *The Politics of Military Rule*, 171; Curi, "Os barões do açúcar", 78.

13. Hammond, "Alcohol," 565.
14. Hammond, "Alcohol," 565; "Geisel autoriza contratos de risco, aumenta barreiras para importações, e passa gasolina comum a Cr$3,19,"*Jornal do Brasil* 85, no. 185, (1975): 1. Other measures included the expansion of domestic oil exploration through the controversial use of risk contracts with foreign companies.
15. "O petróleo da cana," *Veja* 562 (June 13, 1979), 97.
16. Santos, "Alcohol as Fuel," 259.
17. "Para Severo, prioridades são álcool e metalurgia," *ESP* (October 12, 1976), 43. See also Gilberto Felisberto Vasconcellos and J. W. Bautista Vidal, *Poder dos Trópicos: Meditação sobre a alienação energética na cultura brasileira* (São Paulo: Casa Amarela, 1998), 32.
18. Silva and Fischetti, *Etanol*, 67–70.
19. Silva and Fischetti, *Etanol*, 67–70. Lead was a common additive used to reduce corrosion and boost combustion energy. The US too began replacing lead in its car fuel with its own ethanol program in the 1970s. However, the US ended up using the toxic MTBE (methyl tertiary buthyl ether) as its primary booster replacement. American ethanol would only replace MTBE in 2005. See Marcos Jank, "Perspectives for Hemispheric Cooperation in Agro-energy," at the Seminar "Energy Cooperation in the Americas," December 11, 2006 in Rio de Janeiro.
20. Ueki remained a staunch advocate of the smaller version of Proálcool, even as the program expanded. See,for example, "Ueki e Calmon: dois destinos para o álcool," *Diário Comércio e Indústria* (December 14, 1978) and "Ueki nega ter mudado prioridade para álcool," *ESP* (December 14, 1978), as cited in Barzelay, *The Politicized Market Economy*, 178.
21. Szmerscányi, *O planejamento*, 314–315; Santos, "Alcohol as Fuel," 277; "Disputa atrasa a divulgação do texto do álcool" *FSP* (November 13, 1975), as cited in Santos, "Alcohol as Fuel," 277.
22. Jorge Wolney Atalla, "O perigo da estatização da comercialização do álcool," *ESP* (November 6, 1975), 5.
23. Triner, *Mining and the State*, 5.
24. Atalla, "O perigo da estatização da comercialização do álcool," 5. See also Jorge Wolney Atalla, "Considerações economicas da COPERSUCAR sobre o Plano Nacional do Álcool," *ESP* (November 6, 1975), 11. Copersucar published these articles in all major newspapers. Broader debate about the "statization" of the national economy emerged in this era as government-led companies such as telephones, water, and other services dominated economic development. See Barzelay, *The Politicized Market Economy*, 92–93; Szmerscányi, *O planejamento*, 314–15.
25. Barzelay, *The Politicized Market Economy*, 195n70.
26. Decree no. 76.593, November 14, 1975, *Diario Oficial.*
27. "Meta: equilibrar o balanço," *ESP* (November 15, 1975), 30; Szmrecsányi, *O planejamento*, 436–437.
28. Commissão Executivo Nacional do Álcool (CENAL), *Proálcool: Informações Básicas para Empresários* (Rio de Janeiro: BNDE, 1980), 21. Private businessmen had to secure banking support from a number of different institutions, which

divided credit between industrial and agricultural investments. All agricultural credit came through banks related to the Sistema Nacional de Crédito Rural, which included the Bank of Brazil. Industrial credit financiers included the following institutions (in the order listed): Banco Nacional do Desenvolvimento Economico (BNDE), Banco do Brasil, Banco da Amazonia, Banco do Nordeste do Brasil, Banco Nacional de Crédito Cooperativo, state and regional development banks, and official state banks where there were no state development banks. Despite the long list of possible bank financiers, most successful projects were tied to the Bank of Brazil.

29. CENAL, *Proálcool*, 17–19.
30. "Meta: equilibrar o balanço," *ESP* (November 15, 1975), 30.
31. Baer, *The Brazilian Economy*, Statistical Appendix, Table A5.
32. The President of the Republic presided over the Economic Development Council, which included high-level ministers. Santos notes that this is another way in which President Geisel repeatedly intervened with executive authority to ensure Proálcool successfully got off the ground. See Santos, "Alcohol as Fuel," 520.
33. "O plano, afinal", *Veja* 376 (November 19, 1975), 120–121. See also "Sai, enfim, o programa do álcool," *ESP* (November 15, 1975), 30.
34. CENAL, *Proálcool*, 5.
35. In 1975, residual ethanol processed from sugarcane to sugar to molasses to ethanol yielded 7 liters of ethanol per 60 kg of sugar. See "Sai, enfim, o programa do álcool," 30.
36. The first three projects approved by the National Ethanol Commission (CNAl) in December 1975 were for sugarcane-based autonomous distilleries. See Szmerscányi, *O planejamento*, 316.
37. Usina Santa Elisa Proálcool Application, CNAl no. SP06/76. BR RJANRIO IY A6.16 Caixa 0443.
38. Project Summary in the Usina Santa Elisa Proálcool Application, CNAl no. SP06/76. BR RJANRIO IY A6.16 Caixa 0443.
39. CNAl-Act no. 30. Letter to the Director of the Usina Santa Elisa S.A., April 1, 1976. BR RJANRIO IY A6.16 Caixa 0443.
40. Barzelay, *The Politicized Market Economy*, 12.
41. "Como conter as dificuldades?" *Veja* 426 (November 3, 1976), 74–75, with quotation on p. 75. See also "Plano de álcool um ano depois, poucos resultados," *Visão* (November 22, 1976).
42. Dias de Moraes, *A desregulamentação*, 71.
43. CNAl Report no.100/80, Processo CNAl/SP-06/76 and Letter to the Director of the Usina Santa Elisa S.A., April 1, 1976. BR RJANRIO IY A6.16 Caixa 0443.
44. Letter from the Bank of Brazil to the Commissão Nacional do Álcool (CNAl), July 14, 1978. BR RJANRIO IY A6.16 Caixa 443.
45. Letter from Maurilio Biagi Filho to the IAA president General Alvaro Tavares Carmo, June 28, 1976. BR RJANRIO IY A6.16 Caixa 443.
46. Letter from the IAA president Tavares Carmo to the Usina Santa Elisa S.A., July 16, 1976. GPCt-205/76, BR RJANRIO IY A6.16 Caixa 443.

47. The inflation rate and interest rates connected to these loans are important in assessing the program's real value. According to Werner Baer's study of the Brazilian economy, nominal interest rates were 41.15% in 1976, but when adjusted for inflation, which averaged 47% and higher that year, the real interest rate was -3.63%. See Baer, *The Brazilian Economy*, Statistical Appendix, Table A5, 392–393.
48. See J. G. Baccarin, "O papel do estado no Proálcool," *Ciencia Agronomica- Jaboticabal* 3, no. 2 (1988): 17–18.
49. "Álcool: 3 bilhões até dezembro," *ESP* (November 8, 1977), 28.
50. Usina Santa Elisa Proálcool Application, CNAl no. SP06/76. BR RJANRIO IY A6.16 Caixa 0443; Barzelay, *The Politicized Market Economy*, 195, n. 70; Hasse, *Filhos do Fogo*, 170.
51. Confúcio Pamplona, *Proálcool: Technical-Economic and Social Impact of the Program in Brazil* (Belo Horizonte: Ministry of Industry and Commerce and Sugar and Alcohol Institute, 1984), 20.
52. CENAL Report no.100/80; Letter to Dr. Getúlio Valverde de Lacerda of CNAl from the Bank of Brazil financial manager José Vasquez Rodriguez on July 14, 1978. Ref.: GERFI/GEPRO-78/268. BR RJANRIO IY A6.16 Caixa 443; CENAL, *Proálcool*, 15–20.
53. CENAL Report no.100/80.
54. Zanini itself set up a multinational subsidiary company to produce turbines with the German company AEG Kanis in 1976. See Hasse, *Filhos do fogo*, 156 and 171. These multinational agreements align with Evans and Eakin's arguments about the nature of Brazilian development, but I am highlighting how keeping these companies on the periphery permitted the sugar and ethanol industry to remain domestically controlled in opposition to their arguments about other industries.
55. Letter to Dr. Getúlio Valverde de Lacerda of CNAl from the Bank of Brazil financial manager José Vasquez Rodriguez on July 14, 1978. Ref.: GERFI/GEPRO-78/268. BR RJANRIO IY A6.16 Caixa 443.
56. Biagi Filho response to OF/CNAl no. 84 of April 18, 1978 sent to the General Secretary of the Ministry of Industry and Commerce on May 3, 1978. BR RJANRIO IY A6.16 Caixa 443.
57. Letter from Maurilio Biagi Filho to the IAA president Tavares Carmo, March 7, 1978. BR RJANRIO IY A6.16 Caixa 443. Biagi notes that the inauguration was also a symbolic inauguration of the Cia. Açucareira Vale do Rosário and Irmãos Biagi S.A. Açúcar e Álcool, which also received support and financing from Proálcool. Both companies are affiliated with the Usina Santa Elisa and owned by other members of the Biagi family. Together, the three units accounted for 10% of all ethanol production in the state of São Paulo in the 1976/1977 harvest.
58. "Técnicos dizem que custo da terra atrasa Proálcool," *ESP* (January 18, 1977), 36.
59. Paulo Cesar de Araújo, "Dívida agrícola já preocupa o governo," *ESP* (August 19, 1977), 23.
60. "Álcool: 3 bilhões até dezembro," *ESP* (November 8, 1977), 28.
61. "Só dia 1o começa venda de combustível misturado," *ESP* (May 24, 1977), 22.
62. "Só dia 1o começa venda de combustível misturado," 22.

63. "Proálcool ultrapassa meta de produção," *ESP* (February 24, 1978), 25; "Em abril, aumento de 8,6% no refino," *ESP* (May 30, 1978), 36.
64. Cesar de Araújo, "Dívida agrícola já preocupa o governo," 23.
65. As STI secretary from 1974 to 1979, Bautista Vidal was known for his "passion and combative defense" of Proálcool; however, Barzelay claims that Bautista Vidal "chose to promote the program so ardently that he gained a reputation among auto producers as a clown." See J.W. Vidal, *O esfacelamento da nação* (Petrópolis: Editora Vozes Ltda, 1994), 10; Barzelay, *The Politicized Market Economy*, 175; Vasconcellos and Vidal, *Poder dos tropicos*, 82.
66. "CTA diz que carro movido a álcool passou no teste," *ESP* (October 30, 1976), 26. See also "O petróleo da cana."
67. Codistil, " Atenção, equipe do 1o circuito nacional motor 100% álcool," *ESP* (November 12, 1976), 17.
68. "1ª usina do Proálcool já está pronta," *ESP* (November 10, 1977), 34. That Germany and Brazil found mutual interest on the topic is somewhat unsurprising as both of their historically limited oil reserves had pushed the countries toward alternative fuels early in the twentieth century.
69. "Volkswagen do Brasil testa motores a álcool," *ESP*–Suplemento de Turismo (October 31, 1976), 204; Bernton, Kovarik, and Sklar, *The Forbidden Fuel*, 152–153.
70. "Governo pode dar incentivo," *ESP* (August 25, 1978), 25.
71. Wolfe, *Autos and Progress*, 164.
72. Rogério de Simone and Rogério Ferraresi, *Fiat 147* (São Paulo: Alaúde Editorial, 2016), 14–18, 47–48.
73. "Telesp inicia hoje programa do álcool," *ESP* (May 25, 1977), 17; "O petróleo da cana."
74. "O petróleo da cana."
75. Cesar de Araújo, "Dívida agrícola já preocupa o governo," 23. On Brazil's auto parts industry, see Caren Addis, *Taking the Wheel: Auto Parts Firms and the Political Economy of Industrialization in Brazil* (University Park, PA: Pennsylvania State University Press, 1999). According to Addis, looming recession pushed the reluctant auto parts industry to invest in research and development in ethanol engines, and, more generally, Proálcool saved the Brazilian auto industry from severe recession in the late 1970s.
76. Barzelay, *The Politicized Market Economy*, 174.
77. Santos, "Alcohol as Fuel," 360.
78. Skidmore, *The Politics of Military Rule*, 162, 210.
79. Secretaria do Planejamento, *Brazil's III National Development Plan 1980–1985* (Brasilia: Presidencia da República, 1979), 44.
80. Paulo Sotero, "Figueiredo e o desafio dos anos 80," *Veja* 562 (June 13, 1979), 93.
81. Ministry of Mines and Energy, *O modelo energético brasileiro* (Brasilia: Ministry of Mines and Energy, 1979), 38–42. For discussion of the second phase in 1978, see "Autos: 1/6 a álcool em 1982," *ESP* (August 25, 1978), 25.
82. According to Castro Santos, poor distribution and storage infrastructure, a delayed approval process connected to a poor administrative structure, complaints about

ethanol pricing, and limited resources to finance expansion were the primary problems with the program. See Santos, "Alcohol as Fuel," 381–383.

83. Decree no. 83.681 of July 4, 1979
84. Decree no. 83.700 of July 5, 1979, *Diario Oficial*, July 5, 1979.
85. Interview with Minister of Industry and Commerce João Camilo Penna by *Veja* reporter Jaime Sautchuk, "O programa que poderá ser sempre revisto," *Veja* 562 (June 13, 1979), 97.
86. "Só dia 1° começa venda de combustível misturado," 22.
87. "Para Mário Garnero, uma revolução de tecnologia," *ESP* (11 Sept 1979), 33; Lauro de Barros Siciliano, "Álcool, um aliado da natureza e do Brasil," *ESP* (January 9, 1977), 34.
88. "Álcool: CNP já tem plano de distribuição," *ESP* (February 7, 1979), 29.
89. Simone and Ferraresi, *Fiat 147*, 47–56; "Telesp vai adquirir 517 Fiats a álcool," *ESP* (August 10, 1979), 30; Decree no. 13.693 of July 11, 1979, *Diário oficial* (July 12, 1979), 7–8.
90. Sérgio Pompeu, "'Elitista!' 'impatriótico!' e o programa emplaca" *Revista Globo Rural* 1, no. 9 (1986), 62.
91. Mário Garnero, *JK: A coragem da ambição* (Campinas, SP: Editora MM, 2011), 13–24, 29.
92. Interview with Mário Garnero by Jennifer Eaglin, December 11, 2013.
93. Petrobras had already formally won control of selling and distributing ethanol through its oil distribution system in 1978. In 1980, it won control of maintaining ethanol stocks. See Randall, *The Political Economy of Brazilian Oil*, 35.
94. Pompeu, "'Elitista!' 'impatriótico!' e o programa emplaca," 62–65; Matthew Veazey, "Brazil's 'Father of Ethanol' Sees Bounty for Biofuel," (February 8, 2012). https://www.rigzone.com/news/oil_gas/a/149425/brazils_father_of_ethanol_sees_bounty_for_biofuel/
95. "Para Mário Garnero, uma revolução de tecnologia," 33.
96. "Camargo Corrêa tem interesse no risco," *ESP* (August 11, 1979), 29.
97. According to Barzelay, various government organs and private companies bought into the program in 1979 and 1980 in ways their diverging interests had previously resisted. Addis also notes that the auto parts sector committed to the program because the alternative, recession, pushed compliance. See Barzelay, *The Politicized Market Economy*, 198; Addis, *Taking the Wheel*, 156.
98. Pedro Lobato, "Pronto o Fiat-Álcool," *Gazeta Mercantil* (September 4, 1978); Barzelay, *The Politicized Market Economy*, 179.
99. João Batista Olivi, "CTA ditará padrões para motor a álcool," *ESP* (April 27, 1979), 30; See also "INPI não aceita royalty sobre motor a álcool," *O Globo* (April 24, 1979), as cited in Santos, "Alcohol as Fuel," 416.
100. Critiquing Brazilian development strategies, Eakin states, "Rather than moving toward continual technological innovation—a true sign of self-sustaining and dynamic industrialization—the Brazilians continue to rely on others for technological advances and innovation." See Eakin, *Tropical Capitalism*, 59.
101. Wolfe, *Autos and Progress*, 12.

102. Hasse, *Filhos do Fogo*, 194. Maurilio Biagi Filho remained the superintendent of the Usina Santa Elisa and the navigator of the Biagi sugar and ethanol holdings, while Luiz Lacerda Biagi led Zanini's holdings.
103. "Anunciada a redução na meta de carros a álcool," *ESP* (May 16, 1980), 25; Skidmore, *The Politics of Military Rule*, 205–206, 212–214, 222–224; Barzelay, *The Politicized Market Economy*, 212–213.
104. Interview with Maurilio Biagi Filho, May 21, 2013.
105. Pompeu, " 'Elitista!' 'impatriótico!' e o programa emplaca," 63.
106. "O petróleo da cana"; "Uma reação nas vendas de autos?," *ESP* (November 13, 1981).
107. Hasse, *Filhos do Fogo*, 171.
108. Barzelay, *The Politicized Market Economy*, 31; Anfavea, *Anuário da Indústria Automobilística Brasileira*, 59; Santos, "Alcohol as Fuel," 201. See also S. Stefani, "Álcool: O susto da guerra provocou o 'boom,'" *Gazeta Mercantil* (November 28, 1980).
109. Anfavea, *Anuário da Indústria Automobilística Brasileira*, 59.
110. "Governo desiste da Alcoolbrás e só vai distribuir," *ESP* (May 23, 1979), 27; See also "Cals veta o plano tripartite," *Gazeta Mercantil* (March 19, 1980), as cited in Santos, "Alcohol as Fuel," 402–403. Ultimately, private interests created an ethanol investment group to promote a similar agenda led by Zanini and Dedini instead of Petrobras. See Barzelay, *The Politicized Market Economy*, 182. On the common "tripartite" development model, see Evans, *Dependent Development*, 32–38.
111. In an *ESP* commentary article, "O nacionalismo e o Proálcool," a critic of the state claimed that the exclusion of foreign capital would lead to the same disaster as the creation of Petrobrás, "a state within a state" whose inefficiencies had led to Brazil's failed oil industry. See "O nacionalismo e o Proálcool," *ESP* (April 9, 1980), 3; "Debatido o interesse do capital externo no álcool," *ESP* (May 27, 1981), 24.
112. As cited in "O nacionalismo e o Proálcool," *ESP* (April 9, 1980), 3.
113. "Serpa prega 'correção de rumo' em quarto setores," *ESP* (April 16, 1980), 5; See also "Serpa condena presença das multis na política energetica brasileira" *FSP* (February 14, 1980), as cited in Santos, "Alcohol as Fuel," 426; "Capital externo fora do Proálcool na distribuição," *ESP* (April 9, 1980), 29.
114. In fact, Garnero's model had already begun at some distilleries in both São Paulo and Minas Gerais. See, for example, "Já há capital externo no Proálcool" *ESP* (April 27, 1980), 54; "Debatido o interesse do capital externo no álcool," 24.
115. CENAL Relatório 169/80; Processo CENAL no.122/80, signed by the President of the IAA, Hugo Almeida, November 19, 1980. BR RJANRIO IY J5.19 Caixa 4634.
116. Ibid.
117. Ibid.
118. This included the largest usina in the country and the neighbor of the Usina Santa Elisa, the Usina São Martinho. The usina submitted a revised expansion application in September 1981. See original proposal, CENAL Relatório 0083/81, submitted July 1981; revised proposal, CENAL Relatório 567/81, submitted September 1981. BR RJANRIO IY D6.16 Caixa 1921.

119. Santos, "Alcohol as Fuel," 422–423; Barzelay, *The Politicized Market Economy*, 183–184.
120. Skidmore, *The Politics of Military Rule*, 67.
121. "O Proálcool, inflacionário," *ESP* (January 6, 1981), 24; Barzelay, *The Politicized Market Economy*, 221–222.
122. Given Proálcool budget cuts, the World Bank loan provided all the funding for projects approved in 1982, and by 1984, about 75% of Proálcool's funds came from the World Bank. See Santos, "Alcohol as Fuel," 430–436; Demetrius, *Brazil's National Alcohol Program*, 100.
123. The aggressive pricing strategy created problems for the company in the mid-1980s when the World Bank financing dried up, after which the company started to fall behind on projects and lose clients. See Hasse, *Filhos do Fogo*, 195–196, 200; Barzelay, *The Politicized Market Economy*, 195, n. 70; Santos, "Alcohol as Fuel," 433–436.
124. "O impasse do álcool," *Veja* 677 (August 26, 1981), 84–86.
125. "A subida da montanha," *Veja* 708 (March 31, 1982), 100–101; "Produtores de álcool acusam as montadores," *FSP* (June 10, 1983); Pompeu, " 'Elitista!' 'impatriótico!' e o programa emplaca," 63; see also Santos, "Alcohol as Fuel," 471.
126. Rubens da Silva, "Assim nasceu Santa Elisa," 15.
127. Anfavea, *Anuário da Indústria Automobilística Brasileira*, 59; Biagi Filho, "O álcool é nosso"; Pedro Zan, "A grande usina: Aqui se produz," *ESP* (June 16, 1985), 20.
128. The political scientist Castro Santos also asserts that private ethanol equipment producers were critical in pushing public opinion in favor of the program and ethanol-fueled cars in periods of waning support in the early 1980s. See Santos, "Alcohol as Fuel," 203.
129. "A cana já rende 5 bilhões de litros," *ESP* (April 24, 1981), 49; "Para Belotti, descrença no álcool é injustificável," *ESP* (June 24, 1981), 27; "Biagi prevê participação estrangeiro no Proálcool," *ESP* (May 14, 1982), 29.
130. Biagi Filho, "O álcool é nosso."
131. Interview with Maurilio Biagi Filho, May 21, 2013.
132. Barzelay, *The Politicized Market Economy*, 31; Anfavea, *Anuário da Indústria Automobilística Brasileira*, 59; Márcia Azanha Ferraz Dias de Moraes, "Considerações sobre a indústria do etanol do Brasil," in *Biocombustíveis: realidade e perspectivas*, ed. Ministério das Relações Exteriores (Brasilia: Ministério das Relações Exteriores, 2007), 143.

Chapter 4

1. Stefani, "Álcool"; "O outro lado da moeda," *Veja* 707 (March 24, 1982), 92–94; "A subida da montanha," 100–101.
2. More traditional analyses of sugar's environmental impact have focused on land degradation and deforestation associated with its monocultural cultivation. See, for example, Dean, *With Broadax and Firebrand*; Monzote, *From Rainforest to Canefield*.

3. Shawn Miller, "Fuelwood in Colonial Brazil: The Economic and Social Consequences of Fuel Depletion in the Bahian Recôncavo, 1549–1820," *Forest and Conservation History* 38, no. 4 (1994): 189.
4. Ordinance/GM/N. 124 of August 20, 1980 in J. de O. Rezende, "Vinhaça: Outra grande ameaça ao meio-ambiente," *Revista-Magistra* 1 (1984): 99.
5. Freyre, *Nordeste*, 60. José Lins do Rêgo's famous semi-fictional work, *Usina* (Rio de Janeiro: Livraria José Olympio Ed., 1936), also called attention to the noxious practice.
6. A pH of 7 is neutral on a scale of 0 to 14. Any reading below 7 is acidic.
7. Franz O. Brieger, "Meio de utilização da vinhaça," *ESP* (November 2, 1960)," 33.
8. Jorge Bierrenbach de Castro, "Usina que ajuda a melhorar a cultura da cana," *ESP–Suplemento Agrícola* (September 15 1965), 48–49.
9. Jayme Rocha de Almeida, "O problema da vinhaça," (Rio de Janeiro: IAA, 1955), 12–16.
10. Margarida Maria de Oliveira, "Vinhoto: Poluição e a grande ameaça," *ESP* (April 27, 1980), 54.
11. IAA, *Anuário Açucareiro 1953–1956* (Rio de Janeiro: IAA, 1956), xi.
12. Hartzmark, "Businesses, Associations and Regions," 278.
13. On guano, see Edward Melillo, "The First Green Revolution: Debt Peonage and the Making of the Nitrogen Fertilizer Trade, 1840–1930," *American Historical Review* 117, no. 4 (2012): 1028–1029.
14. Brieger, "Meio de utilização", 33; "A vinhaça como fertilizante," *ESP* (August 29, 1953), 3.
15. W. Leithe, *The Analysis of Organic Pollutant in Waste and Waste Water*, trans. STS, Inc. (Ann Arbor, MI: Ann Arbor Science Publishers, Inc., 1973), 6–7.
16. Rocha de Almeida, "O problema da vinhaça," 6–7.
17. Brasil, *Códigos de Águas*. Federal Decree no. 24.643 of July 10, 1934, articles 110 and 111. See also articles no. 267 and 271. On the law's history and comparative legislation of the period, see Lise Sedrez, "The Bay of All Beauties: State and Environment in Guanabara Bay, Rio de Janeiro, Brazil, 1878–1975" (Ph.D. diss., Stanford University, 2005), 212. Mexico notably established early water legislation in 1888 and formally claimed public domain over all waterways in 1910. See Mikael Wolfe, *Watering the Revolution: An Environmental and Technological History of Agrarian Reform in Mexico* (Durham, NC: Duke University Press, 2017), 17.
18. Sedrez, "The Bay of All Beauties," 213–214.
19. Ministry of Agriculture, Ordinance no. 69, March 3 1943 as published in *Diario Oficial* (March 16, 1943), 3789–3790.
20. Ibid; Fishing Code, art. 16, Decree no. 794 of Oct 19, 1938.
21. Sedrez, "The Bay of All Beauties," 212.
22. Fishing Code, art. 162.
23. Randolfo Marques Lobato, "Poluição das Aguas: 9: Falta unidade à máquina administrativa," *ESP* (April 18, 1965), 15.
24. "Noticias do Interior," *ESP* (July 19, 1931), 6; "Noticias do Interior," *ESP* (July 26, 1933), 2; "Epizootia entre os peixes," *ESP* (July 1, 1937), 6; "Peixes mortos no Rio Taquary," *ESP* (July 31, 1938), 10.

25. "Noticias do Interior," *ESP* (July 26, 1933), 2.
26. De Melo, *A política do álcool-motor,* Appendix.
27. "Mortande de peixes no ribeirão Chibarro, em Araraquara," *ESP* (October 11, 1938), 7.
28. "Construccão de uma 'cidade ferroviária' em Araraquara," *ESP* (October 14, 1938), 6.
29. "A aproveitamento das caldas das distilarias," *ESP* (November 15, 1942), 1.
30. Memorandum to IAA President Truda, August 7, 1935. BR RJANRIO IY LATA 458.
31. Codiq advertisement, *Brasil Açucareiro* (March 1943), 20.
32. Hasse, *Maurilio Biagi*, 185–186.
33. Urgel de Almeida Lima, "Um resumo histórico sobre a vinhaça em Piracicaba," *Revista Instituto Histórico Geográfico de Piracicaba* 20 (2013): 258.
34. Rocha de Almeida, "O problema de vinhaça," 18.
35. Lima, "Um resumo histórico sobre a vinhaça em Piracicaba," 258.
36. Francisco Bergamin, "A cana e o restilo," *ESP* (September 9, 1953), 9; see also Lima, "Um resumo histórico sobre a vinhaça em Piracicaba," 258–259.
37. Edgar Fernandes Teixeira, "Assuntos Agrícolas: Rei da Agua Doce e outros substitutos da carpa," *ESP* (November 19, 1948), 6.
38. The historian José Augusto Pádua has noted the general ineptitude of regulation in Brazilian environmentalism's development during this period. See José Augusto Pádua, "Environmentalism in Brazil: A Historical Perspective," in *A Global Companion to Global Environmental History*, ed. J. R. McNeill and Erin Stewart Mauldin (Hoboken, NJ: Wiley-Blackwell Publishing, 2012), 459–465.
39. "Aguas poluidas de nossos rios," *ESP* (October 2, 1953), 5.
40. Teixeira, "Assuntos Agrícolas," 6; "Poluição e mortande de peixes," *ESP* (November 19, 1954), 10.
41. Lima, "Um resumo histórico sobre a vinhaça em Piracicaba," 266.
42. "Noticias de Piracicaba," *ESP* (November 16, 1952), 12; "O emprego do restilo como adubo e o problema da poluição dos rios," *ESP* (November 8, 1953), 36; "A vinhaça como fertilizante," *ESP* (August 29, 1953), 3.
43. "Considerada impropria para o consume a agua de rios que recebem restilo," *ESP* (November 15, 1953), 36.
44. "Considerada impropria para o consume a agua de rios que recebem restilo," 36. The experts included Dr. Raul Machado Filho and Professors Domingos Gallo, Desmostenes Santos Corrêa, and Anisio Ferraz Godinho, dean of the Colegio Piracicabano, and Francisco Goçalves Nocetti.
45. "Considerada impropria para o consume a agua de rios que recebem restilo," 36.
46. Peter Maier, "BOD test: History and Description," http://www.petermaier.net/clean-water-act/bod-test-history-and-description-2/ (May 17, 2015), accessed on October 2, 2021.
47. "A vinhaça como fertilizante," *ESP* (August 29, 1953), 3.
48. "Poluição de rios em Piracicaba," *ESP* (December 3, 1953), 10.
49. Lima, "Um resumo histórico sobre a vinhaça em Piracicaba," 267; Bergamin, "A cana e o restilo," 9; "Aguas poluidas de nossos rios," *ESP* (September 17, 1953), 9.

50. "Considerada impropria para o consume da agua de rios que recebem restilo," 36; "Companha contra a poluição: Protesto da UDN contra a comissionamento para a capital de promotor de Piracicaba," *ESP* (December 19, 1953), 8.
51. Thomas Rogers argues that Brazilian caneworkers politicized fire, an easily accessible tool, to contest transformations of the land while employers used fire to terrorize workers in Pernambuco. Gillian McGillivray notes how Cuban workers similarly forced sugar mill owners to extend cane production beyond quotas with arson of additional lands. In truth, the practice reaches further back even to the Haitian Revolution. See Rogers, *The Deepest Wounds*, ch. 5; Gillian McGillivray, *Blazing Cane: Sugar Communities, Class, and State Formation in Cuba, 1868–1959* (Durham, NC: Duke University Press, 2009); Laurent Dubois, *Avengers of the New World: The Story of the Haitian Revolution* (Cambridge, MA: Harvard University Press, 2004).
52. Lima, "Um resumo histórico sobre a vinhaça em Piracicaba," 265–266. Environmental justice is a weighted and anachronistic term often used in a US context today, but I use it here to highlight Brazilian mobilization around environmental issues long before debates about the Amazon won international attention in the 1970s.
53. Law no. 1350 of December 12, 1951. The DAEE later moved to the jurisdiction of the Special Service of Electrical Planning Works (Serviço Especial de Obras do Plano de Eletrificação) in January 1956.
54. Decree no. 2.182 of July 23, 1953, *Diario oficial do Estado de São Paulo* (July 25, 1953).
55. "O problema da poluição dos cursos de agua em Piracicaba," *ESP* (September 9, 1953), 10.
56. "Aguas poluídas de nossos rios," *ESP* (December 22, 1953), 7.
57. Decree no. 2.182 of July 23, 1953; "Denunciados os industriais responsáveis pela poluição das aguas do rio Piracicaba," *ESP* (November 19, 1954), 10.
58. Francisco Bergamin, "Usinas de cana e poluição dos rios," *ESP* (May 3, 1961), 42.
59. "Há solução ao problema da poluição das aguas de Piracicaba," *ESP* (November 14, 1954), 53.
60. "Aguas poluídas de nossos rios," 7; "Solicitada abertura de inquérito sobre a mortandade de peixes no rio Piracicaba," *ESP* (January 23, 1955), 15. See Municipal Law 393 of Piracicaba. Bergamin, "Usinas de cana e poluição dos rios," 42.
61. "O lançamento de restilo nos cursos de agua do município de Piracicaba," *ESP* (January 9, 1954), 4.
62. "Solicitada abertura de inquérito sobre a mortandade de peixes no rio Piracicaba," 15; Lima, "Um resumo histórico sobre a vinhaça em Piracicaba," 266.
63. Rocha de Almeida, "O problema da vinhaça," 5; Lima paraphrasing Lecy in "Um resumo histórico sobre a vinhaça em Piracicaba," 260.
64. Rocha de Almeida, "O problema da vinhaça," 16–17.
65. Bergamin, "Usinas de cana e poluição dos rios," 42.
66. Lobato, "Falta unidade à máquina administrativa,"15.
67. Law no. 4.904 of December 17, 1965.
68. Lobato, "Falta unidade à máquina administrativa,"15.
69. Lobato, "Falta unidade à máquina administrativa,"15.

70. Decree no. 50.079, July 24, 1968.
71. Decree of February 19, 1970, *Diario oficial do Estado de São Paulo* (February 20, 1970), 3. Law 2.182 was lightly amended in Law 3.068 of July 14, 1955, to increase the fine for noncompliance and broaden the category of aquatic life as a victim of pollution.
72. Hochstetler and Keck, *Greening Brazil*, 6; Dean, *With Broadax and Firebrand*, 292.
73. Governo do Estado de São Paulo, *Macrozoneamento das Bacias dos Rios Mogi Guaçu, Pardo, e Médio Grande: Questões Sócio-Ambientais Regionais*, (São Paulo: CETESB, 1995), 7.
74. On international influence, see Ronie Garcia-Johnson, *Exporting Environmentalism: U.S. Multinational Chemical Corporations in Brazil and Mexico* (Cambridge, MA: MIT Press, 2000); Brazilian environmental historians have vigorously opposed this position. For more on the debate, see José Augusto Pádua, "The Birth of Green Politics in Brazil: Exogenous and Endogenous Factors," in *Green Politics Two*, ed. W. Rudig (Edinburgh: Edinburgh University Press, 1992), 134–155; Hochstetler and Keck, *Greening Brazil*, 6, 75–83, 191–195.
75. Law no. 118, "Atos Legislativos," *Diario Oficial do Estado de São Paulo* (June 30, 1973).
76. Decree no. 5.992 and 5.993, *Diario Oficial do Estado de São Paulo* (April 17, 1975).
77. "Aguas poluidas de nossos rios," *ESP* (September 17, 1953), 9.
78. Francisco Bergamin, "Os peixes e a poluição," *ESP* (December 7, 1966), 31.
79. "Usinas paralisem e poluição diminui," *ESP* (October 30, 1968), 15.
80. "Usina oferece explicações," *ESP* (December 1, 1968), 37.
81. Jorge Bierrenbach de Castro, "Usina que ajuda a melhorar a cultura da cana," *ESP* (September 15, 1965), 9.
82. "Usina oferece explicações," 37.
83. "Cetesb sempre optimista," *ESP* (December 3, 1978), 66; see also CETESB, "Avaliação da situação atual de contaminação dos rios Mogi-Guaçu e Pardo e seus reflexos sobre as comunidades biológicas," vol. 1 (São Paulo: CETESB, 1980), 12.
84. "Usina nega poluição de Mogi-Guaçu," *ESP* (November 29, 1973), 38. However, by 1978, the newspaper would identify the usina as one of the largest polluters along the entire Mogi-Guaçu River. "No Tietê existiam peixes: Hoje só esgotos e detritos," *ESP* (December 3, 1978), 66.
85. See, for example, "Há solução ao problema da poluição das aguas de Piracicaba," *ESP* (November 14, 1954), 53.
86. Hermas Amaral Germek, "Aquecimento indireto da coluna de destilação e/ou aquecimento indireto da coluna de destilação com concentração de vinhaça (K1 e K2)." Paper Presented at the VII Seminário dos Têcnicos Açucareiros do Brasil (1979): 1. ESALQ No. 41741.
87. Antônio Celso Gemente, Davi Guilherme Gaspar Ruas, and Cláudio Hartkopf Lopes, "Evolução do rendimento agroindustrial nas usinas de açúcar do Estado de São Paulo," *Caderno Planalsucar, Piracicaba* 2, no. 1 (1983): 15; Bierrenbach de Castro, "A vinhaça proveniente da indústria de álcool," *ESP* (September 23, 1977), 37; de Oliveira, "Vinhoto," 54; José J. R. Moreira, P. U. M. Dos Santos, and G. E. Serra, "Ethanol Fuel: A Use of Biomass Energy in Brazil," *Ambio* 14, nos. 4/5 (1985): 294–295.

88. "Nos rios, a piracema é só tradição," *ESP* (8 Dec 1976), 22; See also Wilson Marini, "Em São Paulo, os rios condenados à morte," *ESP* (December 3, 1978), 66; Newton Castagnolli, "Ainda há tempo de salvar o rio Mogi-Guaçu," *ESP-Suplemento Agrícola* (November 14, 1979), 7.
89. Germek, "Aquecimento indireto da coluna de destilação," 1.
90. De Oliveira, "Vinhoto," 54.
91. J. J. Castellani, "O potássio das vinhaças," *ESP-Suplemento Agrícola* (June 25, 1972), 12; "Estado do Rio vai aproveitar vinhaça," *ESP* (June 9, 1976).
92. Rezende, "Vinhaça: Outra grande ameaça ao meio-ambiente," 49–56.
93. Usina Santa Elisa Proálcool Application, CNAl no. SP06/76. BR RJANRIO IY A6.16 Caixa 0443.
94. See Conger, Zanini, Racional advertisement, "300 mil litros de combustível e 110 mil quilos de fertilizante," n.d. APHRP Caixa 193. Estimates based on Universidade Estadual de Campinas (UNICAMP) estimates of a liter of ethanol to 13 liters of vinasse average in 1980. See de Oliveira, "Vinhoto," 54.
95. Conger, Zanini, Racional advertisement, "300 mil litros de combustível e 110 mil quilos de fertilizante," n.d. APHRP Caixa 193.
96. Usina Santa Elisa Proálcool Application, CNAl no. SP06/76. BR RJANRIO IY A6.16 Caixa 0443.
97. Ricardo Bueno, *Pró-Álcool: Rumo ao desastre* (Petrópolis: Editora Vozes Ltda, 1980), 42.
98. Miller, *An Environmental History of Latin America*, 209.
99. Bierrenbach de Castro, "A vinhaça proveniente da indústria de álcool," 37. Antônio Jose de Carmo, "Região de Araçatuba teme poluição das destilarias," *ESP* (November 28, 1982), 41; The Biagis also complained of valve problems with fuel tanks in the late 1970s. See Letter from Maurilio Biagi Filho to the President of National Petroleum Council on March 27, 1978. BR RJANRIO IY A6.16 Caixa 443.
100. "Técnicos pedem pesquisas para vinhoto," *ESP* (March 8, 1981), 54.
101. Bierrenbach de Castro, "A vinhaça proveniente da indústria de álcool," 37.
102. Bierrenbach de Castro, "A vinhaça proveniente da indústria de álcool," 37; "Mecanização agrícola enfrenta crise," *Química e derivados* 16, no. 190 (1982): 34. For more on vinasse vehicles, see also, Gastão Moraes de Silveira, "Aplicação de vinhaça concentrada," *ESP* (October 14, 1981), 38.
103. De Oliveira, "Vinhoto," 54. See, for example, Eurípedes Malavolta, "A adubação da cana-de-açúcar," *ESP-Suplemento Agrícola* (July 11, 1971); "A vinhaça de cana pode corrigir solo," *ESP* (August 20, 1976), 33.
104. Bueno, *Pro-Álcool*, 42; "Estado do Rio vai aproveitar vinhoto."
105. Ordinance/GM/N. 323 of November 29, 1978, cited in Rezende, "Vinhaça: Outra grande ameaça ao meio-ambiente," 96–98. In 1976, the Ministry of the Interior passed legislation on internal waters in Ordinance GM 0013 of October 15, 1976. Rezende, "Vinhaça: Outra grande ameaça ao meio-ambiente," 102.
106. Other examples include the Fundação Estadual de Engenharia do Meio Ambiente (FEEMA), in Rio de Janeiro, or the Superintendência de Recursos Hídricos e Meio Ambiente in Paraná (Surehma). See "A Sema espera ter meios que faltavam" *ESP* (5 June 1980), 48; "Técnicos pedem pesquisas para vinhoto," 54.

107. Ordinance/GM/N. 323 of November 29, 1978, cited in Rezende, "Vinhaça: Outra grande ameaça ao meio-ambiente," 96–98.
108. See, for example, IAA: Acompanhamento e fiscalização, Relatorio no. 001/82 application by Carlos Eduardo Ferreira Pereira of June 21, 1982.
109. "Lei Áurea dos rios paulistas," *ESP* (December 2, 1978), 20.
110. See, for example, "Proibição de lançamento de resíduos tóxicos nos rios," *ESP* (December 2, 1954), 12; Bergamin, "Usinas de cana e poluição dos rios," 42; Bierrenbach de Castro, "Usina que ajuda a melhorar a cultura da cana," 48–49; "Usinas paralisem e poluição diminui," 15.
111. Germek, "Aquecimento indireto da coluna de destilação," 4.
112. Rezende, "Vinhaça: Outra grande ameaça ao meio-ambiente," 52–53, 79–80, 99; Carlos Alberto Nonino, "Vinhoto: De problema a solução," *ESP* (January 7, 1987), 47.
113. Ordinance GM/n. 124 of August 20, 1980, in Rezende, "Vinhaça: Outra grande ameaça ao meio-ambiente," 76.
114. "Os perigos do vinhoto," *ESP* (March 13, 1983), 27; Rezende, "Vinhaça: Outra grande ameaça ao meio-ambiente," 80–81.
115. Hochstetler and Keck, *Greening Brazil*, 30–31.
116. "Indústria responsável por 90% da poluição," *ESP* (March 19, 1981), 26.
117. Roberto Manera, "O poderoso agente do bem e do mal," *Globo Rural* 1, no. 9 (1986): 72–73; "Agrovale matou peixes; Será multada e fechada," *ESP* (March 27, 1984), 13.
118. Rezende, "Vinhaça: Outra grande ameaça ao meio-ambiente," 105.
119. Joel A. Tarr, *The Search for the Ultimate Sink: Urban Pollution in Historical Perspective* (Akron, OH: University of Akron Press, 1996), 103–104.
120. Lerner adapted the term from American government officials who called radioactive nuclear testing sites "National Sacrifice Zones" in the 1940s. See Steve Lerner, *Sacrifice Zones: The Front Lines of Toxic Chemical Exposure in the United States* (Cambridge, MA: MIT Press, 2010), 2–3.
121. Nancy Langston, *Sustaining Lake Superior: An Extraordinary Lake in a Changing World* (New Haven, CT: Yale University Press, 2017), 14–21; José Augusto Pádua, "The Dilemma of the 'Splendid Cradle': Nature and Territory in the Construction of Brazil," in *A Living Past: Environmental Histories of Modern Latin America*, ed. John Soluri, Claudia Leal, and José Augusto Pádua (New York: Berghahn, 2018), 109.

Chapter 5

1. Biagi Filho, "O álcool é nosso;" Perani, "A greve dos bóias-frias em São Paulo," 17; Interview with Élio Neves, Jennifer Eaglin, May 26, 2020; Ernesto Paglia, *Rede Globo* (June 1984) in "Boias-frias e o Acordo de Guariba após a greve de 1984," (July 24, 2014), https://www.youtube.com/watch?v=9ZiZbF6WYUk, accessed October 4, 2021.
2. Ubaldo Silveira, *Igreja e conflito agrário: A comissão pastoral da terra na região de Ribeirão Preto* (Franca, SP: Unesp, 1998), 14. "Proálcool, quem sai ganhando,"

Cadernos de Estudos, no. 11 (October 1984). Brazilian Popular Groups: Arquivo Edgard Leunroth (BGP: AEL).

3. Rob Nixon, *Slow Violence and the Environmentalism of the Poor* (Cambridge, MA: Harvard University Press, 2011); See also Nancy Scheper-Hughes, *Death without Weeping: The Violence of Everyday Life in Brazil* (Berkeley, CA: University of California Press, 1992), 4; Silveira, *Igreja e conflito agrário*, 69; Silva, *Errantes do fim do século*, 27.
4. See, for example, Welch, *A semente foi plantada*; Antonio Thomaz Júnior, *Por trás dos canaviais, os "nós" da cana: A relação capital x trabalho e o movimento sindical dos trabalhadores na agroindústria canavieira paulista* (São Paulo: Annablume/Fapesp, 2002); Luiz Antonio da Silva, "Sindicalismo, assalariados rurais e a luta pela cidadania," in *Modernização e impactos sociais: O caso da agroindústria sucro-alcooleira na região de Ribeirão Preto (SP)*, ed. Rosemeire Scopinho and Leandro Valarelli (Rio de Janeiro: FASE, 1995), 87–114.
5. For more on the colonato system and its demise, see Stolcke, *Coffee Planters, Workers, and Wives*, esp. ch. 3.
6. See Clifford Welch, *The Seed Was Planted: The São Paulo Roots of Brazil's Rural Labor Movement, 1924-1964* (University Park, PA: Pennsylvania State University Press, 1999), 8–9; Clifford Andrew Welch, "Rivalry and Unification: Mobilising Rural Workers in São Paulo on the Eve of the Brazilian Golpe of 1964." *Journal of Latin American Studies* 27, no. 1 (1995): 172.
7. Welch, *A semente foi plantada*, 108–112.
8. Cliff Welch, "Keeping Communism down on the Farm: The Brazilian Rural Labor Movement during the Cold War," *Latin American Perspectives* 33, no. 3 (2006): 32. The PCB had interest in developing the peasantry into a proletariat to then lead a larger communist uprising, but their efforts directly affected rural labor mobilization.
9. Welch, *A semente foi plantada*, 151.
10. Welch, *A semente foi plantada*, 108–112; Pereira, *The End of the Peasantry*. On industrial workers' path to labor rights, see Wolfe, *Working Women, Working Men*, 2–5; French, *The Brazilian Workers' ABC*; Weinstein, *For Social Peace in Brazil*.
11. Welch, "Keeping Communism down on the Farm," 34–35.
12. Silva, *Errantes do fim do século*, 63–64; da Silva, "Sindicalismo, assalariados rurais e a luta pela cidadania," 87.
13. Thomas Skidmore, *Brazil: Five Centuries of Change* (New York: Oxford University Press, 2010), 150–151, Stepan, *The Military in Politics*, ch. 8. See also Stephen Rabe, *Killing Zone: The United States Wages Cold War in Latin America* (New York: Oxford University Press, 2012), 104–113.
14. Wenceslau Gonçalves Neto, *Estado e agricultura no Brasil: política agricola e modernização economica Brasileira, 1960-1980* (São Paulo: Editora Hucitec, 1997), 53; Skidmore, *The Politics of Military Rule*, 68–70, 90–92; Houtzager, "State and Unions in the Transformation of the Brazilian Countryside, 1964–1975," 112–114. See also Roberto Campos, "Agricultura, reforma agrária e ideologia," *FSP* (November 12, 1995).

15. da Silva, "Sindicalismo, assalariados rurais e a luta pela cidadania," 89; Silva, *Errantes do fim do século*, 115.
16. Stolcke, *Coffee Planters, Workers, Wives*, 113–132.
17. Rosemeire Aparecida Scopinho, "Modernização e superexploração na agroindústria sucroalcooleira," Modernização e impactos sociais: O caso da agroindústria sucro-alcooleira na região de Ribeirão Preto (SP), ed. Rosemeire Scopinho and Leandro Valarelli (Rio de Janeiro: FASE, 1995), 76.
18. Wilson Marini, "Jovem, analfabeto, e inexperiente, é o bóia-fria" *ESP* (May 20, 1984), 18.
19. São Paulo Secretaria da Economia e Planejamento (Seplan), *Trabalho volante na agricultura paulista* (Estudos e pesquisas) no. 25 (1978), 220–225, as cited in Welch, *A semente foi plantada*, 286, n. 81; Welch, *A semente foi plantada*, 298.
20. "Uma vida de muito trabalho e pouco dinheiro," *FSP* (May 17, 1984).
21. "Uma vida de muito trabalho e pouco dinheiro;" "São 40 mil colhendo laranja e outros 110 mil cortando cana," *FSP* (May 17, 1984).
22. "Uma vida de muito trabalho e pouco dinheiro;" "Os canaviais da ira," *Veja* 820 (May 23, 1984): 25. On temporary and permanent labor migration statistics, see São Paulo Secretaria de Economia e Planejamento Coordenaria de Ação Regional, *Plano Regional de Ribeirão Preto*, 7. Silva, *Errantes do fim do século*, 68–72; A. C. C. R. Motta and M. C. Quinteiro, "Repercussões do Proálcool no comportamento migratório do Estado de São Paulo: O caso de Ribeirão Preto," *Informe Demográfico (São Paulo)* (Fundação SEADE, no. 10, 1983), cited in Silva, *Errantes do fim do século*, 69.
23. Silva, *Errantes do fim do século*, 235. See also Weinstein, *The Color of Modernity*, 14; Silva, *Errantes do fim do século*, 230.
24. Maurilio Biagi Filho states that, from 1970 to 1986, jobs in the interior of São Paulo increased by 121% compared with 54% in the metropolitan region of São Paulo. Maurilio Biagi Filho, "A industrialização do interior," *Isto É Senhor* (November 8, 1988), 34.
25. This applies to the macroregion of Ribeirão Preto, which is larger than the administrative region of Ribeirão Preto. However, the administrative region of Ribeirão Preto had the second highest rate of population growth in the same period after the macroregion. See Rosemeire Aparecida Scopinho, "A região de Ribeirão Preto e a agroindústria sucro-alcooleira," in *Modernização e impactos sociais: O caso da agroindústria sucro-alcooleira na região de Ribeirão Preto (SP)*, ed. Rosemeire Scopinho e Leandro Valarelli (Rio de Janeiro: FASE, 1995), 40.
26. "São 40 mil colhendo laranja e outros 110 mil cortando cana," *FSP* (May 17, 1984).
27. Antenor Braido, "A difícil vida de quem corta cana," *FSP* (May 20, 1984).
28. There is some debate on the average amount of cane cut per day. Aparecida de Moraes Silva and others say five tons per day, while other studies suggest the average worker cut closer to 6–10 tons per day. I erred on the conservative side. See "Os canaviais da ira," 24–25; Carlos Alberto Nonino and Galeno Amorim, "Uma manhã de terror em Guariba," *ESP Suplemento-Agrícola* (May 16, 1984), 1; Perani, "A greve dos bóias-frias em São Paulo," 17–23; "Uma vida de muito trabalho e pouco dinheiro;" Silva, *Errantes do fim do século*, 92–93; Silveira, *Igreja e conflito agrário*, 58; Guariba Workers

Agreement in Ana Luiza Martins, ed., *Guariba: 100 anos* (São Paulo, Prefeitura Municipal de Guariba, 1996), 186–187; Welch, *A semente foi plantada*, 426; Rosa Ester Rossini, "Mulheres e homens na força de trabalho na agricultura: O exemplo da macro-área de Ribeirão Preto," Paper Presented at the 15th National Conference on Population Studies (ABEP-2006): 11–12. On inflation, see also Baer, *The Brazilian Economy*, 427.

29. Interview with Maria Conceição D'Incao, "Despertar do bóia-fria", Emanuel Neri, *Veja* 821 (May 30, 1984), 3–6; see also Welch, *A semente foi plantada*, 436–437.
30. Irene Vucovix, "Sob tensão, polícia ocupa Guariba," *ESP* (May 17, 1984), 14.
31. Interview with Padre José Domingos Bragheto, Jennifer Eaglin, April 13, 2013.
32. Scopinho, "A modernização e superexploração," 77; "Uma vida de muito trabalho e pouco dinheiro."
33. Quotation from "Doenças atingem zona canavieira" *ESP* (November 14, 1991), 17; see also José Roberto Ferreira, "A queima dos canaviais aflige Interior paulista," *ESP* (October 24, 1982), 45; "Quiemadas perturbam Interior," *ESP* (July 14, 1985), 28.
34. "Quiemadas perturbam Interior," 28.
35. Paglia in "Boias-frias e o Acordo de Guariba após a greve de 1984" *Rede Globo* (June 1984).
36. Interview with Neves, Eaglin; Federação de Órgãos para a Assistência Social e Educacional, *Boia-fria, Sangue Quente: Mobilização e Resistência dos Assalariados Temporários Rurais* (Jaboticabal: Fase, 1987), i–ii. For examples, see Jau cases, Folder 50z383-J, Arquivo Público do Estado de São Paulo (APESP).
37. Élcio Thenório, *Jornal Rural* (n.d.), Disc-File 5, Copersucar/Museu da Imagem; Federação dos Trabalhadores na Agricultura do Estado de São Paulo (FETAESP), "Epidemia de sarampo surge em 'alojamento' em Guariba: 1 morto" *Realidade Rural* (August 1984): 7. O Centro de Documentação e Pesquisa Vergueiro (CDPV): São Paulo.
38. FETAESP, "Secretarias estouram 'alojamento' em Pitangueiras: Ação exemplar," *Realidade Rural* (August, 1984): 7. CDPV.
39. "Considerada impropria para o consume a agua de rios que recebem restilo," 36; See chapter 3.
40. FETAESP, "Secretarias estouram 'alojamento' em Pitangueiras: Ação exemplar;" FETAESP, "Epidemia de sarampo surge em 'alojamento' em Guariba: 1 morto."
41. "Os canaviais da ira," 25. On sugar workers and the Northeast's environmental issues, see Rogers, *The Deepest Wounds*, and on perceptions of the region and water, see Buckley, *Technocrats and the Politics of Drought and Development in Twentieth-Century Brazil.*
42. Silva, *Errantes do fim do século*, 222–227.
43. Scopinho, "A região de Ribeirão Preto e a agroindústria sucro-alcooleira," 42.
44. "Os canaviais da ira," 20–26; "Sistema de corte da cana e contas de agua levaram crise a Guariba."
45. "Os canaviais da ira," 20–26.
46. "Revolta de bóias-frias provoca destruição e morte," *FSP* (May 16, 1984); José Murilo de Carvalho, "Surpresa é não ter acontecido antes" *FSP* (May 16, 1984).

47. "Uma vida de muito trabalho e pouco dinheiro."
48. Paglia, *Rede Globo* (June 1984).
49. Braido, "A difícil vida de quem corta cana."
50. Interview with Neves, Eaglin.
51. "Sistema de corte da cana e contas de agua levaram crise a Guariba," *FSP* (May 16, 1984).
52. Ícaro Ferracini, Leandro Santini, and Heloisa Zaruh, "O Corte- 30 anos da Greve de Guariba" (December 16, 2013), https://www.youtube.com/watch?v=FYUfU9FDguw, accessed October 4, 2021; See Guariba Workers Agreement in Martins, *Guariba: 100 anos*, 186–187. See also Welch, *A semente foi plantada*, 426.
53. "Uma vida de muito trabalho e pouco dinheiro."
54. Murilo de Carvalho, "Surpresa é não ter acontecido antes." See also "Sistema de corte da cana e contas de agua levaram crise a Guariba"; "Revolta de bóias-frias provoca destruição e morte;" Maria Aparecida de Moraes Silva, "Atrás das cortinas no palco do etanol," *FSP* (February 10, 2007) .
55. "Os canaviais da ira," 21.
56. Interview with Neves, Eaglin.
57. See also Archbishop Paulo Evaristo Arns and the Archdiocese of São Paulo, *Brasil: Nunca Mais* (São Paulo: Vozes, 1985); Catholic Church and the Archdiocese of São Paulo, *Torture in Brazil: A Report by the Archdiocese of São Paulo*, ed. Joan Dassin, trans. Jaime Wright (New York: Vintage Books, 1986), 123–124.
58. Margaret Keck, *The Workers' Party and Democratization in Brazil* (New Haven, CT: Yale University Press, 1992), 47; Skidmore, *The Politics of Military Rule*, 135–137, 180–183.
59. Silveira, *Igreja e conflito agrário*, 94–95.
60. Scott Mainwaring, *The Catholic Church and Politics in Brazil, 1916–1985* (Stanford, CA: Stanford University Press, 1986), 114.
61. Skidmore, *The Politics of Military Rule*, 135. Bishops in the Amazonian region in particular spoke out against the detrimental effects of the military's development programs in the region, which included the construction of the Transamazonian highway and large-scale cattle-grazing schemes. On Amazonian development schemes and land conflict, see Joe Foweraker, *The Struggle for Land: A Political Economy of the Pioneer Frontier in Brazil, 1930 to Present* (Cambridge: Cambridge University Press, 1981); Anthony L. Hall, *Developing Amazonia: Deforestation and Social Conflict in Brazil's Carajás Programme* (Manchester: Manchester University Press, 1989); Acker, *Volkswagen in the Amazon*.
62. Interview with Padre José Domingos Bragheto, Cliff Welch on September 13, 2004. Cliff Welch Personal Collection.
63. Ibid.
64. Ibid. See also Interview with Padre José Domingos Bragheto, Ubaldo Silveira on December 16, 1993, as cited in Silveira, *Igreja e conflito agrário*, 125. The CPT-São Paulo focused on labor rights and land reform.
65. Interview with Bragheto, Eaglin.
66. Interview with Bragheto, Eaglin.

67. Interview with Bragheto, Eaglin.
68. Perani, "A greve dos bóias-frias em São Paulo," 17–23.
69. Interview with Neves, Eaglin.
70. A pelego literally is a type of sheepskin horse blanket. For more on pelegos and their role in industrial unions, see Wolfe, *Working Women, Working Men*, 75–85.
71. Interview with Bragheto, Eaglin.
72. In fact, Bragheto was in Mato Grosso helping with a different land occupation in Ivinhema when the strike broke out, despite claims in the news to the contrary. Interview with Bragheto, Eaglin.
73. Interview with Bragheto, Eaglin. See, for example, "Igreja ao lado dos sindicatos," *ESP* (May 16, 1984), 38; "Os canavias da ira."
74. Perani, "A greve dos bóias-frias em São Paulo," 17–23; On Zilda Bezerra's experience, see Julia Chequer, "Memórias ocultas: Experiências de mulheres canavieiras em Guariba (1975–1985)," Master's thesis Programa de Pós-Graduação em História, Política e Bens Culturais, CPDOC/FGV, 2019: 154–155; See also Maria Antonieta Gomes Penteado, *Trabalhadores da cana: Protesto social em Guariba, maio de 1984* (Maringá: Eduem, 2000), 25–30.
75. Interview with Neves, Eaglin.
76. "Revolta de bóias-frias provoca destruição e morte;" Chequer, "Memórias ocultas," 144; Penteado, *Trabalhadores da cana*, 25.
77. Nonino and Amorim, "Uma manhã de terror em Guariba," 38. "E a greve continuará," *ESP* (May 17, 1984), 14.
78. Silveira, *Igreja e conflito agrário*, 73–75; "Revolta de bóias-frias provoca destruição e morte."
79. Antenor Braido, "Vitoriosos, trabalhadores encerram greves em Guariba," *FSP* (May 18, 1984), 23.
80. "O levante do bóias-fria: medo e tensão no interior," *Veja* 820 (May 23, 1984), 20–26.
81. Alan Riding, "For Brazilian Farmhands, a Notable Victory," *New York Times* (June 10, 1984) ; "Tensão continua e pode faltar comida na cidade," *FSP* (May 17, 1984).
82. Moacyr Castro, "Usineiros temem colapso," *ESP* (May 17, 1984), 15.
83. Welch, *A semente foi plantada*, 422; Companha Nacional Pela Reforma Agrária (CNPRA), "Informa," no. 8 (November/December, 1984), 4. BPG: AEL.
84. "Sistema de corte da cana e contas de água levaram crise a Guariba."
85. "Sabesp nega que tarifa sejam altas," *FSP* (May 16, 1984).
86. "Montoro culpa a crise e Gusmão acusa a 'ganância' " *FSP* (May 16, 1984).
87. "Os canaviais da ira," 26.
88. Interview with Neves, Eaglin.
89. "Revolta de bóias-frias provoca destruição e morte."
90. "E a greve continuará," 14.
91. Interview with Neves, Eaglin.
92. "Sem greve, calma volta ao Interior," *ESP* (May 18, 1984), 10.
93. Interview with Neves, Eaglin.
94. "Guariba começa a esquecer o tumulto," *ESP* (May 18, 1984), 10.
95. Original accord reproduced in Martins, *Guariba: 100 anos*, 186–187; "Sem greve, calma volta ao Interior," 10.

96. “Sem greve, calma volta ao Interior,” 10.
97. Interview with Neves, Eaglin; Interview with Bragheto, Eaglin.
98. CNPRA, “Informa,” 14.
99. “Coordenador da Pastoral da Terra diz que não é líder,” *FSP* (May 17, 1984).
100. “Mil bóias-frias em greve exigem dissídio cumprido,” *ESP* (July 6, 1984), 9.
101. The National Confederation of Agricultural Workers reported this case to the Ministry of Justice. See “Bóias-frias preocupam novamente,” *ESP* (August 16, 1984), 16; CNPRA, “Informa,” 15.
102. Interview with Bragheto, Eaglin; FETAESP, “Secretarias estouram ‘alojamento’ em Pitangueiras: Ação exemplar,” 7.
103. “Temer critica trabalhadores e garante que ordem será mantida,” *FSP* (May 16, 1984); “Os canaviais da ira,” 20; “Comandante PM reafirma que tropa não atirou” *FSP* (May 17, 1984); “Bombas e espancamentos na greve em Bebedouro,” FSP (May 17, 1984); Perani, “A greve dos bóias-frias em São Paulo,” 17.
104. Silveira, *Igreja e conflito agrário*, 79–81; Diário do Município, *Diário Oficial do Estado de São Paulo* (November 30, 1984), Section 1, 61.
105. Interview with Galeno Amorim, Jennifer Eaglin, April 22, 2020.
106. Interview with Neves, Eaglin; see also Interview with Amorim, Eaglin.
107. FETAESP, “Aos domingos a TV fala do trabalhador rural: E qui vai um convite” *Realidade Rural* (August 1984): 3; FETAESP, “Secretarias estouram ‘alojamento’ em Pitangueiras: Ação exemplar,” 3, 7.
108. Interview with Amorim, Eaglin.
109. In fact, the Guariba strikes were so popular they inspired a telenovela, *O Salvador da Patria*, in the late 1980s. See Laura César Muniz, “O Salvador da Patria,” *Rede Globo* (January 9–August 12,1989), https://memoriaglobo.globo.com/entretenimento/novelas/o-salvador-da-patria/, accessed October 4, 2021.
110. “Usina utiliza ônibus para transporte de bóias-frias,” *Jornal do Interior* 86 (1984): 10. Folder 50/028, APESP.
111. Paglia, *Rede Globo* (June 1984).
112. Copersucar, “O álcool não traz apenas economia de divisas: O álcool traz outras soluções,” *Petro & Química* 11, no. 8 (1979): 19.
113. A CPT pamphlet summarized the program's three key objectives: “1. End the oil crisis; 2. End the external debt (debts that were not made by the people nor had their approval); 3. End employment inequality between the north and the south of the country.” See Associação de solidariedade as comunidades carentes de MT (Mato Grosso), Comissão Pastoral da Terra/regional de MT, and Centro de documentação terra e índio, “Pro-álcool: mar de cana, mar de miséria,” (Cuiabá, MT, 1984): 10-11. BPG: AEL; Biagi Filho, “O álcool é nosso.”
114. “O Proálcool, inflacionário,” *ESP* (January 6, 1981), 24; see also Chapter 3.
115. “Produtores de álcool acusam as montadores,” *FSP* (June 10, 1983).
116. Fernando Homem de Melo, “O álcool é nosso, mas quem paga o desperdício?” *FSP* (May 15, 1983), as cited in Cláudio de Araújo Peçanha, “O álcool é do povo brasileiro,” *O Diário* (May 31, 1983).

117. Homem de Melo, "O álcool é nosso, mas quem paga o desperdício?" For more examples, see Fernando Homem de Melo, "Por que o álcool não é a melhor alternativa?" *Revista Exame* 256 (July 28, 1982): 102>>>; Fernando Homem de Melo, "Crise agrícola," *FSP* (February 13, 1983), 18; Homem de Melo, "O álcool é nosso, mas quem paga o desperdício?" 40; Fernando Homem de Melo "O problema é mais sério do que se imagina" *ESP–Suplemento Agrícola* (October 26, 1983), 3. For a more comprehensive account, see also Homem de Melo, *Proálcool, energia e transportes* (São Paulo: Enio Matheus Guazzelli & Cia. Ltda., 1981), 5–31.
118. CNPRA, "Informa," 15.
119. FETAESP, "José Gomes da Silva volta ao batente: E Secretarias querem disciplinar Proálcool," *Realidade Rural* (July 1984): 8. CDPV.
120. Rubens Rodrigues dos Santos interview with the engineer and industrialist João Augusto do Amaral Gurgel, "Valeu a pena investir tanto?" ESP (May 20, 1984), 48.
121. Rubens Rodrigues dos Santos interview with Minister of Industry and Commerce Camilo Penna, "Penna rebate as críticas ao Proálcool," ESP (May 22, 1984), 41.
122. Barzelay, *The Politicized Market Economy*, 300, n. 20; Santos, "Alcohol as Fuel," 254; Ruben Rodrigues dos Santos interview with Lamartine Navarro Júnior, "Pretende-se socializar Proálcool em São Paulo," ESP (May 23, 1984), 22.
123. Ibid.
124. Rubens Rodrigues dos Santos interview with Luiz Lacerda Biagi, "Salário pouco pesa no Proálcool," ESP (May 27, 1984), 42.
125. Ibid.
126. Maurilio Biagi Filho, "O balanço positivo do Proálcool," *FSP* (October 6, 1985).
127. Richard White, *The Organic Machine: The Remaking of the Columbia River* (New York: Hill and Wang, 1996), 4.

Chapter 6

1. Leonencio Nossa, "Lula diz que tornou usineiros 'heróis mundiais,'" *ESP* (March 21, 2007), 7.
2. Pompeu, "'Elitista!' 'impatriótico!' e o programa emplaca," 62–65.
3. "O problema do abastecimento de álcool," *ESP* (July 15, 1989), 3; Bob Sharp, "Carro a álcool," *ESP* (August 16, 2001), 3.
4. Scholars have noted the promotional shift from economic savings to environmental benefits in the 1990s, but not examined how and why interest groups, particularly the sugar sector and the auto industry, intentionally did this. Hochstetler and Keck, *Greening Brazil*, 207; Brilhante, "Brazil's Alcohol Program," 435–449.
5. Anne Hanley, Julio Manuel Pires, Maurício Jorge Pinto de Soua, Renato Leite Marcondes, Rosne Nunes de Faria, and Sérgio Naruhiko Sakurai, "Critiquing the Bank: 60 Years of BNDES in the Academy," *Journal of Latin American Studies* 48, no. 4 (2016): 823–850; Triner, *Mining and the State*, 5.
6. While this book has laid out this case in the sugar sector, on the auto industry, see Ioris, *Transforming Brazil*. On the social and political importance of the car in

Brazil, see Wolfe, *Autos and Progress* and Owensby, *Intimate Ironies*; on its cultural and spatial importance, see Miller, *The Street Is Ours*.

7. "Seca agravará crise economia do Sul," *ESP* (February 16, 1986), 52.
8. "Seca agravará crise economia do Sul," 52. See also Eaglin, "The Demise of the Brazilian Ethanol Program," 104–129.
9. Cley Scholz, "Bois invadem canaviais e poderá faltar álcool," *ESP* (November 11, 1986), 41; "Elogiada a limitação do álcool," *ESP* (February 26, 1986), 28; United States Department of Agriculture, *Sugar and Sweetener Yearbooks*, https://www.ers.usda.gov/data-products/sugar-and-sweeteners-yearbook-tables/. Accessed December 1, 2021. See also Table 6.1.
10. WTI Cushing Crude Oil Prices in "Spot Prices for Crude Oil and Petroleum Products," US Energy Information Administration (EIA) https://www.eia.gov/dnav/pet/PET_PRI_SPT_S1_A.htm Accessed December 1, 2021; Dermot Gately, "Lessons from the 1986 Oil Price Collapse," *Brookings Papers on Economic Activity* 17, no. 2 (1986): 237–284.
11. "Como restituir? A Seplan não sabe," *ESP* (July 25, 1986), 24.
12. Scholz, "Bois invadem canaviais e poderá faltar álcool;" Ministry of Mines and Energy, O *modelo energético brasileiro*, 41; Anfavea 2015 Annual Report.
13. "Petrobras racionaliza as compras de álcool," *ESP* (January 29, 1983), 27.
14. "Conta álcool tem definido o saneamento," *ESP* (June 14, 1988), 30; Ricardo Boechat, "Nordeste poderá ficar sem combustíveis," *ESP* (September 11, 1988), 47.
15. "Em maio, álcool pode custar 65% da gasolina," *ESP* (January 6, 1984), 22; "Álcool a 70,00 sobe mais que a gasolina," *ESP* (June 23, 1988), 1.
16. "Nos postos de gasolina, muitas criticas às medidas do governo," *ESP* (May 21, 1988), 26.
17. Marli Olmos, "Nas retíficas, moda agora é gasoline," *ESP* (June 26, 1988), 49.
18. Boechat, "Nordeste poderá ficar sem combustíveis," 47. See also "Seca afetou os estoques," *ESP* (September 11, 1988), 47.
19. "No Interior, postos já fazem racionamento," *ESP* (May 12, 1989), 24.
20. "Produção de carros a álcool terá limite," *ESP* (May 17, 1989), 21.
21. "Produção de carros a álcool terá limite," 21; "Governo reduz a 50% produção de carro a álcool," *ESP* (May 17, 1989), 1; "Escassez de álcool vai durar até julho," *ESP* (May 19, 1989), 25.
22. "Pedido congelamento do Proálcool até 95," *ESP* (May 19, 1989), 25.
23. Anfavea, *Anuário da Indústria Automobilística Brasileira*, 59; see Table 6.2.
24. João Borges, "Problema previsto há 4 anos", *ESP* (May 19, 1989), 25.
25. "Um sonho corroído," *Veja* 1080 (May 24, 1989), 103.
26. Márcio de Moraes, "Cotas para o racionamento," *ESP* (December 21, 1989), 70; Interview with Werther Annicchino, president of Copersucar, "Crise chega ao fim," *Globo Rural—Economia* (July 1990), 24.
27. "Produtores de cana pedem mais crédito," *ESP* (November 15, 1990), 51; "Mais álcool para o Rio," *ESP* (November 15, 1990), 51.
28. György Miklós Böhm, Eduardo Massad, Paulo Hilário Saldiva, Maria Alice Gouveia, Carlos Augusto Pasqualucci, luiza Maria Nunes Cardoso, Marina Pires do

Rio Caldeira and Débora Fernandes Calheiros, "Comparative Toxicity of Alcohol and Gasoline Fueled Automobile Exhaust Fumes," in *Developments in the Science and Practice of Toxicology*, ed. A. W. Hayes, R. C. Schnell, and T. S. Miya (Elsevier, Amsterdam and New York, 1983), 480. See also P. H. N. Saldiva , E. Massad, M.P.R. Caldeira, D.R. Calheiros, C.D. Saldiva, M.A.L. Nicolelis, and G.M. Böhm, "Pulmonary Function of Rats Exposed to Ethanol and Gasoline Fumes," *Journal of Brazilian Medical Biological Research* 18 (1985): 573–577; Eduardo Massad et al, "Toxicity of Prolonged Exposure to Ethanol and Gasoline Autoengine Exhaust Gases," *Environmental Research* 40 (1986): 479–486; György Miklós Böhm, Paulo Hilário Nascimento Saldiva, Carlos Augusto Gonçalves Pasqualucci, Eduardo Massad, Milton de Arruda Martins, Walter Araújo Zin, Wellington Veras Cardoso, Patricia Martins Pereira Criado, Márcia Komatsuzaki, Regina Silvia Sakae, Elnara Márcia Negri, Miriam Lemos, Vera del Monte capelozzi, Cassiana Crestana, and Ruberval da Silva, "Biological Effects of Air Pollution in São Paulo and Cubatão," *Environmental Research* 49 (1989): 208–216.

29. Eduardo Massad, György M. Böhm, and Paulo H.N. Saldiva, "Ethanol Fuel Toxicity," in *Handbook of Hazardous Materials*, ed. Morton Corn (San Diego, CA: Academic Press, 1993), 274; Pedro Jacobi, Denise Baena Segura, and Marianne Kjellén, "Governmental Responses to Air Pollution: Summary of a Study of the Implementation of *rodízio* in São Paulo," *Environment and Urbanization* 11, no. 1 (1999): 79–82.
30. See, for example, José Goldemberg, "Brazil: Energy Options and Current Outlook," *Science* 200, no. 158 (1978): 158–164; José Goldemberg, "Renewable Energy Sources: The Case of Brazil," *Natural Resources Forum* 3, no. 3 (1979): 253–262; José Goldemberg, *Energia no brasil* (Rio de Janeiro: Livros Técnicos e Científicos, 1979); José Goldemberg, J. R. Moreira, P. U. M. Dos Santos, and G. E. Serra, "Ethanol Fuel: A Use of Biomass Energy in Brazil," *Ambio* 14, nos. 4–5, Energy in Developing Countries (1985): 293–297.
31. José Goldemberg, "Solving the Energy Problems in Developing Countries," *Energy* 11, no. 1 (1990): 19–24.
32. Walter Reid, Oswaldo Lucon, Suani Teixeira Coelho, and Patricia Guardabassi, *No Reason to Wait: The Benefits of Greenhouse Gas Reduction in São Paulo and California* (Menlo Park, CA: Hewlett Foundation, 2005), 19; Jacobi, Segura, and Kjellén, "Governmental Responses to Air Pollution," 80.
33. Henrique Amorim, "Réquiem para o Proálcool," *ESP* (November 20, 1996), 48.
34. Hochstetler and Keck, *Greening Brazil*, 207. See also Reid, Lucon, Coelho, and Guardabassi, *No Reason to Wait*, 6.
35. Shawn William Miller, "Fuelwood in Colonial Brazil: The Economic and Social Consequences of Fuel Depletion in the Bahian Recôncavo, 1549–1820," *Forest and Conservation History* 38, no. 4 (1994), 189.
36. José Coronado, "Bagaço aquece a indústria," *Química e derivados*, 16, no. 190 (1982), 45, 50, 53.
37. Galeno Amorim, "Simpósio discute alternativa para energia," *ESP* (August 18, 1989), 22. See also José Roberto Moreira and José Goldemberg, "O álcool como

combustível: considerações econômicas," *ESP—Suplemento Cultural* 2, no. 97 (September 10, 1978), 10-11; "Companhia de Sertãozinho aposta-se em co-geração há 53 anos," *ESP* (November 18, 2001), 18.

38. "Agonia das águas," 72.
39. Amorim, "Simpósio discute alternativa para energia," 22.
40. Governo do Estado de São Paulo, *Macrozoneamento das bacias dos rios Mogi Guaçu, Pardo, e Médio-Grande*, 113.
41. "Queimadas perturbam Interior," *ESP* (July 14, 1985), 28.
42. "A colheita mecânica da cana," *ESP* (October 7, 1973), 300; "Queimadas perturbam Interior," 28.
43. José Roberto Ferreira, "A queima dos canaviais aflige Interior paulista," *ESP* (October 24, 1982), 45.
44. "Queimadas perturbam Interior," 28.
45. Decree no. 28.848 of August 30, 1988, *Diario Oficial* (August 31, 1988), 7.
46. Moacyr Castro, "Documento explica a queimada," *ESP* (September 4, 1988), 26.
47. Castro, "Documento explica a queimada," 26.
48. Decree no. 28.895 of September 20, 1988. *Diario Oficial* (September 21, 1988), 2.
49. See, for example, "Uso do fogo é defendido por usineiros," *ESP* (November 4, 1991), 17; Galeno Amorim, "Queimadas de cana provocam poluição," *ESP* (November 4, 1991), 17; "Doenças atingem zona canavieira," *ESP* (November 14, 1991), 17; Patrícia Carvalho with Maria Aparecida P. Ramos, "O fogo à prova," *Globo Rural—Economia* (July 1993), 56–59; "Fuligem é o pior problema" *Globo Rural—Economia* (July 1993), 58–59.
50. Carvalho with Ramos, "O fogo à prova," 56–59.
51. Carvalho with Ramos, "O fogo à prova," 56–59.
52. Mário Duarte of São Paulo, "Temas de debates," *ESP* (December 14, 1995), 2.
53. "Usineiros apóiam consumidores," *ESP* (December 23, 1989), 18.
54. Galeno Amorim, "Governo e usineiros brigam com números," *ESP* (December 31, 1989), 51; Galeno Amorim, "Fabricantes farão campanha," *ESP* (December 30, 1989), 34; Luiz Guilhermino, "Petrobrás vai enfrentar usineiros," *ESP* (December 30, 1989), 34.
55. Amorim, "Fabricantes farão campanha," 34.
56. Rosane de Souza, "Estatal não vai abandonar usuário," *ESP* (December 30, 1989), 34.
57. "Beer defende importação do metanol," *ESP* (December 23, 1989), 18; "Gasolinas são parecidas," *ESP* (December 30, 1989), 34; Laura Tetti, "A crise de álcool," *ESP* (December 6, 1989), 38; João Jamil Zarif, "Álcoolina, combustível único," *ESP* (October 10, 1990), 38.
58. "Collor manda estudar extinção do Proálcool," *ESP* (March 8, 1990), 55.
59. See, for example, "Um sonho corroído;" "Gurgel prepara dossiê para enviar a Collor," *ESP* (December 23, 1989), 18; Uziel Nogueira, "Proálcool: A solução é a de Mercado," *ESP* (April 13, 1990), 22.
60. "Governo reduz a 50% produção de carro a álcool," *ESP* (May 17, 1989), 1; Odete Pacheco, "Agora, muitos querem um carro a álcool," *ESP* (August 26, 1990), 87.
61. "O maior critico do Proálcool," *ESP* (August 19, 1990), 96.

62. "Pesquisadores aplaudem indicação," *ESP* (March 16, 1990), 22.
63. Dean, *With Broadax and Firebrand*, 292 and, more broadly, ch. 13.
64. See World Commission on the Environment and Development, *Our Common Future* (Oxford: Oxford University Press, 1987), 12.
65. Hochstetler and Keck, *Greening Brazil*; Angela Alonso and Débora Maciel, "From Protest to Professionalization: Brazilian Environmental Activism after Rio-92," *The Journal of Environment and Development* 19, 3 (September 2010): 300–317; Pádua, "Environmentalism in Brazil: A Historical Perspective," 468–469. See also Acker, *Volkswagen in the Amazon*, 5–15.
66. "Conferência muda imagem do Brasil," *ESP* (April 20, 1990), 13.
67. José Goldemberg, "O Brasil em 1992," *ESP* (June 28, 1990), 54.
68. Galeno Amorim, "Álcool volta a ser bom negócio," *ESP* (September 2, 1990), 95.
69. "Collor reabilita o Proálcool," 72.
70. Fernando Collor de Mello, "Desenvolvimento é o objetivo," *ESP* (August 30, 1990), 6.
71. Other efforts included increased use of hydroelectricity and nuclear energy, intensified domestic oil exploration, and expanded trade relationships with other oil-producing countries such as Mexico, Venezuela, Angola, and China. See João Paulo dos Reis Velloso, *O último trem para Paris: De Vargas a Sarney, "milagres", choques e crises do Brasil moderno* (Rio de Janeiro: Nova Fronteira, 1986), 250, 369.
72. Collor, "Desenvolvimento é o objetivo," 6.
73. Pacheco, "Agora, muitos querem um carro a álcool," 87.
74. "Collor anuncia hoje estímulos ao Proálcool."
75. João Camilo Penna, "Chega de inverdades," *ESP* (February 27, 1990), 38; Maurilio Biagi Filho, "O merecido valor do Proálcool," *ESP* (March 16, 1991), 46.
76. "Collor reabilita o Proálcool," 72; Collor, "Desenvolvimento é o objetivo," 74.
77. Galeno Amorim, "Proálcool divulga conquistas na Rio-92," *ESP* (June 7, 1992), 93; "Hoje no Fórum Global," *ESP* (June 6, 1992).
78. Hochstetler and Keck, *Greening Brazil*, 114–126.
79. "Subprodutos que só poluíam agora representam lucros," *ESP* (June 7, 1992), 93.
80. "Usineiros tentam abrir Mercado de exportação," *ESP* (June 7, 1992), 93.
81. "A energia verde," *ESP* (June 11, 1992), 44.
82. Amorim, "Álcool volta a ser bom negócio," 95; Biagi Filho, "O merecido valor do Proálcool," 46.
83. "Opinião: Para quem o Proálcool 2?" *ESP* (July 25, 1991), 56.
84. Converting cars from ethanol to gasoline engines cost consumers between NCr$13,000 and NCr$20,000 (while new gasoline cars cost more than NCr$200,000). "Beer defende a importação do metanol," 18; on comparable car prices, see "Carro novo é vendido com ágio de 40%," *ESP* (January 28, 1990), 58.
85. Wolfe, *Autos and Progress*, 166; "País poderá até exportar carro popular," *ESP* (January 2, 1993), 21.
86. Homem de Melo, *Proálcool, energia e transportes*, 160.
87. "Projeto pode ficar pronto em 5 meses," *ESP* (February 3, 1993), 36; see also Bernhard Rieger, *The People's Car: A Global History of the Volkswagen Beetle* (Cambridge, MA: Harvard University Press, 2013), 68.

88. "País poderá ate exportar carro popular," 21; "Itamar quer financiamento para o Fusca," *ESP* (February 3, 1993), 36; Asdrubal Figueiró Junior, "Falta definir o conceito de carro popular brasileiro," *ESP* (March 7, 1993), 100; Alzira Rodrigues Marli Olmos, "Assinatura de protocolo acirra polemica no setor," *ESP* (March 31, 1993), 31. See also Presidencia da Republica, Decree no. 755 of February 19, 1993 and Decree no. 799 of April 17, 1993, http://www.planalto.gov.br/ccivil_03/decreto/1990-1994/D0799.htm, accessed October 6, 2021.
89. The historian Joel Wolfe has noted how important car ownership was to entry into the Brazilian middle-class before the 1970s. See Wolfe, *Autos and Progress*, 166–67.
90. Wolfe, *Autos and Progress*, 166–67.
91. "Opinião: Para quem o Proálcool 2?," 56; Cleide Silva, "Aumenta a procura para carros a álcool," *ESP* (April 26, 1999), B4; Anfavea, *Anuário da Indústria Automobilística Brasileira*, 59.
92. Baer, *The Brazilian Economy*, 116–118, 128, 425.
93. Maurilio Biagi Filho, "Sobriedade na política do álcool," *ESP* (March 2, 1993), 40.
94. Biagi Filho, "Sobriedade na política do álcool," 40. See also "Subprodutos que só poluíam agora representam lucros," 93; "Proálcool terá US$1,17 bilhão," *ESP* (February 6, 1993), 43.
95. Baer, *The Brazilian Economy*, 125–127, 428.
96. Francisco Vidal Luna and Herbert S. Klein, *The Economic and Social History of Brazil since 1889* (Cambridge: Cambridge University Press, 2014), 273.
97. Biagi Filho, "Sobriedade na política do álcool," 40; "Futuro incerto para o Proálcool," *ESP* (November 25, 1995), 3.
98. "Cana-de-açúcar mostra bons resultados," 71; Baer, *The Brazilian Economy*, 236–239.
99. Maurilio Biagi Filho, "O Brasil caiu na conta da globalização" *Imprensa* (April 1997) . APHRP Caixa 193; Baer, *The Brazilian Economy*, 130, Table 7.2 GDP Growth Rates, 1985–1999, particularly Table 7.2b, Brazil's Sectorial GDP Growth Rates, 1993–1999. Brazil's soy industry grew exponentially in the 1970s. By the 1990s, increased trade with China pushed exports ahead of those of Argentina so that Brazil became the second largest soy exporter after the US. Today it it is the largest exporter. Herbert S. Klein and Francisco Vidal Luna, *Feeding the World: Brazil's Transformation into a Modern Agricultural Economy* (New York: Cambridge University Press, 2019), 59–62 and ch. 3.
100. Galeno Amorim, "Usineiros querem a volta dos incentivos ao programa," *ESP* (February 13, 1995), 35.
101. Isabel Dias de Aguiar, "Carro a álcool terá imposto menor," *ESP* (February 13, 1995), 34.
102. Dias de Aguiar, "Carro a álcool terá imposto menor," 34.
103. Alberto Cavalcanti de Figueiredo, "O Proálcool e as montadoras," *ESP* (February 10, 1995), 34.
104. Cley Scholz "Transito vira um inferno," *ESP* (October 1, 1995), 167; Jacobi, Segura, and Kjellén, "Governmental Responses to Air Pollution," 80.
105. Marisa Folgato, "Diretor do AIAA condena restrição," *ESP* (August 24, 1995), 24.

106. "EUA já usam álcool, afirma especialista," *ESP* (August 24, 1995), 24; Edson Chaves Filho, "Preço faz consumo de combustível bater recorde," *ESP* (October 1, 1995), 167. The *rodízio* was later implemented for a month in 1996 and from June to September in 1997 and 1998. On the results, see Jacobi, Segura, and Kjellén, "Governmental Responses to Air Pollution," 79–88.
107. "Futuro incerto para o Proálcool," 3.
108. "Destino do Proálcool será definido esta semana," *ESP* (November 20, 1995), 42.
109. "O álcool sabotado," *ESP* (October 21, 1995), 48.
110. "Ministros não chegam a consenso sobre como salvar o Proálcool," ESP (March 6, 1996), 45.
111. Dias de Moraes and Zilberman, *Production of Ethanol from Sugarcane in Brazil*, 48.
112. Riomar Trindade and Dinise Neumann, "Malan terá de explicar estímulo ao Proálcool," *ESP* (June 26, 1997), 114; Mariángela Herédia, "Governo vai punir quem burlar preço oficial do álcool," *ESP* (June 5, 1998), 48; "Preço da cana provoca insatisfação," *ESP* (July 22, 1998), 70.
113. "Proálcool volta a consumidor faz fila pelo modelo," *ESP* (April 17, 1999), 28.
114. "Usineiros cobram ações do governo e fazem ameaças," *ESP* (April 26, 1999), 38.
115. Dow Jones & Company, http://www.forecast-chart.com/chart-crude-oil.html, accessed October 6, 2021. US first purchase prices were a little lower but saw an even bigger price increase of nearly 40% in the same time period. See https://www.eia.gov/dnav/pet/hist/LeafHandler.ashx?n=pet&s=f000000__3&f=m, accessed October 6, 2021.
116. "Número de bombas a álcool caiu pela metade em dez anos," *ESP* (April 17, 1999), 28.
117. "Proálcool volta a consumidor faz fila pelo modelo," 28; Silva, "Aumenta a procura para carros a álcool," 38.
118. "Número de bombas a álcool caiu pela metade em dez anos," 28; "Proálcool volta a consumidor faz fila pelo modelo," 28.
119. "O governo do estado de São Paulo e a iniciativa privada saem na frente na retomada do programa do carro a álcool," *ESP* (September 13, 1999), 31. See also Pedro Cafardo and Isabel Dias de Aguiar, "Acordo traz de volta o carro a álcool," *ESP* (March 20, 1992), 33.
120. "Os erros da nossa política de petróleo," *ESP* (January 8, 1999), 3; Alexandre Carvalho, "Carro a álcool perde interesse e agora está com mais desconto," *ESP* (January 27, 2000), 53.
121. Eduardo Magossi and Kelly Lima, "Após leilão, preço do álcool nos posto fica estabilizado," *ESP* (January 17, 2000), 35.
122. Carvalho, "Carro a álcool perde interesse e agora está com mais desconto," 53.
123. Herton Escobar and Eduardo Cerioni, "País já tem carro flex fuel, que funciona com álcool ou gasoline," *ESP* (March 30, 2003), 16.
124. Cleide Silva, "Motor flex: Paternidade disputada," *ESP* (November 4, 2004), 37; Celso Ming, "A confiabilidade do álcool" *ESP* (January 27, 2003), 14; David Luhnow and Geraldo Samor, "As Brazil Fills Up on Ethanol, It Weans off Energy Imports," *Wall Street Journal* (January 9, 2006), https://www.wsj.com/articles/SB11367694753

3241219, accessed October 6, 2021. The German company Bosch also developed the technology, and the two companies dominated the Brazilian market.

125. IMF, "The Impact of Higher Oil Prices on the Global Economy" (December 8, 2000). http://www.imf.org/external/pubs/ft/oil/2000/, accessed October 6, 2021.
126. Vera Rosa, "'Não queremos cair na vala comum', diz Lula," *ESP* (February 6, 2000), 9.
127. Vera Rosa, "Lula propõe pacto de convivência a usineiros," *ESP* (June 5, 2002), 5; see also Rosa, " 'Não queremos cair na vala comum', diz Lula" 9.
128. Kyoto Protocol, http://unfccc.int/kyoto_protocol/items/2830.php, accessed October 6, 2021.
129. Renata Veríssimo, "Acordo prevê 100 mil carros a álcool da Volks," *ESP* (August 23, 2002), 41; "Driven to Alcohol" *The Economist* 364 (September 7, 2002); Mario Osava, "Brazil-Germany: Kyoto Protocol Gets a Ride in Fuel-Alcohol Car," *Inter Press Service* (August 22, 2002), http://www.ipsnews.net/2002/08/brazil-germany-kyoto-protocol-gets-a-ride-in-fuel-alcohol-car/, accessed October 6, 2021; "The 'Car Chancellor' Loses Some of His Sheen," *Deusche Welle* (November 25, 2002), https://p.dw.com/p/2sDM, accessed October 6, 2021.
130. Cleide Silva, "A Volks, ao 50, quer renascer," *ESP* (March 16, 2003), 33. See also Anfavea, *Anuário da Indústria Automobilística Brasileira*, 69; Veríssimo, "Acordo prevê 100 mil carros a álcool da Volks," 41; It is worth noting that Germany and Brazil made over fourteen other such market-based agreements as part of Germany's efforts to abide by the Kyoto Protocoland the more recent Doha Agreement. Among these fourteen projects is a bagasse cogeneration project in the greater Ribeirão Preto region, located about 110 km directly north of the city. Implemented in May 2002, the program was to provide credit over the next seven years. The Netherlands, Finland, France, Japan, the UK, Norway, Sweden, and Canada all invested in the project, which provided a reduction in CO_2 equivalents of 12,024 metric tonnes per year (84,165 over the course of the crediting period) by selling bagasse-based cogeneration to the national electricity grid. See BR-181, Alta Mogiana Bagasse Cogeneration Project (AMBCP), http://cdm.unfccc.int/Projects/DB/TUEV-SUED1134666922.78/view, accessed October 6, 2021.
131. "Gol muda: É a VW abrindo espaço para o Tupi," *ESP* (February 16, 2003), 54.
132. Nelson Carrer Jr. "Carro movido a álcool ou gasolina chega em um ano," *ESP* (September 17, 2002), 25; Ming, "A confiabilidade do álcool," 14
133. "Montadora anuncia adesão ao Fome Zero," *ESP* (March 25, 2003), 6; "Na Volks, discurso para 'animar auditório,' " *ESP* (March 25, 2003), 6.
134. Igor Thomaz, "Novo Palio chega com motor bicombustível," *ESP* (November 9, 2003), 46; Carlos Franco and Lucia Camargo Nunes, "Ford entra na briga dos bicombustíveis," *ESP* (September 29, 2004), 26.
135. Nossa, "Lula diz que tornou usineiros 'heróis mundiais,' " 7; Cleide Silva, "Briga do bicombustível chega aos 1.0," *ESP* (March 16, 2005), 29; Anfavea, *Anuário da Indústria Automobilística Brasileira*, 59.
136. "Em Sertãozinho, quanto o petróleo sobe, mais o povo ri," *ESP* (August 14, 2005), 33.
137. David Luhnow and Geraldo Samor, "Alta do petróleo aumenta atenção mundial para o álcool," *Wall Street Journal*, as published in *ESP* (January 9, 2006), 19.

Chapter 7

1. Clemens Höges, "A 'Green Tsunami' in Brazil: The High Price of Clean, Cheap Ethanol," *der Speigel* (January 22, 2009), https://www.spiegel.de/international/world/a-green-tsunami-in-brazil-the-high-price-of-clean-cheap-ethanol-a-602951.html#:~:text=A%20%27Green%20Tsunami%27%20in%20Brazil%20The%20High%20Price,plantation%20workers%20harvest%20the%20cane%20at%20slave%20wages, accessed December 1, 2021.
2. Stavros Afionis, Lindsay C. Stringer, Nicola Favretto, Julia Tomei, Marcos S. Buckeridge, "Unpacking Brazil's Leadership in the Global Biofuels Arena: Brazilian Ethanol Diplomacy in Africa," *Global Environmental Politics* 16, no. 3 (August 2016): 127–150; Stephanie Hanson, "Brazil's Ethanol Diplomacy," *Council on Foreign Relations* (July 9, 2007). http://www.cfr.org/publication/13721/brazils_ethanol_diplomacy.html?breadcrumb=%2Fregion%2F245%2Fbrazil
3. Jad Mouwad, "Oil Prices Pass Record Set in '80s, but then Recede," *New York Times* (March 3, 2008)..
4. Marcos Sawaya Jank, "A Fuel Matrix for Brazil," in *Ethanol and Bioelectricity: Sugarcane in the Future of the Energy Matrix*, ed. Eduardo Leão de Sousa and Isaias de Carvalho Macedo (São Paulo: UNICA, 2011)," 11.
5. Anfavea, 2015 Annual Report, 59.
6. Daniel Budny, "The Global Dynamics of Biofuels: Potential Supply and Demand for Ethanol and Biodiesel in the Coming Decade," Wilson Center: Brazil Institute Special Report (2007), 4–5. For consumers, ethanol burns faster than gasoline in standard vehicles, and thus drivers require more fuel to travel similar distances; in higher-compression engines this differential is less pronounced. See Jason Delborne, "Biofuels: Streams and Themes," *Controversies in Science and Technology Vol. 3*, ed. Daniel Lee Kleinman, Jason A. Delborne, Karen A. Cloud-Hansen, and Jo Handelsman (New Rochelle, NY: Mary Ann Liebert, Inc., 2010), 176–177.
7. "The New Face of Hunger," *The Economist* (April 19, 2008), 32; David Adams, "Chavez, Castro Bash U.S. Ethanol Plan," *Tampa Bay Times* (May 16, 2007), https://www.tampabay.com/archive/2007/05/15/chavez-castro-bash-u-s-ethanol-plan/, accessed October 6, 2021; C. Ford Runge and Benjamin Senauer, "How Biofuels Could Starve the Poor," *Foreign Affairs* 86, no. 3 (May/June 2007), 44.
8. Jean Ziegler, "Report of the Special Rapporteur on the Right to Food," Interim Report Submitted to the UN General Assembly (August 22, 2007). http://www.righttofood.org/wp-content/uploads/2012/09/A62289.pdf, accessed October 6, 2021.
9. Höges, "A 'Green Tsunami' in Brazil."
10. José Goldemberg, "O programa do álcool e os ambientalistas," *ESP* (February 18, 2008), 2; Höges, "A 'Green Tsunami' in Brazil;" Hanson, "Brazil's Ethanol Diplomacy."
11. Carmen Gentile, "Analysis: Brazil's Leader Defends Ethanol," *Energy Daily* (June 11, 2008). https://www.energy-daily.com/reports/Analysis_Brazils_leader_defends_ethanol_999.html, accessed October 6, 2021. On ethanol and deforestation, see Bernton, Kovarik, and Sklar, *The Forbidden Fuel*, xxvi–xxviii.

12. "World News: Brazil's President Defends Biofuels," *Wall Street Journal* (April 18, 2008), A11.
13. Riordan Roett, *The New Brazil* (Washington, DC: Brookings Institution Press, 2010), 134–135; Höges, "A 'Green Tsunami' in Brazil."
14. Marcos S. Jank, "Etanol: Entendendo o mercado e os preços," *ESP* (January 22, 2010), 2; José Goldemberg, "A ciência e a odisseia do etanol," *ESP* (August 17, 2015), 2.
15. Maurilio Biagi Filho, "O etanol na hora da verdade." *ESP* (October 17, 2011), 16.
16. Jank, "Etanol: Entendendo o mercado e os preços," 2; "Sugar prices hit 30-year peak," *Korea Times* (November 6, 2010), 5.
17. Gustavo Porto, "Produção de etanol cai 15,7% no Centro-Sul," *ESP* (October 26, 2011).
18. Jonathan Watts, "Operation Car Wash: Is This the Biggest Corruption Scandal in History?" *The Guardian* (June 1, 2017), https://www.theguardian.com/world/2017/jun/01/brazil-operation-car-wash-is-this-the-biggest-corruption-scandal-in-history.
19. Bob Dinneen and Joel Velasco, "Não à volta do protectionismo ao etanol," *ESP* (July 22, 2017), 2. On fracking, see Anthony Ladd and Richard York, "Hydraulic Fracking, Shale Energy Development, and Climate Inaction: A New Landscape of Risk in the Trump Era," *Human Ecology Review* 23, no. 1 (2017), 65–79.
20. Mahdi Mazuchi, "Life Cycle Assessment of Sugarcane Biorefinery," *Advances in Sugarcane Biorefinery: Technologies, Commercialization, Policy Issues and Paradigm Shift for Bioethanol and Byproducts*, ed. Anuj Kumar Chandel and Marcos Henrique Luciano Silveira (Cambridge, MA, 2018), 213–233.
21. Interview with Dr. Raffaella Rossetto of the São Paulo Agency of Agibusiness Technology (Agência Paulista de Tecnologia dos Agronegócios), *Bioen Newsletter* 1, http://bioenfapesp.org/news-69/news/newsletter/bioen-newsletter-1-full-interview-raffaella-rossetto, accessed October 6, 2021.
22. Interview with Rossetto.
23. Eli Elias, "A incrível invasão dos pernilongos," *ESP* (September 29, 1979), 17; Josmar Verillo, "Usina emite comunicado oficial sobre vazamento de vinhaça," *Dourados News* (June 29, 2009), http://www.douradosnews.com.br/noticias/usina-emite-comunicado-oficial-sobre-vazamento-de-vinhaca-96e20babba89/362661/, accessed October 6, 2021; "Usina é autuada e embargada após acidente poluir rio e matar peixes em MT," *globo.com* (July 30, 2018), https://g1.globo.com/mt/mato-grosso/noticia/2018/07/30/usina-e-autuada-e-embargada-apos-acidente-poluir-rio-e-matar-peixes-em-mt.ghtml, accessed October 6, 2021.
24. Interview with Rossetto; See also CETESB Normative P 4.231 of February 12, 2015, *Diário Oficial Estado de São Paulo: Caderno Executivo I*, no. 125 (30) (February 13, 2015): 51–53.
25. De Andrade and Miccolis, "The Expansion of Sugarcane Ethanol in Brazil," 215–219.
26. Mônica Scaramauzzo, "Volta ao campo: O homem melhor que a máquina," *ESP* (July 28, 2019), https://arte.estadao.com.br/economia/trabalho-rural/volta-ao-campo/, accessed October 6, 2021.
27. Scaramauzzo, "Volta ao campo: O homem melhor que a máquina."

28. See, for example, Mitchell, *Carbon Democracy*; Jones, *Routes of Power*; Malm, *Fossil Capital.*
29. "Story of Change: The Rise of Brazil's Sugarcane Cars," *Rapid Transition Alliance* (December 2, 2018), https://www.rapidtransition.org/stories/the-rise-of-brazils-sugarcane-cars/, accessed October 6, 2021.
30. Schwartz, *Sugar Plantations in the Formation of Brazilian Society.*
31. Gerard Ostheimer, "Sustainable Biofuels: The Leading Edge of Sustainable Transport," *Stanford Energy Journal* (April 7, 2014), https://sej.stanford.edu/sustainable-biofuels-leading-edge-sustainable-transport, accessed October 6, 2021.
32. J. R. McNeill and Peter Engelke, *The Great Acceleration: An Environmental History of the Anthropocene since 1945* (Cambridge, MA: Belknap Press of Harvard University Press, 2014), 1–5; Gareth Austin, *Economic Development and Environmental History in the Anthropocene: Perspectives on Asia and Africa* (London: Bloomsbury Publishing, 2017), 1.
33. McNeill and Engelke, The Great Acceleration, 1–5; Austin, Economic Development and Environmental History in the Anthropocene, 1.
34. Christopher Wells, *Car Country: An Environmental History* (Seattle, WA: University of Washington Press, 2012), 180.
35. Roberto Godoy, Interview with Cícero Junqueira Franco: Director of Santaelisa Vale, " 'A Santaelisa não vai perder; ela vai deixar de ganhar,' " *ESP* (November 1, 2008), 44
36. Santiago, *The Ecology of Oil.*
37. For example, on the car industry in the United States, see Tom McCarthy, *Auto Mania: Cars, Consumers, and the Environment* (New Haven, CT: Yale University Press, 2007), 110–112; Wells, Car Country, ch. 6; on petroleum in Mexico, see Santiago, *The Ecology of Oil*, ch. 6.
38. Naomi Klein, "The Violence of Othering in a Warming World," *London Review of Books* 38, no. 11 (2016): 3; See also David Farrier, *Anthropocene Poetics: Deep Time, Sacrifice Zones, and Extinction* (Minneapolis, MN: University of Minnesota Press, 2019), 52.
39. On sacrificial zones of alternative energy infrastructure, see Dayna Nadine Scott and Adrian A. Smith, "'Sacrifice Zones' in the Green Energy Economy: Toward an Environmental Justice Framework," *McGill Law Journal* 62, no. 3 (2017): 861–898.
40. See, for example, Madrigal, *Powering the Dream*; See also Eaglin, "Fuel in the Age of the Great Acceleration."
41. Eaglin, "The Demise of the Brazilian Ethanol Program."
42. Scholars have long critiqued environmental histories for their exclusive focus on human destruction. However, historians such as Connie Chiang and Nancy Langston have reimagined stories of destruction as histories of human reclamation of waterways previously destroyed by industries. See Connie Chiang, *Shaping the Shoreline: Fisheries and Tourism on the Monterey Coast* (Seattle, WA: University of Washington Press, 2008); Nancy Langston, *Sustaining Lake Superior: An Extraordinary Lake in a Changing World* (New Haven, CT: Yale University Press, 2017).
43. Dinneen and Velasco, "Não à volta do protectionismo ao etanol," 2.
44. Intergovernmental Panel on Climate Change, *Climate Change 2021: The Physical Science Basis* (Cambridge: Cambridge University Press, forthcoming).
45. Höges, "A 'Green Tsunami' in Brazil."

Bibliography

Journals, Magazines, Newspapers, and News Websites

Anuário Açucareiro
Brasil Açucareiro
British Broadcasting Corporation (BBC)
Deutsche Welle
Diário Oficial do Estado de São Paulo
The Economist
Energy Daily
Estado de São Paulo
Folha de São Paulo
Forbes Magazine
Globo Rural
The Guardian
IstoÉ Senhor
Jornal do Interior
New York Times
Rede Globo
Reuters
Der Spiegel
Tampa Bay Times
Veja
Wall Street Journal

Archives

Arquivo da Associação de Comércio e Indústria Ribeirão Preto, Ribeirão Preto, SP
Arquivo Edgard Leunroth, Campinas, SP
Arquivo Nacional, Brasilia
Arquivo Nacional, Rio de Janeiro
Arquivo Público do Estado de São Paulo, São Paulo
Arquivo Público e Histórico de Ribeirão Preto, Ribeirão Preto, SP
Assembleia Legislativa do Estado de São Paulo (online)
Biblioteca da Canaoeste, Sertãozinho, SP
Biblioteca da Escola Superior de Agricultura "Luiz Queiroz" (ESALQ), Piracicaba, SP
Biblioteca Prof. Dr. Lucas Nogueira Garcez do CETESB, São Paulo
O Centro de Documentação e Pesquisa Vergueiro (CDPV), São Paulo
Cliff Welch Personal Collection, São Paulo
Copersucar/Museu da Imagem, Ribeirão Preto, SP

Ministério de Agricultura, Brasilia
Ministério da Fazenda, Rio de Janeiro
New York Public Library, New York, NY
Senado Federal (online)
UCLA Southern Regional Library Facility, Los Angeles, CA
UCLA Thayer Collection, Los Angeles, CA

Interviews by Author

Amorim, Galeno. Skype. April 22, 2020.
Biagi Filho, Maurilio. Ribeirão Preto, SP. May 20, 2013; March 18, 2017.
Bragheto, José Domingos. São Paulo, SP. April 13, 2013.
Garnero, Mário. São Paulo, SP. December 11, 2013.
Neves, Élio. Skype. May 26, 2020.

Secondary Sources

Abreu, Marcelo de Paiva, , ed. A ordem do progresso: Cem anos de política econômica republicana, 1899–1989. Rio de Janeiro: Campus, 1989.

Acker, Antoine. *Volkswagen in the Amazon: The Tragedy of Global Development in Modern Brazil.* Cambridge: Cambridge University Press, 2017.

Addis, Caren. *Taking the Wheel: Auto Parts Firms and the Political Economy of Industrialization in Brazil.* University Park, PA: Pennsylvania State University Press, 1999.

Afionis, Stavros et al. "Unpacking Brazil's Leadership in the Global Biofuels Arena: Brazilian Ethanol Diplomacy in Africa." *Global Environmental Politics* 16, no. 3 (2016): 127–150.

Alonso, Angela and Débora Maciel. "From Protest to Professionalization: Brazilian Environmental Activism after Rio-92." *The Journal of Environment and Development* 19 (September 2010): 300–317.

Alves, Maria Helena Moreira. *State and Opposition in Military Brazil.* Austin, TX: University of Texas Press, 1985.

Anfavea (Associação Nacional dos Fabricantes de Veículos Automotores). *Anuário da Indústria Automobilística Brasileira,* 2015, https://anfavea.com.br/anuarios, accessed October 6, 2021.

Arns, Archbishop Paulo Evaristo and the Archdiocese of São Paulo. *Brasil: Nunca Mais.* São Paulo: Vozes, 1985.

Atalla, Jorge Wolney. *Reflexões e sugestões para o desenvolvimento brasileiro.* Brasilia: Confederação Nacional da Agricultura, 1979.

Austin, Gareth, ed. *Economic Development and Environmental History in the Anthropocene: Perspectives on Asia and Africa.* Oxford: Bloomsbury Publishing, 2017.

Baer, Werner. *The Brazilian Economy: Growth and Development.* 7th edn. Boulder, CO: Lynne Rienner, 2008.

Barzelay, Michael. *The Politicized Market Economy: Alcohol in Brazil's Energy Strategy.* Los Angeles, CA: University of California Press, 1986.

Bernton, Hal, William Kovarik, and Scott Sklar. *The Forbidden Fuel: A History of Power Alcohol*. Lincoln, NE: University of Nebraska Press, 2010.

Blanc, Jacob. *Before the Flood: The Itaipu Dam and the Visibility of Rural Brazil*. Durham, NC: Duke University Press, 2019.

Böhm, György Miklós. *O álcool combustível e a saúde da população*. 3rd edn. Edição Associação das indústrias de açúcar e de álcool do Estado de São Paulo (AIAA), 1991.

Böhm, György Miklós et al. "Biological Effects of Air Pollution in São Paulo and Cubatão." *Environmental Research* 49 (1989): 208–216.

Böhm, György Miklós, Eduardo Massad, Paulo Hilário Saldiva, et al. "Comparative Toxicity of Alcohol and Gasoline Fueled Automobile Exhaust Fumes." In *Developments in the Science and Practice of Toxicology*, edited by A. W. Hayes, R. C. Schnell, and T. S. Miya, 479–482. New York: Elsevier, 1983.

Brieger, Franz O. *Noções básicas e métodos analíticos para a indústria açucareira*. Ribeirão Preto, SP: Copereste, 1964.

Brilhante, Ogenis Magno. "Brazil's Alcohol Program: From an Attempt to Reduce Oil Dependence in the Seventies to the Green Arguments of the Nineties." *Journal of Environmental Planning & Management* 40, no. 4 (1997): 435–449.

Brown, Lester R, Christopher Flavin, and Colin Norman. *The Future of the Automobile in an Oil-Short World*. Worldwatch Paper 32. Washington DC: Worldwatch Institute, 1979.

Brown, Lester. *Food or Fuel: New Competition for the World's Cropland*. Worldwatch Paper 35. Washington DC: Worldwatch Institute, 1980.

Buckley, Eve. *Technocrats and the Politics of Drought and Development in Twentieth-Century Brazil*. Chapel Hill, NC: University of North Carolina Press 2017.

Budny, Daniel. "The Global Dynamics of Biofuels: Potential Supply and Demand for Ethanol and Biodiesel in the Coming Decade." Wilson Center: Brazil Institute Special Report, 2007.

Bueno, Ricardo. *Pró-Álcool: Rumo ao desastre*. Petrópolis: Editora Vozes Ltda, 1980.

Cardoso, Fernando Henrique and Enzo Faletto. *Dependency and Development in Latin America*. Berkeley, CA: University of California Press, 1979.

Castro, Moacyr. "Pedro Biagi." In *Os desbravadores*, edited by Galeno Amorim, 127–132. Ribeirão Preto, SP: Palavra Mágica, 2001.

Catholic Church and the Archdiocese of São Paulo. *Torture in Brazil: A Report by the Archdiocese of São Paulo*, edited by Joan Dassin and translated by Jaime Wright. New York: Vintage Books, 1986.

Chequer, Julia. "Memórias ocultas: Experiências de mulheres canavieiras em Guariba (1975–1985)." Master's thesis Programa de Pós-Graduação em História, Política e Bens Culturais, CPDOC/FGV, 2019.

Chiang, Connie. *Shaping the Shoreline: Fisheries and Tourism on the Monterey Coast*. Seattle, WA: University of Washington Press, 2008.

Collier, David. "The Bureaucratic-Authoritarian Model." In *The New Authoritarianism in Latin America*, edited by David Collier. Princeton, NJ: Princeton University Press, 1979.

Commissão Executivo Nacional do Álcool (CENAL). *Proálcool: Informações Básicas para Empresários*. Rio de Janeiro: BNDE, 1980.

Coronil, Fernando. *The Magical State: Nature, Money, and Modernity in Venezuela*. University of Chicago Press, 1997.

da Silva, Luiz Antonio. "Sindicalismo, assalariados rurais e a luta pela cidadania." In *Modernização e impactos sociais: O caso da agroindústria sucro-alcooleira na região de*

Ribeirão Preto (SP), edited by Rosemeire Scopinho and Leandro Valarelli, 87–114. Rio de Janeiro: FASE, 1995.

Dean, Warren. *With Broadax and Firebrand: The Destruction of the Brazilian Atlantic Forest*. Los Angeles, CA: University of California Press, 1995.

de Andrade, Renata Marson Teixeira and Andrew Miccolis. "The Expansion of Sugarcane Ethanol in Brazil and Controversies Surrounding Human Rights." In *Controversies in Science and Technology: From Evolution to Energy, Vol. 3*, edited by Daniel Lee Kleinman, Jason A. Delborne, Karen A. Cloud-Hansen, and Jo Handelsman, 214–228. New Rochelle, NY: Mary Ann Liebert Inc., 2010.

Delborne, Jason. "Biofuels: Streams and Themes." In *Controversies in Science and Technology: From Evolution to Energy, Vol. 3*, edited by Daniel Lee Kleinman, Jason A. Delborne, Karen A. Cloud-Hansen, and Jo Handelsman, 175–190. New Rochelle, NY: Mary Ann Liebert, Inc., 2010.

de Melo, Joaquim. *A política do álcool-motor no Brasil*. Rio de Janeiro: Instituto de Açúcar e do Álcool, 1942.

Demetrius, F. Joseph. *Brazil's National Alcohol Program: Technology and Development in an Authoritarian Regime*. New York: Praeger, 1990.

Dias de Moraes, Márcia Azanha Ferraz. A desregulamentação do setor sucroalcooleiro do Brasil. Americana, SP: Caminho Editorial, 2000.

Dias de Moraes, Márcia Azanha Ferraz. "Considerações sobre a indústria do etanol do Brasil." In *Biocombustíveis: Realidade e perspectivas*, edited by Ministério das Relações Exteriores, 137–157. Brasilia: Ministério das Relações Exteriores, 2007.

Dias de Moraes, Márcia Azanha Ferraz and David Zilberman. *Production of Ethanol from Sugarcane in Brazil: From State Intervention to a Free Market*. New York: Springer, 2014.

D'Incao e Mello, Maria Conceição, *O bóia-fria: Acumulação e miséria*. Petrópolis: Editora Vozes, 1975.

Duarte, Regina Horta. "Nature and Historiography in Brazil, 1937–1945." *Iberoamericana* 3, no. 10 (2003): 23–36.

Dubois, Laurent. *Avengers of the New World: The Story of the Haitian Revolution*. Cambridge, MA: Harvard University Press, 2004.

Eaglin, Jennifer. "The Demise of the Brazilian Ethanol Program: Environmental and Economic Shocks, 1985–1990." *Environmental History* 24 (2019): 104–129.

Eaglin, Jennifer. " 'More Brazilian than Cachaça': The Development of the Brazilian Sugar-Based Ethanol Industry." *Latin American Research Review* 54, no. 4 (2019): 927–943.

Eaglin, Jennifer. "Fuel in the Age of the Great Acceleration." In *A Cultural History of the Environmental*. Oxford: Bloomsbury, forthcoming.

Eakin, Marshall. *Tropical Capitalism: The Industrialization of Belo Horizonte, Brazil*. New York: Palgrave, 2001.

Eisenberg, Peter L. *The Sugar Industry in Pernambuco: Modernization without Change, 1840–1910*. Berkeley, CA: University of California Press, 1974.

Escobar, Arturo. *Encountering Development: The Making and Unmaking of the Third World*. Princeton, NJ: Princeton University Press, 1995.

Evans, Peter. *Dependent Development: The Alliance of Multinational, State, and Local Capital in Brazil*. Princeton, NJ: Princeton University Press, 1979.

Farrier, David. *Anthropocene Poetics: Deep Time, Sacrifice Zones, and Extinction*. Minneapolis, MN: University of Minnesota Press, 2019.

Federação de Órgãos para a Assistência Social e Educacional. *Boia-fria, Sangue Quente: Mobilização e Resistência dos Assalariados Temporários Rurais*. Jaboticabal: Fase, 1987.

Federative Republic of Brazil. *First National Development Plan 1972–1974*. Brasilia, 1971.

Fraginals, Moreno and Teresita Pedraza Moreno. "The Ten Million Ton Sugar Harvest," https://snimsib.files.wordpress.com/2017/11/ten-million-ton-sugar-harvest.pdf, accessed September 30, 2021.

French, John. *The Brazilian Workers' ABC: Class Conflict and Alliances in Modern São Paulo*. Chapel Hill, NC: University of North Carolina Press, 1992.

Freyre, Gilberto. *Nordeste: Aspectos da influencia da cana sobre a vida e a paisagem do nordeste do Brasil*. Rio de Janeiro: J. Olympio Editora, 1937.

Fischer, Brodwyn. *A Poverty of Rights: Citizenship and Inequality in Twentieth-Century Rio de Janeiro*. Stanford, CA: Stanford University Press, 2008.

Foweraker, Joe. *The Struggle for Land: A Political Economy of the Pioneer Frontier in Brazil, 1930 to Present*. Cambridge: Cambridge University Press, 1981.

Furtado, Celso. *A operação nordeste*. Rio de Janeiro: Ministério da Educação e Cultura, Instituto Superior de Estudos Brasileiros, 1959.

Furtado, Celso. *Formação econômica do Brasil*. São Paulo: Companhia das Letras, 2006.

Garcia-Johnson, Ronie. *Exporting Environmentalism: U.S. Multinational Chemical Corporations in Brazil and Mexico*. Cambridge, MA: MIT Press, 2000.

Garfield, Seth. *A luta indígena no curação do Brasil: Politica indigenista, a marcha para o oeste e os índios xavante (1937–1988)*. São Paulo: UNESP, 2011.

Garnero, Mário. *JK: A coragem da ambição*. Campinas, SP: Editora MM, 2011.

Gately, Dermot. "Lessons from the 1986 Oil Price Collapse." *Brookings Papers on Economic Activity* 17, no. 2 (1986): 237–284.

Goldemberg, José. "Brazil: Energy Options and Current Outlook." *Science* 200, no. 158 (1978): 158–164.

Goldemberg, José. *Energia no brasil*. Rio de Janeiro: Livros Técnicos e Científicos, 1979.

Goldemberg, José. "Renewable Energy Sources: The Case of Brazil." *Natural Resources Forum* 3, no. 3 (1979): 253–262.

Goldemberg, José. "Solving the Energy Problems in Developing Countries." *Energy* 11, no. 1 (1990): 19–24.

Goldemberg, José, J. R. Moreira, P. U. M. Dos Santos, and G. E. Serra. "Ethanol Fuel: A Use of Biomass Energy in Brazil." *Ambio* 14, nos. 4–5 (1985): 293–297.

Gordinho, Margarida Cintra. *Do álcool ao etanol: Trajetória única*. São Paulo: Terceiro Nome, 2010.

Governo do Estado de São Paulo. *Estudo do macrozoneamento das bacias do rios Mogi Guaçu Pardo e Médio-Grande*. São Paulo: SMA/SAA/SEP, 1995.

Governo do Estado de São Paulo. *Macrozoneamento das Bacias dos Rios Mogi Guaçu, Pardo, e Médio Grande: Questões Sócio-Ambientais Regionais*. São Paulo: CETESB, 1995.

Haber, Stephen, ed. *How Latin America Fell Behind: Essays on the Economic Histories of Brazil and Mexico*. Stanford, CA: Stanford University Press, 1997.

Hall, Anthony L. *Developing Amazonia: Deforestation and Social Conflict in Brazil's Carajás Programme*. Manchester: Manchester University Press, 1989.

Hanley, Anne et al. "Critiquing the Bank: 60 Years of BNDES in the Academy." *Journal of Latin American Studies* 48, no. 4 (2016): 823–850..

Hartzmark, Amanda. "Businesses, Associations, and Regions in the Brazilian Sugar Industry, 1920–1990." Ph.D. diss., University of Chicago, 2014.

Hasse, Geraldo. *Filhos do fogo: Memória industrial de Sertãozinho, 1896–1996*. Ribeirão Preto, SP: Editora Ceu e Terra, 1996.

Hasse, Geraldo. *Maurilio Biagi: O semeador do sertão*. Ribeirão Preto, SP: Editora Ceu e Terra, 2003.

Hecht, Gabrielle. *The Radiance of France: Nuclear Power and National Identity after World War II*. Cambridge, MA: MIT Press, 2000 [2009].

Hochstetler, Kathryn and Margaret Keck. *Greening Brazil: Environmental Activism in State and Society*. Durham, NC: Duke University Press, 2007.

Holston, James. *Insurgent Citizenship: Disjunctions of Democracy and Modernity in Brazil*. Princeton, NJ: Princeton University Press, 2009.

Houtzager, Peter. "State and Unions in the Transformation of the Brazilian Countryside, 1964–1975." *Latin American Research Review* 33, no. 2 (1998): 103–142.

Intergovernmental Panel on Climate Change. *Climate Change 2021: The Physical Science Basis*. Cambridge: Cambridge University Press, forthcoming.

International Monetary Fund (IMF), "The Impact of Higher Oil Prices on the Global Economy." (December 8, 2000), http://www.imf.org/external/pubs/ft/oil/2000/, accessed October 6, 2021

Ioris, Rafael. *Transforming Brazil: A History of National Development in Postwar Brazil*. New York: Routledge 2014.

Jacobi, Pedro. "Perspectives for Hemispheric Cooperation in Agro-Energy: Energy Cooperation in the Americas." Seminar, 11 December 2006, Rio de Janeiro, Brazil.

Jacobi, Pedro et al. "Governmental Responses to Air Pollution: Summary of a Study of the Implementation of *rodízio* in São Paulo." *Environment and Urbanization* 11, no. 1 (1999): 79–88.

Jones, Christopher. *Routes of Power: Energy and Modern America*. Cambridge, MA: Harvard University Press, 2014.

Keck, Margaret. *The Workers' Party and Democratization in Brazil*. New Haven, CT: Yale University Press, 1992.

Klein, Herbert S. and Francisco Vidal Luna. *Feeding the World: Brazil's Transformation into a Modern Agricultural Economy*. New York: Cambridge University Press, 2019.

Klein, Naomi. "The Violence of Othering in a Warming World." *London Review of Books* 38, no. 11 (2016): 1–6.

Kovarik, Bill. "Henry Ford, Charles Kettering and the Fuel of the Future." *Automotive History Review* 32 (1998): 7–27.

Ladd, Anthony and Richard York. "Hydraulic Fracking, Shale Energy Development, and Climate Inaction: A New Landscape of Risk in the Trump Era." *Human Ecology Review* 23, no. 1 (2017): 65–79.

Langston, Nancy. *Sustaining Lake Superior: An Extraordinary Lake in a Changing World*. New Haven, CT: Yale University Press, 2017.

Lasso, Marixa. *Erased: The Untold Story of the Panama Canal*. Cambridge, MA: Harvard University Press, 2019.

Leão, Regina Machado. *Álcool: Energia verde*. São Paulo: IQUAL, 2002.

Leão de Sousa, Eduardo L. and Isaias de Carvalho Macedo, eds. Ethanol and Bioelectricity: Sugarcane in the Future of the Energy Matrix, translated by Brian Nicholson. São Paulo: Unica, 2011.

Leite, Alberico. "A nova política." In *II Encontro Nacional dos Produtores de Açúcar*, edited by COPERFLU, 71–100. Campos, RJ: COPERFLU, 1974.

Leithe, W. *The Analysis of Organic Pollutant in Waste and Waste Water*, translated by STS, Inc. Ann Arbor, MI: Ann Arbor Science Publishers, Inc., 1973,

Lerner, Steve. *Sacrifice Zones: The Front Lines of Toxic Chemical Exposure in the United States*. Cambridge, MA: MIT Press, 2010.

Lima, Léo da Rocha and Aluizio de Abreu Marcondes. Álcool carburante: Uma estratégia brasileira. Curitiba: Editora UFPR, 2002.

Lima, Urgel de Almeida. "Um resumo histórico sobre a vinhaça em Piracicaba." Revista Instituto Histórico Geográfico de Piracicaba 20 (2013): 246–290.

Love, Joseph. *São Paulo in the Brazilian Federation, 1889–1937*. Stanford, CA: Stanford University Press, 1980.

Love, Joseph. *Crafting the Third World: Theorizing Underdevelopment in Rumania and Brazil*. Stanford, CA: Stanford University Press, 1996.

Madrigal, Alexis. *Powering the Dream: The History and Promise of Green Technology*. Cambridge, MA: Da Capo, 2011.

Mainwaring, Scott. *The Catholic Church and Politics in Brazil, 1916–1985*. Stanford, CA: Stanford University Press, 1986.

Malm, Andreas. *Fossil Capital: The Rise of Steam Power and the Roots of Global Warming*. London: Verso, 2016.

Marchesi, Ida Pizzoli. *João Marchesi: História de um imigrante*. Ribeirão Preto, SP: Editora Colégio, 1987.

Martins, Ana Luiza, ed. *Guariba- 100 anos*. São Paulo: Prefeitura Municipal de Guariba, 1996.

Massad, Eduardo et al. "Toxicity of Prolonged Exposure to Ethanol and Gasoline Autoengine Exhaust Gases." *Environmental Research* 40 (1986): 479–486.

Massad, Eduardo et al. "Ethanol Fuel Toxicity." In *Handbook of Hazardous Materials*, edited by Morton Corn, 265–277. San Diego, CA: Academic Press, 1993.

Mazuchi, Mahdi. "Life Cycle Assessment of Sugarcane Biorefinery." In *Advances in Sugarcane Biorefinery: Technologies, Commercialization, Policy Issues and Paradigm Shift for Bioethanol and Byproducts*, edited by Anuj Kumar Chandel and Marcos Henrique Luciano Silveira, 213–240. Cambridge, MA: Elsevier, 2018.

McCarthy, Tom. *Auto Mania: Cars, Consumers, and the Environment*. New Haven, CT: Yale University Press, 2007.

McGillvray, Gillian. *Blazing Cane: Sugar Communities, Class, and State Formation in Cuba, 1868–1959*. Durham, NC: Duke University Press, 2009.

McNeill, J. R. and Peter Engelke. *The Great Acceleration: An Environmental History of the Anthropocene since 1945*. Cambridge, MA: Belknap Press of Harvard University Press, 2014.

Médici, Emilio Garrastazu. *A verdadeira paz*. Brasilia: Departamento de Imprensa Nacional, 1971.

Melillo, Edward. "The First Green Revolution: Debt Peonage and the Making of the Nitrogen Fertilizer Trade, 1840–1930." *American Historical Review* 117, no. 4 (2012): 1028–1060.

Miller, Shawn William. "Fuelwood in Colonial Brazil: The Economic and Social Consequences of Fuel Depletion in the Bahian Recôncavo, 1549–1820." *Forest and Conservation History*, 38, no. 4 (1994): 181–192.

Miller, Shawn William. *An Environmental History of Latin America*. Cambridge: Cambridge University Press, 2000.

Miller, Shawn William. *Fruitless Trees: Portuguese Conservation and Brazil's Colonial Timber*. Palo Alto, CA: Stanford University Press, 2000.

Miller, Shawn William. *The Street is Ours: Community, the Car and the Nature of Public Space in Rio de Janeiro*. New York: Cambridge University Press, 2018

Ministry of Mines and Energy. *O modelo energético brasileiro*. Brasilia: Ministry of Mines and Energy, 1979.

Miranda, Maria Augusta Tibiriça. *O petróleo é nosso: A luta contra o "entreguismo" pelo monopólio estatal, 1947–1953*. Petrópolis: Vozes, 1983.

Mitchell, Timothy. *Carbon Democracy: Political Power in the Age of Oil*. London: Verso, 2011.

Monzote, Reinaldo Funes. *From Rainforest to Canefield: An Environmental History Since 1492*. Raleigh, NC: University of North Carolina Press, 2008.

Nixon, Rob. *Slow Violence and the Environmentalism of the Poor*. Cambridge, MA: Harvard University Press, 2011.

Nunberg, Barbara. "State Intervention in the Sugar Sector in Brazil: A Study of the Institute of Sugar and Alcohol." Ph.D. diss., Stanford University, 1979.

Nunberg, Barbara. "Structural Change and State Policy: The Politics of Sugar in Brazil since 1964." *Latin American Research Review* 21, no. 2 (1986): 53–92.

O'Donnell, Guillermo. *Modernization and Bureaucratic-Authoritarianism: Studies in South American Politics*. Berkeley, CA: University of California Press, 1973.

Osava, Mario. "Brazil-Germany: Kyoto Protocol Gets a Ride in Fuel-Alcohol Car." *Inter Press Service* (August 22, 2002), http://www.ipsnews.net/2002/08/brazil-germany-kyoto-protocol-gets-a-ride-in-fuel-alcohol-car/, accessed October 7, 2021.

Owensby, Brian. *Intimate Ironies: Modernity and the Making of Middle-Class Lives in Brazil*. Stanford, CA: Stanford University Press, 2002.

Pádua, José Augusto. "Natureza e projeto nacional: As origens da ecologia política no Brasil." In *Ecologia e política no Brasil*, edited by José Augusto Pádua, 11–59. Rio de Janeiro: Espaço e Tempo, 1987.

Pádua, José Augusto. "The Birth of Green Politics in Brazil: Exogenous and Endogenous Factors." In *Green Politics II*, edited by W. Rudig, 134–155. Edinburgh: Edinburgh University Press, 1992.

Pádua, José Augusto. "Environmentalism in Brazil: A Historical Perspective." In *A Global Companion to Global Environmental History*, edited by J. R. McNeill and Erin Stewart Mauldin, 455–473. Hoboken, NJ: Wiley-Blackwell Publishing, 2012.

Pádua, José Augusto. "Brazil in the History of the Anthropocene." In *Brazil in the Anthropocene: Conflicts Between Predatory Development and Environmental Policies*, edited by Liz-Rejane Issberner and Philippe Léna, 19–40. New York: Routledge, 2017.

Pádua, José Augusto. "The Dilemma of the 'Splendid Cradle': Nature and Territory in the Construction of Brazil." In *A Living Past: Environmental Histories of Modern Latin America*, edited by John Soluri, Claudia Leal, and José Augusto Pádua, 91–114. New York: Berghahn, 2018.

Pamplona, Confúcio. *Proálcool: Technical-Economic and Social Impact of the Program in Brazil*. Belo Horizonte: Ministry of Industry and Commerce and Sugar and Alcohol Institute, 1984.

Penteado, Maria Antonieta Gomes. *Trabalhadores da cana: Protesto social em Guariba, maio de 1984*. Maringá: Eduem, 2000.

Pereira, Anthony W. *End Of The Peasantry: The Rural Labor Movement in Northeast Brazil, 1961–1988*. Pittsburgh, PA: University of Pittsburgh Press, 1997.

Pereira, Moacyr Soares. O problema do álcool-motor. Rio de Janeiro: Livraria José Olympio Editora, 1942.

Pinheiro, Murilo et al. *Ribeirão Preto*. Ribeirão Preto, SP: MIC Editorial Ltda, 1996.

Prado Júnior, Caio. *História econômica do Brasil*. São Paulo: Brasiliense, 1967.

Prebisch, Raúl. *The Economic Development of Latin American and Its Principal Problems*. Lake Success, NY: United Nations Department of Economic Affairs, 1950.

Rabe, Stephen. *Killing Zone: The United States Wages Cold War in Latin America*. New York: Oxford University Press, 2012.

Ramos, Pedro. *Agroindústria canavieira e propriedade fundiária no Brasil*. São Paulo: Editora Hucitec, 1999.

Reid, Walter et al. *No Reason to Wait: The Benefits of Greenhouse Gas Reduction in São Paulo and California*. Menlo Park, CA: Hewlett Foundation, 2005.

Rieger, Bernhard. *The People's Car: A Global History of the Volkswagen Beetle*. Cambridge, MA: Harvard University Press, 2013.

Rogers, Thomas. *The Deepest Wounds: A Labor and Environmental History of Sugar in Northeast Brazil*. Chapel Hill, NC: University of North Carolina Press, 2010.

Rossini, Rosa Ester. "Mulheres e homens na força de trabalho na agricultura: O exemplo da macro-área de Ribeirão Preto." Paper Presented at the 15th National Conference on Population Studies (ABEP-2006).

Runge, C. Ford and Benjamin Senauer. "How Biofuels Could Starve the Poor." *Foreign Affairs* (May/June 2007).

Sabino de Oliveira, Eduardo. *Álcool motor e motores a explosão*. Rio de Janeiro: Ministério do trabalho, indústria, e comercio, Instituto de tecnologia, 1937.

Saldiva, Paulo Hilario et al. "Pulmonary Function of Rats Exposed to Ethanol and Gasoline Fumes." *Journal of Brazilian Medical Biological Research* 18 (1985): 573–577.

Santiago, Myrna. *Ecology of Oil: Environment, Labor, and the Mexican Revolution, 1900–1938*. Cambridge: Cambridge University Press, 2010.

Santos, Adriano Pereira. *A usinagem do capital e o desmonte do trabalho: Reestruturação produtiva nos anos de 1990, o caso da Zanini S/A de Sertãozinho-SP*. São Paulo: Editora Expressão Popular, 2010.

Santos, Maria Helena de Castro. "Alcohol as Fuel in Brazil: An Energy Policy Analysis." Ph.D. diss., Massachusetts Institute of Technology, 1984.

Santos, Maria Helena de Castro. *Política e políticas de uma energia alternativa: o caso do Proálcool*. Rio de Janeiro: Notrya, 1993.

Scheper-Hughes, Nancy. *Death without Weeping: The Violence of Everyday Life in Brazil*. Berkeley, CA: University of California Press, 1992.

Schwartz, Stuart. *Sugar Plantations in the Formation of Brazilian Society: Recôncavo, Bahia, 1550–1835*. Cambridge: Cambridge University Press, 1985.

Schwartz, Stuart. *Sea of Storms: A History of Hurricanes in the Greater Caribbean from Columbus to Katrina*. Princeton, NJ: Princeton University Press, 2015.

Schwartzman, Simon. *A Space for Science: The Development of the Scientific Community in Brazil*. University Park, PA: Pennsylvania State University Press, 1991.

Scopinho, Rosemeire Aparecida. "Modernização e superexploração na agroindústria sucroalcooleira." In *Modernização e impactos sociais: O caso da agroindústria sucro-alcooleira na região de Ribeirão Preto (SP)*, edited by Rosemeire Scopinho and Leandro Valarelli, 21–49. Rio de Janeiro: FASE, 1995.

Scott, Dayna Nadine and Adrian A. Smith. "'Sacrifice Zones' in the Green Energy Economy: Toward an Environmental Justice Framework." McGill Law Journal 62, no. 3 (2017): 861–898.

Scott, James. *Seeing like a State: How Certain Schemes to Improve the Human Condition Have Failed*. New Haven, CT: Yale University Press, 1998.

Secretaria do Planejamento. *Brazil's III National Development Plan 1980–1985*. Brasilia: Presidencia da República, 1979.

Sedrez, Lise. "The Bay of All Beauties: State and Environment in Guanabara Bay, Rio de Janeiro, Brazil, 1878–1975." Ph.D. diss., Stanford University, 2005.

Showers, Kate B. "Biofuels' Unbalanced Equations: Misleading Statistics, Networked Knowledge and Measured Parameters." *International Review of Environmental History* 5, no. 1 (2019): 61–83.

Sikkink, Kathryn and Margaret E. Keck. *Activists beyond Borders: Advocacy Networks in International Politics*. Ithaca, NY: Cornell University Press, 1998.

Silva, Maria Aparecida de Moraes. *Errantes do fim do século*. São Paulo: Fundação Editora da UNESP, 1999.

Silveira, Ubaldo. *Igreja e conflito agrário: A comissão pastoral da terra na região de Ribeirão Preto*. Franca, SP: Unesp, 1998.

Skidmore, Thomas. *Politics in Brazil, 1930–1964: An Experiment in Democracy*. New York: Oxford University Press, 1967.

Skidmore, Thomas. *Brazil: Five Centuries of Change*. New York: Oxford University Press, 2010.

Soluri, John. *Banana Cultures: Agriculture, Consumption, and Environmental Change in Honduras and the United States*. Austin, TX: University of Texas Press, 2005.

Stepan, Alfred. *The Military in Politics: Changing Patterns in Brazil*. Princeton, NJ: Princeton University Press, 1971.

Stolcke, Verena. *Coffee Planters, Workers, and Wives: Class Conflict and Gender Relations on São Paulo Coffee Plantations, 1850–1980*. New York: St. Martin's Press, 1988.

Szmrecsányi, Tamás. *O planejamento da agroindústria canavieira do Brasil 1930/1975*. São Paulo: Edição Hucitec, 1979.

Tan, Yan. *Resettlement in the Three Gorges Project*. Hong Kong: Hong Kong University Press, 2008.

Tarr, Joel A. *The Search for the Ultimate Sink: Urban Pollution in Historical Perspective*. Akron, OH: University of Akron Press, 1996.

Thomaz Júnior, Antonio. *Por trás dos canaviais, os "nós" da cana: A relação capital x trabalho e o movimento sindical dos trabalhadores na agroindústria canavieira paulista*. São Paulo: Annablume/Fapesp, 2002.

Topik, Steven. "State Enterprise in a Liberal Regime: The Bank of Brazil, 1905–1930." *Journal of Interamerican Studies and World Affairs* 22, no. 4, Special Issue: Public Enterprise in Latin America (1980): 401–422.

Topik, Steven. *The Political Economy of the Brazilian State, 1889–1930*. Austin, TX: University of Texas Press, 1987.

Triner, Gail D. *Banking and Economic Development: Brazil, 1889–1930*. New York: Palgrave, 2000.

Triner, Gail. *Mining and the State in Brazilian Development*. London: Pickering & Chatto, 2011.

Tucker, Richard. *Insatiable Appetite: The United States and the Ecological Degradation of the Tropical World*. Berkeley, CA: University of California Press, 2000.

United Nations Framework Convention on Climate Change. The Kyoto Protocol, http://unfccc.int/kyoto_protocol/items/2830.php, accessed October 6, 2021.

Vasconcellos, Gilberto Felisberto and J. W. Bautista Vidal. *Poder dos Trópicos: Meditação sobre a alienação energética na cultura brasileira*. São Paulo: Casa Amarela, 1998.

Velloso, João Paulo dos Reis. *O último trem para Paris: De Vargas a Sarney, "milagres", choques e crises do Brasil moderno*. Rio de Janeiro: Nova Fronteira, 1986.

Viton, Albert. *The International Sugar Agreements: Promise and Reality*. West Lafayette, IN: Purdue University Press, 2004.

Walker, Thomas. "From Coronelismo to Populism: The Evolution of Politics in a Brazilian Municipality, Ribeirão Preto, São Paulo, 1910–1960." Ph.D. diss., University of New Mexico, 1974.

Weinstein, Barbara. *For Social Peace in Brazil: Industrialists and the Remaking of the Working Class in São Paulo, 1920–1964*. Chapel Hill, NC: University of North Carolina Press, 1996.

Weinstein, Barbara. *The Color of Modernity: São Paulo and the Making of Race and Nation in Brazil*. Durham, NC: Duke University Press, 2015.

Welch, Clifford Andrew. "Rivalry and Unification: Mobilising Rural Workers in São Paulo on the Eve of the Brazilian Golpe of 1964." *Journal of Latin American Studies* 27, no. 1 (1995): 161–187.

Welch, Clifford Andrew. *The Seed Was Planted: The São Paulo Roots of Brazil's Rural Labor Movement, 1924–1964*. University Park, PA: Pennsylvania State University Press, 1999.

Welch, Clifford Andrew. "Keeping Communism down on the Farm: The Brazilian Rural Labor Movement during the Cold War." *Latin American Perspectives* 33, no. 3 (2006): 28–50.

Welch, Clifford Andrew. *A semente foi plantada: As raízes paulistas do movimento sindical camponês no Brasil, 1924–1964*. São Paulo: Editora Expressão Popular, 2010.

Wells, Christopher. *Car Country: An Environmental History*. Seattle, WA: University of Washington Press, 2012.

Wirth, John. *The Politics of Brazilian Development, 1930–1954*. Stanford, CA: Stanford University Press, 1970.

Wolfe, Joel. *Working Women, Working Men: São Paulo and the Rise of Brazil's Industrial Working Class, 1900–1955*. Durham, NC: Duke University, 1993.

Wolfe, Joel. *Autos and Progress: The Brazilian Search for Modernity*. Oxford: Oxford University Press, 2010.

Wolfe, Joel. "Change with Continuity: Brazil from 1930–1945." In *The Great Depression in Latin America*, edited by Paulo Drinot and Alan Knight, 81–101. Durham, NC: Duke University Press, 2014.

Wolfe, Mikael. *Watering the Revolution: An Environmental and Technological History of Agrarian Reform in Mexico* (Durham, NC: Duke University Press, 2017.

Wright, Angus and Wendy Wolford. *To Inherit the Earth: The Landless Movement and the Struggle for a New Brazil*. Oakland, CA: Food First Books, 2003.

Ziegler, Jean. "Report of the Special Rapporteur on the Right to Food." Interim Report Submitted to the UN General Assembly (August 22, 2007), http://www.righttofood.org/wp-content/uploads/2012/09/A62289.pdf, accessed October 6, 2021.

Index

For the benefit of digital users, indexed terms that span two pages (e.g., 52–53) may, on occasion, appear on only one of those pages.